AQUINAS
ACADEMY
2370 Red Lion Road
Bear, Delaware 19701
(302) 838-9601

The
FACTS
of LIFE

AN AUTHORITATIVE GUIDE
TO LIFE AND FAMILY ISSUES

BRIAN CLOWES, PhD

Human Life International
Front Royal, Virginia
1997

© 1997 Human Life International

Human Life International
4 Family Life
Front Royal, Virginia 22630
Phone: (540) 635-7884 • Fax: (540) 636-7363
E-mail: hli@hli.org • World Wide Web: http://www.hli.org

Cover design by Christy Sharafinski
Cartoons by Chuck Asay

ISBN 1-55922-043-0

Library of Congress Catalogue number 96-80003
Printed in the United States of America.

This book is dedicated to St. Michael the Archangel,
prince of the heavenly host.

St. Michael,
lead us into battle against
the Culture of Death
and protect us against Satan and all his snares.

The Facts of Life

Table of Contents

Acknowledgements

This book is one of the concrete results of hard work by Human Life International's worldwide team.

I would especially like to thank Fathers Paul Marx and Matthew Habiger, whose long and diverse experience in the pro-life movement made the writing of this book a true education. Their guidance was crucial to its completion and contributed immensely to my pro-life education.

Mike Engler's intense editorial scrutiny greatly improved the readability of *The Facts of Life* and made me a much better writer. Thanks, Mike — it may be said that you have permanently cured me of using the passive voice.

Christy Sharafinski and Don James did the layout and artwork, giving plain pages of text eye-pleasing photographs and charts that illustrate important concepts. Vern Kirby, director of HLI's Publications Department, orchestrated the entire project from beginning to end.

I would also like to thank those experts who carefully reviewed parts of the book and made specific comments that were very helpful: Eleanor Drechsel, Rudolf Ehmann, M.D., Pat Farley, Thomas Hilgers, M.D., Father Germain Kopaczynski, Magaly Llaguno, Sister Renee Mirkes, OSF, Ph.D., William M. Petty, M.D., David Reardon, Dr. Charles Rice, Monsignor William Smith, William Toffler, M.D. and Father Richard Welch.

Finally, I must express my profound gratitude to my dearest bride of 22 years and fellow pro-life activist, Kathy, not only for her patience but for the benefit of her in-depth expertise. She caught all the mistakes that everyone else missed.

The Facts of Life

Foreword

"It ain't ignorance that's our problem. It's everything we know that ain't true."
—*American humorist Will Rogers*

When I was an educator, ignorance *was* the problem. And it was difficult enough dealing with *that*.

I thank God I'm not in the classroom today. Because today's young people, like the rest of Western society, suffer from a malady far worse than *lack* of education: deliberate *mis*education.

Our schools, our news media, our entertainment media, government officials, special-interest groups and even some of our pulpits have taught millions that pre-born children with beating hearts are mere "lumps of cells." That vivisecting babies in their mother's wombs is "women's health care." That teaching kids how to "have sex" won't tempt them to try it. That contracepted fornication prevents abortions. That natural birth regulation is "Vatican Roulette." That we're about to fall off the planet because of "overpopulation." That a test tube can be a good parent. That being killed like a sick old dog is "dignified." And that people who stand up for God's laws "just want to control people's lives."

After decades of 'round-the-clock "disinformation," trying to get these notions out of people's heads can be like trying to pull an old stump. But from now on it will be easier, thanks to Brian Clowes' astonishing new book, *The Facts of Life*.

I'm giving fair warning to anti-lifers: my friend Brian doesn't fight fair. He has a habit of citing documented facts. *Lots* of documented facts. He uses airtight logic, too. On every page. Worst of all, he reveals little-known quotes from people on your side admitting that you're wrong. On issue after issue.

I beg you, dear pro-life friend, to make maximum use of this Heaven-sent book. Read it and dog-ear it. Give copies to young people, to priests, ministers and rabbis, to nuns and brothers, to seminarians and novices, to teachers and professors, to journalists, to health professionals, to politicians, to school, church and public libraries, to pro-lifers in other countries. Use it to prepare talks and debates, sermons, letters to the editor, talk-show call-ins, classroom lectures, news releases, pro-life brochures, school papers, testimonies before lawmakers, and pro-life training sessions. Do not—repeat, do not—let it sit on your bookshelf. Wear it out—then get another copy!

The Facts of Life is the first major pro-life educational tool "born" at Human Life International's new central office. I congratulate its "father," Brian Clowes, on a breathtaking feat of research. And I promise you, it's only the first of many enlightening "children" to come from the talented people now at work in our new building.

Our Lord said Satan was a liar and a murderer from the beginning. With God's help and yours, HLI will unmask every lie the enemy uses to murder God's children, until the Culture of Life triumphs over the Culture of Death in the New Millennium.

Rev. Paul Marx, OSB, PhD
Founder, Human Life International

Introduction

More than 2,500 years ago, the great Chinese military strategist Sun Tzu observed in his classic treatise *The Art of War* that information is crucial to winning any battle. Since Sun's time, every successful general, CEO, lawyer and coach has proven time and again the wisdom of his words.

Nowhere is information so critical as it is in the struggle between the Culture of Life and the Culture of Death. All anti-life movements — whether they are promoting abortion, euthanasia, "gay" rights, pornography or population control — thrive in an atmosphere of deception and lies. The weapon that tears away the thick shroud of misperception and propaganda cloaking the Culture of Death, the implement that exposes the evil inherent in such a culture, is accurate *information*.

Every pro-life activist should know the basic facts and arguments surrounding the life issues of our day. This will allow him to dispel the concerns of family members and friends, inform the public, recruit people into the pro-life movement, and, most importantly, save lives.

All effective pro-lifers must consider themselves eternal students and must be dedicated to a study of these issues. This book will help deepen your understanding of the most crucial issues surrounding the worldwide struggle over abortion and other evils, giving you then the information you need to educate others on the *facts of life.*

The Facts of Life

Chapter I

Abortion Definitions, Methods and Effects

1. What Is the General Definition of "Abortion?"

The general term "abortion" has traditionally meant the intentional or unintentional expulsion of the preborn child from the uterus before he or she reached the age of viability (defined as the point after which the preborn child can survive outside the womb with or without medical assistance). In practice, though, abortion in a number of countries (including the United States, Canada and the People's Republic of China) is legal until the moment of birth. In fact, some abortion methods such as dilation and extraction (D&X), the "partial birth" abortion, are designed to kill the preborn child when the birth process is almost complete.

At the other end of the spectrum, more and more drugs are now being developed whose only purpose is to destroy the life of preborn children after fertilization (the union of the sperm and ovum) and before implantation of the embryo or zygote in the mother's uterus.

The Planned Parenthood Federation of America (PPFA), the United Nations World Health Organization (UNWHO), the American Medical Association (AMA), the American College of Obstetricians and Gynecologists (ACOG), and other pro-abortion organizations now falsely define pregnancy as beginning at implantation, and not at fertilization. In this manner, these groups claim that abortifacient drugs and devices such as the birth control pill and the intrauterine device (IUD) do not cause early abortions, because they say that a pregnancy does not exist before actual implantation. Their motives for this subterfuge are explained further in Question 38.

The Catholic Church teaches that abortion is not only "the expulsion of the immature fetus," but is also "the killing of the same fetus in any way and at any time from the moment of conception."[1]

1

Therefore, the honest, accurate and complete definition of the general term "abortion" would be "the intentional *or* unintentional expulsion of the preborn child at any time after fertilization and before the natural birth process is completed."

1 The Pontifical Commission for the Authentic Interpretation of the Code of Canon Law, Statement of 24 November 1988, quoted in "Church Elaborates Definition of Abortion." *National Catholic Register*, 11 December 1988, p.3.

2. What Is the Definition of "Abortionist?"

The current definition of "abortionist" used by the medical profession is "one who performs criminal abortions."[1]

However, the logical, truthful and complete definition of "abortionist" is "anyone who commits direct surgical or chemical abortions, legal or illegal, whether they be a medical doctor, nurse, midwife, or lay person."

This definitional divergence exists because the primary focus of the medical profession is the *legality* of the procedure, while the primary concern of pro-lifers is the stark reality that an abortion, whether it is legal or not, always takes the life of a human person.

The medical profession insists that only those who commit criminal (illegal) abortions should be called abortionists. It has two reasons for such semantic subterfuge: (1) The term "abortionist" carries with it the strong connotation of an unskilled and unprincipled hack and must therefore be avoided, and (2) The term "abortion" and all of its derivatives denote a bloody and barbarous procedure, and therefore must be shunned as well.

Because abortion is entirely incompatible with the healing mission of the medical profession, it is *intrinsically* disreputable. Abortion is not medicine or health care. Therefore, pro-lifers should *always* use the term "abortionist" to describe someone who commits abortions, whether the procedures are legal or criminal. Terms such as "abortion doctor," "abortion provider," and "abortion clinic" should always be strictly avoided, because they lend an air of respectability and even benevolence to those who have murderously betrayed an honorable profession.

1 Benjamin F. Miller, M.D., and Claire Brackman Keane. *Encyclopedia and Dictionary of Medicine, Nursing, and Allied Health* (Third Edition). Philadelphia: W.B. Saunders Company, 1983.

3. What Are the Different Types of Abortions?

There are a number of medical and legal terms for the different types of abortion, both intentional and unintentional. These are listed below.[1]

The different types of surgical abortion procedure are described in Questions 5 through 14.

- **Complete abortion:** When all of the contents of the uterus (i.e., the preborn child and the placenta) have been expelled from the uterus.

- **Criminal [illegal] abortion:** Any abortion committed outside the parameters set by law. For instance, an abortionist commits a criminal abortion if he aborts a minor without her parent's permission in a state with parental consent laws, or if he commits a D&X abortion on a woman at 28 weeks gestation for convenience purposes in a state where third-trimester abortions are banned except in the case of severe fetal anomalies.

■ **Early abortion:** An abortion within the first trimester (i.e., first 12 weeks) of a pregnancy.

■ **Habitual abortion:** Spontaneous abortion (i.e., miscarriage) occurring in three or more consecutive pregnancies. Women who suffer from habitual abortions account for the majority of miscarriages.

■ **Incomplete abortion:** An intentional or unintentional abortion in which parts of the preborn child and/or placenta remain within the uterus.

■ **Induced abortion:** An intentional abortion brought on by mechanical (surgical) or chemical (abortifacient) means.

■ **Inevitable abortion:** A condition marked by vaginal bleeding and cervical dilation which indicates an impending miscarriage that cannot be prevented, and follows a condition of threatened abortion (see below).

■ **Infected abortion:** An abortion associated with, and possibly caused by, an infection of the uterus or the genital tract, such as a venereal disease.

■ **Missed abortion:** When a woman does not miscarry a preborn child who died more than eight weeks previously.

■ **Septic abortion:** An abortion associated with, and possibly caused by, an infection of the uterus.

■ **Spontaneous abortion:** The medical term for a miscarriage. This term is very important for pro-life activists to remember because many medical statistical categories and subsequent medical treatments (such as delivery of a child) do not distinguish between intentional and spontaneous abortion.

■ **Therapeutic abortion:** The current medical literature equates "legal abortion" with "therapeutic abortion." However, the definition of the word "therapeutic" means "treatment of disease."[1] The use of the term "therapeutic" is another pro-abortion attempt to sanitize a repulsive act, and it also implies that pregnancy is a disease, an assertion many pro-abortionists have made directly.[2]

■ **Threatened abortion:** A condition that usually includes vaginal bleeding but not cervical dilation, and may or may not lead to a condition of inevitable abortion.

1 Benjamin F. Miller, M.D., and Claire Brackman Keane. *Encyclopedia and Dictionary of Medicine, Nursing, and Allied Health* (Third Edition). Philadelphia: W.B. Saunders Company, 1983.

2 Just three of many examples of the pro-abortion assertion that "pregnancy is a disease:" (1) Alan Guttmacher, M.D., former Medical Director of the Planned Parenthood Federation of America (PPFA), asserted, "The [birth control] pill, in my opinion and that of my colleagues, is an important prophylaxis, perhaps the most important, against one of the gravest sociomedical illnesses extant. That, of course, is unwanted pregnancy." (Senator Gaylord Nelson's (D-Wi.) Hearings on Competitive Problems in the Drug Industry, by the Senate Subcommittee on Monopoly, Select Committee on Small

Business, Part 16, p. 6,572, 25 February 1970). (2) Mary S. Calderone, M.D., another former Medical Director of PPFA and co-founder and President of the Sex Information and Education Council of the United States (SIECUS), said "We have yet to beat our public health drums for birth control in the way we beat them for polio vaccine; we are still unable to put babies in the class of dangerous epidemics, even though that is the exact truth." (*Medical Morals* Newsletter, February-March 1968). (3) Abortionist Warren Hern has said "[Pregnancy] is an episodic, moderately extended, chronic condition ... [and] may be defined as an illness ... treated by evacuation of the uterine contents" ("Is Pregnancy Really Normal?" Alan Guttmacher Institute's *Family Planning Perspectives*, January 1971, p. 9.) In his book *Abortion Practice* (Philadelphia: J.B. Lippincott, 1990), Hern, on pp. 14-17, describes pregnancy as an "illness" and a "host-parasite relationship."

4. What Are the Different Types of Surgical Abortions?

Depending upon the gestational age of the preborn child and the physical condition of the mother, the abortionist has a variety of abortion methods in his arsenal.

Early abortions (those in the first trimester) are usually done with dilation and curettage (D&C) or suction. Abortionists use more complex methods to kill preborn babies in the second and third trimesters. These include dilation and evacuation (D&E), saline, dilation and extraction (D&X), prostaglandin, hysterotomy, and intercardiac injection abortions, as described in the following Questions. See also the Color Plates depicting several different types of abortion later in this Chapter.

5. How Is a Suction Abortion Done?

Abortionists use this method (also known as "suction curettage") in most first-trimester abortions, and can also use it up to 16 weeks. The abortionist begins by dilating the cervix. Then, he inserts a suction curette of the appropriate size, which consists of a hollow tube with a sharp tip, into the cervix and then into the uterus. The suction machine then tears the developing baby apart, sucks the pieces through the tube, and deposits them into a bag. Either the abortionist or an assistant assembles or checks the body parts to ensure a complete abortion.[1]

1 For a complete explanation of first-trimester abortion methods, including suction abortions, D&Cs, and menstrual extraction, see Warren Hern. *Abortion Practice*. Philadelphia: J.B. Lippincott Company, 1990, pp. 108-122.

6. How Is a Dilation and Curettage (D&C) Abortion Done?

Abortionists use D&C (also known as "sharp curettage") most often during the first trimester of pregnancy. The abortionist inserts a sharp looped knife (curette) into the uterus to scrape its walls. He then cuts the preborn baby apart, removes the body parts, and checks them for completeness.

Unlike other abortion methods, D&C has an alternative and entirely legitimate use. Physicians often perform curettage after a miscarriage to ensure that the uterus is "clean," thereby avoiding the infection that may result from the retention of necrotic [decaying] tissue, either from the baby or from the placenta, or from other uterine conditions or disorders.

However, it is vitally important to ensure that a baby does not remain in the uterus before this type of D&C is performed; many times, women have thought they had miscarriages because they passed blood clots or tissue, but subsequent sonograms or other tests have revealed that they were still pregnant.

In some cases, the woman actually lost a recognizable baby during a miscarriage, but ultrasound revealed that she was still pregnant with the lost baby's twin. Many doctors assert that ultrasound testing should precede any D&C, or the woman risks having an unintentional surgical abortion.

7. How Is a Dilation and Evacuation (D&E) Abortion Done?

The D&E method of abortion is most commonly used during the first half of the second trimester (13 to 20 weeks), but is employed up to about 28 weeks. The baby is dismembered, and the pieces are removed one by one. In many cases, the abortionist cuts off one or more of the baby's limbs and waits until he or she bleeds to death before proceeding with the abortion. Larger babies must have their heads crushed so the pieces can pass through the cervix.

Abortionist Warren Hern, who specializes in late-term abortions, has said that "We have reached a point in this particular [D&E] technology where there is no possibility of denial of an act of destruction by the operator. It is before one's eyes. The sensations of dismemberment flow through the forceps like an electric current."[1]

Pro-abortion groups are particularly enthusiastic about D&E because, unlike other second-trimester abortion methods such as saline and prostaglandin, there is absolutely no chance that the baby will survive.

Hern also authored the how-to book *Abortion Practice*, in which he describes some of the more grisly aspects of the D&E abortion: "The procedure changes significantly at 21 weeks because the fetal tissues become much more cohesive and difficult to dismember.... A long curved Mayo scissors may be necessary to decapitate and dismember the fetus...."[2]

Usually, the cervix must be dilated for one to three days before a D&E abortion. The most popular method of cervical dilation involves the insertion of dried seaweed sticks called laminaria, which absorb fluids and swell, thereby expanding the cervical diameter. The abortionist may also forcibly dilate the cervix over a period of just a few minutes with a series of stainless steel rods of increasing diameter.

It is a common ploy for abortionists to tell their patients that, once the laminaria are inserted, the abortion process cannot be reversed. Pro-life activists in general, and sidewalk counselors in particular, must be aware of the fact that laminaria can be removed by any emergency room physician if the woman changes her mind about having an abortion.

1 Warren Hern, address before the Association of Planned Parenthood Physicians convention in San Diego, "WHAT ABOUT US? Staff Reactions to the D&E Procedure." 26 October 1978.

2 Warren Hern. *Abortion Practice*. Philadelphia: J.B. Lippincott Company, 1990, p. 154.

8. How Is a Saline Abortion Done?

Also known as the "intra-amniotic injection," "saline solution method," or the "amnio abortion," this method is used for second trimester and early third trimester abortions, but has become less popular due to possible harm to the mother brought on by accidental injection of saline solution into a blood vessel.

To begin with, about 200 milliliters of amniotic fluid is withdrawn and replaced with saline or urea solution.[1] The baby breathes and swallows this concentration and dies painfully over a period of hours from salt poisoning, dehydration, brain hemorrhage and convulsions. The baby's skin is often severely burned by the solution, and delivery occurs 24 to 48 hours after the baby dies. The skin of the baby is either completely burned or turned a cherry-red color, which is why some abortionists and nurses refer to them as "candy-apple babies."

Many mothers who have undergone saline abortions report feeling the baby's movements increase to a desperate frenzy as its skin and mucous membranes are scalded and it dies in unspeakable agony.

Another reason the salt poisoning method has become less popular is that it occasionally results in a hardy baby who survives the torture—the so-called "dreaded complication." Therefore, abortionists now generally use hysterotomy or a modified D&E method that guarantees the baby's death.

1 Warren Hern. *Abortion Practice.* Philadelphia: J.B. Lippincott Company, 1990, p. 124.

9. How Is a Dilation and Extraction (D&X) Abortion Done?

More than any other abortion, the D&X killing method exposes the cruel and inhumane nature of both abortion in general and abortionists in particular.

Abortionist Marvin Haskell originated the D&X procedure because "... most surgeons find dismemberment [i.e., D&E] at twenty weeks and beyond to be difficult due to the toughness of fetal tissues at this stage of development."[1]

Haskell, who boasted at a 1992 National Abortion Federation (NAF) conference that he has committed more than 700 late second-trimester and third-trimester D&X killings, describes his technique:

At this point [after the baby has been entirely delivered except for the head], the right-handed surgeon slides the fingers of the left hand along the back of the fetus and "hooks" the shoulders of the fetus with the index and ring fingers (palm down). Next he slides the tip of the middle finger along the spine towards the skull while applying traction to the shoulders and lower extremities. The middle finger lifts and pushes the anterior cervical lip out of the way.

While maintaining this tension, lifting the cervix and applying traction to the shoulders with the fingers of the left hand, the surgeon takes a pair of blunt curved Metzenbaum scissors in the right hand. He carefully advances the tip, curved down, along the spine and under his middle finger until he feels it contact the base of the skull under the tip of his middle finger.

Reassessing proper placement of the closed scissors tip and safe elevation of the cervix, the surgeon then forces the scissors into the base of the skull or into the *foramen magnum* [the large opening in the occipital bone between the cranial cavity and the spinal canal]. Having safely entered the skull, he spreads the scissors to enlarge the opening.

The surgeon removes the scissors and introduces a suction catheter into this hole and evacuates the skull contents. With the catheter still in place, he applies traction to the fetus, removing it completely from the patient."[1]

Dry medical terminology cannot begin to convey the true horror of this type of killing.

In layman's terms, an abortionist considering a D&X has two problems. He wants to abort a viable preborn baby of seven or eight months gestation who has an 80 percent chance of surviving birth. This baby's muscles and cartilage have toughened to the point where it is virtually impossible to chop him or her apart without harming the mother. Since the baby is probably viable, the abortionist also faces the prospect of the "dreaded complication"—a live, crying newborn baby. Therefore, he must make sure the baby dies before he or she is fully "delivered."

He therefore uses forceps to twist one of the baby's legs and pull it out through the birth canal, which tears muscles and breaks bones and must cause the baby unspeakable agony, since even pro-abortionists acknowledge that seven-month and eight-month preborn babies definitely feel pain (see Question 80). Then he punctures the back of the baby's head with sharp scissors and spreads the blades, tearing a massive hole in the soft part of the baby's skull. Finally, he *vacuums out the baby's brains* and completes the delivery in just a few seconds.[1]

During the heated Congressional debate over banning the D&X procedure in early 1996, every major pro-abortion group vigorously defended the D&X procedure on the grounds that crushing the baby's skull and vacuuming out his or her brains was necessary to make the head "smaller" so the mother could deliver the dead child with less danger to herself. This is obviously a fraudulent claim, because the entire baby is delivered except for the head before he or she is killed. Obviously, the only purpose of a D&X abortion is to kill the child.

Pro-abortionists also claimed that the baby always dies of anesthesia overdose before the D&X, but abortionists who use the method admit, "the majority of fetuses aborted this way are alive until the end of the procedure."[2]

Finally, pro-abortionists say the D&X is only used in extreme cases of fatal birth defect. Abortionist Marvin Haskell, who invented the method, decisively refuted this claim, saying that about 80 percent of the D&X procedures he has committed have been purely for convenience purposes.[3]

Bill Clinton, the 42nd President of the United States, vetoed the bill that allegedly would have banned most D&X abortions. Many pro-lifers realized that this bill, which included an exception for the life of the mother, would have saved few babies, because abortionists claim that *all* pregnancies threaten the life—or life*style*—of the mother in one way or another (see Question 84).

7

Figure I

Partial Birth Abortion

These medical drawings depict the partial-birth abortion procedure. They have been validated as technically accurate by medical experts on both sides of the abortion issue. The partial-birth abortion procedure is used after 20 weeks (4½ months) of pregnancy—often to 6 months, and later.

(Illustrations by Jenny Westberg.)

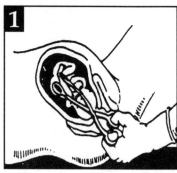

Guided by ultrasound, the abortionist grabs the baby with forceps.

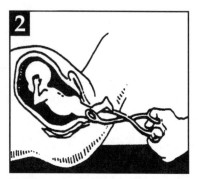

The baby's leg is pulled out into the birth canal.

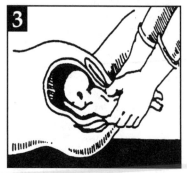

The abortionist delivers the baby's entire body, except for the head.

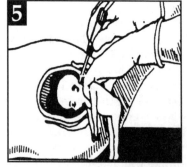

The abortionist jams scissors into the baby's skull. The scissors are then opened to enlarge the hold.

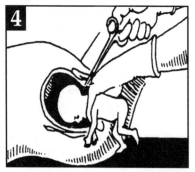

The scissors are removed and a suction tube is inserted. The child's brains are sucked out, causing the skull to collapse. The dead baby is then removed.

The protracted, highly publicized wrangling over the D&X abortion produced one substantial good. Pro-abortionists, who unanimously supported the D&X method, will never again be able to hide behind their facade of sympathetic "moderation." In every public and private debate, in every sidewalk discussion, and in every attempt to persuade a nominally "pro-choice" relative or fellow churchgoer, pro-life activists have the pro-abortionist's support of the D&X procedure as a vivid illustration of just how Satanic and uncompromising the anti-life mentality truly is.

1 Martin Haskell, M.D. "Dilatation and Extraction for Late Second Trimester Abortion." National Abortion Federation conference proceedings *Second Trimester Abortion: From Every Angle*, 13-14 September 1992, Dallas, Texas.

2 Diane Gianelli. "Shock-Tactic Ads Target Late-Term Abortion Procedure." *American Medical News*, 5 July 1993.

3 Marvin Haskell, quoted in *Sixty Minutes* episode of 2 June 1996 entitled "Partial Birth Abortion Ban."

10. How Is a Prostaglandin Abortion Done?

Prostaglandin abortions are used during the late second trimester and third trimester. About eight milliliters of prostaglandin hormone is injected into the uterine muscle, which contracts to expel the baby in an artificially-induced and extremely violent premature labor that takes about 20 hours. Alternatively, 20 to 40 milligrams of a prostaglandin analogue (Prostin F2 Alpha, dinoprost tromethamine) are infused following the placement of laminaria. Sometimes, saline or urea are combined with prostaglandin for infusions.[1]

This method of abortion is now rarely used, because up to seven percent of preborn babies are born alive during the procedure.[1] In such cases, the abortionist must clandestinely kill the baby or risk a so-called "wrongful life" situation and a possible lawsuit and bad publicity.

1 Warren Hern. *Abortion Practice*. Philadelphia: J.B. Lippincott Company, 1990, pp. 125-126.

11. How Is a Hysterotomy Abortion Done?

A hysterotomy is actually a Cesarean section done during the last trimester of pregnancy when other types of abortion may be too dangerous to the mother. The mother's uterus is surgically opened and the baby is lifted out.

The helpless baby is then either left to die or is killed by the abortionist or his staff. According to Planned Parenthood's Alan Guttmacher Institute, abortionists commit about 1,000 hysterotomy abortions every year in the United States alone.[1]

1 Alan Guttmacher Institute figures, quoted by Richard D. Glasow, Ph.D. "Abortion Statistics Paint Grim Picture." *NRL News*, 28 May 1987, pp. 5, 16.

12. How Is an Intercardiac Injection Abortion Done?

At about 16 weeks, ultrasound imagery is used to pinpoint the location of the baby so that a long needle may be guided into its heart. The abortionist injects potassium chloride or some other fluid which causes an immediate heart attack in the preborn baby.[1] After a period of days, the dead preborn child is delivered naturally, or the process can be accelerated with cervical dilation followed by prostaglandin injections.

This method is most commonly used for "pregnancy reduction" abortions, which are described in more detail in Question 14.

1 "Selective Abortion, AKA Pregnancy Reduction." *New England Journal of Medicine*, 21 April 1988.

13. What Is "Menstrual Extraction" (ME)?

Definitions and Terms

"Menstrual extraction" is basically an early suction abortion using either a standard abortion suction machine with a flexible cannula or a homemade contraption made of Mason jars, aquarium tubing, corks, and syringes.

ME serves three very important purposes, in both developed and developing countries:

■ It lets abortionists circumvent legal clauses that include statements such as "woman known to be pregnant," and thus lets them avoid legal liability. This aspect of ME is critical when it is used in countries with abortion laws that protect preborn children, and it will become more significant as some developed nations with permissive abortion laws move to outlaw or restrict abortion in the future.

■ ME insulates women from knowing whether they are pregnant. They may *suspect* they are pregnant, but ME allows them to remain ignorant, and therefore lets the mechanism of self-denial operate.

■ It allows nations to "fudge" their abortion statistics for various purposes. For example, ME is frequently used in Holland, but they are not counted as abortions. This allows Dutch statisticians to claim that the nation's abortion rate is low due to widespread contraception and sex education.[1]

The Pathfinder Fund outlines the devious "logic" behind menstrual extraction in both developed and developing countries: "Today, a woman faced with a possible but unconfirmed and unwanted pregnancy can walk into a health services clinic or doctor's office and often within twenty minutes have her endometrial lining extracted ... and since menstrual extraction can be performed before a positive pregnancy test is obtainable, it is hard to prove that menstrual induction is an abortion procedure."[2]

There are two very important reasons why pro-life activists should be familiar with menstrual extraction. First, in Western countries where lawmakers are trying to place limits on abortion, feminists have vowed to disseminate crude ME technology and know-how so that "self-abortion" becomes popular. For example, Cynthia Pearson of the National Women's Health Network (NWHN) predicts that "Anyone who could get their hands on an electric suction machine would be in business."[3] And Frances Kissling of "Catholics" for a Free Choice seems to be smacking her lips in anticipation of the prospect of widespread "self-help" abortion whom she says: "I would like to see a huge underground of activist women learning how to do menstrual extractions and vacuum aspiration abortions, mothers teaching their daughters, *sub rosa* [covert] classes at campus women's centers...."[3]

The second reason that pro-lifers should be familiar with ME is that, in most developing countries where abortion is illegal, population control organizations do ME on a widespread scale in order to bypass and undermine pro-life laws.

Alternative names for ME include "endometrial extraction," "menstrual shedding," "menstrual regulation" (MR), "menstrual induction," "early uterine evacuation," and "bringing on the menses."

ME in Developed Countries

Before abortion was legalized in the United States, feminists routinely referred women to illegal abortionists, operated a "Jane" network to route women to abortionists, and constructed ME devices such as the "Del-Em," made of local materials and used for self-abortions.

Since the legalization of abortion, feminists have promoted a series of ME programs designed to put complete control of the abortion process in the hands of the woman, regardless of the legality of the act.

Rebecca Chalker and Carol Downer, in their book *A Woman's Book of Choices,* demonstrate vividly how pro-abortionists twist any law to suit their purpose: "Women who do menstrual extraction consider it and other home health-care techniques to be completely legal, since an individual woman or a group of women cannot make a medical diagnosis of pregnancy; in fact, they are not attempting to do so. Therefore, they would not have the necessary intent required to constitute a criminal act of abortion."[4]

Cindy Pearson, who has been promoting self-abortion for nearly a decade, also displayed the feminists' utter contempt for preborn human life when she enthused that "this is so [much] fun; this is so great, that we can do this ourselves.... It's just joyful."[5]

If surgical abortion is outlawed in the United States, pro-lifers will face a diffused, twofold battle against abortifacient drugs and ME. This fact was highlighted when Susan Landau of the Redding Feminist Women's Health Center boasted that "the technology is here—you can't take that away. They may make abortion illegal, but they can't control it."[6]

ME in Developing Countries

The largest promoter of menstrual extraction in developing countries is the International Planned Parenthood Federation (IPPF). IPPF, in its *Vision 2000* document, outlined its plan to make legal abortion available in every country of the world.

In pursuit of this goal, IPPF has provided thousands of suction machines for early abortions to the Philippines, Bangladesh, Korea, Singapore, Hong Kong, Thailand, Vietnam, India, and other countries, regardless of the status of the target nation's abortion laws.[7]

Malcolm Potts, former IPPF Medical Director, admitted nearly 30 years ago that menstrual extraction is indeed an abortion method, and that it is a simple and convenient way to do abortions that are difficult to prosecute:

Using the name "menstrual regulation" alters the name of the game. It is not practical to write about abortion in a Bangladesh newspaper in a straightforward way, but it has proved acceptable to hold a much-publicized conference on menstrual regulation in Dacca. ... It is not prudent to have even a whispered discussion of the role of abortion in family planning in the Philippines; but it generates immediate and widespread interest to discuss menstrual regulation.... Menstrual regulation is probably safer than any other pregnancy termination procedure ... there will be no proof of pregnancy unless the tissue removed from the uterus is subjected to microscopic examination. The point is of crucial importance in countries where abortion is illegal.[8]

In its *Family Planning Handbook for Doctors,* IPPF describes the value of the ME/MR procedure to pro-abortion activists: "In some countries, menstrual regulation has proved remarkably popular, and individual practitioners sometimes perform several thousand operations a year. In certain countries menstrual regulation is legal, even when therapeutic abortion is illegal, as in many Latin American countries, where prosecution for abortion requires proof that a pregnancy was terminated."[9]

Health professionals are not the only people using ME/MR in developing countries. A number of "family planning" manuals have described how to assemble a homemade suction machine in order to do early abortions, and this makes ME an ideal tool for midwives and "neighborhood abortionists" in Latin America, Asia and Africa.

Abortionists in some countries use menstrual extraction extensively, and MEs in these countries are not counted as abortions. Therefore, pro-abortion statisticians in Holland and other countries claim that the "lower" abortion rates in these countries are a direct result of their mandatory, comprehensive sex education and contraceptive distribution programs. This is a critical point for pro-lifers opposing permissive sex education programs to remember.

The Dangers of ME

The "menstrual extraction" procedure is extremely dangerous, particularly when done by lay people. Depending upon the equipment used and the experience level of the lay abortionist, women can suffer injuries ranging from punctured uteri and severe infections to incomplete abortions and undiagnosed ectopic pregnancies. In fact, ME is so hazardous that even the National Abortion Federation (NAF), the abortionists' trade union, has labeled it "... dangerous to the health of the women we seek to assist."[10]

Abortionist Grant Bagley of Salt Lake City pointed out the racism and hypocrisy of feminists and the United States government when he said, "No one has been particularly alarmed that we're exporting this [ME] technology to Third World countries, but somehow if women in the U.S. are going to be using the same techniques, it's dangerous."[10]

ME/MR is just one facet of the United States' "contraceptive imperialism." When a contraceptive, abortifacient, or abortion technique is in the research phase or is deemed to be too dangerous for American women to use, testing or production is simply shifted to women in developing countries.

The Catholic Church Teaching on ME

"Catholic" dissenters in Asian and Latin American countries often claim that menstrual extraction does not really fall under the Catholic Church's teachings against abortion, since it is not really possible for a woman to know whether she is pregnant at the time she undergoes ME.

This argument is as dishonest as claiming that firing a rifle randomly in a city is harmless because the shooter cannot really know whether he is going to hit anyone.

The Vatican's *Declaration on Procured Abortion* (14) states that "divine law and natural reason, therefore, exclude all right to the direct killing of an innocent man." On 24 November 1988, The Pontifical Commission for the Authentic Interpretation of the Code of Canon Law declared that abortion is not only "the expulsion of the immature fetus," but is also "the killing of the same fetus in any way and at any time from the moment of conception."[11]

This definition of abortion includes the use of all menstrual extraction techniques and all abortifacients.

1 Personal communication with Father Paul Marx of Human Life International, 4 June 1996.

2 Holtrop and Waife. *Uterine Aspiration Techniques in Family Planning* (Second Edition). The Pathfinder Fund, 1979.

3 Brett Harvey. "The Morning After." *Mother Jones*, May 1989, pp. 28-31, 43.

4 Rebecca Chalker and Carol Downer. *A Woman's Book of Choices: Abortion, Menstrual Extraction, RU-486.* Four Walls Eight Windows Press, Post Office 548, Village Station, New York, New York 10014. 1992, pp. 37, 166.

5 Candy Berkebile. "Feminists Teach "Do-It-Yourself" Abortions." Quoted in *Family Voice* [a publication of Concerned Women for America], June 1992, pp. 12-13.

6 Susan Landau of the Redding Feminist Women's Health Center, quoted in Lisa M. Krieger. "Clinics Teaching Women to Do Home Abortions." San Francisco *Examiner,* 21 July 1989.

7 Donald Page Warwick. "Foreign Aid for Abortion," *The Hastings Center Report,* Volume 10, Number 2, p. 33, April 1980.

8 Malcolm Potts, Peter Diggory and John Peel. *Abortion.* London: Cambridge University Press, 1970, pp. 230-232.

9 *IPPF Family Planning Handbook for Doctors.* Chapter 15, "Menstrual Regulation," pp. 241, 242, 247-248, date not given, but post-1987.

10 Janice Perrone. "Controversial Abortion Approach." *American Medical News,* January 12, 1990, pp. 9, 18-19.

11 "Church Elaborates Definition of Abortion." *National Catholic Register,* 11 December 1988, p. 3.

∙∙

14. What Is a Selective Abortion (Pregnancy Reduction)?

The "pregnancy reduction" abortion has been in use since about 1980 and is now generally standardized. The most common method involves inserting a needle through the mother's abdominal wall into her uterus and injecting potassium chloride into the hearts of the most accessible "surplus" babies. They subsequently die and are reabsorbed by the mother's body.

The *New England Journal of Medicine* recently described this method:"Using ultra-sound to locate each fetus, the doctors would insert a needle into the chest cavity of the most accessible fetus and place the needle tip directly into the heart of the baby. Potassium chloride was then injected into the heart and the heart was viewed on the ultrasound screen until it stopped beating."[1]

"Pregnancy reduction" is often used after *in-vitro* fertilization (IVF) procedures, because up to six embryos are often implanted in order to ensure that a pregnancy results. The United States Congress Committee on Small Business found that many unregulated IVF enterprises deliberately implant an excessive number of embryos during transfer procedures just to increase their chances of success:

> IVF success rates are so discouraging that there are some centers trying to do better in terms of creating babies by using multiple [embryo] implants. It shows at the forty-one [leading] centers there were an average of three embryos used. Some centers use more than that. When they do, they some-times create multiple pregnancies, three, four, five, or six babies ... Then they use fetal reduction, which is killing some fetuses to preserve the health of the mother and to help the other fetuses survive. That is a serious procedure. But because of the lack of pressure to standardize, routinize, and assure quality in the centers out there, we have this kind of dubious activity going on out there.[2]

The above quote highlights one of the primary reasons that pro-life activists oppose artificially-assisted reproduction techniques such as IVF that result in the creation of so-called "spare" embryos that are then disposed of or experimented upon. Another reason is that the women who go through all of the pain, trouble and expense of IVF in order to have a baby, must suffer intense heartbreak when they are told that one or more of them must be deliberately killed in order to spare the lives of the others.

For further information on IVF and other assisted reproduction techniques, see Chapter 9.

1 "Selective Abortion, AKA Pregnancy Reduction." *New England Journal of Medicine*, 21 April 1988.

2 Committee on Small Business. *Consumer Protection Issues Involved in* In-Vitro *Fertilization Clinics.* Washington, D.C.: United States Government Printing Office, 1988, pp. 26-27.

....

15. How Do Abortion Centers Dispose of the Remains of Aborted Babies?

There are two common methods of disposing of the bodies of first-trimester aborted babies: Flushing them down a garbage disposal or "Insinkerator" or dis-posing of them as biological waste in special plastic bags. Larger aborted babies are frequently sold for research purposes.

Pro-abortionists do not want the remains of aborted babies (especially late-term aborted babies) to fall into the hands of pro-life activists, who then can reveal the bloody reality of abortion to the world. In Wichita, Kansas, and other cities, pro-lif-ers have discovered aborted preborn babies as large as six pounds (full-term) being burned as garbage along with dead dogs, cats, and birds thrown out by local Humane Society offices.[1] Some abortionists have even used meat grinders and garbage disposals to dispose of the bodies of aborted preborn babies.[2]

Warning!

**The photographs on the following
two pages graphically depict
the horrible truth of abortion.**

In order to completely eliminate the bodies of late-term aborted babies, some abortuaries that specialize in third-trimester abortions possess on-site crematoria.[3] An example of such an incinerator is shown in Figure 2.

It is very important for pro-abortionists to deny the humanity of the preborn child, even after he or she is dead, in order to maintain a grisly consistency. In several instances, when pro-life activists have tried to bury dead preborn babies, the American Civil Liberties Union (ACLU) and other pro-abortion groups have sued them because such funerals would allegedly "violate the separation of Church and State."[4]

For more information on fetal experimentation and fetal organ harvesting, see Chapter 10.

1 Dave Andrusko. "Fetal Bodies Incinerated Along With Animal Remains in Wichita, Kansas." *NRL News*, 18 August 1983, pp. 1, 11.

2 "Abortionist Uses Meat Grinder." *HLI Reports*, October/November 1992, p. 26. "Delaware Officials Probe Claims of "Improper Disposal" of Aborted Babies." *The Wanderer*, 23 December 1993, p. 6.

3 Mary Kay Culp. "George Tiller Specializes in Late-Term Abortions." *NRL News*, 24 September 1991, p. 5.

4 For one example, see Leslie Bond. "16,500 Aborted Babies Buried, but without Religious Services." *NRL News*, 26 September 1985, p. 6.

Figure 2

Nazi and Abortion Ovens

One of the many stark similarities between the Nazi and abortion holocausts is seen in how bodies are disposed of. The small oven to the right below is specifically designed to incinerate the bodies of aborted preborn babies up to full-term size.

Nazi ovens for dead slave laborers (1945).

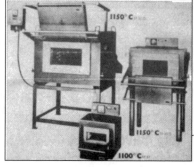

Contemporary Austrian ovens for dead babies (1987).

16. How Many Women Died from Illegal Abortions in the United States Before *Roe V. Wade?*

Pro-Abortion Claims

Pro-abortion groups commonly claim that anywhere from 5,000 to 140,000 women died annually from illegal surgical abortions before *Roe v. Wade.*

Dr. Bernard Nathanson was one of the founders of the National Association for the Repeal of Abortion Laws (now NARRAL), and the former operator of the largest abortion clinic in the world in New York City. He was one of the originators of the popular "5,000 to 10,000 deaths" figure.

After he converted to the pro-life movement, he revealed the deception behind these figures:

> How many deaths were we talking about when abortion was illegal? In NARAL, we generally emphasized the frame of the individual case, not the mass statistics, but when we spoke of the latter it was always "5,000 to 10,000 deaths a year." I confess that I knew the figures were totally false, and I suppose the others did too if they stopped to think of it. But in the "morality" of our revolution, it was a useful figure, widely accepted, so why go out of our way to correct it with honest statistics? The overriding concern was to get the [anti-abortion] laws eliminated, and anything within reason that had to be done was permissible."[1]

Many other American pro-abortionists have acknowledged that they vastly inflated the numbers of maternal deaths. For example, author Marian Faux confirms the lie supporting what she labels "propaganda" in her book *Roe v. Wade:* "An image of tens of thousands of women being maimed or killed each year by illegal abortion was so persuasive a piece of propaganda that the [pro-choice] movement could be forgiven its failure to double-check the facts."[2]

Malcolm Potts, former Medical Director of the IPPF, who helped promote abortion throughout the world, claimed in 1970: "Those who want the [abortion] law to be liberalized will stress the hazards of illegal abortion and claim that hundreds, or thousands, of women die unnecessarily each year—when the actual number is far lower."[3]

When American illegal abortion statistics were examined closely, the actual number of women dying before legalization turned out to be much lower than pro-abortionists claimed.

The late Dr. Christopher Tietze of the Population Council, the country's most experienced abortion statistician, believed that the illegal abortion death rate in the United States was about 100 deaths for every 100,000 abortions in the mid-1960s.[4] The U.S. government's Centers for Disease Control (CDC) estimate that about 150 women died annually from illegal abortions before Colorado, California, and North Carolina legalized it in 1967. Using Tietze's illegal abortion death rate figure, this results in a total of perhaps 150,000 annual illegal abortions in the early and mid-1960s.[5]

These estimates are typical of a number of approximations that have been made by experts in the field of abortion epidemiology and statistics. Higher estimates of maternal deaths are invariably accompanied by little or no documentation.

A Problem with Documentation?

Pro-abortionists argue that the "official" CDC illegal abortion-death figures are much too low because almost all of the deaths caused by illegal abortion before 1973 were not reported or properly documented.

This obviously cannot be the case. As described in Question 18, the maternal death rate has declined steadily over the last fifty years. If a major cause of maternal deaths was suddenly removed by the 1973 *Roe v. Wade* decision, there would have been a sharp drop in the absolute numbers of maternal deaths. Yet no such drop occurred.[6]

According to the U.S. government's Bureau of Vital Statistics and the CDC, the last time 1,000 women died of illegal abortions in the United States was in the year before penicillin became widely available to the public—1942. The number of maternal deaths from illegal abortions declined steeply until it stabilized at about 90 to 150 per year during the decade before *Roe v. Wade*.[5]

1 Bernard Nathanson, M.D. *Aborting America*. Doubleday, 1979, p. 193.

2 Marian Faux. *Roe v. Wade: The Untold Story of the Landmark Supreme Court Decision That Made Abortion Legal*. MacMillan Publishers, 370 pp., 1990.

3 Malcolm Potts, Peter Diggory and John Peel. *Abortion*. Cambridge University Press, 1970.

4 Christopher Tietze, M.D. *Induced Abortion: A World View, 1983*. New York: The Population Council, 1983.

5 CDC figures and other quotes are extracted from Matthew J. Bulfin, M.D. "Deaths and Near Deaths with Legal Abortions." Presented at the American College of Obstetricians and Gynecologists (ACOG) Convention at Disney World, Florida, 28 October 1975.

6 U.S. Bureau of Commerce, Department of the Census. National Data Book and Guide to Sources, *Statistical Abstract of the United States 1990*. Washington, DC: U.S. Government Printing Office. Table 80, "Live Births, Deaths, Marriages, and Divorces: 1950 to 1988," and Table 110, "Infant, Maternal, and Neonatal Mortality Rates, and Fetal Mortality Ratios, By Race: 1980 to 1987."

17. How Many Women Currently Die from Illegal Abortions Worldwide?

The Pro-Abortion Claims

When pro-abortionists find a lie that works, they use it all over the world. One of the most effective tactics the abortion movement has used in almost every nation is to greatly exaggerate the numbers of women who die from illegal abortions, in order to generate sympathy for their cause and make pro-lifers seem heartless.

Many pro-abortion claims about numbers of maternal deaths from illegal abortions in various developing countries exceed the total number of deaths of *all* women of childbearing age for *all* reasons in those respective nations.

For instance, before legalization, Indian pro-abortionists commonly claimed that the total number of women dying of illegal procedures was an incredible 600,000 annually.[1] African medical professionals have recently claimed that as many as 74,000 African women currently die of illegal abortions each year.[2] And abortion promoters have alleged that 140,000 women die of illegal abortions every year in Mexico.[3]

Perhaps the most extreme example of exaggeration is the BEMFAM estimate of 400,000 annual deaths in Brazil. BEMFAM is the Brazilian affiliate of the International Planned Parenthood Federation (IPPF). Brazilian Institute of Geography and Statistics (IBGE) figures have showed that only 55,066 Brazilian women between the ages of 14 and 50 died *of all causes* in 1980. The IBGE figures were confirmed by World Health Organization (WHO) statistics showing that 41,685 Brazilian women between the ages of 15 and 41 died in 1986 and, of these, 241 died of complications from both legal and illegal abortions.[4]

This means that Planned Parenthood grossly inflated the actual number of illegal abortion deaths in Brazil by 166,000 percent!

It is a simple matter to add up pro-abortion claims of deaths from illegal abortions in a number of nations to produce an aggregate claimed total number of worldwide deaths. These include current figures in countries where abortion is now illegal, and pre-legalization figures in countries where abortion is now legal.

The resulting total number of deaths would be more than two million, which would make illegal abortion the number one cause of death among women of childbearing age on this planet.[5]

The usual number of total worldwide illegal abortion deaths currently claimed by pro-abortionists is comparatively modest, but is still a gross exaggeration.

The Worldwatch Institute has claimed that 200,000 women die from illegal abortions each year, and from six million to eight million more "suffer serious, often life-long health problems."[6] This number is echoed by virtually every pro-abortion group from the Fund for a Feminist Majority to the Revolutionary Communist Party of the United States.[7]

The magic "200,000" seems to carry the same cachet for pro-abortionists on a worldwide level as their discredited "5,000 to 10,000" figure did for the United States. IPPF is the worst offender in this area, and the 200,000 figure is repeated so frequently in its literature that it approaches the status of a mantra: "It is conservatively estimated that 200,000 women worldwide die every year from abortions that are illegal and unsafe."[8] "Hospital records alone show that 200,000 women die from such non-clinical abortions worldwide each year; the real total is estimated to be much higher."[9] "Illegal abortions in developing countries result in as many as 200,000 maternal deaths each year."[10]

Despite the occasional pro-abortion claim that the figure of 200,000 deaths was derived from "hospital records" (which would have been a mammoth international accounting task indeed!), no original documentation or impartial verification of this number is ever provided. In fact, such proof would be impossible, given the extremely rudimentary quality of census and hospital statistics in many developing countries.

One must question why IPPF continues to use this number, particularly because the Alan Guttmacher Institute, closely associated with the Planned Parenthood Federation of America (PPFA), employs the most experienced abortion statisticians in the world.

An Estimate of Worldwide Maternal Deaths from Illegal Abortion

The pro-abortion claim that 200,000 women currently die from unsanitary illegal abortions is a persuasive piece of unsupported and unverified propaganda. However, the question remains: How many women *really* die from illegal abortions in the world today?

A few simple calculations will yield a fairly accurate estimate.

Two reasonable assumptions about abortion mortality rates must first be established. The Alan Guttmacher Institute estimates that the current worldwide mortality rate for legal abortions is about 0.6 per 100,000.[11] For the purposes of this estimate, it is assumed that illegal abortions are 20 times as dangerous as legal abortions on a worldwide basis—12 per 100,000, or twice the illegal/legal mortality ratio commonly quoted by Planned Parenthood and the National Abortion Rights Action League (NARAL).

The Alan Guttmacher Institute also estimates that 26 to 31 million legal abortions are done annually in these countries, and 10 to 22 million clandestine abortions are done in these and other countries each year.[11]

The above statistics lead to the conclusion that a maximum of

$$22,000,000 \times (12/100,000) = 2,640 \text{ women die each year from illegal abortions.}$$

Remember that these numbers are calculated entirely from *pro-abortion* statistics, thereby making them immune to charges of pro-life bias.

This means that the common pro-abortion claim of 200,000 annual maternal deaths from illegal abortion is an exaggeration of 7,500 percent.

1 Priya Darshini. "Abortions Increase in India." *The Oregonian* [Portland, Oregon], 3 September 1989, p. A9.

2 Khama Rogo. "Induced Abortion in Africa" (unpublished draft), prepared for the Population Association of America annual meeting in Toronto, Canada, 2 May to 3 May 1990.

3 See Dr. Salvador Sandoval's letter in the 2 April 1992 issue of the *Merced Sun-Star*, and James A. Miller's rebuttal in the 30 April 1992 issue of the same publication.

4 30 December 1991 letter of Dr. Geraldo Hideu Osanai, President, *Associacao Pro-Vida de Brasilia* to Andrew M. Nibley and Thomas D. Thompson of the Reuters News Agency in New York City.

5 In addition to the exaggerated claims illegal abortion deaths in India, Brazil, Mexico, Africa and the United States, there have been allegations of 20,000 deaths in Italy, 15,000 deaths in West Germany (D. Kurchoff, *Deutsches Arztblatt*, Volume 69, Number 27, 26 October 1972) and 2,000 deaths in Portugal (*Portuguese Anuario Estatistico*, Tables 11, 16, and 111).

6 Jodi L. Jacobson. "Coming to Grips with Abortion," pp. 114-131. In the Worldwatch Institute's *State of the World* 1991 Report. W.W. Norton Publishers, London, 1991. Also issued as Worldwatch Paper #97, "The Global Politics of Abortion."

7 The Fund for the Feminist Majority claimed that "Illegal Abortion Kills One Woman Every 3 Minutes Worldwide" in the title of an advertisement for its "Abortion for Survival" propaganda video in the July/August 1989 issue of *Ms. Magazine*, p. 47. The Revolutionary Communist Party of the United States alleges on pp. 4 and 40 of its booklet entitled "Women Are Not Incubators!: The Assault on Abortion Rights" that "Today some 200,000 women a year die in Third World countries—one woman every three minutes. And the anti-abortion policy of the U.S. is making the situation even worse."

8 1989 Planned Parenthood Federation of America pamphlet titled "The Bush Administration: Dragging Us Back to the Back Alley."

9   6 February 1989 Planned Parenthood Federation of America advertisement in the *New York Times* titled "How Can You Explain That Her Mother Died of Politics?"

10 International Planned Parenthood Federation, Western Hemisphere Region, Inc. *Annual Report,* 1989. New York: PPFA, 1989. pp. 2-3.

11 Stanley K. Henshaw. "Induced Abortion: A World Review, 1990." *Family Planning Perspectives,* March-April 1990, pp. 76-89.

....

18. Does the Legalization of Abortion Contribute to Overall Improvements in Maternal Health?

One of the most common arguments of pro-abortionists in support of legal abortion is the allegation that "safe and legal" abortion contributes to improved overall maternal health, mainly because the dangers of "back-alley" abortions are eliminated. In support of this claim, they point out that the maternal death rate in the United States after abortion was legalized was lower than it was before it was legalized.

The International Planned Parenthood Federation (IPPF) repeats this argument several times in its *Vision 2000* document as a justification for legalizing abortion worldwide.

This is a classic pro-abortion half-truth. The maternal death rates after abortion was legalized in the United States and other countries are indeed lower than before; but abortion has little or nothing to do with the change, which is always the result of more significant factors.

It is important to note that the most significant drop in the U.S. maternal mortality rate occurred *prior* to the legalization of abortion in 1973. The United States' maternal mortality rate (which includes all deaths due to abortion, childbirth, and ectopic pregnancies) was 37.1/100,000 live births in 1960. The rate was 16.4/100,000 in 1973, the year of the *Roe v. Wade* decision. This means that the average annual decline in the maternal mortality rate before abortion was fully legalized (between 1960 and 1973) was 1.59/100,000.[1]

This rate of decline remained nearly constant even after the first several states legalized abortion during the time period 1967-1969. The maternal mortality rate was 9.6/100,000 in 1978, which means that the average annual decline in the rate *after* abortion was legalized (during the period 1973 to 1978) was 1.36/100,000, *less* than the rate of decline before abortion was legalized.

In 1987, the rate was beginning to level out at 6.6/100,000 as it approached its lowest practicable level.[1]

This steady trend reflects advances in all areas of medicine. The introduction of abortion methods, both legal and illegal, that pose fewer dangers to the mother, have had a negligible impact on the decline in the maternal mortality rate.

Dr. Bernard Nathanson has said:

In fact, the lowering of maternal mortality has been due largely, if not entirely, to advances in anesthesia techniques; the development of new and more powerful antibiotics; the emergence of realtime ultrasound; major strides in laboratory technology with a deeper understanding of the mechanisms of infectious disease; more sophisticated transfusion techniques and—perhaps most important—a higher and more standardized level of training of nurses, medical students and resident physicians in obstetrics and gynecology.[2]

1 U.S. Bureau of Commerce, Department of the Census. National Data Book and Guide to Sources, *Statistical Abstract of the United States 1990*. Washington, DC: U.S. Government Printing Office. Table 110, "Infant, Maternal, and Neonatal Mortality Rates, and Fetal Mortality Ratios, by Race, 1960 to 1987."

2 Bernard N. Nathanson, M.D., FACOG. "A Pro-Life Medical Response to ACOG's January 1990 Publication: "Public Health Policy Implications of Abortion'" presented by William F. Colliton, M.D., *et. al.* American Life League, 1990.

19. What Are Common Physical Dangers of Surgical Abortion?

It is interesting to note that pro-abortionists exaggerated the physical risks of illegal abortion for the purpose of political gain, and now understate and cover up the dangers of legal abortion for exactly the same reason.

Warren Hern, one of the most prolific abortionists in the United States, has admitted that "in medical practice, there are few surgical procedures given so little attention and so underrated in its potential hazards as abortion. . . . It is a commonly held view that complications are inevitable."[1]

Despite what Hern and other abortionists have revealed, many pro-abortion organizations—including the Planned Parenthood Federation of America (PPFA), the National Abortion and Reproductive Rights Action League (NARRAL) and the National Abortion Federation (NAF)—circulate glossy "fact sheets" purporting to "show" that abortion is extremely safe for the mother, both physically and mentally.

These groups do not mention that their "fact sheets" include only very conservative estimates of those injuries that occur during or immediately after the abortion itself in countries with modern medicine. These are commonly referred to as "on-the-table" complications. The pro-abortion "fact sheets" also ignore problems that occur after women leave abortion centers, and do not mention those due to ancillary causes such as resulting ectopic pregnancies and severe nervous system and brain damage from "anesthetic misadventures."

Some of the more common physical dangers of abortion are:[2]

■ **Death.** As many as 100 women currently die from legal abortions in the United States every year. However, the vast majority of these deaths are not reported as being caused by abortion. Instead, coroners attribute them to other causes, such as "blood poisoning," "anesthetic misadventure," or "spontaneous gangrene of the ovaries."

■ **Uterine Perforation.** Between two and three percent of aborted women suffer perforations of the uterus. Most of the perforations caused during first-trimester abortions go undiagnosed, and may lead to problems that may require a hysterectomy or other major corrective surgery, which in itself entails physical and psychological complications. Perforations occurring during late-term abortions are more frequent and are always serious in nature.

■ **Cervical Lacerations.** Cervical lacerations requiring sutures occur in about one percent of all first-trimester abortions. Less severe undiagnosed cervical damage may result in subsequent cervical incompetence, premature delivery and labor complications. Cervical damage and scarring of the endometrium from abortion may also increase the risk of abnormal development of the placenta in subsequent pregnancies, thus increasing the risk of birth defects.

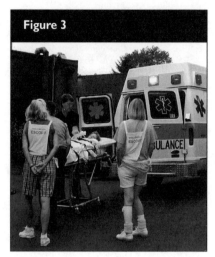

Figure 3

■ **Breast Cancer.** As described further in Question 20, the risk of breast cancer more than doubles after one abortion and grows even greater with subsequent abortions.

"It is a commonly held view that complications are inevitable."—Abortionist Warren Hern

■ **Cervical, Ovarian and Liver Cancer.** Women who have had one abortion more than double their risks of cervical, ovarian, and liver cancer, and women with more than one abortion quadruple their risks.

■ **Placenta Previa.** Placenta previa involves a placenta being superimposed upon the os, and causes severe hemorrhage during labor. Abortion increases the risk of this condition by a factor of from 700 to 1,500 percent. Placenta previa also increases the risks of subsequent fetal malformation and perinatal death.

■ **Ectopic Pregnancies.** Abortion is related to an increase in ectopic pregnancies in future pregnancies, which can seriously threaten the mother's future fertility and even her life. Abortionists may also "abort" a mother who has an ectopic pregnancy at the time, thereby allowing the condition to continue and placing her life in danger.

■ **Pelvic Inflammatory Disease (PID).** PID is life-threatening, and can lead to subsequent infertility and an increased risk of ectopic pregnancy. Twenty-five percent of mothers who have chlamydia [the most common female venereal disease] at the time of their abortions will develop PID, and five percent of those who do not have chlamydia at the time will develop PID.

■ **Endometriosis.** Endometriosis is inflammation of the endometrium (the mucous membrane lining the uterus). Abortion increases the risk of endometriosis, especially among teenagers.

There are two primary reasons why the rates of legal abortion injuries are always underreported.

First, abortion centers do not legally require licensing, and most states (including California, New York, Texas and Florida, which account for 40 percent of all abortions in the United States) do not require the reporting of abortion-related injuries. This allows many abortion deaths and injuries discovered after the woman leaves the abortuary to be attributed to other causes. Therefore, any rate of legal abortion morbidity and mortality in many states must necessarily be an estimate and must therefore be suspect.

Second, less than 40% of women who require post-abortion emergency care return to the abortionist, but instead go to their own gynecologist or to an emergency room when they begin to suffer delayed abortion problems such as infections.[3] Aggravating this situation is the fact that only 30% to 40% of women who have had abortions return for the abortion center's follow-up examinations (even if required), thereby letting many injuries go undetected until they cause serious problems.[4]

1 Warren Hern. *Abortion Practice*. Philadelphia: J.B. Lippincott Company, 1990, p. 101, 103.

2 The information in this section is extracted from two excellent summaries of current research on the physical and psychological complications arising from legal abortion. These are recommended to anyone who is doing any type of in-depth research on this topic. (1) David C. Reardon. *Abortion Malpractice*. Life Dynamics, PO Box 2226, Denton, Texas 76202, telephone: (817) 380-8800, FAX (817) 380-8700. (2) Thomas Strahan. *Major Articles and Books Concerning the Detrimental Effects of Abortion*. Rutherford Institute, PO Box 7482, Charlottesville, Virginia 22906-7482, telephone: (804) 978-3880.

3 Schonberg, "Ectopic Pregnancy and First Trimester Abortion." *Ob.Gyn.* 49 (1S):73S-75S, January 1977.

4 Major & Cozzarelli. "Psychosocial Predictors of Adjustment to Abortion." *Journal of Social Issues* 48(3):121-142 (1992).

··

20. What Is the Connection Between Breast Cancer and Abortion?

The Likely Abortion/Breast Cancer Mechanism

Cancers seem to begin in immature, undifferentiated breast cells, which are those that have not yet specialized. These cells proliferate in the first trimester of pregnancy, stimulated by increased concentrations of the female hormone estrogen. In the second half of pregnancy, these tissues grow under the influence of human placental lactogen and other hormones, and differentiate rapidly into specialized milk-producing tissue which is less susceptible to malignancies than undifferentiated cells.

This process is cut short if the mother has an abortion.

Some studies show that miscarriages do not appear to increase the risk of breast cancer, possibly because a miscarriage is a natural process that takes place over several days, whereas abortion is an abrupt interruption of the pregnancy that does not allow the body's hormones enough time to adjust properly.

The Increased Risks of Breast Cancer

More than 50 studies on a possible abortion-breast cancer link have been performed as of August of 1996, and the medical community is beginning to lend greater credence to the possibility of a connection between the two, despite the loud protests of pro-abortion groups.

None of these studies have shown a conclusive link between abortion and breast cancer because of the extraordinary difficulties inherent in carrying out such an investigation. These problems arise from several sources;

- The study must cover a period of at least 20 years in the lives of a large number of women in order to account for women who drop out of the study and to attain the required level of statistical reliability.

- The influence of many parallel lifestyle indicators (i.e., diet, sexual habits, general health, genetic predispositions, addictions, etc.) must be identified and accounted for in the risk factors.

- The study must be reproducible; that is, the same methodology must yield approximately the same results in other studies.

The abortion-breast cancer link has been suspected since about 1970, but since the methodology for the study of such a connection is only now being developed, the 50 studies mentioned above have yielded understandably varied results. Some have shown an increase in risk, some have shown no statistically significant connection, and a few have even shown a small *decrease* in breast cancer risk among women who have had abortions.

However, a careful review of the studies reveals that the largest and most rigorously-conducted investigations—and those performed by organizations without a vested interest in the abortion industry—imply a definite link between abortion and breast cancer.

A 1994 study published in the *Journal of the National Cancer Institute* concluded that, if a woman aborts her first pregnancy, her chances of developing breast cancer before she turns 45 increase by 50 percent. Because about 10 percent of women contract breast cancer, and because about 1.6 million women have surgical abortions in the United States every year, this would mean that abortion ultimately causes about 80,000 "surplus" cases of breast cancer each year.[1]

An earlier study found that if a woman aborts her *first* baby after the age of 30, her chances of getting breast cancer jump 110 percent. If she has an abortion before the age of 18, her risk escalates by 150 percent.[2]

The results of these studies were confirmed by a 1993 survey of African-American women. Those women who abort a child at any time in their lives had a 180 percent greater risk of developing breast cancer by age 40 and a 370 percent greater risk by age 50.[3]

Will the Public Learn the Truth?

Although the results of the body of studies on the abortion-breast cancer link have been inconclusive as of mid-1996, this certainly does not rule out proof of a definitive link in the future. At the very least, the medical community is acknowledging that a connection may indeed exist.

However, pro-abortionists strenuously deny that such a link is even *theoretically* possible, even though there is no way that their conclusion can possibly be proven at this time.

This reaction is very interesting, considering that liberals and the media immediately sound a general alarm over any suspected cancer cause, no matter how tenuous the connection may be. This has happened repeatedly with Alar, electromagnetic fields (EMFs), saccharin, cellular phones, chlorine, and asbestos, to name just a few.

Only continued neutral study by epidemiologists will ultimately prove or disprove the suspected abortion-breast cancer link.

1   Janet Daling, M.D. "Risk of Breast Cancer Among Young Women: Relationship of Induced Abortion." *Journal of the National Cancer Institute,* 2 November 1994.

2   H.L. Howe, et. al. "Early Abortion and Breast Cancer Risk Among Women Under Age 40." *International Journal of Epidemiology,* February 1989, pp. 300-304. M.C. Pike. "Oral Contraceptive Use and Early Abortion as Risk Factors for Breast Cancer in Young Women." *British Journal of Cancer* 43:72 (1981).

3   "Breast Cancer Risk Factors in African-American Women: The Howard University Tumor Registry Experience." *Journal of the National Medical Association,* December 1993.

••

21. What Are the Common Psychological Problems Abortion Causes to Mothers?

The Definition of Post-Abortion Syndrome (PAS)

A large percentage of women who have had one or more illegal or legal surgical abortions report having one or more of a cluster of psychological symptoms that resemble those suffered by victims of post-traumatic stress disorder (PTSD). Pro-life psychologists and activists call this cluster of symptoms "post-abortion syndrome," or PAS.

Does PAS Exist?

Pro-abortionists often simply deny that women suffer at all as a result of abortion. For example, the Planned Parenthood Federation of America (PPFA) has claimed that "[Post-abortion syndrome is a] largely non-existent phenomenon [circulated by] anti-family planning extremists ... emotional responses to legally induced abortions are largely positive."[1] Other pro-abortionists, despite evidence to the contrary, simply insist that there are absolutely *no* adverse psychological impacts from abortion and claim that PAS is a "myth."[2]

Their allegations were buttressed in January of 1989 when then-Surgeon General C. Everett Koop reported on the psychological and physical impacts of abortion. His report, which had been ordered by the Reagan Administration, concluded that not enough data currently existed on the harmful effects of abortion to make a firm conclusion either way.

Pro-abortionists and media spokespersons immediately twisted the conclusions of the report. While the report claimed "inconclusive" or "insufficient" evidence on the matter of PAS, the media reported instead that the report found "*no* evidence."

Dr. Koop was enraged by this deception and manipulation. He told an interviewer that, "Instead of saying 'the Surgeon General could not find sufficient evidence to issue a scientifically statistically accurate report that could not be assailed,' the Associated Press said, 'He could find no evidence.' I *know* there are detrimental effects [from abortion]. I have counseled women with this problem over the last fifteen years. There is no doubt about it."[3]

Many leading pro-abortionists admitted the existence of psychological trauma from abortion even before it was legalized. In 1960, Dr. Mary Calderone, the founder of the Sex Information and Education Council of the United States (SIECUS), said that "Aside from the fact that abortion is the taking of a life, I am mindful of what was brought out by our psychologists—that in almost every case, abortion, whether legal or illegal, is a traumatic experience that may have severe consequences later on."[4]

Thirty years later, *The Journal of Social Issues* confirmed this conclusion when it stated that "There is now virtually no disagreement among researchers that some women experience negative psychological reactions postabortion."[5]

In light of this unanimity, it is grossly unethical, uncaring and typically irresponsible for pro-abortionists to blithely insist that a problem does not exist.

Stresses Caused by Abortion

In 1986, J. Lawrence Jamieson and Martin H. Stein of Dominion Hospital and Sleepy Hollow Psychiatric Center in Falls Church, Virginia, produced a fascinating scale of stress caused by various events in the lives of American women. This "stress ladder," titled "The Holmes Personal Stress Scale," ranked all events that a woman might encounter.

Abortion ranked ninth on this scale, behind such events as forcible rape, suicide of a husband or lover, divorce, sexual abuse, or death of a parent, and *above* pregnancy, fear of nuclear war, breakup with a steady boyfriend, and rejection by a college.[6]

Other surveys and studies have confirmed that abortion consistently ranks at or near the top of the scale as a life event that causes extremely high levels of emotional distress. A 1992 Gallup Poll showed that, of all events or situations that would make a person feel "bad about himself," 67% of the women questioned and 55% of the men questioned in the age group 18 to 29 years old stated that having or being involved in an abortion tops the list.[7]

The Psychological Impacts of Abortion

More than 400 studies on the psychological effects of abortion have been performed over the last two decades. The findings of these studies have ranged from those alleging that few women suffer from abortion to those that claim that *all* women suffer to some extent.

A comprehensive analysis of 239 articles on the psychological effects of abortion showed that reports with a greater number of methodological flaws (such as small sample size, attrition, and invalidity) tended to produce lower percentages of women suffering from abortion, and the more rigorous studies produced higher percentages.

The ranges of psychological stress quoted by the studies varied from 6% to more than 80%.[8]

There are several reasons why pinning down the exact percentages is very difficult. Most women are ashamed of their abortions and feel guilt because they believe that abortion represents a failure of some kind. Most women also basically believe abortion is wrong (nearly two-thirds of all women who obtain abortions give false phone numbers to their abortion centers). Also, more than half of all women who have had abortions conceal this fact when completing even *anonymous* surveys.[9]

As shown above, there is a huge amount of conflicting evidence available on PAS. Therefore, although there is little doubt that many or most women suffer emotionally after abortion, very little solid evidence exists regarding the exact percentages of women who incur this harm. This is due to many factors, chiefly the reluctance of women to participate in studies of the psychological impacts of abortion, and their hesitation to give accurate answers for various reasons.

However, perhaps the figures given by PPFA can be taken as baseline, because the PPFA operates the largest chain of abortion centers in the United States and can be expected to try to protect its sources of income.

Planned Parenthood admits that "Women can have a variety of emotions following an abortion (grief, depression, anger, guilt, relief, etc.)."[10]

Although there is disagreement on the percentages of women who suffer psychological harm from abortion, most researchers agree that certain factors increase the probability of damage. The PPFA states that about five percent of all women who abort will endure *severe* psychiatric disturbances, and that several categories of women are at high risk.[10]

These categories include:

■ Women who are ambivalent (according to pro-abortionists, abortion is a "difficult choice" for almost *all* women, so almost all aborted women should fall into this category);

■ Women who are under pressure from boyfriends, husbands, parents, teachers, or profit-hungry abortion "counselors" to abort (a 1988 Alan Guttmacher Institute survey showed that virtually *all* women are under one or more external or internal sources of pressure to abort ("My parents want me to abort," "I don't want others to know I was having premarital sex," "my boyfriend forced me," etc.).[11] More than 80 percent of women who have abortions in the United States are unmarried, and therefore feel pressure from a variety of sources to abort (see Chapter 13).

■ Women having abortions because of fetal defects (the prevalent anti-life mentality has persuaded many men and women that they cannot cope with a handicapped baby);

■ Second-trimester abortions (second- and third-trimester abortions account for about 10 percent of all abortions in the United States);

■ Women having abortions because of contraceptive failure (this is a particularly important point, since an amazing 58 percent of all women who have abortions in the United States were using some method of contraception at the time they conceived). See Chapter 13 for details.

■ Teenage girls, because of their immaturity and possible inability to understand the full ramifications of their decisions. Teenage girls have about 25
percent of all abortions in the United States (see Chapter 13).

Judging by the high-risk categories outlined above, virtually every woman who
has an abortion in the United States is at risk for subsequent psychological trauma.
Many (such as unmarried teenagers whose contraception failed) may fall into three
or more high-risk categories.

Despite these obvious risks to women's mental health, every major pro-abortion
group continues to fight any attempt to enact laws that allow women more time or
information to further consider their abortion decisions, such as 24-hour waiting periods, mandatory counseling, or even informed consent provisions that outline the
physical and psychological risks of abortion. This proves that these organizations are
truly so *pro*-abortion that they do not care at all about the health of women, but only
for the continued availability of abortion.

Because of the very nature of the study material, it is very difficult to prove that
a precise number of women suffer a specific psychological consequence of abortion. However, even with a moderately-sized study sample, we can make reasonably accurate *comparisons* between groups of women who abort and groups of
women who do not abort.

■ Women who abort have more psychological problems than women who
carry to term, and can be expected to require psychiatric help up to eight
times more frequently than women who do not abort.[12]

■ Twenty percent of women who abort consider suicide at some time, compared with 12 percent of women who do not abort.[13]

■ One-fourth of women who abort are heavy alcohol users, compared with
one-eighth of women in general.[13]

■ David Reardon's 1994 study found that women who abort have a cluster
of psychological symptoms that occur much more frequently than among
women who do not abort. These symptoms include flashbacks (63%); suicide attempts (28%); hysterical outbreaks (51%); loss of self-confidence and
self-esteem (82%); eating disorders such as anorexia or bulimia (39%); illegal drug use (41%); and loss of pleasure during intercourse (59%).[14]

It is an axiom of psychotherapy that it is not healthy to "bottle up" one's emotions.
There is no doubt that most women who have abortions feel ashamed of their
decisions and believe that they must keep their secrets to themselves.[9]

This is not surprising in light of current attitudes in Western society. How can a
woman share her mourning or negative feelings over having removed a "blob of
tissue" that is morally equivalent to (as the pro-abortionists like to say) "fingernail
clippings" or "warts?" After all, women do not mourn over having an appendix
removed. When an aborted child cannot be discussed or even *acknowledged*; when
she cannot talk to her husband or boyfriend, fellow churchgoers, pastor or co-
workers about the child; when everyone tells her that she has done the "best thing

she could do at the time;" a woman who has had an abortion lives in total isolation with her feelings.

Her friends may tell her to "buck up," because it was only "a little blob" that she had removed. And when a woman cannot or does not admit or acknowledge having killed her own child and feels that she does not have "permission" to mourn, her bottled-up emotions may lead to multiple consequences later.

And so the conspiracy of silence claims another victim.

The Role of the American Psychiatric Association

One particularly curious sequence of actions by the American Psychiatric Association (APA) inevitably comes up in any protracted discussion about PAS.

In 1987, the APA listed abortion as a psycho-social stressor in its *Diagnostic and Statistical Manual of Mental Disorders - III-Revised (DSM-III-R)*. This meant that abortion can cause post-traumatic stress disorder (PTSD). The APA did not specifically mention PAS in its 1987 *DSM-III*, but many women who have had abortions met every one of the criteria listed therein for PTSD.

The APA apparently was deeply troubled by pro-lifers drawing parallels between PAS and "traditional" PTSD, since it vocally supports every part of the abortion agenda.

Therefore, the APA took the easy way out: It purged its 1994 *DSM-IV* of any references to abortion, miscarriage, children, and surgery of any type. The APA even went so far as to completely redefine the categories of psychosocial stressors that cause mental trauma (i.e., problems associated with the economy, family, litigation, education, access to health care, and so on). The APA seems to have done this in order to make it more difficult to categorize abortion as a stressor.

The obvious question is this: Why did the APA consider abortion to be a psychological stressor in 1987 but not in 1994? This change was certainly not due to the findings of new medical studies on PAS, because no conclusive research was done during this period.

The only logical explanation is that the APA could not continue to endorse something that is generally admitted to cause significant psychological damage. Therefore, it took the easy way out. The APA simply removed all evidence of psychological trauma caused by abortion from its *DSM-IV,* thereby "erasing" the problem from its professional consciousness.

1 Planned Parenthood "fact sheet," described in Keith J. Finnegan. "Post-Abortion Syndrome: An Emerging Crisis." American Family Association *Journal,* August 1988, pp. 4-6.

2 See for example N. Stotland. "The Myth of the Abortion Trauma Syndrome." *Journal of the American Medical Association,* 268, 2078 (1992).

3 Dr. C. Everett Koop. Interview with the Rutherford Institute, Spring 1989. Also recounted in *The Abortion Injury Report* (a publication of the American Rights Coalition, PO Box 487, Chattanooga, Tennessee 37401). Spring 1990, p. 2.

4 Dr. Mary Calderone. "Illegal Abortion as a Public Health Problem." *American Journal of Public Health,* Volume 50, Number 7, p. 951 (1960).

5 G. Wilmouth. "Abortion, Public Health Policy, and Informed Consent Legislation." *Journal of Social Issues,* 48, 3, p. 5 (1992).

6   J. Lawrence Jamieson, Ph.D., and Martin H. Stein, M.D. "The Holmes Personal Stress Scale." This study is described in *The Oregonian*, 28 December 1986.

7   "The Curse of Self-Esteem." *Newsweek* Magazine, February 17, 1992. Also see a letter by John Leonardi entitled "Abortion and "Self-Esteem"." *ALL About Issues*, September/ October 1992, p. 6.

8   V. Rue, A. Speckhard, J. Rogers, and W. Franz. "The Psychological Aftermath of Abortion: A White Paper." Presented to the Office of the Surgeon General, Department of Health and Human Services, Washington, D.C., 1987. Also see E. Posavac and T. Miller. "Some Problems Caused by Not Having a Conceptual Foundation for Health Research: An Illustration from Studies of the Psychological Effects of Abortion." *Psychology and Health*, 5, 12-13. Also see Dagg. "The Psychological Sequelae of Therapeutic Abortion - Denied and Completed." *American Journal of Psychiatry*, 148:5 (May 1991), Table 2.

9   Center for Epidemiological Studies Depression Scale, Applied Psychological Measurement, 1993. C. Everett Koop, January 9, 1989 Letter to President Ronald Reagan concerning the health risks of induced abortion. In *Medical and Psychological Impact of Abortion* (Washington, D.C., U.S. Government Printing Office), pp. 68-71.

10 Planned Parenthood Federation of America. "The Emotional Effects of Induced Abortion." *Fact Sheet*, New York, NY, 1993.

11 Aida Torres and Jacqueline Darroch Forrest. "Why Do Women Have Abortions?" *Family Planning Perspectives*, July/August 1988, pp. 169-176.

12 Badgely, *et. al. Report of the Committee on the Operation of the Abortion Law*. Ottawa: Supply and Services, 1977, pp. 313-321.

13 Louis Harris & Associates. "The Health of American Women." The Commonwealth Fund, Table 418, p. 451. 20 April 1993.

14 "Psychological Reactions Reported After Abortion." *The Post-Abortion Review*, Fall 1994, pp. 4-8.

....

22. What Are the Common Psychological Problems Abortion Causes to Fathers?

The *Danforth* Decision

The U.S. Supreme Court ruled on father's rights regarding abortion in its *Planned Parenthood of Central Missouri v. Danforth* decision of 7 July 1976.

In this court case, James Bopp of the National Right to Life Committee (NRLC) represented Erin Andrew Conn of Elkhart, Indiana, who won a court order in June 1988 barring his wife, Jennifer, six weeks pregnant, from having an abortion. She defied the court injunction and had an abortion with the help of the American Civil Liberties Union (ACLU). Her lawyer, Richard A. Waples of the Indiana ACLU, stated in legal papers that "she did what she had to do to protect both her physical and emotional health."

This document made it sound as if Jennifer Conn had her back against the wall, and that abortion was the only way out for her. However, *all* abortions are "hard cases" to pro-abortionists. Why did Jennifer Conn need an abortion "to protect both her physical and emotional health?" Court documents showed that she had the abortion because she had planned a trip to the beach and wanted to look good in her new bathing suit![1]

Among other findings, the Court held that any requirement that a husband or parent be even *informed* about a wife's or minor's abortion is unconstitutional.

This decision stripped fathers of any legal right whatever to protect their own preborn children. The father therefore has less of a right to protect his *own child* than abortion referral agents have to arrange its death, the abortionists to kill it, or the State to declare his slightest opposition unconstitutional and punishable. His relationship to his own child is deemed much less important than his relationship to a piece of property—say a car stereo.

On the other hand, the *Danforth* decision enforced "mandatory fatherhood" for those men who did *not* want a child. In summary, a father has literally no voice whatever in the decision to have or not have a child. And this glaring and hurtful inequality is ignored by the same feminists who are demanding equality themselves.

The *Conn v. Conn* case was the first pure "father's rights" litigation brought to the attention of the Supreme Court of the United States, and decisively demonstrated that fathers have no rights whatever regarding their preborn children.

Impacts on Fathers and Relationships

According to a national poll, more than half of all fathers—including married men—are *not even told* that their children have been aborted.[2]

While feminists demand total control over the abortion decision, they callously disregard the feelings and needs of men, whom they lock out of the process with grim determination. And while they demand that men be more "sensitive" and "caring," they mandate that men may have no say in the decision regarding whether or not their own child lives.

The reaction of Louise Tyrer, vice-president of medical affairs at Planned Parenthood, is typical of the utter callousness that pro-abortionists show toward any rights other than their own: "But it doesn't matter how much men scream and holler that they are being left out [of the abortion decision]. There are some things that they are never going to be able to experience fully. I say, 'tough luck.'"[3] And Marjorie Reiley Maguire and Daniel C. Maguire, members of the anti-religious group 'Catholics' for a Free Choice, counsel that "Nor is [abortion] a question of the man's rights. You have no moral obligation to consult him or to consider his desire that you continue the pregnancy."[4]

This callous hypocrisy can only lead to anger and hurt on the part of men and a subsequent tremendous strain on relationships.

Researcher Arthur Shostak surveyed 1,000 men waiting in abortion mills while their wives and girlfriends were being aborted. He tallied and analyzed their responses to his questions on their feelings and concluded the following;

- 42% of the boyfriends had offered to marry the woman;

- 25% of those who did not offer to marry the woman offered child support;

- Most of the men, regardless of their feelings toward abortion, offered to pay the costs of the abortion "procedure;"

- 39% of the men believed that life began at conception or when the nervous system began to function; and

- 26% believed that the abortion was the "killing of a child."

Shostak's study, not surprisingly, found a vast range of emotions among the men. They feared for the women's health, felt guilty about the abortion or the pregnancy, felt self-doubt, and also anguish and pain over the loss of their children and over the entire abortion "experience."[5]

Just as childbirth is not a trivial issue for a woman, abortion is not a trivial issue for a man. University of Maryland psychologist Arnold Medvene says that "Abortion is one of the major death experiences that men go through. It resurrects very important, very primitive issues, memories, and feelings."[6]

When men are purposely and systematically shut out of such an important decision, they (being men) must take some kind of *action* to relieve their frustrations. Clinical studies have shown that men become angry when they are purposely omitted from an important decision that involves their own family, and they feel deceived and manipulated. The man may not show his anger at the time of the abortion, but it will eventually express itself through "hooking," a process of reacting angrily to a situation that he associates with the abortion.[7] In other words, he may feel strong emotions when he sees a child that is the same age as his aborted child would have been, or when he sees a pregnant mother. This kind of reaction is remarkably similar to those of women suffering from post-abortion syndrome (PAS).

Most commonly, however, a man reacts to an abortion that was committed over his objections by dumping his wife or girlfriend. One study showed that three-fourths of the relationships between married *and* unmarried couples fell apart within *one month* of the abortion.[8] Not surprisingly, feminist groups object strenuously to the men abandoning relationships without any input from women, while they fully support the "right" of women killing their preborn children without any input from men.

1 In re Unborn Baby H., No. 84C01 8804JP185, slip opinion at 1-2 (Vigo County, Indiana Circuit Court, April 8, 1988). Also see "Woman Defies Court, Father, Aborts Child." *Washington Times*, 15 April 1988.

2 Marie Shelton. "Abortion Often Causes Guilt, Regret, Poll Finds." *Sacramento Bee*, 19 March 1989, p. A7.

3 Quoted in John Leo. "Sharing the Pain of Abortion." *Time* Magazine, 26 September 1983, p. 78. For more information on men's role in abortion, see the book by Arthur Shostak, Gary McLouth and Lynn Seng. *Men and Abortion: Lessons, Losses, and Love*. Praeger Publishers, 1984.

4 Marjorie Reiley Maguire and Daniel C. Maguire. "Abortion: A Guide to Making Ethical Decisions." 'Catholics' for a Free Choice, September 1983.

5 Arthur B. Shostak. "Abortion as Fatherhood Glimpsed: Clinic Waiting Room Males as [Former] Expectant Fathers." Presented to the Eastern Sociological Society Meeting in Philadelphia, Pennsylvania in March of 1985, p. 4.

6 Tamar Jacoby. "Doesn't a Man Have Any Say?" *Newsweek* Magazine, 23 May 1988, pp. 74-75.

7 Jane Steinhauser, M.D. "Abortion's Impact on the Father and Familial Relationships." Presented at a conference titled "Healing Visions II, the Second National Conference on Post Abortion Counseling", at the University of Notre Dame, on 20 July 1987.

8 Vincent M. Rue, Ph.D. "Forgotten Fathers: Men and Abortion." Life Cycle Books, PO Box 792, Lewiston, New York 14092-1792. 1986, $1.00.

23. What Organizations Help Women and Men Who Have Been Injured by Abortion?

There are more than one hundred pro-life organizations, local, national and worldwide, that are dedicated to offering emotional support to women and men injured by abortion. In addition to direct support, these groups also perform research on post-abortion syndrome and pursue litigation against abortion clinics that physically or emotionally injure women.

The addresses and telephone numbers of these organizations are listed in Appendix A. See also Appendix D for a listing of Human Life International's major Branches.

The Facts of Life

Chapter 2

Contraception

....

24. What Is the Definition of "Contraception?"

The classical definition of the word "contraception" comes from the Latin (*contra* = opposed to, and *concepto* = conceive).[1] This definition was generally accepted by the medical profession until the beginning of large-scale development of scores of different abortifacients in the late 1960s.

At about that time, pro-abortion and population control groups intentionally began to blur the line between contraceptives (which prevent the union of sperm and egg) and abortifacients (which end the life of the early developing human being *after* the sperm and egg have been united).

This semantic subterfuge was committed for three purposes: (1) to anticipate the shift in abortions from surgical butchery to silent chemical killings, which are much more acceptable to the public; (2) to protect the availability of abortifacients should surgical abortion be outlawed; and (3) to promote the use of abortifacients, which, as a class, have a higher effectiveness rate than do contraceptives.

As a result, all medical dictionaries now simply lump contraceptives and abortifacients together into a single category. For example, Miller and Keane's *Encyclopedia and Dictionary of Medicine, Nursing, and Allied Health* (3rd Edition, 1983) defines "contraception" as "prevention of conception or impregnation," and lists among various methods of "contraception" all birth control pills and intrauterine devices, which are both abortifacients.

The only true contraceptives that exist are surgical sterilization and the barrier methods, which include the male and female condom, diaphragm, vaginal sponge, cervical cap, and spermicidal foams, gels, creams, and suppositories.

1   Charlton T. Lewis, Ph.D. *A Latin Dictionary.* Oxford: Clarendon Press, 1989.

....

25. What Is the Difference Between the "Method Effectiveness Rate" and the "User Effectiveness Rate?"

Overview

When referring to the effectiveness or failure rates of contraceptives and abortifacients, terms are usually expressed in percentages per year.

For example, if 100 women use a certain contraceptive method for one year and 18 of them become pregnant, the effectiveness rate of the contraceptive method is 0.82 or 82% for one year, and the failure rate is 0.18 or 18% for one year.

The Pearl Index is also often used to quantify contraceptive failures. It is a measure or the number of pregnancies per 100 woman-years of exposure. Therefore, the Pearl Index for the above-mentioned contraceptive would be 18.

Method Effectiveness Rate

The "method effectiveness rate" is the rate at which a contraceptive or abortifacient method prevents or ends pregnancy if used *exactly* as directed (i.e., perfectly, with absolutely no user error). The "method *failure* rate" is the rate at which a contraceptive or abortifacient method *fails* to prevent or end pregnancy. These two rates always add up to 100%. For example, if the method effectiveness rate of a certain brand of condom is 88%, the method *failure* rate would be 12%.

User Effectiveness Rate

The "user effectiveness rate"—also known as the "actual effectiveness rate"—accounts for both method failure and user errors and is therefore the "real-world" measurement of how effective a contraceptive or abortifacient method really is. The actual effectiveness rate is *always equal to or lower* than the method effectiveness rate, and accounts for such user errors as improper usage and forgetfulness.

Some methods, such as sterilization and the IUD, preclude user error, so their method and actual effectiveness rates are identical.

....

26. What Are the Effectiveness Rates of the Various Types of Birth Control?

One of the reasons that abortion rates are so high in countries where contraceptives are common is that the people have come to believe "family planning" propaganda alleging that contraceptive methods are reliable.

As Figure 4 and Table 1 show, the user effectiveness rate for the various types of nonsurgical (temporary) contraception range from 88% to 64%. These rates sound impressive until one considers that, if a woman uses a contraceptive method with a 12% failure rate, she has a 47% chance of an unintended pregnancy in five years and a 72% chance of a pregnancy in 10 years.[1]

"Family planning" experts have always recognized that the high failure rate of contraceptives would lead to more abortions. In fact, they *demand* that abortion be made available as a "backup" to widespread contraception.

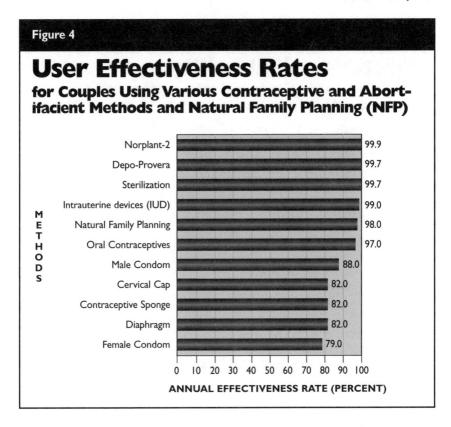

Figure 4

User Effectiveness Rates
for Couples Using Various Contraceptive and Abortifacient Methods and Natural Family Planning (NFP)

METHODS

Method	Annual Effectiveness Rate (Percent)
Norplant-2	99.9
Depo-Provera	99.7
Sterilization	99.7
Intrauterine devices (IUD)	99.0
Natural Family Planning	98.0
Oral Contraceptives	97.0
Male Condom	88.0
Cervical Cap	82.0
Contraceptive Sponge	82.0
Diaphragm	82.0
Female Condom	79.0

ANNUAL EFFECTIVENESS RATE (PERCENT)

Abortion statistician Christopher Tietze stated baldly that women who use contraception are inevitably going to have several "failures" during their reproductive lives: "The safest regimen of control for the unmarried and for married child-spacers is the use of traditional methods [of contraception] backed up by abortion; but if this regimen is commenced early in the child-bearing years, it is likely to involve several abortions in the course of her reproductive career for each woman who chooses it."[2]

The method and user effectiveness rates for the various types of contraceptives and abortifacients are shown in Table 1.

1 Accumulated failure rates can be calculated with the formula $1-(1-e)^n$, where e equals the effectiveness rate and n equals the number of years.

2 C. Tietze, J. Bongaarts, and B. Schearer. "Mortality Associated with the Control of Fertility." *Family Planning Perspectives*, January-February 1976, pp. 6-14.

Table I

First-Year Failure Rates
for Couples Using Various Contraceptive and Abortifacient Methods and Natural Family Planning (NFP)[a]

Method Used	Failure Rates in Percent	
	Method	User
Contraceptives		
No method used	85%	85%
Spermicides only [b]	6%	21%
Withdrawal	4%	19%
Cervical cap with spermicide		
Women with previous children	26%	36%
Women with no previous children	9%	18%
Contraceptive sponge		
Women with previous children	20%	36%
Women with no previous children	9%	18%
Diaphragm with spermicide	6%	18%
Male condom	3%	12%
Female condom ("Reality")	5%	21%
Female sexual sterilization	0.4%	0.4%
Male sexual sterilization	0.2%	0.2%
Abortifacients		
Oral contraceptives		
Progestin	0.5%	3.0%
Combined OC	0.1%	3.0%
Intrauterine devices (IUDs)		
Progesterone T	1.5%	2.0%
Copper T 380A	0.6%	0.8%
LNg 20	0.1%	0.1%
Depo-Provera	0.3%	0.3%
Norplant-2 (6 capsules)	0.1%	0.1%
RU-486 abortion pill [c]	N/A	N/A
Natural Family Planning (NFP)		
Calendar rhythm	9%	N/A
Billings Ovulation Method (BOM)	3%	N/A
Sympto-Thermal Method (STM)	2%	N/A
Post-ovulation	1%	N/A

a   Robert A. Hatcher, et. al. Contraceptive Technology (16th Revised Edition). New York: Irvington Publishers, Inc., 1994. Table 5-2, "Percentage of Women Experiencing a Contraceptive Failure During the First Year of Typical Use and the First Year of Perfect Use and the Percentage Continuing Use at the End of the First Year, United States," p. 113.

b   Includes foams, creams, gels, vaginal suppositories, and vaginal films.

c   Annual rates are not applicable since RU-486 effectiveness is measured on a per-use basis. For further information on the RU-486 abortion pill, see Question 44.

27. What Are the Costs of the Various Methods of Birth Control?

Table 2 shows the initial costs, annual costs, and total costs over five years for the various types of contraceptive and abortifacient methods, with a comparison to the cost of natural family planning (NFP). All costs shown are in 1996 U.S. dollars.

28. How Effective Are Condoms at Preventing AIDS and Venereal Diseases?

Overview

Due to the highly charged aspects of the issues related to contraception (i.e., school-based clinics, the teen pregnancy "epidemic," and the spread of AIDS), there is much conflicting information on the effectiveness of the most commonly-used nonpermanent contraceptive method in the world—the condom—at preventing pregnancy, AIDS, and venereal diseases.

Two types of male condom are commonly available today. These are the latex condom and the animal membrane (skin) condoms.

Experts generally agree that skin condoms are not effective at preventing AIDS and venereal diseases. There is disagreement over the efficacy of latex condoms at preventing AIDS and VDs.

A Complicated Question

There is much debate today over whether latex condoms provide protection against the HIV virus.

The Centers for Disease Control (CDC) assert that unbroken and *properly used* latex condoms can block the AIDS virus.[1] The basis for this claim is a series of studies that show that latex condoms are 99%+ effective at stopping the AIDS virus.

However, there are two serious flaws inherent in each of these studies:

(1) An extremely small sample size was used in each study (only one to 10 condoms of each brand); and

(2) *In-vivo* conditions of actual intercourse were not simulated.

The inherent, naturally occurring flaws in natural rubber (latex) are up to 5 microns (0.0002) inches in size. The average sperm cell is about 50 microns in diameter, and the average AIDS virus is about 0.1 micron in size.[2] This means that, in terms of size, an AIDS virus can pass through a latex flaw as easily as a house cat can walk through a garage door.

This would seem to imply that latex condoms do not protect against the AIDS virus. However, there are two factors that must be taken into account:

(1) The effects of surface tension are extremely powerful at the molecular level. It is very doubtful that an AIDS virus in a water-based suspension of any type would be able to pass through a hole even 100 times its own diameter.

39

Table 2

Costs
of Contraceptive and Abortifacient Methods and Natural Family Planning (NFP)

	Initial Cost	Annual Cost	Total 5-Year Cost
Contraceptive Methods			
Cervical cap with spermicide	$ 130	$ 95	$ 605[a]
Male condom with spermicide	—	150	750[a]
Female condom with spermicide	—	365	1,825[a]
Diaphragm with spermicide	130	95	605[a]
Contraceptive sponge	—	145	725
Female sexual sterilization	2,730	—	—
Male sexual sterilization	820	—	—
Abortifacient Methods			
Depo-Provera	50	155	825[b]
Intrauterine device (IUD)	165	—	265[c]
Norplant	550	—	650[c]
Oral contraceptive	50	215	1,125[b]
Natural Family Planning (NFP)			
Natural Family Planning	75	8	115[d]

[a] Annual cost of spermicide alone is $85.

[b] Includes $50 for initial examination.

[c] Includes $100 removal cost.

[d] Initial cost includes books, instructor fees, thermometer and charts for the sympto-thermal method. Annual cost includes charts ($1) and one thermometer ($7).

Reference (except for NFP): Robert A. Hatcher, *et. al. Contraceptive Technology* (16th Revised Edition). New York: Irvington Publishers, Inc., 1994. Table 5-8, "Cost of Contraceptive Methods, Based on Assumption of 100 Acts of Intercourse Annually," p. 133, and Table 15-2, "Cost of Sterilization," p. 382. Costs updated from 1993 dollars to 1996 dollars at three percent per year.

(2) Latex condoms are "double-dipped," meaning that all or most of the voids left from the first layer will be filled by the second. Repeated SEM (scanning electron microscope) photos of stretched condoms show no apparent voids, even at a magnification of 2,000X.[3]

An Engineering Analysis of an SEM Image

Point (2) above is repeatedly used by condom advocates to argue that latex condoms are extremely effective at blocking the HIV virus.

Indeed, when a latex condom is stretched and viewed under the extreme magnification possible with a scanning electron microscope, no pores seem to be present.

However, when an SEM image of stretched latex shows no pores, we must remember that stretching applies only one type of stress on a material: Uniform lateral stress. It is not possible to get an accurate "picture" of pores in a condom

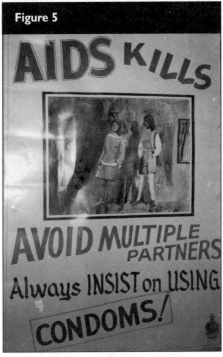

Figure 5

People all over the world are exposed to propaganda implying that condoms are adequate protection against AIDS. If they knew how frequently condoms leak and tear, they would think twice. This poster is from Kenya.

under an SEM, because it is physically impossible to simultaneously simulate for an SEM picture the other four types of stress that are applied to a condom during intercourse: (1) pressure stress (perpendicular to the axis of the lateral stress); (2) shear stress (high twisting or angular stresses at critical points); (3) friction stress (abrasion occurring during lateral movement between two surfaces in contact); and (4) corrosion stress caused by a mixture of body fluids and lubricants, whose effect is greatly enhanced by the repeated and simultaneous application of mechanical stresses.

To say that a latex condom is safe because it shows no pores when only one out of five types of stress is applied is like saying that a new type of car is safe for highway use because it can be driven in a straight line at 25 MPH on a smooth and level road without falling apart.

The fact that latex condoms do indeed contain pores was highlighted by a major 1992 Food and Drug Administration (FDA) study, the first to simulate actual conditions of sexual intercourse. This study showed detectable leakage of HIV-sized particles in one-third of the condoms tested.[4]

The Facts of Life

Those who debate the merits and demerits of condoms should remember that the head of a human sperm cell is approximately 50 microns (0.002 inches) in diameter, and the head of an HIV virus is about 0.1 microns in diameter.[2] This means that a sperm cell, which is effectively blocked by a latex condom, is about 100 million times more massive than an HIV virus.

This contrast in size is proportional to a five-ton bull elephant standing next to a small housefly.

The Primary Danger

Although latex condoms appear to be permeable to the AIDS virus, the greatest danger of infection lies in the propensity of condoms to burst, tear, and slip off frequently.

Even if a few AIDS viruses *can* pass through a porous condom, the risk of infection would still be extremely small; but in those cases where condoms fail catastrophically, massive exposure to the HIV virus is inevitable. In cases of failure during intercourse with an HIV-infected person, there is the distinct possibility of a protracted and painful death.

The frequency of condom breakage depends upon many factors, including the type of lubricant used and the brand of condom. *Contraceptive Technology* tallied the results of seven recent studies and found that 60 of 2,414 condoms broke, or 2.5 percent.[5]

There have been few studies that actually use live couples to test HIV transmission rates. However, a University of Miami Medical School study showed that three out of 10 women whose HIV-infected husbands faithfully used condoms contracted AIDS-Related Complex (ARC) in an 18-month period.[6]

This translates into an infection rate of 11.2% per year, 21 percent in two years, 30 percent in three years, 45 percent in five years, and 70 percent in 10 years. One article in *The Lancet* concluded that "The possible consequences of condom failure when one partner is HIV infected are serious enough and the likelihood of failure sufficiently high that condom use by risk groups should not be described as 'safe sex'.... Condoms have a substantial failure rate: 13-15% of women whose male partners use condoms as the sole method of contraception become pregnant within one year."[7]

Effectiveness Against Venereal Diseases

Most health authorities agree that condoms (when used perfectly and when they do not break) effectively block such venereal diseases as gonorrhea and syphilis. However, condom misuse or breakage can cause massive exposure to these diseases, just as with the HIV virus.

What's more, even perfect use of unbroken condoms will not protect against VDs that are spread by skin-to-skin contact, such as human papillomavirus (HPV) and herpes simplex virus (HSV), which frequently infect the entire genital area. Finally, many VDs, such as gonorrhea and herpes, are transmitted by oral sex, which is usually practiced with multiple sexual partners.[8]

These problems partly account for a resurgence in certain VDs. Genital chlamydial infection is the most common bacterial VD in the United States, and is the leading cause of preventable infertility and ectopic pregnancies. Four million new cases of chlamydia (the most common venereal disease) are reported each year.

Genital warts (*condyloma acuminata*) are caused by human papillomavirus (HPV), the most common viral VD in the United States, accounting for three million new cases each year. HPV is present in an estimated 50 percent of all fornicating young women, and, as with other VDs, is associated with multiple sexual partners and with earlier intercourse.

There are about 1.5 million new cases of gonorrhea in the United States each year, and up to one-fourth of all infected men have no symptoms. Gonorrhea can also infect other mucous membranes, including the mouth. The disease can have extremely serious consequences if left untreated, including sterility, pelvic abscesses, and severe health problems for infants born to infected mothers.

Hepatitis B is a particularly dangerous problem in some developing countries. It can lead to chronic hepatitis, cirrhosis, cancers, hepatic (liver) failure, and death. There is no cure for Hepatitis B, and up to 20 percent of the general population in many developed countries shows signs of infection.

Herpes genitalis is caused by the herpes simplex virus (HSV), and infects about 30 million people in the United States today, most of whom show no symptoms. Those who do show symptoms may have painful ulcers in the genital or mouth area.

Pelvic inflammatory disease (PID) is a result of infection with other VDs and viruses/bacteria such as gonorrhea and *E. Coli.* There are one million episodes among American women each year, 20 percent of which result in hospitalization. PID inflames the Fallopian tubes and is a leading cause of ectopic pregnancy.

Syphilis, one of the deadliest VDs, has reached its highest level in 40 years, with 40,000 people in the United States newly infected each year. Untreated syphilis can lead to rashes, lesions, paralysis, aneurisms, blindness, and death.

Health professionals often assert that there are "epidemics" of teen pregnancy, AIDS, alcoholism, drug use, and of course, violence against abortion centers. Most of these allegations are exaggerated and are are not supported with proper statistical analysis.

But declarations of an epidemic of VDs are certainly *not* exaggerated. With more than 100 million people infected with one or more of 20 VDs in the United States alone, it is unrealistic to expect that a paper-thin, nearly weightless sheath of polyurethane or latex will slow down the epidemic.

The only way to completely eradicate all VDs is to follow God's plan for our sexual lives: Abstinence before marriage and fidelity after.

Of course, the sex educators and condom sellers tell us that this is not a "realistic" solution.

They are wrong, of course. Because abstinence/fidelity is the *only* solution that will work, it is the only *realistic* solution as well. Perhaps if the health professionals struggle unsuccessfully for another decade or two trying to contain the VD epidemic with impractical means, they too will reach the same conclusion.

1 Lauran Neergaard. "CDC: Condoms Can Block AIDS." *The Philadelphia Enquirer*, 6 August 1993, p. E10.

2 C.M. Roland, Ph.D., Editor, *Rubber Chemistry and Technology* and Head of the Polymer Properties

Section, Naval Research Laboratory. Letter entitled "Do You Want to Stake Your Life on a Condom?" *Washington Times*, 22 April 1992.

3   "From the Surgeon General, US Public Health Service." *Journal of the American Medical Association*, 9 June 1993, p. 2,840.

4   Ronald F. Carey, William A. Herman, Stephen M. Retta, Jean E. Rinaldi, Bruce A. Herman, and T. Whit Athey. "Effectiveness of Latex Condoms as a Barrier to Human Immunodeficiency Virus-Sized Particles under Conditions of Simulated Use." *Sexually Transmitted Diseases*, July-August 1992, pp. 230-233.

5   Robert A. Hatcher, *et. al. Contraceptive Technology* (Sixteenth Revised Edition). New York: Irvington Publishers, 1994. Table 7-3, "Prospective Studies of Condom Breakage During Vaginal Intercourse— Developed Countries: A Review of the Literature," p. 157.

6   "Evaluation of Heterosexual Partners, Children and Household Contacts of Adults With AIDS." *Journal of the American Medical Association* (JAMA), 6 February 1987.

7   Jeffrey A. Kelly and Janet S. St. Lawrence. "Cautions about Condoms in Prevention of AIDS." *The Lancet* (Journal of the English Medical Society). 7 February 1987, p. 323.

8   Robert A. Hatcher, *et. al. Contraceptive Technology* (Sixteenth Revised Edition). New York: Irvington Publishers, 1994. For an excellent and complete discussion of the major venereal diseases, see Chapter 4, "Sexually Transmitted Diseases."

29. What Are the Other Types of Barrier Contraception?

The male condom is the most commonly used barrier contraceptive in the world. There are now four other types of barrier contraceptives in general use: The diaphragm, the contraceptive sponge, the cervical cap, and the female condom.[1]

A diaphragm is a dome-shaped rubberized cup with a metal spring rim. After the user applies a spermicidal cream or jelly to the diaphragm, she positions it so that the rim spans the distance between the posterior fornix and the pubic bone, thus covering the cervix. The diaphragm comes in a series of sizes and several types, including flat spring, wide seal rim, coil spring, and arcing spring. The user failure rate of the diaphragm is about 18 percent (see Table 1 in Question 26).

The first vaginal contraceptive sponge was approved by the Food and Drug Administration (FDA) for use in the United States in 1983. It is a small, pillow-shaped polyurethane sponge containing spermicide. The dimple on one side of the sponge fits over the cervix. The sponge comes in one size, and is available over the counter in pharmacies. It works for up to 24 hours. The user failure rate of the contraceptive sponge ranges from 18 percent to 36 percent.

The first cervical cap, the Prentif, was approved by the FDA for use in the United States in 1988. The cervical cap is made of soft rubber and roughly resembles a large rubber thimble. It fits around the base of the cervix, and is inserted by the user after being partly filled with spermicide. It works for up to 48 hours, and, like the contraceptive sponge, must not be left in too long because of the risk of deadly toxic shock syndrome (TSS). The user failure rate of the cervical cap ranges from 18 percent to 36 percent.

The first female condom, which goes by the brand name Reality, was approved by the FDA for sale in the United States in 1993. It consists of a loose polyurethane sheath containing two flexible rings. One of these rings serves as an internal anchor, and the other remains outside the vagina after insertion. The user failure rate of the female condom is 21 percent.

There is much ongoing research into new methods of barrier contraception, most of which will probably be variations on the methods listed above. Under study at this time are disposable diaphragms, a silicone rubber cap named FemCap, spermicide-releasing polymer caps, new spermicides, and germicides to combat VDs.

1 The information in this Question is from Robert A. Hatcher, *et. al. Contraceptive Technology* (16th Revised Edition). New York: Irvington Publishers, Inc., 1994. Chapter 9, "The Diaphragm, Contraceptive Sponge, Cervical Cap, & Female Condom."

30. What Are the Different Types of Female Surgical Sterilization?

Introduction
Through all of recorded history, the paramount goal of the medical profession has been to repair the body and restore organ systems to their normal levels of healthy function—with a single exception.

The only "medical procedures" that are done to *destroy* or *inhibit* healthy organs are those aimed at the male and female reproductive systems.

The most obvious example is abortion, the most commonly done "medical procedure" in the world today.

The *second* most common "medical procedure" in the world is male and female sexual sterilization. Since 1970, about 25 million sterilizations have been performed in the United States.[1]

Methods of Female Sexual Sterilization
Female sexual sterilization mechanically blocks the Fallopian tubes to prevent the sperm and ovum from uniting.

The most common female sterilization method is laparotomy. In this method, the woman's Fallopian tubes are sealed with electrocoagulation, in which an electric current burns the tubes and causes them to clot to prevent bleeding. In other, non-electric methods, a clip or band compresses and divides the tubes.[2]

In a minilaparotomy (or "minilap"), the Fallopian tubes are pulled through a small incision of one to two inches length and are sealed. Complications are slightly less than for laparoscopy, but the hospital stay may be longer.[2]

The death rate for female sterilization is about three per 100,000 for tubal ligation laparotomies and about 5-25 per 100,000 for other types of sterilization.[3]

Half of all women who are sterilized have it done postpartum—that is, immediately after having their last baby. After a Cesarean birth, the sterilization can be done through the same incision through which the baby was delivered.

Less than 50% of female sterilizations can be reversed, and, even if the reversal is successful, the risks of subsequent problems such as tubal pregnancies are greatly increased, because reconnecting the tubes is delicate and often difficult.

The Facts of Life

Problems Associated with Female Sterilization

Immediate ("on-the-table") injuries associated with female sterilization include anesthesia-related complications, bowel burns from electrocoagulation, uterine, intestinal, and bladder perforation, and tears and transections of the Fallopian tube.

Ectopic pregnancies comprise 4 to 73 percent of all pregnancies resulting after sterilization, depending upon the method used. Other problems include changes in hormonal feedback, changes in menstrual patterns, psychological problems, and possible subsequent hysterectomy.[1]

Sterilization: Ideal Weapon for Eugenicists

Surgical sterilization is an ideal tool for eugenicists, racists, and population controllers, because its effects are permanent, it cannot be tampered with, and its effectiveness rate is so high.

In the mid-1920s, American eugenicists found that the simplest and most effective way of preventing the "less desirable classes" from reproducing was widespread forcible surgical sterilization. In the United States, from 1907 to 1941, more than 36,000 persons were forcibly sterilized, mostly in California, Virginia and Indiana, usually for "feeblemindedness" or for having been born into large welfare families.[4]

Population controllers continue to use sterilization on a massive scale to curb population growth. Many sterilizations in developing countries are performed without women's consent or knowledge when they give birth. Tens of thousands of mentally handicapped people have been forcibly sterilized in the People's Republic of China (PRC). The government of Indira Gandhi was brought down in popular reaction to India's forced sterilization camps. Other countries that have suffered forced sterilization programs include Honduras, Brazil, the Dominican Republic, Mexico, Nigeria, Tibet, Vietnam, Bangladesh, and Indonesia. In some cases, people protesting forced sterilization programs have been slaughtered by the score.[5]

1   Robert A. Hatcher, *et. al. Contraceptive Technology* (16th Revised Edition). New York: Irvington Publishers, Inc., 1994. Chapter 15, "Voluntary Surgical Contraception (Sterilization)."

2   American College of Obstetrics and Gynecology, Committee on Patient Education. "Patient Education Pamphlets." P-011, "Voluntary Sterilization for Men and Women" (June 1983), P-035, "Sterilization by Laparoscopy (June 1983), and P-052, "Postpartum Sterilization" (June 1984).

3   Robert A. Hatcher, *et. al. Contraceptive Technology* (16th Revised Edition). New York: Irvington Publishers, Inc., 1994, p. 382.

4   Gregory E. Pence, M.D. *Classic Cases in Medical Ethics: Accounts of the Cases That Have Shaped Medical Ethics, with Philosophical, Legal, and Historical Backgrounds.* New York: McGraw-Hill Publishers, 1990. Chapter 14, "Preventing Undesirable Teenage Pregnancies," pp. 286-302.

5   See L.C. Landman. "Birth Control in India: The Carrot and the Rod?," *Family Planning Perspectives*, May-June 1977, pp. 101-110; "Uncle Sam Goes to Mexico," *ALL About Issues*, November-December 1987, p. 12; "India Seeks Progress Through Mutilation and Murder," *ALL About Issues*, September 1985, p. 43; "Vietnam Preparing a "Chinese Solution"," *ALL About Issues*, July 1985, p. 40; "Dreadful Manipulation Suggested By Dominican Republic Figures," *ALL About Issues*, April 1985, p. 36; "Forced Sterilization at AID-Funded Clinic," *HLI Reports*, January 1988, p. 4; "Forced Sterilization Protestors Killed," *NRL News*, December 1976, p. 3; and "Catholic Bishops Critical Of Sterilization Requirement," *PRI Review*, July/August 1991, p. 10.

31. What Are the Different Types of Male Surgical Sterilization?

The Methods

Vasectomy blocks the *vas deferens* (*ductus deferens*), the small vessel that transports sperm, at a point between the testes, where the sperm are made and where it joins with the duct that transports fluid from the seminal vesicle.

Methods of vasectomy include clamping the *vas*, fulguration (burning it with electrical sparks), and cutting a segment out of it and then tying, clipping or bending back each end.[1]

Pregnancies after vasectomy are usually due to the wrong structure being cut or blocked, congenital duplication of the *vas* unnoticed during the vasectomy or spontaneous regrowth of the *vas*.

The effectiveness rate of vasectomy is 99.8 percent, or one pregnancy in 500 years. Pregnancies after vasectomy are usually associated with intercourse before the male reproductive tract is cleared of sperm.

Other Problems Associated with Vasectomy

A comprehensive study of 11,205 sterilized men in 156 United States medical centers found a significant relationship between vasectomy and the development of urolithiasis (urinary tract stones), immunological changes such as the production of anti-sperm antibodies, and tumors of the testes.[2]

About five percent of all vasectomized men can expect hematoma (blood clots), infection, granuloma (a tumor-like mass or nodule caused by chronic inflammation), and epididymitis (inflammation of the epididymis).[1]

Reversibility of Vasectomy

The reversibility of vasectomy depends upon several factors, primarily the original method of vasectomy used. Clipping of the *vas* has the highest rate of successful reversal, followed by cutting, and then by fulguration.

The rate of reversal also depends upon the interval between the vasectomy and the attempted restoration, the fertility of the wife, and the method of vasovasectomy (vasectomy reversal) used. In large samples, pregnancy is achieved in about 50 percent of all reversals.

Success rates of epididymovasostomy (the surgical reconnection of the epididymis to the *ductus deferens*) are in the 5 to 10 percent range, probably because of the immaturity of sperm in the head of the epididymis.[1]

Methods of vasovasectomy include splinted and nonsplinted end-to-end anastomoses (surgical construction of a connection), and side-to-side anastomoses with elliptical incisions.

Reversible vasectomy devices include plugs, intravasal valves, clips applied to the external surface of the *vas*, chemicals, and intravasal threads.

1 Robert A. Hatcher, *et. al. Contraceptive Technology* (16th Revised Edition). New York: Irvington Publishers, Inc., 1994. Chapter 15, "Voluntary Surgical Contraception (Sterilization)."

2 N.R. Rose and P.L. Lucas. "Immunological Consequences of Vasectomy II: Two-Year Summary in a Prospective Study." In I.H. Lepow and R. Crozier (editors), *Vasectomy: Immunological and Pathophysiologic Effects in Animals and Man.* New York: Academic Press, 1979, pp. 533-539.

32. What Is Chemical Sterilization?

At least 20 different methods of chemical (non-surgical) female sterilization have been intensively investigated since about 1975. Among the most-studied compounds are chloroquine, an antimalarial and lupus erythematosus suppressant; methyl cyanoacrylate (MCA); and quinacrine hydrochloride, which is an antimalarial and antiprotozoal compound used to treat giardiasis and tapeworm infections.[1]

As described in Question 30, surgical sterilization has led to enormous abuses by population controllers in developing countries. The great danger inherent in chemical sterilization is that it may be used on a massive scale to sterilize women in developing nations without their knowledge or consent. In fact, the danger of coercion involved in chemical sterilization is much greater than that with surgical sterilization, because the methods used are much cheaper, and are so easy to employ that a minimum of training is required.

Abuses involving chemical sterilization have already been documented.

Elton Kessel, founder of Family Health International (FHI), and Stephen D. Mumford of the Center for Research on Population and Security say they have tested quinacrine on 100,000 women in 15 developing countries.[2] Quinacrine has not been studied in a laboratory, nor has it been approved by any health regulatory body. Kessel and Mumford essentially travel around the world with quinacrine in a suitcase and without supervision, using third-world women as guinea pigs.

Quinacrine is inserted into the fundus of the uterus where it causes inflammation and scarring in the Fallopian tube, in theory blocking the tube with scar tissue and preventing the sperm from reaching the egg.

However, studies have shown that this may cause a tenfold increase in the risk of uterine cancer and a large increase in ectopic pregnancies (when the Fallopian tube is scarred closed to the point where a sperm can be passed but not a blastocyst, which is thousands of times larger).[3] Needless to say, a woman suffering from an ectopic pregnancy in a remote village is almost certain to die before her problem is diagnosed properly.

Interestingly, Kessel and Mumford's work is being funded by the Federation of American Immigration Reform (FAIR), which itself is receiving money from the Leland Fikes Foundation.

1 H. Chandra, S.C. Nigam, S. Zutshi, and B. Malaviya. "Chemical Occlusion of Rhesus Monkey Oviducts with Chloroquine," *Contraception*, September 1978, pp. 233-238; "The Use of Methyl Cyanoacrylate (MCA) for Female Sterilization," *Contraception*, March 1985, pp. 243-252; and A. Benoit, J. Melancon, and M.A. Gagnon, "Chemically Induced Tubal Occlusion in the Human Female Using Intrauterine Instillation of Quinacrine." *Contraception*, July 1975, pp. 95-101.

2 Stephen D. Mumford and Elton Kessel, "Quinacrine Sterilization in the United States?" *Fertility and Sterility*, letter, March 1996, pp. 679-681.

3 "The Human Laboratory." British Broadcasting Corporation's *Horizon* Television Show, aired in Great Britain on 7 November 1995.

33. What Is the Historical Teaching of the Christian Church on Contraception?

From the Beginning

From the time of its founding, the Christian Church has universally condemned contraception. Among the early Church Fathers who wrote and spoke against contraception were Athenagoras, St. Ambrose, St. Augustine Barnabas, St. Basil the Great, Caesarius, Clement of Alexandria, Ephraem the Syrian, Epiphanius, St. Jerome, St. John Chrysostom, Hippolytus, Lactantius, Minucius Felix, Origen of Alexandria, Tertullian and the assembled Bishops at the First Council of Nicaea.[1]

As the various Protestant denominations formed, their founders and leaders also condemned contraception in the most forceful terms imaginable. John Calvin called the sin of contraception "condemned" and "doubly monstrous," and saw abortion as "a crime incapable of expiation." John Wesley said contraception is "very displeasing to God, and the evidence of vile affections." Martin Luther called those who used contraceptives "logs," "stock," and "swine."[2]

Virtually every leader of every Protestant denomination condemned contraception explicitly in sermons and writings. These included Anglicans Henry Alford, William Dodd, Joseph Hall, Richard Kidder, John Mayer, Simon Patrick, Arthur W. Pink, Thomas Scott, Jeremy Taylor, W. H. Griffith Thomas, James Usher and Christopher Wordsworth; Calvinists Jacob Alting, Robert S. Candlish, Franciscus Junius, Cotton Mather, Teunis Oldenburger, David Paraeus, Franklin P. Ramsay, Andre Rivet and Sebastian Scmidt; Evangelicals Keith Leroy Brooks and Thomas H. Leale; Huguenot Jean Mercier; Lutherans Johann Albrecht Bengel, Johannes Brunneman, Abraham Calovius, Conrad Dannhauer, Franz Delitszch, John H.C. Fritz, Johann Gerhard, Johann Karl Friedrich Keil, Paul Kretzmann, Theodore F.K. Laetsch, Herbert Carl Leupold, Walter Arthur Maier, Wolfgang Musculus, Johannes Olearius, Lukas Osiander, and J. Heinrich Richter; Methodists Adam Clarke and Richard Watson; Nonconformists Henry Ainsworth, Daniel Defoe, John Gill, Matthew Henry, George Hughes, William Jenkyn and Matthew Poole; Presbyterians John Brown, George Bush, Robert Dabney, Alfred Edershei, and Melanchton W. Jacobus; and Puritans Richard Stock and John Trapp.[2]

Until 14 August, 1930, all Christian churches were unanimous in their opposition to artificial means of birth prevention. However, the first crack in the dam was Resolution 15 of the Anglican Bishop's Lambeth Conference of 15 August, 1930. Just as the "hard cases" were used to impose abortion on demand—and just as they are now being used to lobby for euthanasia on demand—they were used 65 years ago to pave the way for easy access to contraception.

The United States Federal Council of Churches (now the National Council of Churches) had been waiting eagerly for someone else to take the lead in "modernizing" the Christian's stand on birth prevention. In March of 1931, it endorsed "the careful and restrained use of contraceptives by married people," while at the same time conceding that "serious evils, such as extramarital sex relations, may be increased by general knowledge of contraceptives."

Interestingly, even the secular press ridiculed the FCC's position. As one example, the 22 March 1931 *Washington Post* editorialized: "Carried to its logical conclusion, the committee's report, if carried into effect, would sound the death-knell of marriage as a holy institution by establishing degrading practices which would encourage indiscriminate immorality. The suggestion that the use of legalized contraceptives would be 'careful and restrained' is preposterous."

Of course, the expansion of approval of contraception from just the "hard cases" to *all* cases continued unabated down its smooth and obstacle-free road. The National Council of Churches (NCC) proclaimed on 23 February 1961: "Most of the Protestant churches hold contraception and periodic abstinence to be morally right

Figure 6

The author of Humanae Vitae, *Pope Paul VI, and one of its greatest defenders, Fr. Paul Marx, OSB, meet on 26 January 1973, four days after* Roe v. Wade.

when the motives are right.... Protestant Christians are agreed in condemning abortion or any method which destroys human life, except when the health or life of the mother is at stake."

As the 20th Century draws to a close, almost all of the mainline Protestant denominations (to include Methodist, Church of Christ, Episcopal, Presbyterian, and Lutheran) accept not only contraception, but abortion for almost all reasons. However, a bright ray of hope is shining, as more and more Christians of every denomination see the connections between contraception, abortion, sexual promiscuity and family problems.

Teaching of the Catholic Church

The teaching of the Catholic Church on abortion and contraception could not be clearer. Only a person who willfully blinds himself or herself to the facts could make the ridiculous claim that there is "room for a diversity of opinion" within the Catholic Church on abortion and artificial contraception.

The Church is the guardian of our interpretation of the Natural Law. Since the Natural Law was given to us by God, the Church does not have the authority to change its fundamental moral principles. The Church, of course, does clarify certain matters in the light of new knowledge, but the fundamental principles remain unchanged.

The self-proclaimed "Catholic" dissenters who are waiting for a change will be waiting for a very long time indeed.

When Subversion Fails...

If infiltration and subversion do not work, pro-abortionists are certainly not above direct coercion or bribery.

Edouard Cardinal Gagnon, then-president of the Pontifical Council on the Family, revealed at a 27 June 1989 lecture in Washington, D.C. that the Vatican was offered "millions of dollars" in a bribe to change Church teachings on artificial contraception when the Vatican took up the issue in the late 1960s. The Church would receive this "gift" if She would not formally proclaim Her teaching in the encyclical *Humanae Vitae*. Interestingly, the bribe was offered by retired U.S. General William Draper, who at the time directed the International Planned Parenthood Federation (IPPF).[3]

Sad But True

A favorite anti-life tactic is to parade results of various polls and surveys showing that about 80 percent of Catholic couples use contraception, or that a large percentage of all priests or theology professors support or condone its use. Therefore, they argue, it must be all right for Catholics to use contraception.

Sadly, it is true that most Catholic married people in the United States use contraception. The most comprehensive study on the birth control habits of U.S. Catholics was the 1988 National Survey of Family Growth (NSFG), which showed that, of all married Catholic women:

- 40 percent use oral contraceptives;

- 24 percent rely on male or female sterilization;

- 8 percent use barrier methods, IUDs, or other methods;

- 24 percent use no form of fertility control, because they are either infertile or are trying to get pregnant; and

- Only 4 percent of married Catholic women of childbearing age use natural family planning (NFP).[4]

This survey shows that American Catholics are woefully ignorant of Church teachings in the critical area of sexual morality. To be sure, there are many who are informed but simply ignore the position of the Church; but it may truthfully be said that most U.S. Catholics have never heard contraception condemned from the pulpit.

On Using Our Consciences

Those who dissent from Church teachings in sexual matters are the most likely to claim they are only following their own consciences. But they leave out a vital part of the equation: It is only licit to follow one's conscience when that conscience is *properly formed* and the conclusions reached are in accord with the teachings of the Church.

Father John Courtney Murray, S.J., principal author of the Second Vatican Council's *Declaration on Religious Freedom*, described how this dangerous attitude can lead to the moral anarchy of subjectivism:

The Facts of Life

The *Declaration* [on Religious Freedom] does not base the right to the free exercise of religion on "freedom of conscience." Nowhere does this phrase occur. And the Declaration nowhere lends its authority to the theory for which the phrase frequently stands, namely, that I have the right to do what my conscience tells me to do, simply because my conscience tells me to do it. This is a perilous theory. Its particular peril is subjectivism—the notion that, in the end, it is my conscience, and not the objective truth, which determines what is right and wrong, true or false.[5]

The Popes Speak

The Pope does not live in a vacuum, as many dissenters and anti-Catholic bigots would like us to believe. He is, more than anyone else in the world, completely aware of the currents of dissent and apostasy in the Catholic Church today, because he is surrounded by the finest body of practical and moral theologians in the world, and because he continuously receives accurate and complete information on developments all over the globe.

Perhaps no questions divide theologians more than contraception and abortion. This should not be the case, because the Vatican has issued more than 100 official denunciations of these practices during the 20th Century alone.

Of all of the many clear statements against contraception, perhaps the most definitive is that of Pope Pius XI in his great encyclical *Casti Connubii* (4,4):

But no reason, however grave, may be put forward by which anything intrinsically against nature may become conformable to nature and morally good. Since, therefore, the conjugal act is destined primarily by nature for the begetting of children, those who in exercising it, deliberately frustrating its natural power and purpose, sin against nature and commit a deed which is disgraceful and intrinsically vicious.... In order that she [the Catholic Church] may preserve the chastity of the nuptial union from being defiled by this foul stain, she raises her voice in token of her divine ambassadorship and through our mouth proclaims anew: Any use *whatsoever* of matrimony exercised in such a way that the act is deliberately frustrated in its natural power to generate life is an offense against the law of God and of nature, and those who indulge in such are branded with the guilt of a grave sin.

The teaching of the Church has not changed. On 12 November 1988, Pope John Paul II addressed the final session of a three-day meeting of 300 Catholic moral theologians at the Pontifical Lateran University to celebrate the 20th anniversary of *Humanae Vitae*. There, he summarized the Church's teaching against birth control in a single sentence; "No personal or social circumstances have ever or can ever justify such an [contraceptive] act."

During this talk, the Pope also firmly stated that the ban on contraception "cannot be questioned by the Catholic theologian," much to the consternation of dissenting theologians in the Western world.[6]

1   St. Ambrose, Bishop of Milan (c. 339-397), *Hexameron*, 5.18.58; Athenagoras of Athens, letter to Marcus Aurelius in 177, *Legatio pro Christianis* ("Supplication for the Christians"), p. 35; St. Augustine, Bishop of Hippo (354-430), *De Nuptius et Concupiscus* ("On Marriage and Concupiscence"), 1.17; Barnabas (c.

70-138), *Epistle,* Volume II, p. 19; St. Basil the Great, *First Canonical Letter,* Canon 2 (A.D. 374); Caesarius, Bishop of Arles (470-543), *Sermons,* 1.12; Clement of Alexandria, "The Father of Theologians" (c. 150-220), *Christ the Educator,* Volume II, p. 10. Also see *Octavius,* c.30, nn. 2-3; Ephraem the Syrian, *De Timore Dei,* p. 10; St. Jerome, *Letter to Eustochium,* 22.13 (A.D. 396); St. John Chrysostom, *Homilies on Romans* 24 (A.D. 391); *Letter of Barnabas* 19 (A.D. 74); Hippolytus, *Refutation of All Heresies* (A.D. 228); Lactantius, *Divine Institutes* 6:20 (A.D. 307); Minucius Felix, *Octavius,* 30 (A.D. 226); Origen of Alexandria (185-254), *Against Heresies,* p. 9; Tertullian, *Apology,* 9:8 (A.D. 197), and *The Soul,* 25,27 (A.D. 210).

2   The original quotes are provided in Charles Provan. *The Bible and Birth Control.* Monongahela, PA: Zimmer Press, 1989.

3   William Bole. "Cardinal Says Vatican Was Offered Bribe On Birth Control." *The Wanderer,* 13 July 1989, p. 8.

4   Alan Guttmacher Institute Survey described in Catholic News Service. "Most Catholic Women Ignore Church-Accepted Form of Birth Control." The Portland, Oregon *Catholic Sentinel,* 24 January 1992, p. 7.

5   Father John Courtney Murray, S.J., quoted in Russell Shaw. "Answers." *National Catholic Register,* 13 September 1992, p. 4.

6   "Pope Warns Theologians not to Question Ban on Contraception." *The Wanderer,* 24 November 1988, p. 1.

34. What Is the Teaching of the Catholic Church on Sexual Sterilization?

Introduction
Sexual sterilization is sometimes referred to as "Catholic birth control" or "permanent contraception." These terms, and the misguided assertions of a number of well-known dissenters, has led to confusion regarding Catholic Church teaching on sterilization.

For the simple reason that it closes off the marital act to the transmission of human life, sterilization is condemned on the same grounds as other methods of contraception.

The Authentic Teachings of the Church
In his address to the Congress of Urology on 8 October 1953, Pope Pius XII outlined the specific conditions under which sterilization (or any amputation, for that matter) may be performed:

Three things condition the moral permission of a surgical operation requiring an anatomical or functional mutilation;

(1) that the preservation or functioning of a particular organ provokes a serious damage or constitutes a threat to the complete organism [this is the "principle of totality"];

(2) that this damage cannot be avoided, or at least notably diminished, except by the amputation in question and that its efficacy is well assured; and

(3) that it can be reasonably foreseen that the negative effect, namely, the mutilation and its consequences, will be compensated by the positive effect: exclusion of a damage to the whole organism, mitigation of the pain, etc.

[As far as sterilization is concerned], the conditions which would justify disposing of a part in favor of the whole in virtue of the principle of totality are lacking. It is not therefore morally permissible to operate on healthy oviducts if the life or [physical] health of the mother is not threatened by their continued existence.

Pope Paul VI's 1968 encyclical *Humanae Vitae* held sterilization and abortion to be equally sinful: "Above all, direct abortion, even for therapeutic reasons, is to be absolutely excluded as a lawful means of controlling the birth of children. Equally to be condemned as the Magisterium of the Church has affirmed on various occasions, is direct sterilization, whether of the man or the woman, whether permanent or temporary."

In response to a query on sterilization by the United States National Conference of Catholic Bishops (NCCB), the Congregation for the Doctrine of the Faith's statement of 13 March 1975 replied:

Any sterilization which of itself, that is, of its own nature and condition, has the sole immediate effect of rendering the generative faculty incapable of procreation, is to be considered direct sterilization, as the term is understood in the declarations of the pontifical magisterium, especially of Pius XII. Therefore, notwithstanding any subjectively right intention of those whose actions are prompted by the care or prevention of physical or mental illness which is foreseen or feared as a result of pregnancy, such sterilization remains absolutely forbidden by the doctrine of the church.

The Catholic Church also recognizes that sterilization is not only evil when done to individual persons, but that it is a vital part of the "conspiracy against life" waged by a "culture of death" when used for population control. *Evangelium Vitae* (91) states that: "It is therefore morally unacceptable to encourage, let alone impose, the use of methods such as contraception, sterilization and abortion in order to regulate births. The ways of solving the population problem are quite different."

The Catholic Church has consistently condemned sexual sterilization for any reason whatever except to save the life of the man or woman.[1] In such cases, the principle of the "double effect" may apply, as described in the next Question.

1 Some of the Church's pronouncements against sexual sterilization include *Casti Connubii*, Pope Pius XI, 31 December 1930, 68-71; *Decree of the Sacred Congregation of the Holy Office* (Topic: Sterilization for Eugenics), 18 March 1931; Pope Pius XI, "Pronouncement to the Cardinals in Response to Recent Nazi Legislation in Germany," 23 December 1933; *Decree of the Congregation for the Holy Office*, 24 February 1940; Pope Pius XII, "Address to the Congress of the Italian Association of Midwives," 29 October 1951, 24-26; "Address to the Symposium on Medical Genetics," 7 September 1953; "Address to the Seventh Congress on Hematology," 12 September 1958; USCC Administrative Board, *Statement on Sterilization Procedures in Catholic Hospitals*, 22 November 1977; and USCC, *Statement on Tubal Ligation*, 9 July 1980.

35. Does the Principle of the "Double Effect" Apply to Certain Cases of Sexual Sterilization?

As described in Question 85, the Catholic Church allows abortion for no reason whatever, not even to save the life of the mother. However, a fine distinction must be made in the extremely rare case where a pregnant mother's life is directly and immediately threatened by a condition such as an ectopic pregnancy, carcinoma of the uterine cervix, or cancer of the ovary or uterus.

In such cases, under the principle of the "double effect," attending physicians intend to save the life of the mother by correcting the condition. However, they also must do everything in their power to save *both the mother and the child*. If the physicians decide that, in the case of an ectopic pregnancy, the mother's life can only be saved by the removal of the Fallopian tube (and with it, the unborn baby), or by removal of some other tissue essential for the preborn baby's life, the baby will of course die. But this would not be categorized as an abortion; it would be categorized as a tubectomy. The critical difference between deliberate killing (abortion) and unintentional natural death is that the intention is not to kill the child but to save the mother.

This principle of the "double effect" also applies to sterilization. If a woman must have a hysterectomy to remove a dangerously cancerous uterus, this will result in her sterilization. Because the intent was not to sterilize, the operation is not sinful. But if the *primary purpose* is merely to sterilize, then the act is intrinsically evil and is always a mortal sin.[1]

Some dissenters may claim that *all* sterilizations can be justified by the principle of the "double effect," since, as they say, all "unwanted" pregnancies threaten the mother's life in some way. This is obviously an abuse of the principle and is an illicit statement.

1 Pope Paul VI, *Humanae Vitae*, 25 July 1968, No. 15, and Pope Pius XII, "Allocution to Midwives," No. 27, 29 October 1951.

36. Is There Such a Thing as a "Male Contraceptive?"

In this context, a "male contraceptive" means a chemical compound that renders men temporarily sterile.

There is currently no compound commercially available as a male contraceptive, but about 50 compounds, devices, and methods are being investigated in depth. These include benzoquinone, buserelin, various chlorinated antifertility agents, copper, danazol, Depo-Provera, ethanol, glycerol, infrared radiation, the intravas device (IVD), levonorgestrel, microwaves, mifepristone, oxytocin, and ultrasonography.

Research into a male contraceptive has been done for 20 years but has not progressed significantly for three reasons. First, researchers know men would be reluctant to use a contraceptive and women would be reluctant to *trust* them to use it. Second, it is far easier to "target" a single egg released every month or to cause an early chemical abortion than it is to suppress the production of hundreds of millions of spermatozoa every day. Third, some researchers think the investigation of a male contraceptive is redundant, because so many female contraceptives and abortifacients already exist.

One of the most effective male anti-fertility agents is gossypol, a toxic phenolic pigment in cottonseed, being researched mainly in the People's Republic of China and India.

Trials of testosterone compounds are also being conducted in the United States. These involve an injection of testosterone enanthate weekly or testosterone bucyclate quarterly, or progestagen, which inhibits gonadotropin secretion and subsequently suppresses spermatogenesis. Weekly male testosterone injections stopped sperm production (azoospermia) in two-thirds of men and dramatically dropped it (oligospermia) in the other third who were experimented on.[1]

In a 1990 trial, the failure rate among azoospermic men was 0.8 percent, and about 2 percent for all of the men tested. About 10 percent of men had to drop out because they experienced severe acne, increased aggressiveness and blood lipid abnormalities. There was some speculation as to whether the increased rate of aggressiveness caused a much higher rate of divorce than usual during the trials.[2]

1   "Men's Contraception Injection Match Pill's Effectiveness." *Australian Associated Press*, 1 August 1995.

2   Dorothy Bonn. "What Prospects for Hormonal Contraceptives for Men?" *The Lancet*, 3 February 1996, p. 316.

....

37. What Are the Similarities and Connections Between Contraception and Abortion?

Introduction

The most crucial issue for pro-life activists today concerns the growing recognition of the many connections between abortion and contraception.

The pro-life movement is currently divided into two schools of thought on this link.

The first group either sees no connection, or takes a "no official position" stance on contraception in order to avoid controversy or to focus their efforts on abortion. These organizations and individuals include the National Right to Life Committee (NRLC), Dr. James Dobson's Focus on the Family, the 700 Club and D. James Kennedy.

But more and more pro-life groups and individuals have seen the many connections and realize that, as long as contraception is widely available and the underlying anti-life mentality reigns, abortion will never be defeated. These groups include Human Life International (HLI), American Life League (ALL) and Protestants Against Birth Control (PABC).

Regardless of what pro-life activists think about the links between abortion and contraception, they should consider the following points and reflect on their truthfulness—and their relevance to their own lives.

(1) The Sequential Connection Between Contraception and Abortion

Setting the Stage. In Western nations, pro-abortion groups work for school-based birth prevention clinics and comprehensive sex education programs that include training in contraceptive use. Alan Guttmacher revealed one of the primary purposes of value-free sex education when he admitted: "The only avenue the International Planned Parenthood Federation and its allies could travel to win the battle for abortion on demand is through sex education."[1]

In developing nations, population control groups spend hundreds of millions of dollars annually in attempts to saturate indigenous cultures with every available contraceptive and abortifacient. Malcolm Potts, former Medical Director of the International Planned Parenthood Federation (IPPF), said in 1973: "No society has controlled its fertility without recourse to a significant number of abortions. In fact, abortion is often the starting place in the control of fertility."[2]

Pro-abortionists, population controllers, "family planners" and sex educators all over the world assert that, as contraceptive and abortifacient use increases, "unwanted pregnancies" and both illegal and legal abortions will decrease.

At first glance, this position seems logical. After all, authentic contraception is designed to stop conceptions, and, if more conceptions are prevented, fewer abortions will occur.

But this theory does not work in the real world, because the large-scale use of contraceptives and abortifacients leads to a tremendously increased rate of fornication, which, combined with method failures, leads to a huge increase in the number of "unplanned pregnancies."

More Contraception Leads to More Abortion ... *Always*. Pro-abortionists say increased contraceptive use reduces the number of abortions, knowing that this "logic" will appeal to the large segment of the public that uncritically accepts their assertions.

But they *know* that the opposite is true. For more than 40 years, pro-abortion leaders have admitted that an increase in contraceptive availability inevitably leads to an increase in promiscuity and therefore abortions.

In 1955, America's most famous "sexologist," Alfred Kinsey, said:

> At the risk of being repetitious, I would remind the group that we have found the highest frequency of induced abortion in the group which, in general, most frequently uses contraceptives ... I think it is just too much to hope that we can ever have any contraceptive practice, outside of temporary sterilization, which is going to prevent this occasional slip that accounts for a high proportion of undesired pregnancies and abortions, especially among those of the upper socioeconomic levels.[3]

The two men most often credited with developing the birth control pill now admit that their invention has led to widespread promiscuity. Dr. Robert Kirstner of Harvard Medical School has said: "For years I thought the pill would not lead to promiscuity, but I've changed my mind. I think it probably has."[4] And Dr. Min-Chueh Chang, the other co-developer of the Pill, has acknowledged: "[Young people] indulge in too much sexual activity ... I personally feel the pill has rather spoiled young people. It's made them more permissive."[5]

One of the people most qualified to speak on the relationship between rising contraceptive use and abortion rates is undoubtedly Malcolm Potts, who predicted:

"As people turn to contraception, there will be a rise, not a fall, in the abortion rate."[2] And Christopher Tietze, one of the world's most experienced abortion statisticians, said:

> A high correlation between abortion experience and contraceptive experience can be expected in populations to which both contraception and abortion are available ...women who have practiced contraception are more likely to have had abortions than those who have not practiced contraception, and women who have had abortions are more likely to have been contraceptors than women without a history of abortion.[6]

If the population controllers and pro-abortionists *know* contraception leads to more abortion, why do they lie and say exactly the opposite?

Because they *know* that contraception is unreliable, and because they *know* that the only secular "family planning" program that will definitely cut population growth must include both contraception *and* abortion, either voluntary or coerced. Population statistician Emily C. Moore reflected the consensus when she said: "Since contraception alone seems insufficient to reduce fertility to the point of no-growth, and since population experts tell us that eliminating unwanted fertility [is necessary], we should permit all voluntary means of birth control (including abortion) so as to avert the necessity for coercive measures."[7]

And Dr. Alan Guttmacher said: "Each country will have to decide its own form of coercion and determine when and how it should be employed. At present, the means available are compulsory sterilization and compulsory abortion. Perhaps someday a way of enforcing compulsory birth control will be feasible."[8]

Note that, more than four decades ago, the leading experts of the pro-abortion movement admitted that the widespread availability of contraception inevitably leads to abortion. This proves that their push for easy access to contraception was a cover for abortion agitation in North America and Europe in the past and in developing countries all over the world today.

A Natural Phenomenon? The above quotes prove that pro-abortionists and population controllers fully recognize that the wide availability of contraception *must* lead to vastly increased abortion rates, mainly because of the unreliability of contraceptives.

But we must not think for one moment that the pro-abortionists would stop pushing for abortion if a perfect contraceptive method could be found, or if the world's population began to decline. Population controllers and pro-abortionists see abortion as much more than a useful "surgical procedure"—they see it as an absolute and immutable *right*, a paramount privilege that supersedes all other rights, including the right to life and the right to free speech and dissent.

Article 15 of *Humanist Manifesto II* states: "It is the *moral obligation* of the developed nations to provide ... birth control techniques to the developing portions of the globe." Lawrence Lader, co-founder of the National Abortion Rights Action League (NARAL), said: "The right to abortion, an *inalienable right* of all women, is an integral part of population control."[9]

Beneath the anti-lifer's veneer of compassion and understanding lies a total commitment to separation of all people from God and His plan for our lives. Threads of secular humanism, "New Age" theology and radical environmentalism are at the core of the anti-life mentality, which will never rest until contraception and abortion are freely available to every human being on the planet, so everyone can have sex with everyone else, regardless of whether they are married or unmarried.

Molly Yard, former president of the National Organization for Women (NOW), neatly tied abortion and radical environmentalism together when she said: "The abortion question is not just about women's rights, but about life on the planet—environmental catastrophe awaits the world if the population continues to grow at its present rate."[10] Many radical "animal rights" activists and environmentalists, including Ingrid Newkirk, founder of People for the Ethical Treatment of Animals (PETA), actually see humanity not as the greatest creation of God, but as the polar opposite. Newkirk has said: "We [humans] have grown like a cancer. We're the biggest blight on the face of the earth."[11]

The Only Possible Conclusion. The attitudes described above show beyond the shadow of a doubt that pro-abortionists consider abortion an absolute and fundamental human right. The wide availability of contraception has only "softened up" more than 100 countries for legalized abortion by greatly increasing the demand for illegal abortion. This, of course, is a situation custom-made for pro-abortionists, who then wildly exaggerate the public health problems caused by "women dying at the hands of back-alley butchers," and demand the legalization of abortion.

(2) The Chemical Connection Between Contraception and Abortion

The "Advantages" of Abortifacients. The primary mission of the vast "family planning" field is the search for more and more abortifacients. Even now, fewer and fewer women are using true contraceptives and surgical abortion, and more are using abortifacient chemicals.

The ultimate goal of the "family planners" is to see all women using chemical abortifacients in tandem with anti-VD vaccines.

Why are abortifacients preferable to contraceptives from a "family planning" point of view?

(1) Abortifacients are much more effective at *ending* pregnancies than contraceptives are at *preventing* them. The best user ("real world") effectiveness rates of the birth control pill, the IUD, Norplant, and Depo-Provera average about 98 percent, and the best user effectiveness rates for the male and female condoms, cervical cap, diaphragm, and sponge average only 83 percent (see Table 1 in Question 26 for individual method rates).

(2) Abortifacients put more control into the hands of the medical profession and mean more money for the international pharmaceutical cartel. In developed countries, all abortifacients must be prescribed or inserted by health professionals (in developing countries, physicians exert less control over the distribution of abortifacients). By contrast, all contraceptives are

controlled by the user in all countries. Total use of abortifacients will ensure that physicians (and, in some cases, the State) will be able to strictly monitor and, if "necessary," control the fertility of the people. This is now happening in the People's Republic of China, and has happened on a smaller scale in more than 20 other countries. This point in particular concerns feminists, who would like to see as much reproductive control as possible transferred to the user.

(3) From the user's point of view, abortifacients are more convenient, and there is no fiddling around with jams, jellies, and rubber contraptions, which interrupts foreplay.

(4) Most important of all, the widespread use of abortifacients dulls individual and national consciences even more than does the use of contraceptives. If a woman is conscious of the abortifacient nature of the method she is using, and is still willing to kill the preborn child in his or her first week of life, she will not hesitate to kill the child in its first trimester of intrauterine life. And a nation that has grown accustomed to chemical abortion will resist any controls whatsoever on surgical abortion.

The only serious roadblock to the accelerated changeover to abortifacients is that they do not protect against venereal diseases. For this reason, researchers have placed a very high priority on finding "vaccines" and treatments for these diseases as well.

The Psychology of Chemical Abortion. Chapter 3 describes the ongoing intensive pro-abortion campaign designed to confuse the distinction between abortion and contraception. The elements of this campaign are the redefinition of the word "conception," lawsuits designed to group abortifacients and contraceptives into one classification, insistence that all nonsurgical means of birth prevention are "contraceptive" in nature, and a linking of surgical abortion and "contraception" as one "super-right" in the public mind.

Since the frontier of tomorrow's abortion battle will be chemicals, every pro-life activist must become intimately familiar with the various abortifacients and their exact modes of action. And, if the pro-lifer learns that he or she is using any type of abortifacient, a clear choice results: Stop using the abortifacient, or quit the pro-life movement, because to fight against surgical abortion while knowingly committing chemical abortion is the worst kind of hypocrisy.

(3) The Legal Connection Between Contraception and Abortion

Frank Susman, the lawyer who represented the pro-abortion side in the U.S. Supreme Court's 1989 *Webster v. Reproductive Health Services* case, stated in his opening argument that the "rights" of abortion and contraception now actually merge:

For better or for worse, there no longer exists any bright line between the fundamental right that was established in *Griswold* and the fundamental right of abortion that was established in *Roe*. These two rights, because of advances in medicine and science, now overlap. They coalesce and merge and they are not distinct. The most common forms of contraception today—IUDs, low-dose birth control pills, which are the safest type of birth control pills available—act as abortifacients.[12]

The principle used to justify all anti-life practices in the United States is the "right to privacy," which appears nowhere, in any form, in the Constitution of the Unites States. The U.S. Supreme Court first stumbled upon this mythical "right" in its 1965 *Griswold v. Connecticut* decision, which legalized contraception for married couples nationwide. Three years later, the Court extended this "right" to unmarried people. And, of course, five years after that, it quickly applied the "right to privacy" to abortion in its *Roe v. Wade* decision.

The "right to privacy" is now being invoked all over the world in both passive and active euthanasia cases. In the United States alone, more than 250 court decisions, including those involving euthanasia, have been based upon *Roe v. Wade* since 1973 (see Question 68 for details on how the principles outlined in *Roe* are now being used to legalize euthanasia).

Every American values personal privacy. Everyone wants the government to interfere with their private lives as infrequently as possible. So the "right to privacy" is used as a cover to justify practices that the public will not accept until it has been exposed to them for years. We can see this principle at work in the seamless progression from contraception to abortion to euthanasia. And the "right to privacy" is also used to justify sodomy, adultery, infanticide, and all kinds of pornography.

The public has "evolved" to accept acts that were once universally seen as immoral and loathsome. Anti-lifers now label any opposition to abortion, sodomy, euthanasia, pornography, and other evils "anti-choice," "anti-freedom," and "anti-American."

Pro-lifers and other pro-family activists must not feel guilty in the least when opposing abortion, euthanasia, sodomy, "kiddie porn," and other hideous sins/crimes advocated by organized anti-lifers. After all, anti-lifers simply use the "right to privacy" as a cloak to abuse—or kill—other human beings.

If the anti-lifers have their way, the "right to privacy" will continue to expand until it destroys any chance human beings have of living together without seeing each other as objects to be exploited for personal pleasure and gain.

(4) The Attitude Connection Between Contraception and Abortion

As shown above, there are countless intimate legal, medical and practical connections between contraception and abortion.

But all of these links pale in comparison to the most important connection of all: The fact that the very same belief system and psychology that accepts contraception also readily accepts abortion.

Most people (including most Christians) use contraception for one or more of several reasons: They can't afford a baby, they have problems with their relationships, they want to avoid single parenthood, they aren't ready for the responsibility, they have all the children they want, and they are concerned about how a child (or another child) would change their lives.

These are *exactly the same reasons* that women give to justify having abortions.[13] Underlying them all is the fundamental denial of God's plan for children in our lives. People today want to "plan" their families. But who can better plan a family than God?

Why does a couple contracept? Because they don't want a child. Why don't they want a child? Because they have made Important Plans for Their Lives. And when contraception fails, the resulting "unplanned" child is seen as an intruder, one who will spoil the couple's carefully laid plans.

And when a couple has denied God's plan for their lives once through contraception, it is so much easier to do it again through abortion. As Mother Teresa of Calcutta observes:

> In destroying the power of giving life, through contraception, a husband or wife is doing something to self. This turns the attention to self and so it destroys the gifts of love in him or her. In loving, the husband and wife must turn the attention to each other as happens in natural family planning, and not to self, as happens in contraception. Once that living love is destroyed by contraception, abortion follows very easily.[14]

Conclusion

Evangelium Vitae (13) points out that "contraception and abortion are often closely connected, as fruits of the same tree."

This tree is the same tree that brought about the downfall of our first parents, Adam and Eve. It is the tree of taking it upon ourselves to decide what is right and what is wrong, and it is rooted in the rejection of God's will.

As such, all of its fruits—whether they be contraception, abortion, euthanasia, homosexual activity, masturbation, or pornography—are poisonous to the soul. Everyone who genuinely seeks God's will for his or her life must avoid them.

1   Alan Guttmacher quote of 3 May 1973, *Humanity* Magazine, August/September 1979, p. 11.

2   Andrew Scholberg, "The Abortionists and Planned Parenthood: Familiar Bedfellows." *International Review of Natural Family Planning*, Winter 1980, p. 298.

3   Mary Calderone, M.D. (Editor). *Abortion in the United States*. New York: Paul B. Hoeber, Inc., 1956, p. 157.

4   "In Brief: Harvard, Mass." *ALL About Issues*, June 1981, p. 5.

5   Dr. Min-Chueh Chang, quoted by Charles E. Rice. "Nature's Intolerance of Abuse." *ALL About Issues*, August 1981, p. 6.

6   Christopher Tietze. "Abortion and Contraception." *Abortion: Readings and Research*. Toronto: Butterworth & Co., 1981, pp. 54-60.

7   Emily C. Moore, Ph.D. "The Major Issues and the Argumentation in the Abortion Debate," pp. 33-43. In a looseleaf booklet entitled "Organizing for Action." Prepared by Vicki Z. Kaplan for the National Abortion Rights Action League, 250 West 57th Street, New York, N.Y. 10019, no date.

8   *Medical World News*, June 6, 1969.

9   Samuel L. Blumenfeld. *The Retreat From Motherhood*. New Rochelle, New York: Arlington House, 1975, p. 37.

10 "Women are Not Incubators!" *Proletarian Revolution*, Fall 1989, pp. 7-8.

11 Ingrid Newkirk, quoted in Charles Oliver. "Liberation Zoology," *Reason* Magazine, June 1990, pp. 22-27.

12 "Excerpts of Arguments Before Supreme Court on Missouri Abortion Law." *Washington Post*, 27 April 1989, p. A16.

13 Aida Torres and Jacqueline Darroch Forrest. "Why Do Women Have Abortions?" *Family Planning Perspectives*, July / August 1988, pp. 169-176.

14 Mother Teresa of Calcutta. "Whatever You Did Unto One of the Least, You Did Unto Me." Address given at the National Prayer Breakfast in Washington, D.C., Thursday, 3 February 1994.

The Facts of Life

Chapter 3

Abortifacients

....

38. How Has the Definition of "Conception" Evolved, and Why Is this Important?

The Future of Pro-Life Activism

The current paramount objective of "reproductive" research is to find the ideal abortifacient—one that will kill the preborn child every time without side effects to the woman. This emphasis on abortifacients rather than contraceptives has come about because abortifacients in general eliminate or greatly reduce user error, whereas contraceptives, which always remain under the control of the user, have much higher failure rates than abortifacients and are therefore less effective.

In other words, abortifacients are much more efficient at *ending* pregnancies than contraceptives are at *preventing* them. The average user effectiveness rates of oral contraceptives, IUDs, Norplant, and Depo-Provera are about 98 percent, and the average user effectiveness rates of the male and female condoms, cervical caps, diaphragm, and sponge are only about 83 percent (see Question 26 for individual method and user effectiveness rates).

This means that, as women change their preferences from surgical abortion to chemical abortion, the future of pro-life activism lies not as much outside the abortion mills as it does inside and outside the major pharmaceutical corporations.

How the Definitions Have Evolved

In 1963, the U.S. Department of Health, Education and Welfare (HEW) defined "abortion" as "all the measures which impair the viability of the zygote at any time between the instant of fertilization and the completion of labor."[1]

Until the mid-1960s, scientists universally acknowledged that conception happened at the moment of fertilization of the ovum by the spermatozoa, somewhere in the Fallopian tube. But pro-abortionists and population controllers already had their sights set on a shift from contraceptive to abortifacient methods of birth prevention, and abortifacient research was already ongoing in Japan and several European countries.

In order to make abortifacients acceptable to women, and to circumvent laws designed to prohibit abortion, the pro-abortionists realized that they had to blur the line between contraceptive and abortifacient action.

They could do this only by changing the definition of "conception" from *fertilization* [union of spermatozoa and ovum] to *implantation*. Under the *new* definition of "conception," if a device or drug—such as an IUD or Depo-Provera—prevents implantation, then no abortion takes place. Under the *new* definition, abortion would only occur if a chemical or device killed a preborn child who had already implanted in the endometrium (lining) of the uterus.

The pro-abortionists' continuing agitation for a terminology change finally bore fruit in 1965, when the American College of Obstetrics and Gynecology (ACOG) published its first *Terminology Bulletin*, which stated: "Conception is the implantation of a fertilized ovum." This semantic subterfuge resulted in the *Bulletin* inventing two misleading terms for early abortion: "Post-conceptive contraception" and "post-conceptive fertility control."[2]

The deception by the medical establishment regarding the definition of "conception" coincided exactly with its devaluation of the preborn child. Neither change in attitude nor terminology was based upon some revolutionary discovery in medical technology or knowledge: The changes were made purely to further the anti-life goals of the pro-abortionists within and outside of the medical profession.

Dr. J. Richard Sosnowski, head of the Southern Association of Obstetricians and Gynecologists, a member group of ACOG, clearly highlighted this strategy in his 1984 presidential address:

> I do not deem it excellent to play semantic gymnastics in a profession.... It is equally troublesome to me that, with no scientific evidence to validate the change, the definition of conception as the successful spermatic penetration of an ovum was redefined as the implantation of a fertilized ovum. It appears to me that the only reason for this was the dilemma produced by the possibility that the intrauterine contraceptive device might function as an abortifacient.[3]

Summary of the Changes

Table 3 summarizes the changes that have occurred in medical terminology that are relevant to the early preborn child.

How the New Definitions Work to Kill Preborn Babies

The new (post-1965) definitions in Table 3 have implications far beyond that of the field of abortifacients. The new terms represent "non-inclusive" language that excludes preborn children before implantation. The new definitions will become more and more important, especially if the public and pro-life activists accept them without dispute.

Under the new terminology, few people will object to *in-vitro* fertilization (IVF), through which fertilization takes place in a laboratory dish. The least perfect blas-

Table 3

Changes in Terminology Pertinent to the Beginning of Life

Term	Pre-1965 Definition	Post-1965 Definition
Fertilization	Sperm unites with egg	Sperm unites with egg
Conception	Sperm unites with egg	Implantation (7-10 days after fertilization)
Embryo	The human being from first cell division until 35-40 days after fertilization	The human being after implantation, until 35-40 days after fertilization
Pre-embryo	(Nonexistent term)	The tissue (non-human being) after fertilization, before implantation.

tocysts (very early developing human beings) are simply discarded. If these are mere "pre-embryos," who will care?

What's more, nobody will care if "pre-embryos" are experimented on. And there will be no outcry when, eventually, all "pre-embryos" are systematically screened for all known birth defects, and only the most perfect will be allowed to continue developing. Strong agitation for universal genetic screening shortly after true conception will be one of the inevitable outgrowths of the Human Genome Project, which seeks to map every human chromosome and list every possible defect that can befall human beings.

The Bottom Line

As the battle over abortion shifts from retail surgical baby-killing to wholesale *chemical* baby-killing, pro-lifers must use precise and unchanging language and terms on the ever-changing battlefield. The babies cannot afford sloppy or imprecise language, because confusion and uncertainty always work to the advantage of the pro-abortionists.

Traditionally, pro-life activists have proclaimed: "life begins at conception."

In the Brave New World of silent abortions and shifting terminology, this statement, although it is true, is not specific enough to counter the shifting terminology of the anti-life forces.

The vast majority of preborn children who die at the hands of abortionists are not killed by vacuum machines or curettes, but by injections and pills.

In order to fight for all preborn children, pro-lifers must declare what has always been true, but which is now particularly relevant: "Life begins at *fertilization!*"

1 Public Health Service leaflet No. 1066, U.S. Department of Health, Education and Welfare, 1963, p. 27.

2 American College of Obstetrics and Gynecology. *Terminology Bulletin*, "Terms Used in Reference to the Fetus." Chicago: ACOG, September 1965.

3 J. Richard Sosnowski, M.D. "The Pursuit of Excellence: Have We Apprehended and Comprehended It?" *American Journal of Obstetrics and Gynecology*, 15 September 1984, p. 117.

39. What Is the Definition of "Abortifacient?"

The general definition of "abortifacient" is "a drug or agent that induces an abortion."[1]

A true *contraceptive* agent prevents conception by one or more of four specific actions. It can:

■ place an actual mechanical barrier such as a condom or cervical cap between the sperm and ovum to prevent them from uniting;

■ thicken the cervical mucus;

■ inhibit ovulation, thereby preventing the release of a mature ovum;

■ block the Fallopian tube or *vas deferens* through sexual sterilization.

All of these means prevent a new human being from being created.

By contrast, an *abortifacient* destroys the preborn child who is already conceived. Depending upon the type of abortifacient, this killing can take place at virtually any stage of pregnancy, by preventing implantation of the blastocyst (the very early developing human being), by killing the unborn child shortly after implantation or by killing the child later in pregnancy.

As discussed in the next Question, even the definitions of "abortion" and "abortifacient" are being distorted due to pro-abortion manipulations designed to blur the distinction between true contraceptives and abortifacients.

1 Benjamin Miller and Claire Keane. *Encyclopedia and Dictionary of Medicine, Nursing, and Allied Health* (Third Edition). Philadelphia: W.B. Saunders Company, 1983.

40. What Are the Different Types of Abortifacient?

Hundreds of Lethal Chemical Compounds

It has been said that man's greatest ingenuity is displayed in time of war. This is especially true in the war against his own fertility.

At this moment, extensive research is being conducted on a bewildering array of more than 200 actual and potential abortifacient agents, covering the complete alphabet from alcyonacean soft corals to zoapatle aqueous crude extract, or ZACE.

As one cartoonist noted a few years ago, scientists whose product killed preborn children used to moan "We're ruined!" Now they happily exclaim "We're rich!"

There are generally two classes of abortifacient in existence and under research today. The first type includes drugs and devices designed to continually maintain a certain level of abortifacient in the system and repeatedly kill early preborn children before implantation (without the woman's knowledge), such as birth prevention pills (oral contraceptives), intrauterine devices (IUDs), Depo-Provera and Norplant. The second type is used to kill a preborn child who is *known or suspected* to exist, and includes the RU-486 abortion pill, "doubling up" on oral contraceptives ("emergency contraception") and the methotrexate/misoprostol combination.

Questions 41 through 45 describe the abortifacients most widely used in the world today.

Abortifacients Currently Under Research

As we saw above, the research trend in "family planning" is toward pure abortifacients. Of the more than 200 abortifacients currently under research, the most effective include progestin-carrying IUDs, steroid-containing vaginal rings and diaphragms, and progestin-only creams that could be rubbed on the skin (in other words, an abortifacient skin lotion).[1]

One abortifacient in particular has emerged recently as the next contender for the widespread killing of preborn children—the methotrexate/misoprostol combination under investigation by Dr. Richard U. Hausknecht of the Mount Sinai School of Medicine and funded by the Population Council.

This drug combination is 96% lethal through nine weeks of pregnancy. First the woman receives an injection of methotrexate. This drug inhibits cell growth and division, and works by interfering with the growth of the embryo and placenta by blocking folic acid (Vitamin B) uptake. It has been used since 1985 to successfully treat ectopic pregnancies, cancer, psoriasis and rheumatoid arthritis.

Five to seven days after the methotrexate injection, the woman returns to the abortionist's office for a vaginal suppository containing misoprostol (Cytotec), an ulcer drug that causes uterine contractions. Within two days, cramping and bleeding occur, followed by the abortion, usually at home. Then she returns to the abortionist's office a fourth time to confirm that the pregnancy is ended. In about 10 percent of all cases, a second suppository is required. If this fails as well, a suction abortion is done.

Both methotrexate and misoprostol have been approved by the U.S. Food and Drug Administration for non-abortion purposes. No further government oversight is necessary, because any drug approved by the FDA for any use may be used by any licensed physician for any purpose, although "off-label" uses may expose them to liability.[2]

The confirmed side effects of methotrexate include liver and chromosomal damage, infertility, birth defects, liver toxicity, induced cancer, convulsions, vomiting, diarrhea, stomatitis, severe blood disorders, behavioral abnormalities, pneumonitis, fever, coughing and death. The documented side effects of misoprostol (Cytotec) include spotting, cramps, hypermennorhea, excessive menstrual bleeding, menstrual disorders, nausea, vomiting and severe headaches.[3]

---

1 "New Contraceptives." United Press International, 3 August 1995. Also see Susan Aucott Ballagh, *et. al.* "A Contraceptive Vaginal Ring Releasing Norethindrone Acetate and Ethinyl Estradiol." *Obstetrical and Gynecological Survey*, September 1995, pp. 607-610.

2   Jane E. Brody. "Abortion Method Using Two Drugs Gains in a Study: Vast New Implications." *New York Times*, 31 August 1995, pp. B1 and B12.

3   Pharmacists for Life International. "New Abortion Drugs a Health Threat." News release dated 31 August 1995.

••

41. What Are the Different Types of Birth Prevention Pill (Oral Contraceptive), and How Do They Work?

General Modes of Action of Oral Contraceptives (OCs)

(1) Suppression of Ovulation. When the female reproductive system is functioning normally, the hypothalamus (the part of the brain containing the vital autonomic regulatory centers) controls the release of gonadotropin-releasing hormone (GnRH), which signals the pituitary gland to secrete luteinizing hormone (LH), which in turn assists ovulation and coordinates the release of estrogen and progestin from the ovaries.

When a woman ingests birth prevention pills, they literally hijack her reproductive system. The pills cause the ovaries to maintain a steady high level of estrogen and/or progestin production, depending upon the type and brand of pill being used. Thus, the woman's body is essentially "tricked" into acting as if it is continuously pregnant. The hypothalamus adjusts to this high level of hormone secretion and essentially shuts off GnRH production.

Therefore, the production of luteinizing hormone by the pituitary gland is also inhibited, and ovulation either ceases or is drastically curtailed.

In those months that ovulation is suppressed, the mode of action of the birth prevention pill is contraceptive in nature.

(2) Cervical Mucus Effects. Oral contraceptives also cause changes in the consistency and acidity of cervical mucus, making it more difficult for sperm to penetrate and live in the cervix, a second contraceptive effect.

(3) Endometrial Effects. The third effect of oral contraceptives on the body is to cause certain changes in the endometrium (lining of the uterus), making implantation more difficult. In a cycle where ovulation was not prevented and fertilization takes place, the pill causes a "silent abortion."

Biphasic vs. Triphasic

Most of the older "high-dose" birth prevention pills functioned mainly by inhibiting ovulation and affecting the cervical mucus, making them primarily "biphasic" (two-fold) in function. Sometimes, however, breakthrough ovulation occurred, and so the older pills were occasionally abortifacient in their actions.

All of the newer birth prevention pills on the market today not only often suppress ovulation and affect the cervical mucus, they often make implantation of the developing human being impossible. This "triphasic" (three-fold) function means that all of the newer birth prevention pills function at least part of the time as abortifacients.

The Types of Oral Contraceptive

Overview. There are currently three general classes of birth prevention pill manufactured in the United States and other countries and used worldwide. These are the high-dose pill, the low-dose pill, and the "mini-pill."

The following paragraphs describe these pills and their modes of action.

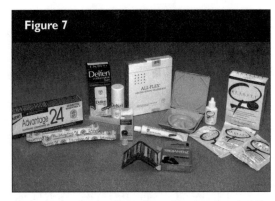

Figure 7

Man's greatest ingenuity is displayed in warfare—not only on the field of battle, but against his own fertility. There exists a bewildering array of methods designed to suppress what we have come to see as an enemy.

The High-Dose Pill.

The Searle Pharmaceutical Corporation developed the first oral contraceptive, Enovid, in the late 1950s. In keeping with its defensive anti-lawsuit strategy, the company tested the pill on Puerto Rican women before concluding in 1961 that it was safe for women on the American mainland to use.[1]

Experimentation on foreign women is a typical tactic of the major pharmaceutical companies. They often test birth prevention chemicals and devices on poor women in developing countries so any mistakes or serious health problems are easier to cover up. Poor women in foreign countries have little recourse when their health is destroyed or damaged by this kind of testing. This is because the companies bring huge amounts of money to their homelands, and protest against the programs can easily be suppressed by local or national governments.

Enovid and other high-dose pills, which have generally fallen out of favor in the United States but are still widely used in developing countries, contained from 1 to 12 milligrams of progestin and/or 60 to 120 micrograms of estrogen, a natural female hormone. This high dosage had a variety of effects, including blurred vision, nausea, weight gain, painful breasts, cramping, irregular menstrual bleeding, headaches and possibly breast cancer.[1]

The high-dose pills were primarily biphasic. Their primary mechanism suppressed gonadotropin production and therefore ovulation. They also caused changes in the consistency and acidity of cervical mucus, making it more difficult for sperm to penetrate and live in the cervix. Finally, they occasionally caused certain changes in the endometrium (lining of the uterus), making implantation more difficult.

When the high-dose pill functioned by this last mechanism, it was an abortifacient if the woman experienced a "breakthrough" ovulation. Although this occurred only during about 1 to 12 percent of all cycles, it was not the primary intent of the manufacturers.

Beginning about 1975, pill makers, in reaction to bad publicity about the severe side effects of the high-dosage pills, steadily decreased the content of estrogen and progestin in their products.

The Low-Dose Pill. Eventually, the older "high-dose" pills gave way to the new, abortifacient "low-dose" pills. Ortho/Johnson & Johnson, G.D. Searle/Monsanto and Syntex, the three largest manufacturers of OCs in the United States, voluntarily withdrew their "high-dose" products from the U.S. market in 1988 on the advice of the U.S. Food and Drug Administration (FDA). These were the last commercially-available pills containing more than 50 micrograms of estrogen.[1]

The low-dose pills contain from 0.35 to 15 milligrams of progestin in the form of norethindrone, norgestrel, ethyndiol diacetate or norethindrone acetate, and from 0.7 to 2.0 micrograms of estrogen in the form of ethinyl estradiol or mestranol, a tremendous drop in estrogenic potency compared to the high-dose pills.[2]

The low-dose biphasic and triphasic pills work in essentially the same manner as the high-dose pill. However, a much higher percentage of ovulation occurs in women who use the low-dose pills, due to the much lower estrogen dose. This means that women who use these pills frequently conceive, and the low-dose pills prevent implantation of the new human life, thereby acting more often as true abortifacients.

The Mini-Pill. Scientists have not pinpointed the primary mechanism of mini-pills (progestin-only pills), although women who use them frequently ovulate. Therefore, these pills function primarily as abortifacients.

It is known that pills that contain only progestin alter the cervical mucus. They also interfere with implantation by affecting the endometrium (lining of the uterus) and suppressing ovulation in some women by reducing the presence of follicle-stimulating hormone (FSH).

This mechanism is confirmed by the U.S. Food and Drug Administration, which has stated: "Progestin-only contraceptives are known to alter the cervical mucus, exert a progestinal effect on the endometrium, interfere with implantation, and, in some patients, suppress ovulation."[3] The U.S. Department of Health and Human Services (HHS), in its 1984 pamphlet "Facts About Oral Contraceptives," compared the action of high-dose pills and mini-pills:

It is possible for women using combined pills (synthetic estrogen and progestin) to ovulate. Then other mechanisms work to prevent pregnancy. Both kinds of pills make the cervical mucus thick and "inhospitable" to sperm, discouraging any entry to the uterus. In addition, they make it difficult for a fertilized egg to implant, by causing changes in Fallopian tube contractions and in the uterine lining. These actions explain why the minipill works, *as it generally does not suppress ovulation* [emphasis added].

The makers of the mini-pills also admit this mode of action. For example, Syntex Laboratories announced that its progestin-only pill Norinyl "... did not interfere with ovulation.... It seems to affect the endometrium so that a fertilized egg cannot be implanted."[4]

In other words, the pill is now truly abortifacient "birth prevention"—*not* conception control, as may have originally been intended when the first oral contraceptives were being developed.

"Emergency Contraceptives"

For 30 years, pro-abortionists and "family planners" have searched for new and better ways to kill early preborn babies with chemical compounds and devices already approved by the FDA. The methotrexate/misoprostol combination described above is one of the results of this ongoing search.

Anti-lifers have also promoted another type of abortifacient potion, the "Yuzpe Regimen," which consists of women taking combined ethinyl estradiol/levonorgestrel pills at a higher than normal dose. This kind of abortifacient is ideal for women who are forgetful or lazy about taking their pills.[5]

Pro-abortionists dishonestly call this "emergency contraception," another attempt to erase the distinction between true contraception and abortifacient action. Pills taken under the Yuzpe and similar regimens are often called "emergency contraceptive pills (ECPs)," "morning-after pills (MAPs)," and "postcoital contraception."

When pro-lifers hear pro-abortionists using these and similar terms, they can be sure that they are referring to abortifacient cocktails.

Pregnancies While Using the "Infallible" Pill

From the very first day that it was introduced, the oral contraceptive has been hailed as the solution to "unwanted pregnancies" and the enabler of the Sexual Revolution. Continued allegations of high efficiency, combined with the easy availability of abortion as a "backup," have inevitably led to widespread careless use of the pill.

Only about 11 percent of all women who use the pill do so correctly, according to a 1989 study.[6]

This carelessness is the major contributor to an incredible number of unintended pregnancies, especially among younger women. There are about 630,000 pregnancies annually among U.S. women who are on the pill, and more than 80 percent of these occur among women 15 to 24 years old.

Among women in this age group, the *method* effectiveness of the birth prevention pill is 96.2 percent per year, significantly lower than the effectiveness for older women. This percentage still sounds very high indeed; but the method effectiveness refers to the efficiency of the pill when a woman is in very good health *and uses the pill without error*. When user error is factored in, the result is the actual *user* effectiveness rate, also known as the overall effectiveness rate.[6]

The overall effectiveness rate for the low-dose pill is 89 percent per year.[6] This still sounds high until you calculate the probability of a woman 15 to 24 years old becoming pregnant over an extended period of time when using the pill, as shown in Table 4.

In summary, if a fornicating girl of 15 starts using the pill, and uses it continuously, *there is a better than 50 percent chance that she will become pregnant by the time she is 22!*

This statistic is verified by pro-abortionists, including Planned Parenthood abortion statistician Dr. Christopher Tietze, who said that "within 10 years, 20 to 50 percent of pill users and a substantial majority of users of other methods may be expected to experience at least one repeat abortion."[7]

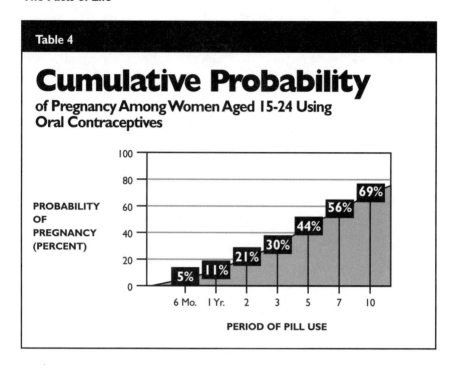

Table 4

Cumulative Probability
of Pregnancy Among Women Aged 15-24 Using
Oral Contraceptives

PROBABILITY OF PREGNANCY (PERCENT)

100 · 80 · 60 · 40 · 20 · 0

5% 11% 21% 30% 44% 56% 69%

6 Mo. 1 Yr. 2 3 5 7 10

PERIOD OF PILL USE

Note that Tietze is speaking about *repeat* (second or more) abortions here. These statistics are significant when one considers that one of the primary goals of school-based clinics is to distribute contraceptives and abortifacients to teenagers without parental consent or knowledge (see Chapter 11 for more information on sex education and school-based clinics).

Implications for Pro-Life Activists

Millions of women in the United States and all over the world use oral contraceptives. Many women who would never even *consider* a surgical abortion now use low-dose birth prevention pills that cause them to abort a new life an average of once or twice every year. A large number of women who say that they are pro-life use these pills, many at the urging of their husbands. These are usually the women who are ignorant of the pill's abortifacient mode of action, those who think that their way of life requires that they use the pill, or those who cannot mentally make the connection between contraception and abortion.

Some researchers (using very conservative figures) have calculated that the birth prevention pill directly causes between 1.53 and 4.15 million chemical abortions per year in the United States—*up to two and a half times the total number of surgical abortions committed every year!*[8]

This means that "pro-life" women who are using an oral contraceptive or some other means of abortifacient birth control are committing abortions themselves on a frequent basis. These abortions are "silent" and unseen, but they are no less abortions in the eyes of God than are gruesome third-trimester D&X abortions. There are many "pro-lifers" who are using these pills and who are involved in their promotion and distribution. These people must consider whether they can, in good conscience, criticize women whose action differs from their own only in that they have to drive to a "clinic" (mill) to commit it.

1 Bogomir M. Kuhar, Ph.D. "Pharmaceutical Companies: The New Abortionists." Reprint 16 from Human Life International, 4 Family Life, Front Royal, Virginia 22630.

2 Robert A. Hatcher, *et al. Contraceptive Technology*, (16th Revised Edition). New York: Irvington Publishers, 1994. Table 10-1, "Relative Potency of Estrogens and Progestins in Currently Available Oral Contraceptives Reflecting the Debate About the Strength of the Progestins," p. 226.

3 *Federal Register*, 41:236, 7 December 1976, p. 53,634.

4 United Press International news release in the *Cincinnati Post*, 11 January 1973.

5 "What are Legalities of Promoting ECPs?" *Contraceptive Technology Update*, November 1995, pp. 137-138.

6 Kim Painter. "Most Users of the Pill Don't Follow Directions." *USA Today*, 21 February 1990, p. D1.

7 Christopher Tietze, quoted in the National Abortion Rights Action League's *A Speaker's and Debater's Guidebook*. June 1978, p. 24.

8 S. Killick, E. Eyong, and M. Elstein. "Ovarian Follicular Development in Oral Contraceptive Cycles." *Fertility and Sterility*, September 1987, pp. 409-413.

42. What Are the Different Types of Intrauterine Devices (IUDs), and How Do They Work?

What is an Intrauterine Device?

The intrauterine device is a foreign body made of a non-reactive plastic, such as polyethylene, inserted into the uterus to prevent implantation of the developing human being. Some IUDs include active chemicals, such as progesterone or copper, which slowly diffuse into the uterus for an enhanced abortifacient effect.

More than 70 different types of IUDs have been manufactured over the last half-century. Some of these have consisted of polyethylene with barium sulfate so they could be detected by X-rays. The Dalkon Shield, which was withdrawn from the market in 1974 due to a number of maternal deaths, was of this type.

Other IUDs, including the Progesterone-T, were loaded with varying doses of progesterone crystals that were usually suspended in silicone oil. This IUD released about 24 milligrams of progesterone a year. It was originally promoted under the truly Orwellian label "The Uterine Therapeutic System."[1]

The copper IUDs (including the "Copper-7," "Copper-T," and "Tatum-T") discharge from 50 to 75 micrograms of ionic copper into the uterus each day. These copper ions interfere with the life-sustaining functions that regulate implantation of the new human life in the uterus. Copper has been proven to be the active agent in these IUDs, because identical devices are ineffective without the element. Each copper IUD is effective at causing early abortions for about four years.[2]

How Do IUDs Work?

IUDs do not interfere with the menstrual cycle, the thickening of cervical mucus, sperm migration, fertilization, or ovulation. That the IUD irritates the endometrium (the lining of the uterus) and makes it inhospitable to the blastocyst (the very early developing human being) is generally accepted among scientists working in this area.

The American Medical Association's Committee on Human Reproduction has said: "The action of the IUDs would seem to be a simple local phenomenon. That these devices prevent nidation [implantation] of an already fertilized ovum has been accepted as the most likely mechanism of action."[3]

The U.S. Food and Drug Administration (FDA), which studies birth control methods before releasing them to the market, has observed that "IUDs seem to interfere in some manner with the implantation of the fertilized egg in the lining of the uterine cavity. The IUD does not prevent ovulation."[4]

The International Planned Parenthood Federation (IPPF) states:

At the end of 1986 the WHO [World Health Organization] Scientific Group on the Mechanism of Action, Safety, and Efficacy of IUDs looked into this aspect [mechanism of action] of the use of IUDs very thoroughly. Their main conclusions stated that all IUDs stimulate a foreign body reaction in the endometrium which is potentiated by the addition of copper, and progestagen-releasing IUDs produce endometrial suppression similar to that seen when the drug is administered by other routes, e.g., orally or by injection.[5]

However, the results of 18 studies of women with IUDs found that the devices do not always prevent implantation. A major study showed that an average of 28.6% of all implanted pregnancies that occurred with the IUD in place were eventually aborted, and another 8.4% resulted in life-threatening ectopic pregnancies that required surgery.[6]

Complications Associated with IUD Use

The Food and Drug Administration's Ad Hoc Committee on IUD Safety met in 1974 for the purpose of summarizing complaints received about the various IUDs on the market at that time.

The Committee received reports of 238 cases of spontaneous septic abortion from women who had become pregnant with IUDs in place. Of these women, 21 died. The Dalkon Shield was involved in 14 of these deaths and 209 cases of septic abortion, and the Lippes Loop caused 5 deaths and 21 septic abortions.[7] Overall, there were about 15,000 IUD-related hospitalizations annually in the early 1970s.[8]

A.H. Robin Pharmaceuticals made the Dalkon Shield IUD from 1971 to 1974. Documented reports of severe injuries began to surface almost immediately after initial distribution, and, on 29 June 1975, the FDA announced it intended to "... require special warning notices for users of the intrauterine devices, the contraceptives that were linked to 43 deaths in recent years."[9] A.H. Robin pulled the Dalkon Shield from the market in 1975. By 1985, 13,000 women had sued the company for damages relating to sterility, miscarriages, and pelvic infections. Incredibly, some population controllers, including Steven Mumford and Elton Kessel, who peddle the dangerous sterilizing chemical quinacrine in developing countries (see Question 32), are trying to sanitize the image of the Dalkon Shield so it can make a comeback.[10]

Ortho Pharmaceuticals withdrew its Lippes Loop from the American market in 1985, and G.D. Searle withdrew its Copper-7 and Tatum-T IUDs in 1986 when its liability insurance lapsed. Searle also faced 775 lawsuits from women who suffered injuries from their IUDs or who conceived malformed babies when the devices did not work properly.

According to a literature review of the journals *Contraception* and *Fertility and Sterility* over the period 1980-1995, harm associated with current IUD use includes (but is not limited to) sterility, hemorrhage, perforation of the uterus, colon, bladder or small or large intestine, ectopic and cervical pregnancies, cervical lacerations, cervical dysplasia (developmental abnormalities), deep embedding of the IUD (a serious problem in developing countries, where women may have had the devices in their uteri for a decade or more), fragmentation of the IUD, dysmenorrhoea (painful menstruation), development of hydatidiform moles, menorrhagia (excessive menstruation), salpingitis (inflammation of uterine tubes), pelvic inflammatory disease (PID, which often leads to infertility or sterility), septic abortion, cervical erosion, cystic masses on the pelvis and tubal infertility.

The IUD and "Contraceptive Imperialism"

IUDs have confronted the anti-fertility industry with a number of insurmountable problems, the greatest of which was the proven danger of the devices. However, this did not stop the IUD manufacturers from turning a tidy profit by dumping their products on the poor women of developing countries.[11]

Despite being faced with nearly 1,000 lawsuits claiming damage from its Copper-7 and Tatum-T IUDs, the Searle company stated that it would continue to make IUDs for women in developing countries (for population control programs funded by the United States and other Western countries).[12] This is yet another example of the West's "contraceptive imperialism"— the willingness to dump unsafe and even lethal products on poor women of other countries; products that are too risky for informed North American and European women.

This is an extremely serious matter with grave implications that are not immediately evident.

Women normally lose an average of 35 to 40 cubic centimeters (cc) of blood during their menstrual period, but women using a loop IUD lose about twice as much blood, and those who use copper IUDs lose about 50 cc of blood. This shows that IUDs are especially ill-suited for use in developing countries, where anemia and malnutrition are often endemic, especially among women and children.[13]

Despite the obvious dangers of IUDs, the American Public Health Association (APHA) backed Searle and other IUD manufacturers by launching a campaign to distribute IUDs to Third World women and to get the U.S. government to assume much of the pharmaceutical company's legal liability for IUD damages, thus letting the corporations act with virtual impunity.[9]

1 E.B. Connell. "The Uterine Therapeutic System: A New Approach to Female Contraception." *Contemporary OB/GYN*, June 1975, pp. 49-55.

2 H.J. Tatum. "The New Contraceptive: Copper Bearing IUDs." *Contemporary Obstetrics and Gynecology*, January 1973, pp. 61-63.

3 American Medical Association Committee on Human Reproduction. "Evaluation of Intrauterine Contraceptive Devices," *Journal of the American Medical Association*, 27 February 1967, p. 155.

4 United States Food and Drug Administration. "Text of Required Patient Information for IUDs." *Federal Register*, 10 May 1977.

5 International Planned Parenthood Federation. *Family Planning Handbook for Doctors*, "Intrauterine Devices." IPPF Medical Publications, p. 104.

6 Thomas W. Hilgers, M.D. "The Intrauterine Device: Contraceptive or Abortifacient?" *Minnesota Medicine*, June 1974, p. 497.

7 "The Dalkon Shield and the Questions of Safety." *Medical World News*, 13 September 1974, pp. 58-61. Also see Catherine Breslin. "Day of Reckoning." *Ms.* Magazine, June 1989, pp. 46-52. This article describes the inside story of the Dalkon Shield disaster.

8 H.S. Kahn and C.W. Tyler. "IUD-Related Hospitalizations: United States and Puerto Rico, 1973." *Journal of the American Medical Association*. 234:53-56(1973).

9 "American Public Health Association Launches Campaign to Save IUD." *ALL News*, 9 March 1987.

10 S.D. Mumford and E. Kessel. "Was the Dalkon Shield a Safe and Effective Intrauterine Device? The Conflict Between Case-Control and Clinical Trial Study Findings." *Fertility and Sterility*, June 1992, pp. 1,151-1,176.

11 Filipino women have probably suffered more abuse from American and European pharmaceutical companies than the women of any other nation. Max Ricketts wrote in the *Mabuhay Times* (16-29 April 1991, p. 12) that "... many drugs and devices which are not even permitted in the United States have found their way to Manila where they are dumped on hapless Filipino women. One example was the IUD (or intrauterine device) which is associated with a great deal of disease and despair."

12 Front Line Updates. "Searle Removes IUDs from U.S. Market." *NRL News*, 27 February 1986, p. 4.

13 F. Hefnawi and H. Aksalani. "Menstrual Blood Loss with Copper Intrauterine Devices." *Contraception*, September 1974, pp. 133-139.

●●●

43. What Is Norplant and How Does It Work?

Origins of Norplant

The Population Council (founded by population controllers John Rockefeller III and Elton Kessel) owns the patent for Norplant, which was developed by embryologist Sheldon Segal of the Rockefeller Foundation.

Wyeth-Ayerst Laboratories of Philadelphia, a subsidiary of American Home Products Corporation, produces the abortifacient, which costs women about $500 to produce about five years of barrenness.[1] The U.S. Food and Drug Administration (FDA) approved the abortifacient "contraceptive" Norplant for public use on 10 December 1990.

Norplant was formally introduced to the American public in February 1991, and sales have vastly exceeded expectations.

As of August 1995, about one million North American women had used Norplant. Many of these women have brought more than 200 lawsuits, including 50 class-action suits, against Wyeth-Ayerst Laboratories.[2] The legal complaints allege inadequate warnings of side effects, prolonged menstrual bleeding, headaches, large weight gains, personality disorders, hair loss and depression.

Implantation and Extraction Procedures

The Norplant carrier consists of six small tubes about the size of matchsticks. These tubes are made of silastic (silicone rubber), the same material used in heart valves and medical tubing.

A physician begins the insertion procedure by making a 1/8-inch incision about six inches above the woman's elbow. He then loads the capsules one by one into her arm in a fan-shaped pattern using an insertion tube.[1] He uses local anesthetic for both the implantation and extraction procedures.

In many cases, removing the six tubes is trickier than implanting them, because they become coated with fibrous tissue and gradually anchor into the surrounding tissue (i.e., they grow into the arm). This is a result of trauma caused by the implants being pushed into the tissue and a low-level inflammatory reaction to the tube's foreign substance (see Figure 8).

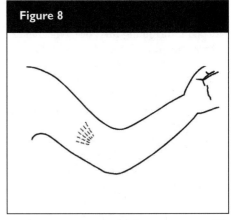

Figure 8

Norplant is easy to insert, but not always easy to remove. This illustration shows the location where the six Norplant implants are inserted into a woman's arm.

How It Works

Norplant is a member of the single-synthetic hormone class of abortifacients that includes the "mini-pill" and the Progestasert intrauterine device (IUD).[3]

Once implanted, the six Norplant carrier capsules slowly release levonorgestrel (low-dosage progestin), an abortifacient that prevents implantation of the developing human being in the uterus.

The "bible" of "family planners," *Contraceptive Technology*, says that Norplant has a triphasic (three-fold) mode of action. It inhibits ovulation, thickens cervical mucus and alters the endometrium (the lining of the uterus) so that its degree of receptivity to the blastocyst (early developing human being) is significantly decreased.[3] Another test of 41 women using Norplant for one year showed that 24 women experienced a suppressed uterine lining, 12 had an irregular uterine lining and only five had normal (unchanged) uterine linings.[4] Thus, Norplant had a clearly abortifacient effect in up to 88 percent of the women tested.

This means that a woman using Norplant will occasionally ovulate and conceive, and will therefore be aborting at least once or twice each year.

The Facts of Life

Norplant Side Effects

Although they naturally vary widely from woman to woman, the range of typical Norplant side effects generally include changes in the endometrium (uterine lining); odd menstrual bleeding patterns; spotting between menstrual periods; missed or prolonged menstrual periods; dizziness; thrombosis (formation of blood clots); liver dysfunction; headaches; sudden weight gain or loss; ectopic pregnancy; nervousness; nausea; breast pain; hirsutism (abnormal body hair growth); high blood pressure; arm numbness; allergic/immune reactions; "migration" of the six polymer capsules; and, ironically, a decreased sexual appetite.[3] One Texas survey showed that eight percent of Norplant users experienced pseudo-tumor cerebri, a condition where increased fluid pressure in the brain crushes the optic nerve and causes partial or complete *permanent* blindness.[5]

Norplant: Targeting the Poor Worldwide

Introduction. It is standard operating procedure (SOP) for contraceptive manufacturers and population controllers to target Third World women with new or untested abortifacients. In addition, the old high-dose birth prevention pills and various IUDs that have proven too dangerous for North American women to use are shipped overseas by the tens of millions, all in the name of population control.

At the turn of the 19th century, the sun never set on the British Empire. If an empire could be defined as control of the wombs of poor women in developing countries, there is a new empire upon which the sun never sets—the empire painstakingly constructed by Western contraceptive imperialists.

Getting with the Program in the United States. Immediately after Norplant was introduced to the public, several U.S. judges ordered women (always poor Blacks) onto the drug because they had been convicted of abusing previous children. In one such case, Tulare County (California) Superior Court Judge Howard R. Broadman gave Darlene Johnson a very simple but coercive choice: Be chemically sterilized with Norplant or go to jail for two to four years.[6]

Nor did it take state legislatures long to perceive the dramatic possibilities of using the drug. Kansas H.B. 2089 identified Norplant by name in an act that would provide help to female welfare recipients *only* if they agreed to be implanted.[7]

Poor Third-World Women as Guinea Pigs. Norplant was the final product of 24 years of Population Council research. In 1990, the United States became the 17th country to accept it for distribution. The abortifacient had been tested continuously since 1972 on women in several developing countries, including Haiti, Indonesia, Brazil and Bangladesh, by the U.S. Agency for International Development (USAID), which provided most of the $20 million in research costs.[8]

At a 1990 meeting of the American Public Health Association (APHA), Dr. Shayam Thapa claimed that, although doctors were eager to implant the drug, only one-fourth of Bangladeshi women who wanted the capsules removed could find a doctor willing or trained to do so.[8]

In 1990, the *Hai News*, a Korean newspaper, reported that UBINIG, a Bangladeshi health advocacy group, had uncovered "gross violations of medical ethics" in the testing and distribution of Norplant under the auspices of the USAID and Family Health International (FHI). Medical personnel did not inform Bangladeshi women that the drug was experimental and that it had possible side effects. They bribed many women to use the drug, and instructed them not to report side effects so the test program results would be skewed to "show" lower rates of health problems. When women became too sick to avoid seeking medical attention, the medics withheld proper care from them, and told them that they would have to refund the cost of the Norplant if it was removed, an impossibility since this sum was more than a year's wage. Many women suffered severe eye problems and even blindness, yet the summary reports on the effectiveness of Norplant contained no mention of these side effects.[5,8]

Whenever a new birth prevention method is invented, population controllers immediately use it on poor women in developing countries in order to test it and to hold down the population. When the method is approved for use in the United States, "family planners" first use it on minorities.

If this is not an overt expression of racism, *what is*?

1 Paul Likoudis. "Five-Year Birth Control Device Approved By FDA." *The Wanderer*, 20 December 1990, pp. 3 and 12.

2 Associated Press. "Publicity Blamed for Drop in Norplant Use." *San Francisco Chronicle*, 12 August 1995, p. A5.

3 Robert A. Hatcher, *et al. Contraceptive Technology*, (16th Revised Edition). New York: Irvington Publishers, 1994. Table 11-1, "Delivery Systems for Progestin-Only Contraceptives and Combined Pills," p. 287.

4 Dale N. Robertson. "Implantable Levonorgestrel Rod Systems: *In Vivo* Release Rates and Clinical Effects." Also see Horacio B. Croxatto, *et al.* "Histopathology of the Endometrium During Continuous Use of Levonorgestrel." Both included in Gerald I. Zatuchini (editor). *Long Acting Contraceptive Delivery Systems*. New York: Harper & Row, 1984, pp. 133-144 and 290-295, respectively.

5 British Broadcasting Corporation. Horizon Television Show titled "The Human Laboratory," broadcast of 7 November 1995.

6 Joe Bigham. "Birth Control Order Stands until Appeal." *The Oregonian* [Portland, Oregon], 11 January 1991, p. A16.

7 "Chemical Warfare." *Communique*, 1 March 1991, p. 1. American Life League.

8 Elizabeth Sobo. "NORPLANT: Lab-Tested on Third World Women." *Our Sunday Visitor*, 3 February 1991, pp. 10-11.

44. What is RU-486 and How Does It Work?

Dreams of an "Ultimate Pill"

At one time, the lives of preborn children had value to the pharmaceutical companies, which actually worked hard to avoid injuring them as they concocted their various chemical mixtures.

However, as national morals loosened, especially after abortion was legalized in the United States, there was simply no need to consider the effects of various "birth control" methods on the life of the developing human being. The only criterion was the health of the mother.

And so, the ideal "contraceptive" gradually evolved into a device or drug that would not only prevent ovulation and fertilization, but eliminate early pregnancies as well. A quarter-century ago, Garrett Hardin and other population theorists dreamed of such a major "contraceptive" of the future, which would most likely take the form of an abortifacient pill.[1]

With RU-486, it seems that the anti-life genie has granted this unholy wish.

The Origin of RU-486

The manufacturer of the RU-486 abortion pill (originally labeled ZK 95.890, but now classified as Roussel-Uclaf 38486, or RU-486 for short) is the French company Groupe Roussel-Uclaf, a subsidiary of the West German pharmaceutical giant Hoechst.

It is a little-known but revealing fact that Hoechst changed its name from the original "I.G. Farben" after World War II in an attempt to shake its loathsome reputation. I.G. Farben made a tidy profit during the war from the manufacture of the cyanide gas Zyklon-B, used to exterminate Jews and other people in the "showers" of the Nazi death camps.

Now Farben's descendant will make a profit by exterminating millions of preborn babies.

Ironically, the pill's inventor, Etienne-Emile Baulieu of France's National Institute of Health and Medical Research, is Jewish. He was born in 1926 to a doctor named Leon Blum, and changed his name in 1942, presumably to avoid being killed by the Zyklon-B gas made by the same company he works for today.

How RU-486 Works

RU-486 imitates progesterone, the hormone that signals the uterus to become receptive to the fertilized egg. The abortion pill is used in tandem with a prostaglandin that prepares the uterus for evacuation.

RU-486 contains a progesterone analogue (imposter) that "plugs in" to the uterine progesterone receptors, but does not deliver the message that progesterone is supposed to transfer naturally. These hormone impostors are commonly labeled "anti-hormones."

Once the anti-hormone has occupied the progesterone receptors, the blastocyst (early growing human being) is denied attachment and simply starves for want of nutrients and oxygen. He or she is expelled after several days. This mechanism of action works to kill preborn children in the first eight weeks of pregnancy.

Most abortion pills, including RU-486, are about 80 percent "effective" when used by themselves, and about 95 percent effective when accompanied by one or two subsequent injections of synthetic prostaglandin E or Sulprotone. The abortion pills are used to kill babies of less than five weeks gestation, and their efficiency decreases dramatically past seven weeks' gestation.

Naturally, pro-abortionists know the RU-486 pill is a true abortifacient, and they know, in fact, that it was *designed* to be a true abortifacient. However, they recognize the value of lying to the public about its intended effects, because they know the public is much more comfortable with contraception than with abortion.

For example, the National Abortion Federation (NAF) says in an article titled "Successful Strategies: Managing the Media":

When polls have been conducted on RU-486, the new French pill, the results vary depending on how the question is asked. If RU-486 is referred to as an 'abortion pill,' it has significantly less support than if it is called a new form of birth control. In many polls, the description can change support by as much as 15-20 points and determine if a majority of those polled are in favor of the pill.[2]

Perhaps even RU-486's inventor, Etienne-Emile Baulieu, feels a little shame and guilt caused by his association with what could very well be the greatest killer of all time. He has said: "I don't like abortion and I don't like talking about it. I am a physician and would rather talk about saving life. I am not really for abortion, I am for women.... I resent it when people present the very early interruption of pregnancy as killing a baby, morally or physically. I think it's a crime to say that."[3]

In order to blur the line between contraception and abortion, anti-lifers commonly call abortion pills "menses regulators," "post-coital contraceptives," "emergency contraceptives" and "contragestives."

RU-486—A Miracle Cure?

The pro-abortion forces that have worked to spread the RU-486 poison pill all over the world consistently use the old "bait and switch" tactic. They insist they are "pro-RU-486"—not because it is an abortifacient, but because it will allegedly cure a wide range of diseases.

As one example, at a 19 November 1990 House subcommittee hearing, pro-abortionists cited a long list of ailments that could supposedly be cured or ameliorated by the abortion pill: AIDS, cancers of the breast and ovaries, Cushing's Syndrome, brain and prostate cancer, diabetes, osteoporosis, hypertension and even obesity.

Note that RU-486 pushers never state categorically that their pill *is* useful for treating illnesses, because no researcher has ever provided any evidence or written any paper showing that RU-486 is useful for anything other than killing preborn babies.[4] So they play on people's emotions and load their sentences with disclaimers. One example stated "... [research] *suggests* that RU-486 *may* have *potential* value in AIDS."[5]

Among many others, Canadian neurologist Paul Ranalli recognizes that the benefits of RU-486 are strictly speculative: "As an antiprogestin agent, RU-486 has properties that might offer theoretical value in Cushing's Disease (an adrenal disorder), meningioma (a largely benign brain tumor) and breast cancer, but despite some of the recent hype, studies to date have failed to show any benefit whatsoever in any of these conditions."[6]

Pro-lifers must not be hoodwinked by the intense glare of publicity surrounding the abortion pill. Pro-abortionists obviously could not care less about the other alleged uses of the abortion pill, or else they would have been involved in fighting other diseases long ago. Their sole purpose in spreading RU-486 all over the world is to promote abortion by making baby-killing even more private and difficult to oppose than it is now.

1 Garrett Hardin. "The History and Future of Birth Control." *Perspectives in Biology and Medicine.* Autumn 1966.

2   National Abortion Federation. *Abortion: Moral Choice and Medical Imperative.* "Abortion Practice Advancement, Sixteenth Annual Meeting Workbook, April 13-14, 1992, San Diego, California," p. 133, "Successful Strategies: Managing the Media."

3   Etienne-Emile Baulieu, quoted in the *New York Times Magazine.* Described in the American Family Association *Journal*, May 1989, p. 8, and quoted in *National Catholic Register.* "France Orders Subsidies for RU-486 Abortion Pill." 1 April 1990, p. 2.

4   Bernard Nathanson, M.D. "Beyond 'Abortion:' RU-486 and the Needs of the Crisis Constituency." *Bernadell Technical Bulletin,* November 1990, pp. 1-3.

5   William Regelson, M.D., Roger Loria, Ph.D., and Mohammed Kalimi, Ph.D. *Journal of the American Medical Association,* 22 to 29 August 1990, pp. 1026-1027.

6   Paul Ranalli. "The Appalling Ordeal of Abortion By Pill." Toronto *Globe and Mail,* 28 August 1992, p. A17.

45. What Is Depo-Provera and How Does It Work?

How Depo-Provera Works

Depo-Provera's active ingredient is depot-medroxyprogesterone acetate (DMPA), a synthetic form of the natural hormone progesterone, originally developed for the treatment of uterine cancer in the 1950s. The woman receives 150 milligrams of DMPA via deep intramuscular injection every three months.

Depo-Provera was approved for use in the United States in October 1992. However, in June of 1993, Canada's Department of Heath and Welfare prohibited the use of Depo-Provera, saying that the drug does not meet Canadian safety standards as a contraceptive.[1] The drug is now available in more than 90 countries and is particularly popular among population controllers in Indonesia, Jamaica, Thailand, Kenya and New Zealand.

As with all other abortifacients that may pose a danger to Western women, Depo-Provera was extensively tested on Third World women first. The World Health Organization (WHO) used Depo on more than 11,000 women in Kenya, Mexico and Thailand, before submitting it to the FDA for approval.[2]

According to Upjohn's information pamphlet on Depo-Provera,[3] the compound "inhibits the secretion of gonadotropins which, in turn, prevents follicular maturation and ovulation and results in endometrial thinning. These actions produce its contraceptive effect." The pamphlet also says that Depo-Provera

■ "[has a] contraceptive effect produced by inhibiting the secretion of gonadotropins (FSH, LH), which prevents follicular maturation and ovulation [and]

■ suppresses the endometrium [the mucous membrane lining the uterus] and changes cervical mucus."

In other words, Upjohn acknowledges that Depo-Provera acts as an abortifacient.

Many women's menstrual cycles continue when using Depo-Provera: 43 percent after 12 months and 32 percent after 24 months.[3] This data shows that the compound does not completely suppress ovulation in a large percentage of women who use Depo-Provera.

Contraceptive Technology confirms that Depo-Provera has a triphasic (three-way) action. It inhibits ovulation and thickens cervical mucus (which are both contraceptive actions), but it also alters the endometrium (the lining of the uterus) so that its degree of receptivity to the blastocyst (very early developing human being) is significantly decreased. According to *Contraceptive Technology*, "Other contraceptive actions include the development of a shallow and atrophic [thinning] endometrium ..."

When Depo-Provera works in this way, it is an abortifacient.[4]

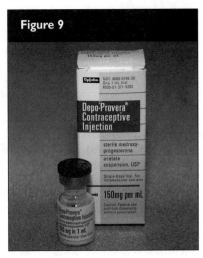

Figure 9

Upjohn's patient information pamphlet for the "contraceptive" Depo-Provera lists more than sixty possible side effects.

Adverse Reactions to Depo-Provera

Upjohn's information pamphlet on Depo-Provera lists more than 60 adverse reactions suffered by various percentages of women who use the compound.[3]

Women on Depo-Provera report an average weight gain of 5.4 pounds in the first year and 16.5 pounds over six years. Depo-Provera users commonly also experience osteoporosis (loss of bone mass). Some users suffer jaundice, a decrease in glucose tolerance and convulsions.

In women who have used Depo-Provera for the first time within the last four years, and who are under 35 years of age, the risk of breast cancer increases 129 percent. There appears to be no increased risk of ovarian, liver or cervical cancer.

Use of Depo-Provera may be associated with ectopic pregnancy, thrombophlebitis (inflammation of blood vessels associated with blood clots), pulmonary embolism (obstruction of the pulmonary artery by a blood clot, air bubble, or other material), cerebrovascular disorders, and partial or complete loss of vision in mothers, and polysyndactyly (webbing and extra digits of the hands and feet), hypospadias (genital tract abnormalities) and chromosomal anomalies among infants born to them.[3]

More than five percent suffer headaches, nervousness, abdominal pain or discomfort, dizziness or asthenia (weakness or fatigue). One to five percent reported one or more of these ailments: Decreased libido (sexual desire) or anorgasmia, depression, nausea, insomnia, leukorrhea (abnormal vaginal discharges), pelvic and breast pain, rashes, hot flashes, edema (swelling), vaginitis and acne.[3]

The information pamphlet lists 48 other symptoms reported by lesser numbers of patients, including chest pains, pulmonary embolus, allergic reactions, anemia, tachycardia (racing heart rate), fever, hoarseness, blood dyscrasia (abnormal blood chemistry), rectal bleeding, breast lumps or nipple bleeding, paralysis, facial palsy, uterine hyperplasia (abnormal growth of the uterus), varicose veins and deep vein thrombosis.[3]

1 *HLI Newswire*, 3 June 1993.

2 *HLI Newswire*, 19 June 1992.

3 Patient information brochure. "Now Available in the U.S.: Depo-Provera Contraceptive Injection." Upjohn Pharmaceutical Company, December 1992.

4 Robert A. Hatcher, *et al. Contraceptive Technology*, (16th Revised Edition). New York: Irvington Publishers, 1994. Narrative on p. 286 and Table 11-1, "Delivery Systems for Progestin-Only Contraceptives and Combined Pills," p. 287.

46. What Is the Teaching of the Catholic Church on Abortifacients?

The Catholic Church recently amended its teaching on abortion to encompass new abortion compounds and methods. This became necessary due to the production of various new abortifacients and fabricated definitions of life promulgated by the medical profession.

On 24 November 1988, The Pontifical Commission for the Authentic Interpretation of the Code of Canon Law declared that abortion is not only "the expulsion of the immature fetus," but is also "the killing of the same fetus in any way and at any time from the moment of conception."

"Conception" in this case refers not to implantation, but to fertilization.

This definition of abortion forbids the use of any of the following:

■ all birth prevention pills, because *every birth prevention pill made today causes early abortions part of the time;*

■ mini-pills, morning-after pills, and true abortion pills such as RU-486;

■ injectable or insertable abortifacients such as Norplant and Depo-Provera; and

■ all intrauterine devices (IUDs), all of which are abortifacients and act by preventing the implantation of the already-fertilized zygote.

As for the RU-486 abortion pill, Albert Cardinal Decourtray of Lyon summed up the feelings of Christians everywhere: "The pill now produces a process which allows abortion to seem like a contraceptive. In other words, it tends purely and simply to numb the conscience about both the act itself and its moral gravity. A follower of Christ cannot accept it."

Chapter 4

Natural Family Planning (NFP)

....

47. How Does the Female Human Reproductive System Work Before and During Conception?

Components of the Female Reproductive System

Introduction. One of the greatest practical advantages of natural family planning is that it lets a woman and her husband learn how her reproductive system works instead of requiring her simply to dominate it with powerful chemicals, which are often accompanied by one or more undesirable side effects. More intimate knowledge of the reproductive system enhances self-reliance, assists in achieving and confirming pregnancy, and allows earlier detection of a wide range of health problems when they occur. It also helps a husband understand his wife's psychology, since a woman's moods are at least partially a function of the hormonal changes that take place during her menstrual cycle.

Five components of the woman's reproductive system are of particular interest to people practicing natural family planning—the breasts, the cervix, the ovaries, the Fallopian tubes and the uterus.

The following paragraphs describe these vital organs.

The Breasts. In most women, breastfeeding on demand helps to suppress ovulation for an interval of three months (if the baby is fed supplements) to as long as 1^{1}/$_{2}$ years (in the case of "ecological" or total breastfeeding). See Question 52 for more information on breastfeeding.

The Cervix. The cervix rises and opens during the fertile time, and closes and descends during the infertile period. These are valuable signs during the practice of natural family planning, because they can confirm other signs (temperature and mucus) and can shorten the period of abstinence.

The Ovaries. The ovaries are a classic example of natural redundancy at work. Although men produce sperm continuously, each newborn girl possesses all of the eggs she will ever need at birth, stored safely in her ovaries.

Three-hundred thousand to 400,000 eggs are contained in protective packages called follicles, which begin to ripen when the girl reaches puberty. All through the fertile years, normally at intervals of anywhere from 24 to 35 days, a follicle (or rarely, follicles) will ripen and burst, ejecting its egg. This process is commonly called ovulation, and usually occurs in alternating ovaries.

The average age of first menstruation/ovulation (menarche) was about 17 to 18 years a century ago. Today, the average age of first menstruation/ovulation for girls who have had sufficient diet and health care is about 13 years of age, although it can happen several years earlier or later in some cases. The typical decline in fertility currently begins at about age forty, culminating in cessation of ovulation at menopause at an average age of about fifty, although there is great variation among individual women.

The Fallopian Tubes. The Fallopian tubes serve as a conduit for the ejected egg as it travels from the ovary to the uterus. These tubes are about five inches long, are about twice the diameter of a human hair, and are extremely delicate. This is why many problems related to infertility stem from blocked or damaged Fallopian tubes. Many infertility treatments, including *in-vitro* fertilization (IVF), fertilization *in vitro* with embryo transfer (FIVET), and gamete intra-fallopian transfer (GIFT) are designed to bypass Fallopian tube blockages.

Chapter 9 discusses both licit and illicit assisted reproduction techniques.

Conception of a new human being (the fertilization of the egg by a spermatozoon) normally takes place in the Fallopian tube.

The Uterus. The uterus is the most powerful and stretchable muscle of either the male or the female body. It is also the residence for the preborn child from implantation until natural (or unnatural) ejection.

At the beginning of a pregnancy, the uterus is about the size and shape of a small pear. The endometrium is the uterine lining constructed each cycle to sustain new human life. It is maintained by the follicle's progesterone. The newly conceived human being implants in this lining and receives its nourishment here.

The endometrium sheds through menstruation 9 to 17 days after ovulation if no conception takes place.[1]

The Reproductive System at Work

Introduction. A brief bio-historical description is usually the easiest way to understand human reproduction. This section describes the female reproductive system at work from the onset of menstruation to post-menopause.

The Beginning and End of Fertility. When a girl reaches sexual maturity, she has her first menstrual cycle, sometimes referred to as the "menarche." This repeating process can begin as early as age 10, and usually occurs by age 15. The menstrual cycle normally continues until anywhere from age 40 to 60, but ovulation and menstruation tend to be more intermittent near the end of menstruation (premenopause), as fertility gradually declines.

When menstruation ceases entirely for a fixed period (usually six to 12 months), fertility has ended. However, beginning in about 1990, scientists have been experimenting with assisted pregnancy even after the menstrual cycle has ended naturally.

The 'Monthly' Cycle. On the average, women have a complete cycle every 28 days. This may range from as little as two weeks to more than two months for any individual woman, especially near the beginning or end of fertility. Some women are extremely regular, and others have very irregular cycles. When a woman takes oral contraceptives (the birth prevention pill), their hormones overpower her natural cycle and cause it to settle into a regular but unnatural 28-day "pseudo-cycle."

Each woman has a relatively regular luteal phase. This is the length of time between ovulation and the following menstruation, and may vary from 10 to 16 days between women. Understanding the luteal phase is one of the keys to using natural family planning.

Sickness, stress and heavy physical activity may cause irregularities in cycle length. Breastfeeding usually causes natural temporary infertility in women, a condition known as amenorrhea.

The cycle begins on the first day of menstruation. Fertility is very low for the first few days of the cycle. The fertile phase follows this period of infertility and, regardless of the length of a woman's cycle, usually lasts five to seven days.

Post-ovulation infertility begins one or two days after ovulation. This phase, lasting about 16 days until the first day of menstruation, is extremely infertile, much more so than the menstruation phase.

Some women experience pre-menstrual syndrome (PMS) before menstruation begins. This group of physical, mental and behavioral symptoms may include some or all of the following: swelling and tender breasts, headaches, clumsiness, irritability, fatigue, bloating, depression and mood swings.

Other women may experience painful cramping or dysmenorrhea. This is caused by contractions of the uterus during menstruation, which are in turn signalled by the secretion of prostaglandins.

The Hormonal Cycle. As a woman experiences various physical symptoms (changes in mucus, temperature, and cervical position and firmness), her body is undergoing a complex and continuous adjustment of a series of hormones that regulate the cycle of fertility.

At the start of the cycle, soon after menstruation begins, the pituitary gland, near the base of the brain, secretes follicle-stimulating hormone (FSH). This hormone stimulates the growth and development of an ovarian follicle and its ovum. The follicle begins to secrete increasing amounts of the hormone estrogen. The most important role of estrogen during the preovulatory phase of the cycle is to stimulate the cervix to produce the mucus which is so critical to human fertility.

FSH reaches peak levels about a day before ovulation. The pituitary gland then secretes luteinizing hormone (LH), which stimulates the follicle into releasing its egg at ovulation.

Upon being ejected, the egg faces a lifespan of only 15 to 24 hours unless it is fertilized. However, the follicle is far from finished with its task. It even takes on a new name: The *corpus luteum,* or "yellow body." It performs several critical functions related to reproduction.

After ovulation, the *corpus luteum* secretes the hormone progesterone for about 10 days to two weeks. This hormone performs five functions. It maintains the lining of the uterus, prevents another ovulation from taking place, and triggers the three indicators used in the sympto-thermal method of natural family planning: (1) the basal (base) body temperature rises from 3/10 to 5/10 of a degree; (2) mucus in the cervix thickens or disappears; and (3) the cervix lowers and closes.

After ovulation, the estrogen level falls sharply, then stabilizes until menstruation.

After 10 to 14 days, the *corpus luteum* stops secreting progesterone. This means the uterine lining is no longer being maintained; it breaks down and sloughs off during menstruation.

The time between ovulation and the beginning of menstruation is called the luteal phase, and usually lasts about 16 days.

Fertilization Age and Gestational Age

The time period relating to milestones in fetal development is described in terms of either fertilization age or gestational age.

Table 5

Landmarks
in Fetal and Gestational Age

	Fetal (Fertilization) Age in Weeks	Gestational Age in Weeks
Fertilization	0	2
Implantation	1	3
First missed menstrual period	2	4
Baby's heart begins to beat	3	5
Baby's brain waves begin	6	8
All body systems present	8	10
Birth	38	40

Fertilization age is a framework of time based upon the preborn child's viewpoint, and begins at the instant of conception. The gestational age timeline begins two weeks earlier, at the beginning of the last menstrual period, and is figured from the mother's viewpoint. Gestational age is most often used in discussions about the development of the preborn child.

In other words, common (gestational) convention holds that the 40 weeks of gestation begin on the first day of the last menstrual period, or two weeks before actual fertilization. Under this system a full-term baby is usually born 38 weeks after fertilization.

These terms are based upon different starting points, and can therefore can be somewhat confusing. Table 5 compares benchmarks of both.

1   Letter from Thomas W. Hilgers, M.D., Pope Paul VI Institute, dated 28 May 1996.

Most of the material in this question is from John and Sheila Kippley's book *The Art of Natural Family Planning*, which is the best available resource for explaining the human reproductive system and its functions in a way that an average person can understand. The book provides the information in a context of respect for God's gift of reproduction. In particular, the material in Chapter 5, "The Basic Physiology of Human Reproduction," is very useful for those who wish to understand human reproduction. You can order this book from the Couple to Couple League, PO Box 111184, Cincinnati, Ohio 45211-1184, telephone: (513) 661-7612.

48. What Are the Different Methods of NFP, and How Do They Work?

Overview

There are four basic types of natural family planning:

(1) the "rhythm" or calendar method, also known as the Ogino-Knaus method;

(2) the Basal Body Temperature (BBT) method;

(3) the ovulation method; and

(4) the Sympto-Thermal Method (STM).[1]

Each of these methods, when used to avoid or postpone pregnancy, take into account sperm viability in the female reproductive tract, which averages three days (with a range of from two to seven days) and the fertile period of the ovum, which is about 24 hours. This means the fertile period may be a maximum of seven days before ovulation to two days after, and is more typically four days before ovulation to two days after.

The following descriptions of these four methods are merely summaries of the similarities and contrasts between them. Anyone who desires more detailed information on any of the methods should consult the NFP teaching groups listed in Question 58.

The "Calendar Rhythm" or Ogino-Knaus Method

During the 1920s, Drs. Kyusaku Ogino of Japan and Hermann Knaus of Germany performed independent research into the menstrual cycles of a number of women, and found the following patterns;

(1) Conception is seldom possible from 20 to 24 days before the next menstruation;

(2) Conception is possible from 12 to 19 days before the next menstruation; and

(3) Conception is impossible during the 11 days before the next menstruation.

The original research of Drs. Ogino and Knaus laid the foundation for the development of modern natural family planning methods that are currently more effective than most contraceptives.

The primary advantage of the calendar method is that it is relatively easy to learn and use. A woman simply keeps a menstrual calendar for several cycles, noting when menstruation begins and ends. She then determines the longest and shortest cycles, and applies the "minus 10, minus 20" rule, which means she uses the shortest cycle to find the first fertile day by subtracting 20 days from its length, and uses the longest cycle to find the last fertile day by subtracting 10 days from its length.

For example, if the longest cycle has been 30 days, and the shortest cycle 25 days, the first fertile day will be Day 5, and the last fertile day will be Day 20.

The disadvantages of the "rhythm" method are obvious. Since it does not reflect the actual nature of the current cycle, but only an average of previous cycles, long periods of abstinence and a relatively high failure rate can be expected, especially if cycles are irregular. The "rhythm" method can be very difficult to use after childbirth and miscarriage, and when menopause is approaching, because cycle lengths can be very irregular during these times.

Despite all of these difficulties, users of the "rhythm" method experience a user effectiveness rate of 91% during the first year, which is far better than most mechanical methods of contraception.[2] The success rate is even better when the method is combined with temperature observations.

The Basal Body Temperature (BBT) Method of NFP

The basal body temperature is the lowest body temperature a person has during the 24-hour day. A woman who takes her temperature with a basal thermometer at about the same time each morning will find there is a definite monthly pattern to her temperatures. She will often also find that her BBT dips before ovulation and rises thereafter until menstruation. Since this does not give adequate advance notice of the impending ovulation in any one cycle, she must chart several cycles in order to narrow the fertile time down to perhaps ten days—about one week before ovulation and three days after a definite "thermal shift."

The Ovulation Method of NFP

This method of NFP is sometimes called the cervical mucus charting method. There are several variations of the ovulation method, including the Billings Ovulation Method (BOM) and Dr. Thomas Hilgers' Creighton Model.

The ovulation method is based upon the regular pattern of changes in the cervical mucus during the menstrual cycle. The quantity and quality of this mucus in terms of slipperiness, stretchiness, wetness and tackiness will change from day to day as a woman approaches ovulation. Ovulation usually occurs within one day before or after the last day of the most slippery or fertile mucus. Beginning users of the ovulation method generally start noting the fertile period starting with the appearance of any external mucus after menstruation has ceased. In order to establish reliable charting of the wife's mucus, it is suggested that the couple abstain from coitus for one cycle in order to avoid confusion between the wife's mucus and the husband's spermatic fluid. The period of monthly abstinence may safely be shortened after several cycles of practice and recording.

Sympto-Thermal Method

The sympto-thermal method combines observations of basal body temperature and cervical mucus, and, as a cross-check, adds an examination of the cervical os (mouth of the cervix) as well. During fertile times, the os expands, becomes softer and rises. Some women also experience regular episodes of *mittelschmerz*, or pain associated with ovulation. During infertile times, the os contracts, closes, becomes firmer and descends.

As a general rule, couples may resume intercourse on the fourth day following peak mucus and the third day following the thermal shift. As with other methods of natural family planning, the period of abstinence may be relatively long for the first few cycles of practice, after childbirth or miscarriage, or after switching from an abortifacient method involving hormones. The average experienced couple using the sympto-thermal method has about 9 or 10 days of abstinence each cycle. Every time that a fertile type of mucus appears before ovulation, they must abstain for three days. Once ovulation occurs, the couple is sterile until menstruation and usually sterile during the first two days of menstruation.

Refinements of Natural Family Planning

Today there are a number of devices available to help couples estimate the day of ovulation. The most practical and effective of these is the Japanese "L-Sophia."

Several other approaches to improving the effectiveness of NFP are under study. One device would measure hormone levels in urine and would therefore be a true ovulation predictor or detector. Another would accurately measure the water level in cervical mucus. Others would detect preovulatory rises in estrogen in saliva and cervical mucus. In addition, changes in breast milk and in the electrical resistance of cervical mucus are under investigation.

One conclusion is certain: 30 years of contraceptive and abortifacient research has shown that there is no way to subdue our fertility without paying a steep price, both on the individual and societal level. The only way to be in harmony with our fertility is to let it take its natural place in our lives as a friend to cooperate with, not as an enemy to be defeated, subdued or snuffed out.

1 For the last twenty years, there has been some discussion regarding the best term that could be applied to the methods used by couples who want to place their reproductive lives in the hands of God. Many pro-lifers object to the term "natural family planning," saying that it smacks of utilitarian Planned Parenthood-type thinking. They prefer instead "natural fertility awareness" (NFA) or "natural fertility regulation" (NFR). NFA refers to the teaching of signs and symptoms of fertility to mature teens in preparation for marriage, and is thus different from NFP. NFR is a term that is certainly appropriate for people who have been using the methods for some time and are therefore knowledgeable enough to avoid the confusion brought on by the use of several different terms for the natural methods.

However, the term "natural family planning" (NFP) has two distinct advantages. First, it appeals strongly to couples using contraception and considering changing to the natural methods, but who still possess lingering traces of the "contraceptive mentality." Pro-lifers should always try to wean their friends and acquaintances away from abortifacients and contraceptives. Secondly, the term "NFP" is used by many teachers in developing countries to draw a sharp contrast between natural methods of fertility regulation and contraceptive/abortifacient methods. These teachers find that their students, who often have little education, are confused by other terms.

For these reasons, the term "natural family planning" (NFP) is used throughout this chapter. This is no way implies that other terms are less appropriate.

2 Robert A. Hatcher, *et. al. Contraceptive Technology* (16th Revised Edition). New York: Irvington Publishers, Inc., 1994. Table 5-2, "Percentage of Women Experiencing a Contraceptive Failure During the First Year of Typical Use and the First Year of Perfect Use and the Percentage Continuing Use at the End of the First Year, United States," p. 113.

49. How Effective Is NFP at Preventing and Achieving Pregnancy?

The only 100 percent effective "birth control" methods are abstinence and complete castration (or hysterectomy). Even surgical sterilization occasionally fails to prevent pregnancy, and abortion sometimes fails to prevent births.

Natural family planning, if learned and used properly, is much more effective than any method of mechanical contraception, including the male and female condoms, cervical cap, cervical sponge and diaphragm. Question 26 shows that barrier methods of contraception have method failure rates of from 3 to 26 percent in the first year of use. The method failure rates for abortifacient methods range from 0.1 to 1.5 percent in the first year of use, and their user failure rates can be as high as 8-12 percent.

According to *Contraceptive Technology*, the ovulation method of NFP has a three percent method failure rate, the sympto-thermal method a two percent method failure rate and the post-ovulation method (intercourse only in the post-ovulation phase) a one percent method failure rate.[1]

As with any method of contraception, user motivation and care figure heavily into how effective a method will really be. The percentages above are *method* failure rates, which apply only if users employ the method perfectly. NFP fails more often when user error is factored in, as does any method of contraception.

The key to any method of NFP is identifying the positive period of peak fertility. This is possible for all women, but it can be more difficult at times, such as when approaching menopause, during the post-breastfeeding transition period, after childbirth or miscarriage, after abandoning a hormone-based abortifacient method or during periods of extended illness.

One important point should be kept in mind: According to the World Health Organization (WHO), sexual "risk taking" during fertile days probably accounts for many more pregnancies than the inability to correctly use the natural methods or interpret charts.[1] In other words, if a husband and wife don't "take a chance" on the first or second day of fertility, all of the NFP methods are much more effective.

Since couples who learn NFP are willing to accept a period of abstinence each month as an expression of responsibility and love, they generally have more self-discipline than couples using contraceptive or abortifacient methods. Therefore, it is reasonable to say the rate of *user* errors will be lower with NFP than with other methods of fertility regulation.

In addition to being effective at avoiding pregnancy, NFP can do one thing that no method of contraception can do: It can help *achieve* pregnancy. In fact, many fertility counselors advise couples who are having trouble conceiving to begin charting their cycles.

The effectiveness of NFP at helping a couple achieve pregnancy depends, of course, primarily upon their individual situation. If the man or woman is physically infertile, no amount of charting will help them to conceive. However, NFP can maximize the probability of conception if there is any possibility of doing so. In addition, learning and using NFP can improve the psychological state of mind of the couple trying to conceive by showing them how the woman's body works and giving them a sense of working with it in a natural way for the purpose of achieving pregnancy.

1   Robert A. Hatcher, *et. al. Contraceptive Technology* (16th Revised Edition). New York: Irvington Publishers, Inc., 1994, p. 328 and Table 5-2, "Percentage of Women Experiencing a Contraceptive Failure During the First Year of Typical Use and the First Year of Perfect Use and the Percentage Continuing Use at the End of the First Year, United States," p. 113.

50. What Are the Advantages of NFP?

The natural methods of fertility regulation offer many advantages over the man-made methods, as listed in Table 6 on page 97.

51. How Does NFP Promote Closeness Between Married Couples when It Requires Periodic Abstinence?

Contrasting Divorce Rates

Recent comprehensive studies have concluded that nearly *one-half* of all marriages now taking place in the United States will end in divorce, annulment or separation.[1]

Contrast this abysmal failure rate with that of married couples who use natural family planning: The divorce/separation rate among these couples is *less than one in eight*[2]. NFP can't take credit for all of this huge discrepancy, of course, but it undoubtedly contributes greatly to marital fidelity and endurance by fostering an atmosphere of knowledge, communication and intimacy between husband and wife. It also manifests a couple's willingness to forego immediate self-gratification for each other, to say nothing of giving a good example of self-control and chastity to their children. The most important feature of NFP is not the method itself, but its *spiritual* aspect. Nothing is more certain than the fact that contraception, abortion and sterilization do *not* make couples happy, and the contrasting divorce rates between contraceptors and NFP users provide stark proof of this fact.

There have been very few statistical studies on how NFP has helped or hindered marriages, but one survey conducted nearly 30 years ago showed that 74% of husbands and 75% of wives thought NFP helped their marriages. Only 9% of husbands and 8% of wives thought it hindered their marriages (17% of both husbands and wives had no opinion).[3]

How NFP Helps

How, exactly, does NFP strengthen marriage?

It increases the husband's respect for his wife's fertility and deepens his understanding of her psychology. It lets husband and wife share the responsibility for their fertility equally, thus living up to the ideal of "conscious parenthood," which is the conceiving and bearing of children by choice and by will, truly the fruit of unselfish love. Finally, the wife appreciates being able to avoid the harmful effects of contraceptives and abortifacients.

Figure 10

"In loving, the husband and wife must turn their attention to each other as happens in natural family planning, and not to self, as happens in contraception." —Mother Teresa of Calcutta, at the 1994 National Prayer Breakfast in Washington, D.C.

When one considers how endearing and unifying it is for a husband or wife to abstain despite their desires, out of consideration for each other or family, abstinence becomes a unifying act of love. In contrast, in a chemically or surgically sterile marriage, abstinence by either husband or wife is considered a burden and becomes a disunifying event.

Finally, studies have shown that a regular period of abstinence helps strengthen marriages by obliging couples to show their affection in other ways for a while every month, thereby improving vital communications skills.

Of course, a person infected with the anti-life mentality thinks this last point is moot, because he basically believes that both animals and humans are simply slaves of their hormones and have no self-control. Two such persons are abortionists Selig Newbardt and Harold Schulman, who assert "the rhythm method is demanding because it requires a couple to surrender their love life in exchange for a sex life."[4]

This statement, of course, simplistically equates "love" and "sex," and even implies that the two are mutually exclusive. This false notion is a primary source of much of the misery afflicting society today.

Setting the Example for Teens

A husband and wife who use natural family planning set a fine example for teenagers. Father Paul Marx of Human Life International often notes that, "contracepting parents beget fornicating teenagers." This is nothing more than common sense. Teenagers are not stupid. You cannot live in the same house with someone and keep even your most intimate secrets from them for 18 years. Teens see what is going on in the family and they can easily deduce their parents' attitudes toward

Table 6

The Advantages
of Natural Family Planning over Contraception

(1) NFP does not interfere with the natural reproductive system and process designed by God.

(2) NFP is morally acceptable to all religions and cultures.

(3) NFP avoids the use of mechanical devices or powerful hormones which may have harmful effects (see Chapters 2 and 3 for information on the harm caused by contraceptives and abortifacients).

(4) NFP is among the most effective methods of nonpermanent fertility regulation known when learned and used properly—up to 99 percent, as described in Question 49.

(5) NFP is virtually free of charge, whereas contraceptive and abortifacient methods cost anywhere from $33 to $365 annually (see Question 27 for the costs of contraceptives and abortifacients). This point is particularly crucial in areas of developing countries where health care is rudimentary and expensive.

(6) NFP strengthens marriage and family, as described in Question 51. It allows husband and wife to have the dignity of actual stewardship of the gift of fertility according to their unique circumstances. It fosters sexual self-control, which is central and essential to human freedom, true love and maturity. It also sets a good example of chastity in married life for teenage children.

(7) NFP is aesthetic. Of all of the methods of fertility regulation, only NFP allows the couple to make love as God and nature intended. It is amusing that "lovemaking manuals" try to work condoms, diaphragms, and various messy jams and jellies into the act of making love—"getting rigged to make love," as one noted gynecologist calls it. It is an enduring contradiction that many of the same people who pride themselves on the "natural" aspects of their lives don't hesitate to pollute their bodies with drugs and devices, and cannot let the most intimate aspect of their existence be *truly* natural and human.

(8) Finally, NFP, unlike all contraceptive and abortifacient methods, lets women and men learn about their bodies and work *with* them, rather than remaining ignorant and subduing them with chemicals. And NFP allows husbands to more intimately understand the psychology of their wives by understanding the nature of their menstrual cycles.

Adapted from "The Advantages of Natural Family Planning," brochure by Father Paul Marx, O.S.B., Ph.D.

sexuality from their actions. Parents who intelligently practice NFP are conscious of their true sexual nature and not only become excellent moral examples to their children, but are the best possible sex educators for them as well.

Teenagers rightly reject the hypocritical attitude, "Do as I say, not as I do." If teens are aware that their mother and father use contraceptives, the parent's admonitions to avoid fornication are not going to carry much weight with their children. However, if parents demonstrate love and affection for each other through respect of fertility and each other's circumstances by the periodic abstinence in NFP, this message will shine bright and clear, in a manner that is unmistakable to their teenagers. It will also help parents—and their children—strengthen and nurture their Faith, for obvious reasons.

1 U.S. Department of Commerce, Bureau of the Census. *Statistical Abstract of the United States*, 1995. Washington, D.C.: U.S. Government Printing Office, 1995. Table 87, "Live Births, Deaths, Marriages and Divorces: 1950 to 1993."

2 Personal communications with 14 major national NFP groups and leaders. Average number is shown (0.6% - 20% range). The lowest figure quoted is 0.6 percent, from Nona Aguilar's book *The New No-Pill No-Risk Birth Control* (New York: Rawson Associates), 1986, p. 188.

3 John Marshall and Beverley Howe. "Psychologic Aspects of the Basal Body Temperature Method of Regulating Births." *Fertility and Sterility*, January 1970, pp. 14-19.

4 Selig Newbardt and Harold Schulman. *Techniques of Abortion*. Boston: Little, Brown and Company. 1977 (Second Edition), p. 123.

··

52. What Advantages Does Breastfeeding Have for Both Mother and Infant?

Breastfeeding and Natural Family Planning

Another important part of the NFP philosophy is "ecological" or total breastfeeding, which is making use of what God has given us for obvious purposes. Traditionally, "educated" women tended to think that only backward, ignorant peasant women breast-fed their children. However, in the last 25 years, a dramatic breastfeeding revolution has taken place in the United States and in other Western nations, where three times as many babies are being breastfed now as in 1970.[1] Many women now allow their children to gradually wean themselves at the age of two or three instead of arbitrarily weaning earlier.

There are many advantages to breastfeeding:

■ Breastfeeding provides babies with the best possible food. Human breast milk contains at least 300 compounds, including 15 elements, eight proteins, 18 amino acids, six forms of nitrogen, six carbohydrates, at least 15 vitamins, and antibodies to protect the baby from various infections. Breast milk even evolves its composition from colostrum to transitional milk and then to "mature" milk over a baby's first 15 days of postnatal life in order to keep pace with the infant's development.[2] This is the primary reason why recent corporate attempts to induce women in developing countries to feed their infants with formula instead of breast milk are so scandalous.

- Breastfeeding provides bonding by allowing extensive skin contact, which helps children thrive physically and emotionally.
- Breastfeeding helps the uterus to contract after childbirth.
- Breastfeeding appears to help reduce the risk of breast cancer.
- The unique "suck and swallow" reflex of breastfeeding reduces tooth decay and encourages optimum jaw, mouth and speech development.
- The high level of calcium contained in human breast milk helps an infant's bones develop quickly and strongly.
- From a natural family planning standpoint, breastfeeding helps suppress ovulation from a period of three months (if the mother feeds the baby supplements) to as long as 1½ years (in the case of ecological breastfeeding).

Figure 11

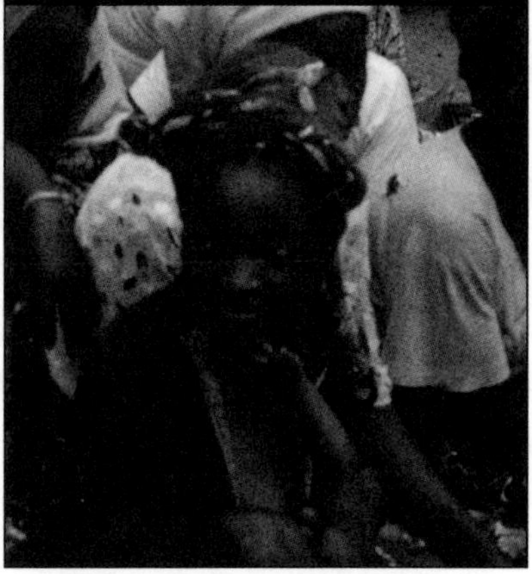

"Ecological" or complete breastfeeding not only contributes significantly to the overall health of mother and child, it helps space children.

For further information on breastfeeding, contact one of the organizations listed in Appendix A.

1 U.S. Department of Commerce, Bureau of the Census. *Statistical Abstract of the United States, 1990.* Washington, D.C.: U.S. Government Printing Office, 1990. Table 92, "Breast-Feeding by Characteristic of Mother and Birth Year of Baby: 1970 to 1981."

2 K. Diem and C. Lentner (editors). *Geigy Scientific Tables* (Seventh Edition). Ardsley, New York: Geigy Pharmaceuticals. 1975, pp. 687-689.

53. How Long Does It Take to Learn and Practice NFP?

Motivation is Everything

As with all worthy efforts, the key to learning and practicing natural family planning is motivation. If a husband and wife truly want to make the Gospel of Life part of *their* lives, they will take the time to learn NFP. With NFP, attitude is everything— the more the couple truly want their relationship with each other and with God to grow in maturity and grace, the easier the methods will be to learn. The secret is to make NFP an integral part of one's life, like a weekly "date" enjoyed by husband and wife or frequent Mass attendance.

Adopting the philosophy of natural stewardship of fertility soon becomes so much a part of one's life that the very *concept* of contraception becomes unnatural and unthinkable.

The Three Primary Concerns

The three primary concerns of couples inquiring about NFP are the result of a pervasive propaganda campaign by medical professionals, pro-abortionists, population controllers and others. These fears are that NFP is ineffective; that too much abstinence is required; and that it is too difficult to learn.

All of these misconceptions can be dispelled by proper instruction.

Question 26 shows that NFP is more effective than all contraceptive methods and as effective as most abortifacient methods. Question 48 shows that the maximum amount of abstinence required each month is about nine days using the most advanced methods of NFP. The only remaining concern voiced by most couples is the difficulty of learning a method of NFP.

The simplest method of NFP is calendar rhythm. Couples need to determine the length of the longest and shortest menstrual cycles over the past twelve months. NFP instructors can quickly teach this method to country women in developing nations, even if they cannot read, because the concepts are very easy to explain.

The most complex and reliable method of natural family planning is the sympto-thermal method. Depending upon the instructor, this method will take up to 12 hours of careful study at first, and will require careful charting thereafter. In addition, if the woman's cycles are in any way atypical, some coaching or consulting with an experienced NFP practitioner will probably be required.

Simply assessing how difficult it is to learn NFP is only a small part of a proper analysis. NFP's great advantages over contraceptives and abortifacients (particularly the intangible benefits) must be carefully weighed.

54. What Physical Complications Are Associated with NFP?

The most commonly used methods of "birth control" are, to put it bluntly, killers. Condoms sometimes break or slip and thus allow the transmission of AIDS and deadly venereal diseases (see Question 28). The intra-uterine device (IUD) has killed scores of women, not to mention the fact that all IUDs are abortifacient. The birth prevention pill has killed more than *twenty thousand* women through cardiovascular problems and other complications over the last 30 years in the United States alone, and has been classified "unavoidably unsafe" by the courts.[1]

Death is only one of the very long list of severe side effects that even feminists recognize as an inescapable result of the widespread use of artificial means of birth control: stroke, severe bleeding, sterility, repeated miscarriages, blindness, perforations, infections, etc.

Even one of the original inventors of the birth prevention pill, Dr. Carl Djerassi, admits that we have gone as far as we can go with contraceptive methods. He said that what the world needs is a "jet-age rhythm method" that can be used to avoid all of the ill effects of his and other "birth control" methods.[2]

Natural family planning is not only free of side effects, but it lets women know and "read" their bodies so well that they may be able to detect certain diseases and injuries to their reproductive systems earlier than they would have been able to otherwise. The ability to track symptoms and anomalies can save lives in cases of various cancers of the female reproductive tract.

Finally, NFP can do one thing that no method of "birth control" can ever do: Help a couple *get pregnant*. In fact, many infertility centers begin their investigations of a couple by teaching them the basics of natural family planning (primarily temperature taking) and having them observe the woman's cycles for several months in order to time intercourse for periods of maximum fertility.

1 Warren Hern. *Abortion Practice*. Philadelphia: J.B. Lippincott Company, 1990. According to Hern, about 750 additional women annually die of coronary thrombosis, strokes and other complications directly related to use of oral contraceptives.

2 Carl Djerassi. *The Pill, Pygmy Chimps, and Degas' Horse*. New York City: Basic Books, 1992, p. 263.

55. Why Does the Catholic Church Permit the Use of NFP?

Until Recently...

Contraception is unacceptable to the authentic tradition of virtually every religious denomination. Today, however, only the Catholic Church and a number of small Protestant and Jewish denominations teach that the only morally acceptable method of birth regulation is natural family planning.

For 1,900 years, all Christian denominations stood united in their condemnation of contraception. Only since 1930 have the "mainline" churches allowed artificial means of fertility regulation.

We must ask ourselves a fundamental question: Which is truly the fruit of the Holy Spirit—the teaching that has endured for more than 1,900 years or the contraceptive mentality that is now only 65 years old?

Common sense should reveal the answer to any person who is being honest with himself.

The Catholic Logic

The Catholic Church has always allowed the use of infertile periods to space children for authentically *serious* reasons. Pope Paul VI said in *Humanae Vitae* (¶10,16):

In relation to physical, economic, psychological and social conditions, responsible parenthood is exercised, either by the deliberate and generous decision to raise a numerous family, or by the decision, made for grave motives and with due respect for the moral law, to avoid for the time being, or even for an indeterminate period, a new birth.... If, then, there are serious motives to space out births, which derive from the physical or psychological conditions of husband and wife, or from external conditions, the Church teaches that it is then licit to take into account the natural rhythms immanent in the generative functions, for the use of marriage in the infecund periods only, and in this way to regulate birth without offending the moral principles which have been recalled earlier.

Some may equate these conditions to those anti-lifers commonly use to justify contraception, sterilization and even abortion. But the truthful answer to the question of what constitutes a truly *serious* impediment to having more children is rooted in honesty and a properly formed conscience. Pro-abortionists, since they lack the virtue of self-sacrifice, interpret any and all reasons as "serious." True followers of Christ can be more honest in their assessments of their own personal situations in light of the natural moral law and Church teaching.

The Catholic Church does not simply make up rules in order to control people, as critics often allege. *The Church uses as its guide the natural moral law instituted by God Himself,* and therefore can never change the teachings rooted in it. Nowhere is the natural moral law more reliable or needed than in matters involving human sexuality. The Church recognizes that contraception is one of the starting points for a true "anti-life mentality" which, once accepted, knows no bounds.

In *Familiaris Consortio* (32), Pope John Paul II explained that the fundamental difference between contraception and NFP lies in the worldview of the people involved:

> ... theological reflection is able to perceive and is called to study further *the difference, both anthropological and moral,* between contraception and recourse to the rhythm of the cycle: It is a difference which is much wider and deeper than is usually thought, one which involves in the final analysis two irreconcilable concepts of the human person and of human sexuality. The choice of the natural rhythms involves accepting the cycle of the person, that is the woman, and thereby accepting dialogue, reciprocal respect, shared responsibility and self-control. To accept the cycle and to enter into dialogue means to recognize both the spiritual and corporal character of conjugal communion and to live a personal love with its requirement of fidelity. In this context, the couple comes to experience how conjugal communion is enriched with those values of tenderness and affection which constitute the inner soul of human sexuality, in its physical dimension also. In this way, sexuality is respected and promoted in its truly and fully human dimension, and is never 'used as an 'object' that, by breaking the personal unity of soul and body, strikes at God's creation itself at the level of the deepest interaction of nature and person.

Humanae Vitae (16) explains that the difference between the practice of contraception and natural family planning lies in the fact that NFP cooperates with the human reproductive system as God designed it, whereas contraception conflicts with it:

> The Church is coherent with herself when she considers recourse to the infecund periods to be licit, while at the same time condemning, as being always illicit, the use of means directly contrary to fecundation, even if such use is inspired by reasons which may appear honest and serious. In reality, there are essential differences between the two cases; in the former, the married couple make legitimate use of a natural disposition; in the latter, they impede the development of natural processes. It is true that, in the one and the other case, the married couple are concordant in the positive will of avoiding children for plausible reasons, seeking the certainty that offspring will not arrive; but it is

also true that only in the former case are they able to renounce the use of marriage in the fecund periods when, for just motives, procreation is not desirable, while making use of it during infecund periods to manifest their affection and to safeguard their mutual fidelity. By so doing, they give proof of a truly and integrally honest love.

In summary, then, when a couple contracepts, they say to God "we will try to frustrate Your will [through contraception] if it is to create a child and will take action to negate it [through abortion] if You *do* create a child." When a couple uses NFP, they instead say "we will allow every instance of our marriage act to be open to Your will, regardless of whether the probability of conception is likely or remote, and will respect Your awesome gift of fertility in exactly the form You gave it to us."

....

56. If NFP Has So Many Advantages, Why Don't More Couples Use It?

Why *Not* Natural Family Planning?

Introduction. Despite constant Church teaching that natural family planning is the only moral means of fertility regulation, studies show that only about four percent of married Catholic couples of childbearing age in the United States use NFP.[1]

If natural family planning boasts all of the advantages referred to in Question 50, why don't more couples use it?

There are five basic reasons: ignorance, laziness, money, fear of abstinence and a failure to understand the nature of true marital love.

Ignorance. NFP does not fit into the anti-life philosophy. It runs counter to the "free sex" philosophy adopted by most people. Pro-abortion groups prefer to contemptuously and dishonestly dismiss this highly scientific method as "rhythm," even though they know better. This pervasive propaganda frightens many men and women into believing that natural family planning is backward and ineffective.

It's a different story for the doctors. Despite their many years of education, most are appallingly ignorant about NFP. A doctor who knows little or nothing about NFP is unlikely to promote it, but will instead prescribe the drugs that are so readily presented to him by the representatives of the major pharmaceutical corporations. Additionally, many doctors believe that women are too unmotivated or unintelligent to learn NFP. Finally, there is great profit to be made in the development, manufacturing and distribution of contraceptives and abortifacients; no such profit motive exists with NFP.

The clergy must share the blame for the ignorance of the faithful regarding NFP. For many years, and in many countries, "this divided position of the clergy [on contraception] has contributed, more than any other factor, to the confusion of the layman—after all, who is the layman to follow except the pastor? In espousing such a position, that the layman must be guided exclusively by his conscience, such clergymen have done more harm to the layman than they imagine, and inestimable disservice to the Church itself."[2]

This point is especially telling in Western countries. How many U.S. or European Catholics have ever heard contraception condemned, even in the vaguest terms, from the pulpit? How many bishops have made pronouncements against it? The primary reason that so many Catholic men and women use contraceptives and abortifacients is that *their bishops and priests have never told them not to.* Often, priests do not preach against anti-life practices because of their faulty seminary education in sexual morality, which is frequently delivered by dissenters from Church teaching.

Figure 12

Natural family planning can be taught easily and effectively to the country people of developing nations under a variety of conditions.

Laziness. NFP takes some time and effort to learn. In this age of instant gratification, the equation "FAST + EASY = GOOD" is an almost inviolable law. If a method of birth regulation requires any effort, most people summarily disqualify it. Most Western women would rather take a long-term gamble on their health than put a short-term effort into learning about their own bodies. And, sadly, most men could not care less which method of contraception their wives use, as long as they themselves aren't inconvenienced and have access to sex at all times.

As Erma Clardy Craven has said, "women are being seen as wombs to be deactivated rather than human beings with lives to be fulfilled."[3]

The Profit Motive. The contraceptive makers and most gynecologists would have the public believe quick 'n easy contraception is the only way to go. The manufacturers say this because they are making huge amounts of money off women who willingly and ignorantly drug their reproductive systems—and the profits from the sale of these drugs amount to more than $5 billion per year! This sum does not include the profits reaped by individual doctors and population control organizations such as the IPPF.

Curiously, NFP practitioners will probably agree with a writer for the Feminist Women's Health Centers, a chain of abortion clinics, as she summarizes the *real* reasons why NFP is not more widespread:

Fertility Awareness poses a big threat to the hormonal contraceptive industry. If women are given the choice of the Pill or implants with their side effects, lack of STD protection, expense, and reliance on doctors; or Fertility Awareness, with or without barrier methods, which seems the more logical choice? Both have the same effectiveness (98.5 - 99.2%). Fertility Awareness costs nothing to use, has no side effects, and puts reproductive responsibility firmly in the hands of the user.[4]

Time is money for busy health professionals. When they are faced with a choice between an easy 20 bucks for a five-minute birth prevention pill prescription or referring a couple to an NFP teacher, the lure of quick money usually wins out.

1   National Survey of Family Growth (NSFG) described in Catholic News Service. "Most Catholic Women Ignore Church-Accepted Form of Birth Control." The Portland, Oregon *Catholic Sentinel*, 24 January 1992, p. 7.

2   Vincent J.A. Rosales, M.D. "The Catholic Choice of Rhythm." *Unitas* [Manila], December 1976, pp. 474-501.

3   Erma Clardy Craven, quoted in *ALL About Issues*, July/August 1980, p. 5.

4   Suzanne Cooper Doyle. "Fertility Awareness: Reclaiming Reproductive Control." *WomenWise* (publication of the New Hampshire Federation of Feminist Women's Health Centers), Summer, 1991, pp. 6-8.

···

57. Can NFP Be Used for Contraceptive Motives?

Most Catholic married couples in developed countries have only one or two children. This is not because they use NFP effectively, but because they use contraceptives and abortifacients at about the same rates as all other groups. Some Catholics will use NFP for a few years and then, when they have had all the children they want, will switch to the Pill or even get sterilized.

As St. Augustine wrote in his treatise *On the Morals of the Manichaeans*:

Sometimes this lustful cruelty or cruel lust goes so far as to seek to procure a baneful sterility, and if this fails, the foetus conceived in the womb is in one way or another smothered or evacuated, in the desire to destroy the offspring before it has life, or if it already lives in the womb, to kill it before it is born. If both man and woman are party to such practices, they are not spouses at all; and if from the first they have carried on thus they have come together not for honest wedlock, but for impure gratification; if both are not party to these deeds, I make bold to say that either the one makes herself a mistress of the husband, or the other simply the paramour of the wife.[1]

More than half a century ago, Mahatma Gandhi illustrated the greatest problem of the 'contraceptive mentality' in marriage when he said:

It is dinned into one's ears that the gratification of the sex urge is a solemn obligation like the obligation of discharging debts.... This sex urge has been isolated from the desire for progeny and it is said by the protagonists of the use of contraceptives that conception is an accident to be prevented except when the parties desire to have children.... Marriage loses its sanctity when its purpose and highest use is conceived to be the satisfaction of the animal passion without contemplating the natural result of such satisfaction.[2]

It is certainly possible to use natural family planning exclusively throughout the reproductive years and still be a victim of the contraceptive mentality. Any method of birth regulation (including NFP) is evil if the intent is to deny God's will for our reproductive lives. A couple who uses NFP to avoid having children that they could properly care for may either be ignorant of the evil of doing so, or may have essentially selfish motivations.

1   St. Augustine, "On the Morals of the Manichaeans" (De Moribus Manichaeorum). Chapter 18, paragraph 65, as quoted in Casti Connubii, 31 December 1930, VII ("Vices Opposed to Christian Marriage.")

2   Mahatma Gandhi, Harijan, 28 March 1936. Louis Fischer (editor). The Essential Gandhi: His Life, Works, and Ideas. New York: Vintage Books, 1962, p. 241.

58. How Can I Obtain Additional Information on NFP?

Overview

In the United States, several national organizations promote the various methods of natural family planning, as described in the following paragraphs.

In addition, the National Conference of Catholic Bishops' *Directory of Diocesan Natural Family Planning Coordinators* lists more than 400 NFP contacts for all 50 states and 63 countries. This volume, updated each year, is available from the Bishops Committee for Pro-Life Activities, NCCB, 3211 Fourth Street N.E., Washington, D.C. 20017-1194, telephone: (202) 541-3070/3240. The NCCB also publishes *Forum*, a diocesan NFP activity report.

Anyone interested in learning about or teaching natural family planning can contact any national or local group.

Couple to Couple League (CCL)

The Couple to Couple League teaches the most up-to-date methods in natural family planning. CCL also distributes information on the hazards of unnatural "birth control," chastity, raising children and related medical news. The group has an extensive catalog of books and pamphlets.

Two of CCL's best pamphlets summarize the advantages of NFP and are suitable for distribution in schools, churches or meetings of any kind: "Good News about Natural Family Planning" and the more detailed "The Case for Natural Family Planning."

CCL is always recruiting for NFP instructors and publicists, and can reliably refer to competent NFP teachers. Anyone interested in attacking abortion and the anti-life mentality at their roots should volunteer to teach NFP.

CCL's newsletter, published six times yearly, is available for a $15 annual donation. It provides detailed information from scientists on the latest NFP findings. For a list and order form, write to or call the Couple to Couple League, 3621 Glenmore Avenue, Post Office Box 111184, Cincinnati, Ohio 45211-1184, telephone: (513) 661-7612.

CCL also publishes the *CCL Family Foundations*, a bimonthly newsletter that covers the technical and "how-to" aspects of natural family planning and information on teen sex clinics, chastity and Planned Parenthood. You can subscribe for a $15 donation.

Pope Paul VI Institute

The Pope Paul VI Institute for the Study of Human Reproduction was founded in 1985 by Thomas Hilgers, M.D., in response to the challenges set forth in the encyclical *Humanae Vitae*.

The Institute provides natural family planning services, teacher education programs and research, primarily in the Creighton Model NFP Medical Systems, a standardized modification of the Ovulation Method. The Pope Paul VI Institute has also developed NaProTechnology (Natural Procreative Technologies), a science which devotes its medical, surgical and allied health energies to cooperating with the natural procreative mechanism and function.

The Institute also offers a free quarterly magazine, *The Love and Life Newsmagazine*, which provides education on NFP developments and the reconnection of love and life.

The Pope Paul VI Institute may be contacted at 6901 Mercy Road, Omaha, Nebraska 68106-2604, telephone: (402) 390-6600; fax: (402) 390-9851.

The Facts of Life

Chapter 5

Euthanasia

<hr>

59. What Is the Definition of "Euthanasia?"

"Euthanasia" means any action committed or omitted for the purpose of causing or hastening the death of a human being after birth, allegedly for the purpose of ending the person's suffering. The Vatican's *Declaration on Euthanasia* states: "By euthanasia is understood an action or an omission which of itself or by intention causes death, in order that all suffering may in this way be eliminated."

In other words, euthanasia is a form of killing, regardless of the motives of the person committing the act.

The critical differences between direct and indirect euthanasia and natural death must be defined precisely before any intelligent discussion on the various "shades" of euthanasia may proceed.

The pro-euthanasia lobby has accomplished many of its goals by using scare tactics involving dramatic anecdotes of people in severe, unrelieved pain, who are being "kept alive by machines" with numerous tubes and devices surrounding them and interfering with their peace and dignity. Pro-euthanasia groups have also confused lawmakers and the public by intentionally blurring the lines between direct and indirect euthanasia and a natural death. Pro-abortionists used precisely the same tactic when they lumped contraceptives, abortifacients and abortion together as described in Question 37.

Anti-euthanasia activists must be intimately familiar with the terms relating to euthanasia, or they will be confused and ineffective in their efforts to save lives.

- **Active (positive, direct) euthanasia** is action *taken* for the purpose of causing or hastening death. These measures may include lethal injection or overdose committed by a physician. "Physician-assisted suicide" indicates that a physician has helped a person kill himself. Specifically, this means that the physician provides a prescription or other means for a person to commit suicide; the person, not the physician, actually performs the lethal act.

■ **Passive (negative, indirect) euthanasia** is action *withheld* for the purpose of causing or hastening death. These measures include the withholding or withdrawal of *non-heroic* measures, including food, hydration (water), and oxygenation. Examples of this type of euthanasia are the many infanticides committed each year in the United States by withholding food and water from handicapped newborn babies who would otherwise have lived. Another example of passive euthanasia is the withholding of food and water from a person in a so-called "persistent vegetative state," or from someone whose health is not improving rapidly enough in the opinions of the attending health care workers. Note that the term "indirect," when applied to a euthanasia case, has a different meaning than when applied to "double effect" cases of abortion and sterilization (see Questions 35 and 85 for a discussion of the "double effect" as applied to abortion and sterilization, and Question 65 for information on the application of the principle to euthanasia and a natural death).

■ **Natural death** means allowing a person to die in comfort and peace by withholding excessive or heroic treatment that would only cause pain and lengthen the person's lifespan by a modest or insignificant amount. Note that, if medical professionals withheld the same treatment from a person in the same circumstances whose lifespan would be significantly lengthened by it, they would be instead committing passive euthanasia. Food, water and oxygen must be provided during the person's progression to natural death, because they are the right of every human being. Letting a person die a natural death is *not* passive euthanasia. As Bishop Rene Gracida has defined it, "if the removal of a life-sustaining procedure is intended to avoid an unreasonable burden of the procedure, so that a quicker death is only an unintended side-effect of the decision, it is not a case of euthanasia."[1]

■ **Voluntary euthanasia** is committed with the willing cooperation of the subject.

■ **Involuntary euthanasia** is committed without the knowledge and/or consent of the subject.

1 Bishop Rene H. Gracida, Corpus Christi, Texas. "A Dissent from the 'Interim Pastoral Statement on Artificial Nutrition and Hydration'" issued by the Texas Conference of Catholic Health Facilities and some of the bishops of Texas. *Diocesan Press*, 25 May 1990, paragraph 2.

··

60. What Is Meant by "Right to Die," "Death with Dignity" and "Mercy Killing?"

The "Right To Die"

Quite simply, there is no "right" to die, according to either the laws of God or the laws of man. Pro-euthanasia activists cleverly fabricated the "right to die" in order to appeal to people who have become used to unthinkingly accepting new and dangerous "rights." The "rights" formulated under the umbrella "right to privacy" include contraception, abortion, direct and indirect infanticide, various homosexual activities, pornography and euthanasia. Courts have used the so-called "right to privacy" repeatedly to legitimize behavior that many people find abhorrent or immoral—quite simply because there is no possible *legitimate* justification for them.

Fundamentally, the "right to die" is *not* a right—*it is the forfeiture of all possible rights*, and, as in the Netherlands and the People's Republic of China, will inevitably become for many people the *duty* to die. As former Colorado Governor Richard Lamm asserted on 27 March 1984: "... we have a duty to die. It's like leaves falling off a tree forming the humus for the other plants to grow out. We've got a *duty to die* and get out of the way with all of our machines and artificial hearts and everything else like that and let the other society, our kids, build a reasonable life."

"Death with Dignity"

All people, whether they support or oppose euthanasia, desire a dignified death for themselves and for their loved ones.

But conflict arises over the definition of "dignity."

Pro-euthanasia activists perceive a loss of *physical* or *intellectual* dignity when a person becomes incontinent, incoherent and confused, suffers intractable pain or feels that he has lost control of his destiny.

Anti-euthanasia activists perceive a loss of *spiritual* dignity when a person loses his focus on God and instead desires only a release from an existence that he or others may find pointless and wasteful.

The terminally ill person's state of mind highlights the difference in viewpoints.

When a person's fear of death is exceeded only by his fear of pain or loss of control, he is in a state of continuous mortal terror and may see death as only a blessed release from his current situation. He may indeed fear what happens after death, but primarily focuses only on his present circumstances. Such a person necessarily defines his degree of dignity by purely physical or emotional criteria.

However, when a person can overcome his fear of both death and pain, and accept and transcend them with a deep peace at the end of his life, he realizes that purely physical measures of "dignity" are inappropriate. True compassion demands that all of us love and support one another regardless of our functional capacity or appearance, and prepare the dying for their ultimate meeting with God. This is the true definition of living with dignity, even when dying.

"Mercy Killing"

"Mercy killing" is an act of *direct* euthanasia usually committed for the alleged purpose of ending the suffering of an unproductive or terminally ill person. In reality, healthy people commit "mercy killings" in order to relieve themselves of the inconvenience and expense of caring for those who have (or will) become an emotional or financial burden on them.

Over the past 20 years, society has defined two classes of born human beings who are not suffering, but who are nonetheless candidates for "mercy killings":

handicapped newborns who could otherwise live long lives, and people in an extended comatose state. Pro-euthanasia groups are now extending this lethal "privilege" to terminal patients and nursing home residents, regardless of their emotional state or level of pain. It is inevitable that the number of people eligible for "mercy killings" will expand rapidly and uncontrollably, just as it did in Nazi Germany, and just as it is doing in the Netherlands today.

"Mercy killing" of both infants and adults is a logical extension of the practice of elective abortion committed to eliminate handicapped preborns. If *healthy* preborn babies can be killed up until the moment of birth because the mother perceives her health or well-being is threatened, then why can they not be killed shortly *after* birth, especially if they have a serious chromosomal defect such as Down's Syndrome? Down's Syndrome children are among the happiest and most contented human beings in existence, often living well into adulthood and giving great joy to others—yet they are frequently murdered *in utero*, not because *they* will suffer, but because their *parents* think they will.

If a person accepts death on God's terms, it is a mercy. However, if others force it on us, or if we strive for it due to the dictates our misguided consciences, it is a dreadful burden, seeming acceptable only because it appears to be less terrible than the pain.

··

61. What Is Meant by "Brain Death" and "Persistent Vegetative State (PVS)?"

"Persistent Vegetative State"

People sometimes use "brain death" and "persistent vegetative state" (PVS) as synonyms, but the terms actually differ greatly in meaning.

Many refer to a person who lapses into an extended coma as one who is suffering from a "persistent vegetative state." This is an inaccurate and demeaning term. To begin with, more than half of all patients in "PVS" eventually regain consciousness, as described below.

Perhaps even more important, pro-life activists should avoid the term "persistent vegetative state" because it is dehumanizing. People are never "vegetables" at any time from fertilization to natural death, and so others should not refer to them as such. We must recognize that all human beings must be afforded dignity and care as basic rights, regardless of the seriousness of their condition.

A more dignified term would be simply "comatose."

Finally, the term "persistent vegetative state" is a very imprecise catch-all term, and its meaning can vary substantially depending upon the outlook *and the intent* of the person using the term. Since it is so open to abuse, the term should be avoided altogether.

"Brain Death"

The Vatican's *Charter for Health Care Workers* (1995, ¶129) defines the exact moment of death:

First with regard to the *biomedical definition of death*: "a person is dead when he has irreversibly lost all ability to integrate and coordinate the physical and mental functions of the body."

Second, with regard to the precise moment of death: "death comes when: a) the spontaneous functions of the heart and breathing have definitively ceased, or b) the irreversible arrest of all brain activity." In reality "brain death is the true criterion of death, although the definitive arrest of cardio-respiratory activity very quickly leads to brain death."

This exacting definition leaves little doubt that a person suffering "brain death" has little or no hope of recovery.[1]

A very important point to remember is that temporary and permanent comas are not in themselves terminal conditions. A person may indeed be unresponsive, but never loses his humanity. He therefore has the inalienable rights to food, water, ventilation and competent medical care.

Pro-Euthanasia Paradoxes

It is a curious fact that most pro-euthanasia activists oppose capital punishment, primarily because judges and juries make mistakes during trials that can result in an unjust sentence of death. In other words, once a person has been executed, not even the most conclusive proof of his innocence can bring him back to life. Those who support euthanasia are therefore willing to spend an average of $800,000 to keep a hardened killer behind bars for the rest of his natural life.[2] However, they are not willing to spend the same amount to keep an *innocent* comatose or ill person alive in the very real hope that he will recover or at least live for an extended period of time.

Pro-life activists may use precisely the same reasoning to oppose euthanasia. As noted below, medical people have judged scores of people "irreversibly comatose," and then they have awakened to lead normal or nearly normal lives.

Recovery from "PVS"

Medical researchers have performed a number of extensive studies to determine how many people in so-called "irreversible comas" actually recover.

One study of 84 people whom physicians considered to be in a "persistent vegetative state" showed that 41% had regained consciousness within six months and 58% had regained consciousness within three years. A second study of 26 children in comas lasting more than twelve weeks found that three-fourths eventually regained consciousness. Another study found that one-third of the 370 patients in a "PVS" for up to one year recovered enough to return to work.[3]

In one dramatic case, physicians had pronounced 79-year old grandfather Harold Cybulski of Barry's Bay, Ontario "brain dead and comatose." They stood by to disconnect his life support systems as soon as his family said their last goodbyes. But when his two-year-old grandson ran into the room and yelled "Grandpa!," Cybulski woke up, sat up, and picked up the little boy!

Six months later, he was leading a completely normal life, including driving the new car he had been looking forward to buying before he became comatose.

Cybulski's doctors could offer "no explanation" for his instant recovery.[4]

1 Blakiston's *Pocket Medical Dictionary* defines "brain death" as "Cessation of neurologic functioning by the criteria of deep unconsciousness without response to painful stimuli, absence of spontaneous breathing, fixed pupils, spontaneous marked hypothermia, absent reflexes except rarely tendon reflexes, and an isoelectric electroencephalogram showing no electrical activity over 2 microvolts at maximum gain even with stimulation by sound, pain, or pressure, recorded for 30 minutes or longer at 24-hour intervals. Excluded are patients under profound central nervous system depressants or hypothermia."

2 Sister Helen Prejean. *Dead Man Walking*. New York: Vintage Books, 1994, p. 130. Figure given is 1985 price; updated at 4 percent per year to 1996 dollars (original figure $516,000).

3 Keith Andrews. "Managing the Persistent Vegetative State: Early, Skilled Treatment Offers the Best Hope for Optimal Recovery." *British Medical Journal*, August 1992, pp. 304-305. "Results of Head Injury Study Released." *Minnesota Physician*, January 1989, p. 5. Lisa Fitterman. "Neurologist Has Cautionary Tales for Euthanasia Fans." *Vancouver Sun* [Canada], 8 September 1993, p. B3.

4 "A Little Child Shall Lead Us." Presbyterians Pro-Life *NEWS*, Summer, 1990, p. 4.

62. What Are Advance Directives?

The Types of Advance Directives

An advance directive is a legal form or document which allows a person to specify the medical treatment he wants and does not want in case he becomes incapable of making his desires known.

There are three general classes of advance directives: The "Living Will," the Durable Power of Attorney for Health Care (DPAHC or DPA), and the Will to Live.

The "Living Will"

What is a "Living Will?" Most versions of the "Living Will" have been written and promoted by The Society for the Right to Die (formerly the Euthanasia Society of America), Americans Against Human Suffering (AAHS), Concern [Compassion] for Dying (formerly the Euthanasia Educational Council), the Hemlock Society and the American Civil Liberties Union (ACLU). Spokesmen for some of these groups have said that the "Living Will" is a publicly acceptable way to introduce the agenda of legalized active euthanasia, suicide and assisted suicide, as described in Question 71.

The primary objectives of the "Living Will" are cost containment and the conditioning of the public to accept the withdrawal of life-saving medical treatment. As described below, the "Living Will" is a woefully inadequate mechanism for safeguarding the rights of patients who have lost the ability to make decisions regarding their own medical care.

"Living Will" legislation goes by many names. It may be called "Directive to Physicians," "Rights of the Terminally Ill" or "Patient's Rights" legislation. All of these titles emphasize understanding and compassion. Since California became the first state to give legal force to "Living Wills" in 1977, all but nine states have passed such laws.

Pro-euthanasia groups define the "Living Will" as a document by which a person can assert in writing a desire not to be kept alive by life-sustaining medical equipment and procedures when his or her condition has been diagnosed as terminal, or under certain other conditions.

Most "Living Wills" signed in the United States today are form-type wills, but, as with any legal document, they can be custom-tailored to meet any actual or perceived need or wish, including:

- requesting or refusing feeding tubes, antibiotics, dialysis, respirators, cardiopulmonary resuscitation (CPR) and other specified treatments;
- requesting pain medication;
- stating the desired place of death, including home;
- designating a proxy to make health care decisions when the individual is incapable of doing so; and
- requesting designation as an organ donor.

Is a "Living Will" Necessary? Many believe the "Living Will" is necessary in order to clarify a patient's legitimate right to refuse *extraordinary* medical treatment. However, the "Living Will" is completely unnecessary because this is a right that all patients *already* possess. Public support for pro-"Living Will" legislation is partly due to the scare tactics of pro-euthanasia groups which highlight the activities of a very small minority of doctors who resist even morally appropriate requests for the withdrawal of treatment.

"Living Wills" are generally unnecessary under present law, because there is nothing to prevent doctors from withholding or withdrawing life-sustaining medical treatment when all reasonable hope for recovery is gone. Patients already have the right to give their doctors and family instructions on how they want to be treated in the event of a terminal illness or grave injury, particularly when they are in no condition to decide for themselves.

What Are the Dangers of the "Living Will?" The primary danger of the "Living Will" is that the person usually signs it long before he knows if or when he will be incapacitated—or what the circumstances of that incapacitation will be. This means that the person cannot specify the desired details of his treatment for future medical conditions. Therefore, anyone who values the sanctity of human life should not sign a "Living Will," which could become an order for assisted suicide in the future. Much better alternatives to the "Living Will" are described later in this Question.

Presumably, one can change or revoke a "Living Will" at any time by making a verbal or written statement to a physician, nurse or other health care worker. However, this can be difficult or impossible for at least four reasons;

- Changes to or revocation of a "Living Will" depend upon an individual's condition. If he should experience a change of heart after he is incapable of communicating, he is out of luck.
- If the presiding health care professional believes the patient's wishes are the result of trauma or some other cause, he can disregard them.
- If a person would like to change or revoke his "Living Will," he may find that it is very difficult to locate all original and duplicated copies of the document.
- The wording of the original "Living Will" may remain the same, but the *law* governing its application may change. For example, Florida "Living Wills" now presume that patients *refuse* food and water unless otherwise specified—a fundamental change from the law's original meaning.

The Facts of Life

If a person signs a "Living Will," it is probably legally binding under prevailing conditions in the U.S. judicial system. It would therefore be difficult or impossible for a family doctor to make the decisions that would be in the patient's best interests.

This set of conditions makes it virtually impossible for the signer of a "Living Will" to define precisely the treatment that he wants—or does *not* want.

No "Living Will" can be made medically and legally secure in every way *even at the time of its signing*. Additionally, there is no way of knowing how the definitions and rules will change as the pro-euthanasia groups lobby for more expansive meanings of such crucial terms as "terminally ill' and "extraordinary treatment."

As an example, the wording of the most common "Living Will," which has been signed by millions, says that "if I am permanently unconscious or there is no reasonable expectation of my recovery from a seriously incapacitating or lethal illness or condition, I do not wish to be kept alive by artificial means."

Figure 13

"A society will be judged on how it treats those in the dawn of life, those in the twilight of life, and those in the shadow of life."
—*Senator Hubert Humphrey*

Ten years ago, "artificial means" would have meant truly extraordinary or "heroic" medical or surgical procedures. However, some states currently define respirators, codes, medication, kidney dialysis, and even *food and water* as "artificial!" In other words, a person might sign a "Living Will" in a state where food and water are a part of standard medical treatment, then travel to a state where they are "extraordinary treatment," and then become incapacitated. Or, the courts or legislature in his home state may quietly redefine food and water as "extraordinary treatment" (which has already happened in Florida), and he will not be aware of the fact.

What happens to him then?

Terms with definitions that are constantly shifting or are difficult to define are tailor-made for anti-lifers of every stripe, and are at the heart of the "Living Will's" problems. Anyone who signs a "Living Will" has placed decisions regarding his medical care not in the hands of medical professionals, but in the hands of people whose overriding concern is the cutting of medical expenses.

Durable Power of Attorney (DPA)

A Durable Power of Attorney for Health Care simply transfers the responsibility for making medical decisions to another person. A DPA allows someone who shares his values regarding the sanctity of life to become his "attorney in fact." The designated person need not be an attorney or health care worker; he or she may be a spouse, relative, priest, rabbi or minister, or fellow churchgoer.

A person who selects another to be the executor of a DPA should be sure that the executor shares his values regarding the sanctity of human life; that he has thoroughly discussed his wishes with the executor regarding medical care should he become incapacitated (these instructions should be detailed enough so that the person executing the DPA can infer decisions regarding medical treatments that are not specifically discussed); and that the executor will be available and capable of making proper decisions under stress.

A DPA is preferable to a "Living Will," because the latter is a static document that simply cannot cover all contingencies, and which may be interpreted incorrectly by someone who does not share the ill person's values regarding the value of human life.

The "Will to Live"

A "Will to Live" is a legal document which is a pro-life alternative to a "Living Will." It specifies that attending health care workers must do what they can to preserve one's life "without discrimination based on age or physical or mental disability or the 'quality' of life" and prohibits "any action or omission that is intended to cause or hasten death."[1] The "Will to Live" defines food and water as basic treatment and allows a person to specify those treatments that he would want withheld or withdrawn under certain circumstances.

The "Will to Live" is a realistic and protective alternative for a person who rejects the utilitarianism of the "Living Will" and who does not want to place the burden of life-or-death decisions on the shoulders of a loved one or friend.

1 A "Will to Live" may be obtained from the Will to Live Project, Suite 500, 419 Seventh Street NW, Washington, D.C. 20004.

••

63. Must Extraordinary or Disproportionate Measures Be Used to Extend a Person's Lifespan?

Introduction

"Extraordinary means" have been defined as " ... all medicines, treatments and operations which cannot be obtained or used without excessive expense, pain or other inconvenience for the patient or for others or which, if used, would not offer reasonable hope of benefit to the patient."[1] Such standard definitions are by their very nature imprecise, and so the terms "proportionate" and "disproportionate" means can be used to further clarify. The Vatican's *Declaration on Euthanasia* clarifies these terms by calling for a balance between the various human and financial costs and benefits of using a particular treatment: "In any case, it will be possible to make a correct judgment as to the means by studying the type of treatment to be used, its degree of complexity or risk, its cost and the possibilities of using it, and comparing these elements with the result that can be expected, taking into account the state of the sick person and his or her physical and moral resources."

Church Teachings

Contrary to what pro-euthanasia propagandists often allege, the Catholic Church has never taught that every life must be extended to the last minute by all means possible. The Church teaches that God determines the time of death of every human being, and that it is just as impermissible to try to extend one's life *beyond* that time as it is to attempt to end it *before* that time.

The Bishops of Ireland have said:

> A very real problem arises when artificial measures of resuscitation and life-support become death-delaying rather than properly life-supporting. There is clearly no moral obligation to keep a body breathing and biologically alive after irreversible brain death has occurred. It is not euthanasia to decline the use of such means or even to discontinue them when it is clear that they are only death-delaying.[2]

The *Declaration on Euthanasia* lays out very specific guidelines for providing or not providing for extraordinary means of life support:

> "In order to facilitate the application of these general principles, the following clarifications can be added:

- If there are no other sufficient remedies, it is permitted, with the patient's consent, to have recourse to the means provided by the most advanced medical techniques, even if these means are still at the experimental stage and are not without a certain risk. By accepting them, the patient can even show generosity in the service of humanity.

- It is also permitted, with the patient's consent, to interrupt these means, where the results fall short of expectations. But for such a decision to be made, account will have to be taken of the reasonable wishes of the patient and the patient's family, as also of the advice of the doctors who are specially competent in the matter. The latter may in particular judge that the investment in instruments and personnel is disproportionate to the results foreseen; they may also judge that the techniques applied impose on the patient strain or suffering out of proportion with the benefits which he or she may gain from such techniques.

- It is also permissible to make do with the normal means that medicine can offer. Therefore one cannot impose on anyone the obligation to have recourse to a technique which is already in use but which carries a risk or is burdensome. Such a refusal is not the equivalent of suicide; on the contrary, it should be considered as an acceptance of the human condition, or a wish to avoid the application of a medical procedure disproportionate to the results that can be expected, or a desire not to impose excessive expense on the family or the community.

- When inevitable death is imminent in spite of the means used, it is permitted in conscience to take the decision to refuse forms of treatment that would only secure a precarious and burdensome prolongation of life, so long as the normal care due to the sick person in similar cases [including the provision of nutrition and hydration] is not interrupted. In such circumstances the doctor has no reason to reproach himself with failing to help the person in danger."[3]

1 J.E. Schowalter, J.B. Ferholt, and N.M. Mann. "The Adolescent Patient's Decision to Die." *Pediatrics*, January 1973, pp. 101-102.

2 The Bishops of Ireland. Joint Pastoral Letter titled "Human Life is Sacred," 1 March 1975. Reprinted in the 22 May 1975 English edition of *L'Osservatore Romano*.

3 Sacred Congregation for the Doctrine of the Faith. *Declaration on Euthanasia*, 5 May 1980. Part IV, "Due Proportion in the Use of Remedies".

....

64. Should Food and Water Be Classified as "Extraordinary Treatment?"

Overview of Principles

How many people, when they are sitting down to eat a bowl of cereal or a hamburger and soft drink, consider themselves to be preparing to undergo medical treatment?

Nobody thinks this way. Yet this is exactly how pro-euthanasia activists want us to think: that food and water are a kind of "medical treatment" for the ill and elderly. They are doing this by trying to reclassify the fundamental right to nutrition and hydration as "extraordinary medical treatment." This goal has already been accomplished in Florida.

Food, water and oxygen are not "treatment"—they are fundamental medical care and they are *basic human rights*. Just as a basic right (to life) was discarded for an artificially manufactured "right" (to privacy) to impose abortion, now another genuine basic right (to food and water) is being jettisoned in order to impose another phony "right" (to die).

The Catechism of the Catholic Church (¶ 2277) states:

> Whatever its motives and means, direct euthanasia consists in putting an end to the lives of handicapped, sick, or dying persons. It is morally unacceptable. Thus an act or omission which, of itself or by intention, causes death in order to eliminate suffering constitutes a murder gravely contrary to the dignity of the human person and to the respect due to the living God, his Creator. The error of judgment into which one can fall in good faith does not change the nature of this murderous act, which must always be forbidden and excluded.

Bishop James T. McHugh of Camden, New Jersey got right to the point when he said:

> Food and water does not cure the PVS patient; it maintains life. It does not cause suffering for the patient nor is it considered exceptional or experimental medical technology. If the nutrition is discontinued then the patient will die because a new cause of death has been introduced, that is, from a deliberately intended deprivation of nourishment, or in common language, from starvation.[1]

Shades of Meaning

No person should be deprived of food and water as long as they can do him good. However, if their provision causes significant pain or discomfort in the very last stages of life—when inevitable death is truly imminent—then it may be permissible to withdraw them to avoid pain and suffering.

Therefore, if a stomach tube is causing a person pain, and the person is near death, nutrition would not be doing him any good, and it would be permissible to remove the stomach tube.

In all cases of withdrawal of nutrition and hydration, two conditions must be met:

(1) The current form of feeding causes significant pain or is contraindicated; and

(2) The person is so close to death that further nutrition will do him no good, and he will die naturally before the resultant hunger and thirst cause significant pain.

The National Council of Catholic Bishops (NCCB) recognized the danger posed by the pro-euthanasia mentality in such cases when it stated

The harsh reality is that some who propose withdrawal of nutrition and hydration from certain patients do directly *intend* to bring about a patient's death, and would even prefer a change in the law to allow for what they see as more "quick and painless" means to cause death. In other words, nutrition and hydration (whether orally administered or medically assisted) are sometimes withdrawn not because a patient is dying, but precisely because a patient is *not* dying (or not dying quickly) and someone believes it would be better if he or she did, generally because the patient is perceived as having an unacceptably low "quality of life" or as imposing burdens on others.[2]

In the United States, there have been many highly-publicized euthanasia cases where people who could have lived a long time if given food and water were deliberately starved to death. These cases include Karen Ann Quinlan, Clarence Herbert, Claire Conroy, Paul Brophy, Elizabeth Bouvia, Hector Rodas, Nancy Ellen Jobes, Marcia Gray, Nancy Cruzan and most of the cases of infanticide that take place in neonatal intensive care units each year (see Question 68 for a more detailed description of these and other euthanasia cases).

Unfortunately, pro-euthanasia activists, just like abortionists, will stretch any exception to the limit. Many abortionists have said that *all* pregnancies "threaten the life of the mother." Some people see tube feeding as extremely expensive and "financially burdensome," but it is usually not much more expensive than mouth feeding, and can often be cheaper. The problem here, of course, is not the cost of feeding the person; it is the withdrawal of *commitment* to the patient and the total cost of *caring* for the person if he should continue to live.

1 Bishop James T. McHugh. Pastoral Letter "Death and Dying Issues," 11 March 1991.

2 National Conference of Catholic Bishops, Committee for Pro-Life Activities. "Nutrition and Hydration: Moral and Pastoral Reflections," April 1992.

65. Can Pain-Killers that Cause Unconsciousness Be Used to Alleviate Severe Pain?

Three questions are commonly asked regarding the use of pain-killing drugs near the end of life:

(1) May they be used if they unintentionally shorten the life of the person?

(2) May they be used if they induce semi-consciousness?

(3) May they be used if they induce unconsciousness?

In general, it is permissible to use pain-killers that dull severe pain, even if they shorten the life of the patient. This is an application of the principle of the "double effect." This states that it is sinful to shorten the life of a person *deliberately*, but if the primary purpose of a drug is to relieve severe pain, and the shortening of life is merely an anticipated side effect, giving the drug is permissible.

That the shortening of life must be *insignificant* in such a case is a very important point; this is not a loophole that allows the administration of lethal overdoses of pain-killers to those who could otherwise live for years.

The Catechism of the Catholic Church (¶ 2279) teaches:

> Even if death is thought imminent, the ordinary care owed to a sick person cannot be legitimately interrupted. The use of pain-killers to alleviate the sufferings of the dying, even at the risk of shortening their days, can be morally in conformity with human dignity if death is not willed as either an end or a means, but only foreseen and tolerated as inevitable. Palliative care is a special form of disinterested charity. As such it should be encouraged.

The Vatican's *Declaration on Euthanasia* further clarifies this point:

> In answer to a group of doctors who had put the question: "Is the suppression of pain and consciousness by the use of narcotics ... permitted by religion and morality to the doctor and the patient (even at the approach of death and if one foresees that the use of narcotics will shorten life)?" the Pope [Pius XII] said: "If no other means exist, and if, in the given circumstances, this does not prevent the carrying out of other religious and moral duties: Yes." In this case, of course, death is in no way intended or sought, even if the risk of it is reasonably taken; the intention is simply to relieve pain effectively, using for this purpose pain-killers available to medicine.[1]

The *Declaration on Euthanasia* states that pain-killing medications may be used even if they induce semi-consciousness:

> Nevertheless it would be imprudent to impose a heroic way of acting as a general rule. On the contrary, human and Christian prudence suggest for the majority of sick people the use of medicines capable of alleviating or suppressing pain, even though these may cause as a secondary effect semi-consciousness and reduced lucidity. As for those who are not in a state to express

themselves, one can reasonably presume that they wish to take these pain-killers, and have them administered according to the doctor's advice.[1]

Physicians may generally use pain-killers, even if they cause a shortening of life or semi-consciousness. In certain cases it can be prudent to use them if they cause complete unconsciousness, if the person has had the opportunity to properly prepare his soul for his meeting with God.

Once again, the *Declaration on Euthanasia* clarifies this point:

However, pain-killers that cause unconsciousness need special consideration. For a person not only has to be able to satisfy his or her moral duties and family obligations; he or she also has to prepare himself or herself with full consciousness for meeting Christ. Thus Pius XII warns: "It is not right to deprive the dying person of consciousness without a serious reason".[1]

1 Sacred Congregation for the Doctrine of the Faith. *Declaration on Euthanasia*, 5 May 1980. Section III, "The Meaning of Suffering for Christians and the Use of Pain-killers".

....

66. Is Assisted Suicide or Euthanasia Permissible if the Person Himself Requests It?

The question of *Who owns us* is at the very heart of the euthanasia debate. Do we own and control our own bodies? If so, then we can do anything we want with them. If not—if our bodies and our souls were brought into existence and nurtured by Someone else—then, of course, our lives belong to Him, and we cannot dispose of them as we wish.

The Catechism of the Catholic Church (¶ 2280) teaches, "Everyone is responsible for his life before God who has given it to him. It is God Who remains the sovereign Master of life. We are obliged to accept life gratefully and preserve it for His honor and the salvation of our souls. We are stewards, not owners, of the life God has entrusted to us. It is not ours to dispose of."

From the beginning, all Christians have looked upon both suicide and murder as grave sins. St. Augustine wrote:

Christians have no authority to commit suicide in any circumstance. It is significant that in the sacred canonical books there can nowhere be found any injunction or permission to commit suicide either to ensure immortality or to avoid or escape any evil. In fact, we must understand it to be forbidden by the law "You shall not kill" (Exodus 20:13), particularly as there is no addition of "your neighbor" as in the prohibition of false witness, "You shall not bear false witness against your neighbor" (Exodus 20:16).[1]

The Vatican's *Declaration on Euthanasia* explains that no person may ask another to kill him in an act currently referred to as "assisted suicide": "Furthermore, no one is permitted to ask for this act of killing, either for himself or herself or for another person entrusted to his or her care, nor can he or she consent to it, either explicitly or implicitly. Nor can any authority legitimately recommend or permit such an action."

Suicide, whether committed alone or in the presence of others, constitutes a grave loss of faith in God. It is the ultimate statement of despair, a loss of belief in the goodness of the world and of the self. *The Catechism* (¶ 2281, 2325) eloquently explains:

Figure 14

> Suicide contradicts the natural inclination of the human being to preserve and perpetuate his life. It is gravely contrary to the just love of self. It likewise offends love of neighbor because it unjustly breaks the ties of solidarity with family, nation, and other human societies to which we continue to have obligations. Suicide is contrary to love for the living God.... Suicide is seriously contrary to justice, hope, and charity. It is forbidden by the fifth commandment.

"The problem with medicine today is that it's under the Dark-Age mentality of mystical religion, which has permeated medicine to the core since Christianity took over" —*Jack Kevorkian. [AP World Wide Photos].*

Finally, *Evangelium Vitae* (¶66) summarizes the reasons that suicide and "assisted suicide" are *intrinsically evil*:

> Suicide is always as morally objectionable as murder. The Church's tradition has always rejected it as a gravely evil choice. Even though a certain psychological, cultural and social conditioning may induce a person to carry out an action which so radically contradicts the innate inclination to life, thus lessening or removing subjective responsibility, suicide, when viewed objectively, is a gravely immoral act. ... In its deepest reality, suicide represents a rejection of God's absolute sovereignty over life and death.... To concur with the intention of another person to commit suicide and to help in carrying it out through so-called "assisted suicide" means to cooperate in, and at times to be the actual perpetrator of, an injustice which can never be excused, even if it is requested.

In summary, God has a plan for all of us, which was formulated long before we were conceived and proceeds to a point far beyond our time on this earth. Just as abortion thwarts His will for lives at their beginnings, euthanasia obstructs His will for lives at their ends.

1 St. Augustine. *The City of God.* Translated by Henry Bettenson. Penguin Books, Book I, Chapter 20, p. 31. Also quoted in *ALL about Issues,* June-July 1986, p. 42.

···

67. Can Hospice Care Be an Alternative to Euthanasia?

Professional hospice care can be given either at home or in special facilities for the dying. Its purpose is to ease the psychological pain of loneliness and the physical pain of dying that many people suffer near the end of their lives.

Hospice care experts agree that the greatest fear of the dying is not physical pain, but the fear of being abandoned—not only by loved ones, but by society in general. The Catholic Bishops of Ireland have pointed out that, "those with experience of nursing the terminally ill and the old know that what they fear is not death so much as being abandoned and left alone. They fear being unloved and unwanted even more than they fear pain. Everything is bearable, even death loses terror, in the presence of those who love us."[1]

Hospice care can be the alternative to the perceived "need" for euthanasia in most cases. At home or in a hospice center, trained professionals, in cooperation with family members, can best attend to the physical and emotional needs of the dying person. In this way, both family and society can join forces to ensure that the death of terminally ill people is truly dignified. The Canadian Conference of Catholic Bishops (CCCB) said:

> As Catholics we strongly recommend that the current debate pay particular attention to the experience of the palliative care units and hospices which have done such extraordinary work in defending the dignity of men and women facing death. Palliation is a form of care that recognizes that cure or long-term control is not possible; is concerned with quality rather than quantity of life; and cloaks troublesome and distressing symptoms with treatment whose primary or sole aim is the highest possible measure of patient care.[2]

When a society cares for its dying and handicapped citizens with tenderness and compassion, everyone benefits. The 1981 *Document of the Holy See for the International Year of Disabled Persons* recognized that "the respect, the dedication, the time and means required for the care of handicapped persons, even of those whose mental faculties are gravely affected, is the price that a society should generously pay in order to remain truly human." This document taught that, if a society begins to treat its handicapped members as animals to be put to sleep rather than human beings to be treated with respect, it is ultimately the society that suffers the most. The same can be said of the dying.

One of the greatest dangers facing the terminally ill today is that the hospice movement is being infected by the pro-euthanasia mindset. As one example of this trend, the American Hospice Association entered an *amicus* brief in the Nancy Cruzan case favoring her starvation.

Anyone considering hospice care should carefully evaluate available programs before choosing one, because there are great differences between individual caregivers. This is particularly important when considering home hospice care, because the dying person is cared for by a single individual. In such cases, the caregiver's attitude toward the sanctity of human life is particularly important.

1 The Bishops of Ireland. Joint Pastoral Letter titled "Human Life is Sacred," 1 March 1975. Reprinted in the 22 May 1975 English edition of *L'Osservatore Romano*.

2 Canadian Bishops Conference position paper "To Live and Die in a Compassionate Community," 26 October 1994.

68. What Is the History of Euthanasia in the United States?

The Courts: Engine for Social Change

The history of euthanasia can be traced through the courts—just as with contraception and abortion.

The Supreme Court of the United States has decisively rejected its role as the interpreter of the Constitution and has transformed itself into the greatest engine for social change our country has ever seen.

The Court started the euthanasia steamroller with its 1965 *Griswold v. Connecticut* decision, in which it discovered a mythical "privacy right" that had somehow escaped the notice of the entire system of government for two centuries. This decision held that married couples should have unrestricted access to contraceptives.

The Court extended this privacy "right" drastically in its 1973 *Roe v. Wade* decision legalizing abortion. And now, the courts are using the "right to privacy" to advance the cause of euthanasia on demand.

Since 1973, many courts have dealt with the question of active and passive euthanasia, and there is an overall pattern tending toward the killing of those whose lives are judged to be "devoid of meaning."

Description of the Euthanasia Cases

Introduction. The following court cases describe with crystal clarity the "slippery slope" from infanticide to passive euthanasia to active euthanasia. Over the past two decades, the controls over euthanasia inevitably became looser and looser, just as they did for abortion. The final result will be, as pro-euthanasia organizations desire, the "right" to kill oneself at any time, for any reason, or the "right" to demand that a licensed "obitiatrist" do the job for you.

In other words, euthanasia on demand.

Karen Ann Quinlan (1976). Karen Ann Quinlan, 21, stopped breathing for unknown reasons and suffered irreversible brain damage. She lapsed into a deep coma, but continued to show minimal brain activity. For this reason, she could not legally be declared dead, and so was kept alive on a respirator. Miss Quinlan's father petitioned the Court to allow her doctors to disconnect her from her life support systems.

The Court ordered that Quinlan be removed from the respirator, if her doctors and the hospital agreed. She lived for nine years after being disconnected. The appended opinion expanded the "right to privacy" found in the *Griswold* decision to include the right of patients to refuse even lifesaving treatment that is not extraordinary. Essentially, the Court ruled that a patient no longer able to communicate may now exercise this "right" through a family member or duly authorized guardian through a doctrine known as "substituted judgment."[1]

Baby Doe of Bloomington (1982). This case involved a tiny baby boy born with Down's Syndrome and a breathing defect that hampered his swallowing as well. Physicians could have corrected the defect easily with surgery, and literally hundreds of couples begged to adopt him.

However, the Supreme Court of Indiana ruled that his parent's *right to privacy* was more important than this *born* baby's *right to live!* The baby died in agony just days before the appeal reached the U.S. Supreme Court. This heartless judgment caused so much consternation that Congress passed legislation 1984 prohibiting the withholding of "medically indicated" treatment from any disabled newborn.

However, a later New York judgment (the *Baby Jane Doe* case) ruled that parents of an infant with spina bifida and other non-life-threatening disabilities could choose to "treat" their little baby "passively" with adequate food, antibiotics and dressings. In other words, all the parents are legally obligated to do is keep the child comfortable and hope that he or she dies.[2]

Claire Conroy (1985). Claire Conroy, at 84 years old, was conscious but confused, and could only be fed intravenously. She could not swallow or communicate, and physicians expected her to die within one year. Her nephew sought to have her feeding tube removed. However, Conroy died while the court deliberated the case.

This court decision set broad limits upon withholding care when the patient clearly would have refused treatment *and* when evidence exists to prove this point; when the cost of care outweighs the benefits; or when no evidence shows that the patient would have refused treatment, but the burdens of care outweigh the benefits, *and* the patient would suffer "inhumane" pain.

The significance of this case is profound: the New Jersey Supreme Court ruled that food and water are in the same category as artificial respirators and other medical treatment and may be classified and withdrawn as "extraordinary measures."[3]

In the Nancy Jobes case, the same Court vastly expanded the pool of patients who could be denied basic care (described below).

Paul Brophy (1986). A blood vessel burst in 45-year-old Paul Brophy's brain, damaging it extensively and plunging him into what physicians described as a permanent coma. His family wanted to have his life support disconnected, but the hospital refused to cooperate. The family filed suit.

The Supreme Court of Massachusetts ruled that Brophy, were he conscious, would want the feeding tube and life support systems disconnected. The court also ruled that he could not be kept alive without his consent, and that the hospital and doctors could not be forced to cooperate in his killing. Brophy was moved out of the hospital, his life support was disconnected, and he died.[4]

Elizabeth Bouvia (1986). Elizabeth Bouvia, a 28-year old quadriplegic with cerebral palsy, bedridden and in unrelieved pain, expressed a desire to die. The hospital staff had earlier begun to feed her intravenously against her wishes. She asked a court to order that the tube be removed. The court refused, and Bouvia appealed.

The resultant frightening decision by the California Court of Appeals took a long step towards legalizing and abetting suicide. This was the first court decision that upheld a "right" to refuse basic care.

The majority opinion argued that the medical profession and the State should be "... permitting and in fact assisting the patient to die with ease and dignity."

The Court ruled that a patient need not be in a coma or near death to decline treatment. The Court decided that motives play no important part in such a decision, and ruled that Bouvia's feeding tube could be removed.[5]

Nancy Ellen Jobes (1987). Nancy Ellen Jobes was 32 years old and severely brain damaged. She could follow people with her eyes and respond to commands and various stimuli. A feeding tube sustained her, but she was not terminally ill.

The New Jersey Supreme Court ordered Jobes' nursing home staff to stop her feeding, and she starved to death in 19 days.

This case vastly expanded the pool of patients whose food and water could be withdrawn, *even if the patient had never expressed a desire for such action.* In other words, third parties who could "best understand the patient's personal values and beliefs" could substitute their judgment for the patient's.

The Court also ruled that, from this point onward, no court hearing was necessary for health care facilities to gain permission to stop the feeding of a patient or patients.[6]

This means that, in New Jersey at least, a family that is awaiting an inheritance or just cannot be bothered to care for an aged or infirm relative any more may starve the patient to death, even if the patient had expressed no such wish.

This fits the definition of involuntary euthanasia.

Marcia Gray (1987). Forty-nine year-old Marcia Gray had been comatose since January 1986. She and her family had expressed a wish that extraordinary measures not be taken to extend her life. Rhode Island District Court Judge Francis Boyle ruled that the state-run General Hospital must remove her feeding tube or transfer her to an institution that would. The hospital then contacted 274 nursing homes and hospitals in the New England area, but none was willing to accept the patient for the sole purpose of having her die of dehydration.[7]

At this point, Rhode Island Gov. Edward DiPrete stepped in and ordered the hospital to disconnect her feeding tube. This order was not appealable. On 17 October 1988, Judge Boyle ruled that Marcia Gray could be starved and dehydrated to death. On 16 November, she was transferred to South County Hospital. Dr. Robert L. Conrad of the hospital was so eager to starve Gray that he removed her feeding tube in the ambulance on the trip to South County!

Marcia Gray took 15 long, agonizing days to die, during which time she lost 50 pounds. Physicians sedated her heavily in order to suppress her severe seizures.

This case and later actions by the State are ominous signs of things to come. It appears that the State will override any hospitals that adhere to a respect for life. What's more, if General Hospital had not been able to find another institution willing to starve Gray, the hospital's personnel would have been forced to starve her over their moral and religious objections—or face jail terms for contempt of court.

John Breguet, general counsel for the Rhode Island Department of Mental Health, Retardation and Hospitals, voiced the fears of many when he said "once we establish as a societal philosophy that society has a right to terminate *some* life that society thinks is not worth living, it is not that far to go to the profoundly retarded, those with severe mental problems, or those with serious physical handicaps."

Of profound significance was Judge Boyle's heavy reliance on the 1973 *Roe v. Wade* abortion decision to affirm the notion "that a person has the right ... to control fundamental decisions involving his or her own body." Thus, the direct link between abortion and euthanasia was, at last, directly and irrevocably drawn for all to see.

Nancy Cruzan (1988). On 11 January 1983, 25-year-old Nancy Cruzan was driving alone on an icy road, lost control of her vehicle, and suffered serious injuries in the resulting accident. She never regained consciousness.

Her medical status was that of a "severely handicapped" person. She required no life support machinery other than a feeding tube implanted in her stomach in early 1983. She was not terminally ill.

She was thus an inconvenience to many people, but the opportunity of a lifetime for pro-euthanasia groups.

Cruzan could not be killed without being dehumanized first, a task expertly performed by Dr. Fred Plum, Chief of Neurology at the Cornell New York Hospital.

During testimony, he called her a mere "collection of organs" and an "artifact of technological medicine."[8]

In an interview with columnist Nat Hentoff, Dr. Ronald Cranford labeled her the "moral equivalent of a biopsy from Nat Hentoff's arm," and said her "legal personhood" should be removed so she could be disposed of or experimented upon without the bother of having to go to court.[8]

Anti-lifers now refer to preborn babies as "pre-human" and comatose people as "post-human."

Nancy's parents petitioned a lower court to order the Missouri Rehabilitation Center at Mount Vernon to starve their daughter. The court granted the petition, but the Missouri Supreme Court overturned the lower court decision, ruling that a decision to withhold or refuse treatment must be an "informed" one, and, most importantly, that the State's interest in human life does not depend on the *quality* of that life.

On appeal, the *Cruzan v. Director of Missouri Department of Health* case became the first to directly address the question of euthanasia at the United States Supreme Court level.

The Court narrowly averted making this case euthanasia's *Roe v. Wade* by denying that the so-called "right to die" is unfettered and absolute. The justices ruled that the States may require "clear and convincing" evidence that comatose persons actually wished to die before they lost their ability to decide their own fates.[9]

The Court essentially held that the States do not have to buckle under to family members' demands when a patient's wishes cannot be concretely proven.

However, the ruling indicated that there is a constitutional right to refuse tube feeding and other life-sustaining measures when patients make their wishes clearly known before they become incompetent.

So a determined Joe and Joyce Cruzan headed back to the Missouri courts, and rounded up a string of Nancy's co-workers who were willing to testify that she would never want to live "like a vegetable." Nobody bothered to explain how her co-workers could all remember such a statement so clearly after eight years.

During this phase, Nancy enjoyed no representation of any kind in the State court; no-one testified for her, because all those who wanted her to live were ruled non-parties by the judge. The outcome of the one-sided hearing was a foregone conclusion.

So the courts essentially sentenced Nancy to death by starvation. Her feeding tube was disconnected on 14 December 1990 at the Missouri Rehabilitation Center in Mount Vernon, Missouri.

In a chilling portent of the future, the first rescue mounted to save a *born* person from death occurred on Tuesday, 18 December 1990. Police arrested nineteen rescuers as they tried to reach Nancy's hospital room and lodged against them the same charges they had encountered at abortion mills: criminal trespass and unlawful assembly.

Scores of armed police officers patrolled the halls of the Missouri Rehabilitation Center until Nancy Cruzan finally died of starvation and thirst after 12 days, on the day after Christmas 1990.

Doron Webster of the New York chapter of the Society for the Right to Die stated ominously, "we feel that Nancy Cruzan has made legal history."[10]

Ninth Circuit Court of Appeals. On 5 November 1991, Washington State voters rejected by a 54-46% margin the first referendum in U.S. history that would have legalized "physician-assisted suicide."

However, pro-euthanasia activists rely heavily on public opinion polls when they favor their positions, and *always* ignore them and rely upon the court system instead when the polls are against them.

Litigation began in 1994 when the pro-euthanasia group Compassion for Dying (CFD), four doctors and three terminally ill people filed suit in federal court challenging the 140-year-old state law against promoting or assisting in another person's suicide. U.S. District Court Judge Barbara Rothstein ruled in May 1994, that the plaintiffs had a constitutional right to help in committing suicide, thus becoming the first federal judge ever to find this right in the Constitution. The State appealed her ruling to the Ninth Circuit Court of Appeals, which in March 1995, voted two to one to overturned Rothstein's ruling. The full Court of 11 judges then reconsidered the case at CFD's request.

Compassion for Dying v. State of Washington was the first euthanasia case any federal court of appeals had ever decided, and the Ninth Circuit exploited this opportunity to strip-mine the Constitution to unearth a new fundamental "right."

On 6 March 1996, the Ninth Circuit decided 8-3 that the Washington State law banning "assisted suicide" violated the Due Process Clause of the U.S. Constitution.

The Facts of Life

The Court used Rothstein's language as it drew a direct parallel between abortion and euthanasia: "Like the decision of whether or not to have an abortion, the decision how and when to die is one of 'the most intimate and personal choices a person may make in a lifetime,' a choice that is 'central to personal dignity and autonomy.' In its decision, the Ninth Circuit extensively quoted the Supreme Court's *Planned Parenthood v. Casey* decision, which established abortion as a fundamental right separate from the "right to privacy."

Roe v. Wade, quoted a dozen times in the decision, held that states may limit abortion if they have a "compelling interest" in preventing it. By stark contrast, in *Compassion for Dying,* the Court stated that a state's interest in preventing suicide *can never exist:*

> No matter how much weight could legitimately be afforded the state's interest in preventing suicide, that weight, when combined with the weight given all of the other state interests, was insufficient to outweigh the terminally ill individual's interest in deciding whether to end his or her agony and suffering by hastening the time of his or her death with medication prescribed by his or her physician.

Many legal scholars agreed that cutting the states out of the picture entirely was a more breathtaking exercise of "raw judicial power" than even *Roe v. Wade.*

The Conclusion

As the above court cases show, the "right to privacy," found nowhere in the U.S. Constitution, has led first to the total legalization of contraception (*Griswold v. Connecticut*), the total legalization of abortion (*Roe v. Wade*), the legalization of infanticide (*Baby Doe*), the legalization of involuntary passive euthanasia (*Cruzan* and *Brophy*), and the legalization of *voluntary* active euthanasia (*Compassion for Dying*).

The progression down the slippery slope could not possibly be clearer.

All Western nations now have the highest proportions of elderly people in their histories. They all have the lowest birthrates, too, which means fewer and fewer workers will be supporting more and more of the retired elderly. And so, pressure will inevitably mount to "cut costs" and "conserve scarce resources" by withdrawing care from the handicapped, the severely ill, and the elderly. Health rationing has already made inroads into North America and Europe; under some of these plans, people above a certain age are disqualified from receiving certain medical treatment.

There is only one step remaining: the legalization of *involuntary* active euthanasia.

As Question 71 explains, this is the final stated goal of the euthanasia movement, which will never stop until it achieves all of its objectives.

1 Debra Braun. "Karen Ann Quinlan Dies of Pneumonia at 31." *National Right to Life News,* 20 June 1985, p. 15.

2 The following articles on the Baby Doe case may be found in *National Right to Life News.* (1) Burke Balch. "Caplan's Criticisms of [Baby Doe] Regs Way Off Mark." 11 April 1985, p. 3. (2) David H. Andrusko. "Breathing Room." 11 April 1985, p. 2. Article on the "Baby Doe" regulations: The 1984 Child Abuse Prevention and Treatment Act. (3) Debra Braun. "Three Years After Infant Doe." 11 April 1985, p. 6. (4) James Bopp, Jr. "Health and Human Services Appeals Verdict in Original "Baby Doe" Regs Case to Supreme Court." 2 May 1985, p. 11.

3   Leslie Bond. "Cases Test Boundaries of *Conroy* Decision." *National Right to Life News*, 21 November 1985, pp. 5 and 9.

4   The following articles on the Paul Brophy case may be found in *National Right to Life News*. (1) Front Line Updates. "Wife Wants to Starve Comatose Husband." 30 May 1985, p. 4. (2) Leslie Bond. "Judge Refuses to Halt Feeding of Man in Comatose Condition." 7 November 1985, pp. 1 and 11. (3) David H. Andrusko. "Brophy Dies Eight Days After Nourishment Withdrawn." 6 November 1986, pp. 1 and 15. (4) David H. Andrusko. "The Bottom of the Slope." 6 November 1986, pp. 2 and 9.

5   The following articles on the Elizabeth Bouvia case may be found in *National Right to Life News*. (1) David H. Andrusko. "Court Opens Gates to Assisted Suicide in *Bouvia* Decision." 1 May 1986, pp. 1 and 17. (2) Paul K. Longmore. "Urging the Handicapped to Die." 12 June 1986, p. 6.

6   The following articles on the Nancy Ellen Jobes case may be found in *National Right to Life News*. (1) Leslie Bond. "Cases Test Boundaries of *Conroy* Decision." 21 November 1985, pp. 5 and 9. (2) Leslie Bond. "New Jersey Court Authorizes Dehydration Death of Patient." 1 May 1986. Back cover. (3) Leslie Bond. "New Jersey High Court Asked to Extend 'Right to Die.'" 20 November 1986, pp. 5 and 10. Nancy Ellen Jobes, Kathleen Farrell, and Hilda Peter. (4) David H. Andrusko. "Catholic Health Association, New Jersey Bishops Clash Over Providing Food and Water." 19 March 1987, pp. 1 and 8.

8   The following articles on the Marcia Gray case may be found in *National Right to Life News*. (1) David H. Andrusko. "Rhode Island Bishop Statement Endorses Withholding of Food and Water." 11 February 1988, back cover. (2) Leslie Bond. "Rhode Island Case Marks First Establishment of Federal Constitutional 'Right' to Starve Incompetent Patients." 17 November 1988, pp. 7 and 11. (3) Nat Hentoff. "Marcia Gray: Legalizing Death By Starvation." 1 February 1989, pp. 4 and 5.

9   David Brockbauer. "Pagan Ethics: The Nancy Cruzan Case." *Fidelity* Magazine, February 1990, pp. 11 to 14.

10 "19 Protestors Halted." *The Oregonian*, 19 December 1990, p. A17. Additionally, the following articles on the Nancy Cruzan case may be found in *National Right to Life News*. (1) Leslie Bond. "State of Missouri Actively Fights Efforts to Starve Nancy Cruzan." 17 December 1987, pp. 1 and 11. (2) David H. Andrusko. "Missouri Supreme Court to Hear Appeal of Death-By-Starvation Sentence for Nancy Cruzan." 25 August 1988, p. 6. (3) Samuel Lee and David H. Andrusko. "Missouri Supreme Court Refuses to Authorize Starvation Death of Nancy Cruzan." 5 December 1988, pp. 1 and 7.

11 Jerry Nachtigal. "Nancy Cruzan Dies Peacefully." *The Oregonian*, 27 December 1990, pp. 1 and 12.

69. What Is the Status of Euthanasia in the Netherlands?

A Matter of Mere Economics

As abortion and population "control" spread across the world, anti-lifers are becoming bolder and bolder in their drive to eliminate any people they consider "useless," or who stand in the way of their self-fulfillment.

Pro-lifers must realize that euthanasia follows abortion just as abortion follows contraception. When people start killing other people and then justify their actions, it can never stop, because the killers can seamlessly apply their justification for killing preborn children to those who are already born.

So, every pro-life activist must be intimately familiar with the various aspects of the euthanasia issue. Students of the anti-life mentality will find it most useful to examine the situation in a country that has fully embraced euthanasia, in order to become familiar with the goals of pro-euthanasia groups based in other nations.

The remainder of this section provides details on the Dutch euthanasia program. When reading it, remember that pro-euthanasia groups and leaders have repeatedly recommended the "Dutch model" of euthanasia not only for the United States, but for the entire world.

Dutch Doctors Have a License to Kill

Every Dutch doctor receives formal "how-to" euthanasia training in medical school, and the Royal Dutch Society of Pharmacology issues a "how-to" euthanasia book to every doctor. This book contains recipes for undetectable poisons that doctors can place in food or inject in such a way that they are almost impossible to detect during an autopsy.[1] The Dutch Euthanasia Society published Dr. Pieter Admiraal's "how-to" euthanasia manual in 1977. Euthanasia groups present this manual to every doctor in Holland, and have also translated it into English and have shipped it to the United States.

Every doctor knows the exact cost of each treatment for every common illness or injury beforehand, because they are written up on charts for easy reference and analysis for each individual case.[2] Hospital administrators instruct their general practitioners to use these charts and then give *involuntary* lethal injections to those elderly patients whose care is deemed "too expensive."[3]

Eighty percent of Dutch doctors have killed people deliberately through *direct*, *active* (not passive) euthanasia.[4] A 1991 government survey found that only one in 10 Dutch doctors would refuse a request for euthanasia.[5]

As in the United States, the *real* motivation behind most Dutch euthanasias is not to relieve the pain of the patients but to enhance the convenience of doctors and families. Dutch pain management techniques are understandably very primitive, since it is easier to simply kill people than it is to analyze their cases and help them. Dr. Pieter Michels, director of a Dutch hospital for terminal patients, said only nine of 3,000 dying people passing through his hospital had asked for euthanasia over twenty years, and most of these requests came because of pressure from their families. One doctor admitted to killing people because the sight of their suffering upset *him*.[6]

As leading Dutch euthanasia practitioner Dr. Pieter Admiraal asserted at the eighth biennial conference of the World Federation of Right to Die Societies, "Every patient has the right to judge his suffering as unbearable and the right to ask his physician for euthanasia. Pain is very seldom a reason for euthanasia."[7]

How It Is Now: The New Abortionists. Dutch doctor Herbert Cohen has described in detail how he kills his patients. It is interesting to note his attention to aesthetic detail, and it is also significant that he is only one of many Dutch doctors who still make house visits—not to heal, but to kill.

Cohen appears on the front doorstep of the "chosen" with a beautiful bouquet of flowers. He chats amiably with the family to put them at ease. Then he approaches his victim, whom he first injects with a sleeping agent and then with the fatal paralyzing agent curare. Cohen is punctual: "If the appointment is for 8 o'clock, I'm there at 7:55, the patient is asleep by 8 and dead by 8:10." Then he calls the police and tells them that a euthanasia has taken place, and a medical examiner comes to the house.[8]

Although he has followed this procedure dozens of times, he has never been prosecuted because he adheres to the notification requirements prescribed by Dutch law.

"Living Wills" Mean Nothing. Patient statements about a desire to live or receive certain treatments, in documents similar in nature to U.S. "Living Wills" and Durable Powers of Attorney (DPAs) mean nothing in the Netherlands.

Physicians often perform *involuntary* euthanasia on patients who have chronic diabetes, rheumatism, multiple sclerosis, AIDS or bronchitis, and upon older accident victims, regardless of the prognosis.[9]

Many Dutch citizens, in self-defense, now carry a "Declaration of a Will to Live" (issued by the aptly-named Sanctuary Society, or *Schuilplaats*), which states that they *do not* want to be euthanized without their knowledge. These documents are also called Life Passports, or "Don't Kill Me" cards. Predictably, these Declarations carry very little weight with the same doctors who introduced—and then ignored—the so-called "Living Wills" in Holland.

Dutch cardiologist Richard Fenigsen notes that "the burden of justifying his existence is now placed upon the patient."[10] And Dutch Attorney General T.M. Schalken said that " ...elderly people begin to consider themselves a burden to the society, and feel under an obligation to start conversations on euthanasia, or even to request it."[11]

Patients Are Pressured. If a person 60 years of age or older cannot avoid entering a Dutch hospital, doctors and nurses will repeatedly suggest euthanasia to him, even if he has not asked for it, and even if he is suffering from only a minor illness.[12]

All of this leads to a chronic fear among elderly Dutch people that they will be put to death if they encounter health professionals in any context. A comprehensive 1987 poll showed that 68 percent of all elderly Dutch citizens feared that they would be killed without their consent *or even their knowledge*.[13]

The number of nursing homes in the Netherlands has decreased more than 80 percent in the last 20 years, and the life expectancy of the few elderly people who remain in such homes is becoming shorter all the time. In some cases, it can be measured in hours.[10] Many elderly people in Dutch nursing homes will only drink water from faucets and will touch no other liquid, because they believe that their orange juice or milk may be spiked with deadly poison.[14]

Doctors and others commit involuntary euthanasia on even non-terminally ill patients in Dutch nursing homes or on those who require intensive home care, including those with multiple sclerosis and even blindness.[15] They also commit involuntary euthanasia on accident victims and those people with rheumatism, diabetes, AIDS and bronchitis.[16]

Even young children are not safe from the "new abortionists." On 9 October 1987, doctor P.A. Voute told the daily newspaper *Het Parool* that he had given a poison pill to a 14-year-old boy. He also asserted that, since 1980, he had given poison pills to many teenagers who have suffered from cancer, even when the disease was non-terminal.[17]

Each year, health care workers commit hundreds or even thousands of infanticides in the Netherlands with impunity. The Amsterdam Court of Appeals dropped charges against Dr. Henk Prins, who directly killed three-day-old Baby Rianne, who suffered from hydrocephaly, spina bifida and leg deformities. This act directly violated Netherlands' loose laws that state that the patient must lucidly and repeatedly ask for death.[18]

No Prosecution for Mass Killings. In Holland, health care workers practice "medicide" on a wide scale, despite it being technically illegal.

A Leeuwarden doctor set the precedent in April of 1973, when she was tried for killing her 78-year-old mother who was lodged in a nursing home. The court found her guilty of murder, but sentenced her to exactly one *week* in jail (suspended).

The presiding judge stated that the Court accepted euthanasia under certain conditions: (1) The disease had to be incurable, (2) the suffering unbearable, (3) the patient terminal and (4) the killing requested by the patient. There was no appeal to a higher court, so this decision set a firm precedent. The virulently pro-euthanasia press hailed the Court's decision as "wise, compassionate and merciful."

Pro-euthanasia activists founded the Dutch Voluntary Euthanasia Society just a few days after this trial. It grew explosively, and in 1978, 20 of the 150 members of Parliament attended its annual meeting. By 1980, a large Parliamentary majority favored the legalization of euthanasia.

On 9 February 1993, after 15 years of pro-euthanasia agitation and lawbreaking, the Parliament finally caved in. It could no longer endure the divergence between national morals and the law, and legalized what was "happening anyway." Apparently unaware of the ghastly irony of its actions, the Parliament codified the Royal Dutch Medical Association's euthanasia guidelines as an appendix to the Disposal of the Dead Act. Naturally, the Parliament tried to craft a law that would allow euthanasia only under the most extreme of circumstances.

However, when a society allows killing for only the "hard cases," it *always* expands to encompass convenience cases as well. The following examples show how meaningless even the most carefully-written laws with "exceptions" are, because anti-lifers all over the world simply ignore laws that do not suit them.

- A doctor embarked on a crusade to "clean out" DeTerp Nursing Home and killed 20 residents without their consent or knowledge. Prosecutors charged him with five murders. Despite the fact that he pleaded guilty, a Dutch court cleared him of all counts—then presented him with an award of $150,000 for "having his name maligned"![19]

- Four nurses at an Amsterdam hospital admitted killing many unconscious patients by injecting them with fatal doses of insulin without their consent or knowledge. The hospital's employee council wholeheartedly supported the "nurses" and excused the murders because of "humane considerations." The district courts agreed with this reasoning and lodged no charges against the nurses. During a sickening media propaganda piece, the children of the victims hugged the nurses and thanked them.[19]

■ Several doctors directly killed 21 men and women at a nursing home in the Hague in Spring, 1985. One doctor admitted killing six of the patients without asking their consent, but investigators did not even charge him with a crime. He said he based his actions on vague statements of patients such as "I don't want to become a vegetable," made as long as four years earlier.[11] This is a fine example of how pro-euthanasia people will seize upon any crumb of "evidence" to kill people—even upon undocumented statements that may never have been made.

■ In total violation of Dutch law, Dr. Frits Schmidt killed a woman who wanted to die merely because she had facial scars. He was not prosecuted or charged with any crime.[20]

These examples give vivid support to this warning by Dutch doctor I. Van der Sluis (an atheist): "Life is not a quality; death is not a right, and it is not realistic to expect that euthanasia will remain voluntary. Euthanasia doctors will kill you with your consent if they can get it; and without your consent if they cannot. Euthanasia is not a right. It is the *abolition* of all rights."[11]

German pro-euthanasia activist Dr. Julius Hackethal confirmed Dr. Van der Sluis' fears that not only are flagrant abuses inevitable under the current legal system in the Netherlands, they are happening *right now* on a wide scale: "I know—based on my 40 years of experience in five hospitals—12 years I spent in university hospitals—that killing by applying death shots to a hopelessly ill patient against his will, or at least without his definite wish, happens much more often than is made public."[21]

All of these examples prove what pro-life activists have been saying all along: pro-euthanasia activists will continue to ignore even the loosest laws. Despite utter contempt of the new law by Dutch euthanasia doctors, not one has ever gone to jail.

The Dutch euthanasia guidelines are firm, clear—and utterly toothless.

What on Earth Happened? The media have subjected Dutch citizens to an intense pro-euthanasia propaganda barrage for more than 20 years. Dutch doctors at first resisted and spoke out against the media, but the press simply destroyed the reputations of prominent anti-euthanasia physicians. Eventually, the resistance of anti-euthanasia doctors was officially punished and suppressed.

This media bombardment has influenced the Dutch public most profoundly. Some 76% of the Dutch public support voluntary euthanasia, which is supposedly the ultimate in "freedom of choice"—but, paradoxically, 77% also support *involuntary* active euthanasia, which is the *denial* of freedom of choice. And fully 90% of university economics students support the *compulsory* (forced) euthanasia of entire classes of people deemed to be a "burden to society" for the purpose of "streamlining the economy."[11]

Dr. Hackethal revealed the root cause of the Dutch ethical disintegration at the Hemlock Society's Second National Voluntary Euthanasia Conference. He showed that the Dutch doctors have abandoned all pretense of restraint and are now a completely independent elite corps with literally unlimited power, unregulated by the courts, the legislative system or even a moral code:

I studied that [Hippocratic] oath exactly. The conclusion of my Hippocratic Oath study is: "A more bad physician's oath doesn't exist!" *One* sentence of the patient-hostile Hippocratic Oath is: "I will never give anyone a deadly poison, not even at their request, nor will I give them any advice as to a deadly poison." But *it* doesn't apply for the last 50 years. Today I judge such an oath to be an act of unmedical patient-hostility, an act of inhumanity.[21]

The Magnitude of the Killing. On 10 September 1991, the Dutch government released a report on the country's euthanasia situation. The two-volume work, titled *Medische Beslissingen Rond Het Levenseinde* (also known as the *Remmelink Report*), reported that 92% of all reported cases of Dutch euthanasia violate the already-permissive "limits" set by Dutch courts. Dutch doctors only commit 200 acts of euthanasia within legal "limits" annually, and the Commission found that *at least* 2,400 illegal mercy killings and assisted suicides happen each year. The Commission estimated that doctors commit a total of about 9,100 legal and illegal mercy killings and assisted suicides (both reported and unreported) in Holland each year, which is equivalent to 7% of all deaths in the country.

The report added the more than 1,000 annual victims of *involuntary* euthanasia to the total number of "mercy" killings, and found that more than 23,000 patients had their lives "significantly shortened" by overdoses of pain-killers each year. Of these, 2,500 overdoses were given with the *specific* goal of shortening or ending life.

Four out of every five Dutch general practitioners have committed active euthanasia. More than one-fourth (28%) actively kill at least two of their patients each year, and one of seven (14%) actively kill at least five of their patients annually.[22] According to the Royal Dutch Academy of Sciences, at least eight Dutch hospitals are committing widespread involuntary euthanasia.[23]

Jack Kevorkian's dream of "obitoriums" staffed by professional "obitiatrists" is a reality in the Netherlands.

In June, 1984, the board of the 30,000-member Royal Dutch Society of Medicine approved a "Position on Euthanasia" paper that supported legalizing both voluntary *and* involuntary active euthanasia.

Three years later, the Committee on Medical Ethics of the European Community unanimously rejected the Dutch medical society's radical proposals on euthanasia: "We hope that this strong reaction will induce our Dutch colleagues to reconsider their move and return to the happy communion of utmost respect for human life."[17]

Dutch serial killer "physicians" completely ignored this "strong reaction." By 1990, Dutch anesthesiologists flatly refused to take part in surgery on Down's Syndrome children. Hospitals starve at least 300 handicapped newborns to death each year, and cardiologists refuse to treat any person over the age of 75.

The Future of Euthanasia in Holland. The Dutch Health Council (*Gezondheidsraad*) is the official medical society advising the Dutch government. This body has proposed a "Model Aid-in Dying Law" that would allow any child six and older to make a death request. According to this "Model" Law, if the child's parents objected to the decision, the child could present himself to a special aid-in-dying board for a final, binding decision. According to the "Model" Law, "Minors have the right to request aid-in-dying whether or not their parents agree."[14]

Note that the child would not have to be terminally ill, or in fact, ill at all—a teenage boy who is depressed over losing his girlfriend or being cut from the soccer team would no longer have to drown or shoot himself; he could be executed "safely and legally" in a Dutch euthanasia clinic under this proposal. A seven-year-old girl who was being teased by her classmates at school could be "put to sleep" as well—and the first her parents would learn about the situation would be when they received a bill from the "obitorium" for "services rendered."

Reaction of the Americans. The topic of runaway health care costs is becoming more and more prominent in the United States. As may be expected, the more utilitarian (or eugenicist) mindset naturally opts for the easy solution: instead of increasing efficiency and cutting waste, simply eliminate the patients who are too costly to care for under the current system.

Pro-abortionist Daniel Callahan of the Hastings Center, says:

> ... a denial of nutrition may in the long run become the only effective way to make certain that a large number of *biologically tenacious* patients actually die. Given the increasingly large pool of superannuated, chronically ill, physically marginal elderly, it could well become the *nontreatment of choice*.... Our emerging problem is not just that of eliminating useless or wasteful treatment, but of limiting even efficacious treatment, because of its high cost. It may well turn out that what is best for each and every individual is not necessarily a societally affordable health care system.

Callahan and others want a "fixed categorical standard" that would flatly deny certain surgeries past specific patient ages, regardless of prognosis. For example, coronary bypass surgery would be banned after age 60. Naturally, those elderly people who have enough money could still buy any surgical procedure they wanted. This situation would thus become a curious reflection of the feminist complaint that, if abortion were to become illegal again, only rich women could afford "safe" ones.

There is growing fear among medical professionals that evils such as those in Holland will quickly become entrenched in U.S health care facilities. Dr. Charles L. Sprung warned in the 25 April 1990 issue of the *Journal of the American Medical Association* (*JAMA*) that "widespread practice of active euthanasia in the United States appears not very far away."

However, others would welcome such "advances" with open arms. Derek Humphry, founder of the Hemlock Society, said of the Dutch euthanasia program: "It's been tested there ... it appears to be working."[24] Margaret Battin, another Hemlock officer, urged the United States to follow the Dutch euthanasia example: "Let's use the Netherlands as a role model."[25] Maurice De Wachter, director of the Institute for Bioethics in Maastricht, said ominously: "The Netherlands is what I would like to call a test case for an experiment in medical ethics. ... There is a practice growing where doctors feel at ease with helping patients to die, in other words killing them."[26] And the *Hemlock Quarterly* reported that "The Netherlands are closest to having achieved their goal of active voluntary euthanasia."[27]

The Netherlands Model certainly *would* save money in the United States. The *Remmelink Report* estimated that 23,000 persons are killed in Holland every year—most of them involuntarily.[28]

Holland has a population of about 15 million, and the United States has a population of about 260 million. If the ratio of euthanasias in the U.S. population were the same as it is in Holland, there would be 400,000 murders by euthanasia every year in the United States—one every *twenty seconds* during working days—equivalent to the total population reaching the age of 80 every year!

1   "The Member's Aid Service of the Dutch Association for Voluntary Euthanasia." *Euthanasia Review*, Fall 1986, p. 153. "Choosing When to End Life." *Albuquerque Journal*, 16 October 1988, p. F1.

2   "Restructuring Health Care." *The Lancet*, 28 January 1989, p. 209.

3   "Involuntary Euthanasia in Holland." *Wall Street Journal*, 29 September 1987, p. 3.

4   "Do Not Go Slowly Into That Dark Night: Mercy Killings in Holland." *The American Journal of Medicine*, January 1984, p. 140.

5   John Henley, Associated Press. "Dutch Euthanasia Rule Stirs Ethical Conflicts." *The Oregonian*, 11 February 1993, p. A9.

6   "Voluntary Euthanasia Common, Accepted in Netherlands." The *Washington Post*, 6 April 1987, p. 3.

7   Dutch physician Pieter Admiraal, at the eighth biennial conference of the World Federation of Right to Die Societies, held in Maastricht, Holland, on June 7-10, 1990. Quoted in Rita L. Marker, "I Only Kill My Friends." *30 Days*, September-October 1990, p. 34.

8   Roddy Ray. "Euthanasia: Netherlands Tolerates It." *The Oregonian*, 21 November 1991, p. A3.

9   "Involuntary Euthanasia in Holland." *Wall Street Journal*, 29 September 1987, p. 3. "Do Not Go Slowly Into That Dark Night: Mercy Killings in Holland." *The American Journal of Medicine*, January 1984, p. 140.

10 Richard Fenigsen, M.D., Ph.D. "A Negative Verdict on Euthanasia." *Medical Economics*, 7 March 1988.

11 "Suicide on Prescription." *Sunday Observer*, London, England, 30 April 1989, p. 22.

12 Richard Fenigsen, M.D., Ph.D., at a 2 November 1990 conference at Seattle University. Quoted in "Holland Euthanasia Experience Described." *Human Life News* (Washington State), November/December 1990, p. 6.

13 Address by Pieter Admiraal to the Voluntary Euthanasia Society in London, England, on 14 April 1985.

14 "Dutch in Agonizing Debate Over Voluntary Euthanasia." The *Pittsburgh Press*, 31 July 1989, p. 1.

15 "Euthanasia in Holland." *Human Life International Reports*, December 1987, p. 1.

16 "Dutch Leaders Address Agonizing Issue of Legislating Mercy Killings." *Los Angeles Times*, March 29, 1987, p. 6.

17 Richard John Neuhaus. "The Return of Eugenics." *Commentary*, April 1988, pp. 15-26.

18 The World. "Dutch Court Drops Charge of Murder in Baby's Death." *The Oregonian*, 8 November 1995, p. A4.

19 "Where Euthanasia is a Way of Death." *Medical Economics*, 23 November 1987, p. 23.

20 Mark O'Keefe. "For Doctors in Netherlands, Death is Part of the Job." *The Oregonian*, 9 January 1995, p. A4.

21 From the transcript of a speech by Dr. Julius Hackethal titled "Medical Help By Suicide—As a Method of Voluntary Euthanasia," presented at the Second National Voluntary Euthanasia Conference of the Hemlock Society on 9 February 1985, in Los Angeles, California.

22 I. van der Sluis, M.D. "The Practice of Euthanasia in the Netherlands." *Living World* (publication of International Life Services, Inc.). Volume 5, Number 2, pp. 18-21.

23 "Is the Physician Allowed to Kill?" (*Mag de Dokter Doden*), *Querido Edition*, Amsterdam, 1986. ISBN: 90-214-5958-2.

24 "Involuntary Euthanasia in Holland." *Wall Street Journal*, 29 September 1987, p. 31.

25 "Dutch Euthanasia Issue May Be a Pandora's Box." Worcester [England] *Sunday Telegram*, 5 July 1987, p. 6A.

26 John Henley, Associated Press. "Dutch Euthanasia Rule Stirs Ethical Conflicts." *The Oregonian*, 11 February 1993, p. A9.

27 Derek Humphry, founder and president of the Hemlock Society, on "Face the Nation," 2 September 1985.

28 Margaret P. Battin, "The Art of Dying in the United States and Holland," presentation given at the Hemlock Conference in Chicago, Illinois, on 20 May 1989. Also see "Report on the World Conference of Right-to-Die Societies," *Hemlock Quarterly*, April 1987, p. 3.

....

70. What Are the Major Pro-Euthanasia Organizations?

Pro-life activists must not believe that euthanasia is a threat only in their own countries. As the rest of this section shows, the Hemlock Society and other U.S. pro-euthanasia organizations are just a small part of a massive, worldwide network of anti-life groups that work together very efficiently towards their goals.

Fortunately, pro-lifers also have a worldwide network with which to oppose the killers, and Appendix A lists some of the main groups in this network. Human Life International Branches are a part of this worldwide pro-life network. Appendix D lists HLI's major Branches.

A point to clarify: pro-euthanasia activists always object to being called "pro-euthanasia." Experienced pro-life activists have heard it all before from pro-abortionists who object to being labeled "pro-abortion." Yet what else can you call a person who works vigorously for the availability of euthanasia, declares it to be a fundamental "right," resists any limitations on it, and labels opponents "fanatics?"

Worldwide. The World Federation of Right to Die Societies—the international umbrella group.

Australia. The Voluntary Euthanasia Society (VES), founded 1974, 5,000 members.

Colombia. *Fundacion Pro-Derecho a Morir Dignamenta* (DMD, Foundation for a Dignified Death), founded 1979, 3,000 members.

Denmark. *Landsforeningen mit Livstestamente* (My Life's Testament Society), founded in 1976, 14,000 members.

France. (1) *Association pour la Droit de Mourir avec Dignite* (ADMD, Association for the Right to Die with Dignity), founded 1980, 20,000 members. Secretary General Madame Paula Caucanas-Pisier committed suicide in 1984. She had commented "AIDS will help us, I'm sure." (2) *Association du Mourir Doucement* (Association for Euthanasia), 11,700 members, 65 departmental delegations. *Association pour la Prevention de L'Enfance Handicappee* (APEH, Society for the Prevention of Handicapped Children). APEH director is French Senator Henri Caillavet, who declared: "If I were to have a retarded child, I would not let it live. I gave it life, and I also have the right to take it away. We must legalize this procedure so that parents are not considered criminals when they demand euthanasia for their abnormal children." Caillavet is also president of the ADMD.

Germany. *Deutsche Gesellschaft für Humanes Sterben* (DGHS, German Society for a Humane Death), founded 1980, 10,000 members. Sponsored by the Humanist Union, which has campaigned against any law that would hobble terrorist activity in the former West Germany. DGHS is staffed with pro-terrorist lawyers, including Heinrich Hannover and Heinreich Albertz. More than 1,000 DGHS members have committed suicide. DGHS member Dr. Julius Hackethal, affectionately known as "Dr. Cyanide," killed a 69-year-old patient because her disfigured face allegedly gave her a "poor quality of life." He made a film of her swallowing his poison and showed it at the 1984 Hemlock Society conference.

Great Britain. The Voluntary Euthanasia Society. Member Dr. Glanville Williams, author of *Beneficent Euthanasia*, is also President of the Abortion Law Reform Association (ALRA), a pro-abortion lobbying group.

India. The Society for the Right to Die and the Indian Society for the Right to Die.

Italy. *Club dell' Euthanasia* (CDE, Group for Euthanasia), founded 1986, 1,600 members.

Japan. Japan Society for Dying with Dignity, 5,200 members. Founded as the Japan Euthanasia Society in 1976 by Dr. Tenrei Ota, who was a primary advocate of "freedom of choice in abortion," and who developed the Ota Ring, an intra-uterine device (IUD).

Netherlands. (1) *Stichting Vrijwillige Euthanasie* (Netherlands Foundation for Voluntary Euthanasia), founded 1973. (2) *Informatie Centrum Vrijwillige Euthanasie* (ICVE, Information Center for Voluntary Euthanasia), founded 1975, 6,000 members. (3) *Nederlandse Verniging voor Vrijwillige Euthanasie* (NVVVE, Netherlands Organization for Voluntary Euthanasia), founded 1973, 26,000 members. Pieter Admiraal wrote the "how-to" euthanasia manual *Justifiable Euthanasia*, sent to 21,000 Dutch physicians and pharmacists.

Spain. *Asociacion Derecho a Morir Dignamenta* (DMD, Association for a Dignified Death), founded in 1984.

Switzerland. (1) *Association pour le Droit de Mourir dans la Dignite Exit* (DMD, Association for Death with Dignity), founded 1982, 1,000 members. (2) *Exit Deutsche Schweiz Vereinigung für Humanese Sterben* (Group Supporting a Humane Death), founded 1982, 1,800 members.

United States. (1) Concern [Compassion] for Dying, (formerly the Euthanasia Educational Council). (2) Americans Against Human Suffering (AAHS), founded with start-up money from the Hemlock Society. (3) Society for the Right to Die (formerly the Euthanasia Society of America), President Emeritus Joseph Fletcher. (4) The Hemlock Society, which publishes *The Hemlock Quarterly*. Contributors have included Joseph Fletcher, Pieter Admiraal, Humanist behaviorist B.F. Skinner, Helge Kuhse, and Rev. William Wendt, who sells coffins for use as coffee tables. The Hemlock Society was founded by Derek Humphry in 1980. Humphry "assisted" in the suicide of his first wife, Jean, and left his second wife, Ann Wickett, pressuring her to kill herself, which she did. Hemlock member psychiatrist Allan Pollack has declared: "Everyone has the right to end their life—even a child. If we do not allow children or the incompetent to commit suicide or have euthanasia administered, we are really practicing age discrimination and illness discrimination." (5) The

Human Betterment Foundation (eugenics and euthanasia). (6) Foundation of Thanatology, founded in 1968 in New York City to promote the Humanistic study of dying. (7) The Death Education Research Group (DERG), founded in 1973 at the School of Education of the University of Massachusetts. One of its main purposes is to prepare a high school death education curriculum. Its national periodicals on suicidology include *Death Education; The Bulletin of Suicidology; Death Studies*; and *Omega—Journal of Death and Dying*. (8) Euthanasia Research and Guidance Organization (ERGO). Maintains the Euthanasia World Directory, one of the most comprehensive World Wide Web sites on euthanasia, an excellent source of information at http://www.efn.org/~ergo. (9) Another comprehensive euthanasia Web site is DeathNet at http://www.islandnet.com/deathnet/.

Other Countries. More than 20 other countries have small but growing pro-euthanasia organizations, including Austria, Belgium, Canada, New Zealand, Norway, Scotland and South Africa.

···

71. What Are the Ultimate Goals of the Pro-Euthanasia Movement?

The Three-Step Strategy

Overview. There can only be one possible ultimate outcome of the utilitarian thinking that brought us contraception, sterilization, abortifacients and abortion. Once society compromises the paramount right to life in any way, once it segregates certain classes of human beings and declares them disposable, once it calculates and assesses the "value" of each human life, the progressive and lethal dehumanization of others by those who hold power will continue unabated until the society either destroys itself or returns to a "sanctity of life" ethic.

The later steps on the road to wholesale killing are always easier, as we found with abortion, contraception and population control. The first step down the slippery slope is the hardest, but, once a society's downward plunge gathers momentum, it will find itself moving so quickly that it will be very difficult to stop or turn back.

Step One: the "Living Will"

Many euthanasia activists consider the "Living Will" just the first step on the road to active, *involuntary* euthanasia of those they deem to be useless to society (Question 62 discusses the "Living Will"). They know that if they can get society to make this first critical step, all of the subsequent steps—no matter how many or how large they are—will be *much* easier.

As Derek Humphry, the founder of the Hemlock Society, has said: "We have to go stage by stage, with the living will, with the power of attorney, with the withdrawal of this; we have to go stage by stage. Your side would call that the 'slippery slope.' ... We would say, proceed with caution; learning as we go along how to handle this very sensitive situation."[1]

The headline of a 16 August 1985 *USA Today* article, which was a compendium of interviews with pro-euthanasia activists, said it all: "Living Wills 1st Step, Euthanasia Group Says."

The Facts of Life

Once a society accepts the "Living Will," it completely changes its yardstick for measuring human worth.

The "sanctity of life" ethic holds that every human being derives his worth from being created in the image and likeness of God—*spiritually*, not physically. Simply put, because everyone has an immortal soul, everyone must be treated equally.

By contrast, the "quality of life" ethic changes the focus from the *spiritual* to the *physical, mental and emotional.* A person's usefulness to society, to his family and even to himself is measured by the condition of his body and his mind.

The change from the "sanctity of life" ethic to the "quality of life" ethic is the most profoundly evil step a people can make. Once they make this transformation, they can justify any atrocity by disguising it behind the alluring masks of "compassion" and "realism." We can truthfully say that, once a society has accepted the "Living Will," it is already nine-tenths of the way down the road to involuntary euthanasia.

Step Two: Voluntary Euthanasia

The "Living Will" is only the first of three major steps in the pro-euthanasia strategy. The second is passive euthanasia followed by assisted suicide and active voluntary euthanasia. The third step is involuntary euthanasia.

Passive voluntary euthanasia—the withholding of food, water and oxygen—is only an intermediate step. People who have been denied the necessities of life will die in agony over a period lasting up to two weeks. Pro-euthanasia activists will then point to this process and say, as Jack Kevorkian has, that "allowing someone to starve to death and to die of thirst, the way we do now, is barbaric. Our Supreme Court has validated barbarism. The Nazis did that in concentration camps. ... It took her [Nancy Cruzan] a week to die. Try it! You think that just because you're in a coma you don't suffer?"[2]

The pro-euthanasia lobby will immediately push on to advocating "physician-assisted suicide" or direct euthanasia, where the patient or his "attorney-in-fact" asks that the patient be killed by injection. This type of direct killing was proposed in Washington State's Initiative 119, which voters rejected in November, 1990.

Dr. Jack Kevorkian has made this second step a reality. The retired Michigan pathologist had assisted in the suicides of scores of people, and has made it perfectly clear that he wants to set up a chain of euthanasia "clinics" ("obitoriums") across the country. Another of the world's leading pro-euthanasia activists, Dr. Julius Hackethal, stated that the ultimate goal is a worldwide "right to die": "Your [Hemlock Society] congress will help that the self-evident human rights for a dignified death will become a fixed and steady law all over the world. Such a vested human right would automatically cause that everybody would be able to determine for himself at what time and in which way he wants to die."[3]

One critical point that must be emphasized here concerns the U.S. Constitution. As we learned with contraception and abortion, when the courts extend a new "fundamental human right" to one group of people, it is unconstitutional to deny it to *other* groups of people. This means that, if incurably ill people receive a "right" to euthanasia, it is inevitable that the courts will quickly expand the "right" to include every citizen in the United States. Anti-lifers first justified the contraception and abortion "rights" under the "hard cases" of rape, incest and fetal deformity, and within five years expanded them to include any reason whatever and at any time during pregnancy. Right now, they are justifying euthanasia for the "hard cases" of terminally ill and comatose people and those suffering unbearable pain.

The anti-lifers will inevitably expand the "right" to euthanasia, just as they did with abortion, so that anyone of any age will be able to kill themselves with the "aid" of a "Doctor Death" for any reason whatsoever.

Step Three: Involuntary Euthanasia

Kill Them... There can no longer be any doubt that the ultimate goal of the euthanasia movement is active *involuntary* euthanasia of those "unfit" people who are either unwilling to die or who are unable to defend themselves.

Many leading pro-euthanasia groups and individuals have admitted this goal. George Crile, M.D., Head of Surgery at the Cleveland Clinic, has declared:

> To view the problem of health rationing objectively, what we need is a concept of man as a colonial creature, similar to ants and bees—which, like ourselves, are so highly specialized and so dependent on one another that no one of them can long survive alone. In the hives and homes of these bees and ants, no special care is given to the aged or infirm. Consideration is for the welfare of the colony as a whole.[4]

Dr. Mark Siegler, Director of the Center of Clinical Ethics at the University of Chicago, has said: "we start off with dispatching the terminally ill and the hopelessly comatose, and then perhaps our guidelines might be extended to the severely senile, the very old and decrepit and maybe even young, profoundly retarded children."[5]

And Dr. William Gaylin, professor of psychiatry and law at Columbia University, has stated: "it used to be easy to know what we wanted for our children, and now the best for our children might mean deciding which ones to kill. We've always wanted the best for our grandparents, and now that might mean killing them."[6]

Finally, Dr. John Goundry described the ultimate goal this way: "A death pill will be available and in all likelihood will be obligatory by the end of this century. In the end, I can see the State taking over and insisting on euthanasia."[7]

...Then Use Them. Just as Nazi and Communist doctors experimented on their victims because they were going to "die anyway," and just as abortionists use the same logic to justify fetal experimentation, a number of pro-euthanasia theorists have called for experimenting upon people who are in a comatose state.

One of these pro-euthanasia "bioethicists," William Gaylin, a former president of the Hastings Institute, would like to see comatose people (he calls them "neomorts") stockpiled in special repositories (called "bioemporiums") for organ "harvesting" and experimentation:

> The idea is based on redefining the concept of death and maintaining banks of bodies with the legal status of the dead but with the qualities we now associate

with the living." "We would have to accept the concept of "personhood" as separate from "aliveness" for adults, as we now do with fetuses.... Various illnesses could be induced in neomorts, and various treatments tried, thus protecting live patients from being "guinea pigs" in experimental procedures and therapies ...

One of Gaylin's colleagues writes approvingly that "neomorts would provide a steady supply of blood, since they could be drained regularly.... Bone marrow, cartilage, and skin could be harvested, and hormones, antitoxins, and antibodies manufactured in neomorts...."[8]

Terms such as "neomort" are excellent examples of verbal engineering used to promote social engineering, just as happened with abortion and contraception.

Figure 15

[Hessisches Hauptstattsarchiv Wiesbaden, courtesy of USHMM Photo Archives].

The smoking chimney of the Hadamar Euthanasia Center. Hadamar, Germany, 1941.
"[The Holocaust] started with the acceptance of the attitude, basic in the euthanasia movement, that there is such a thing as life not worthy to be lived"
—Dr. Alexander, Nuremburg War Crimes staff.

The Lesson to Be Learned

As the euthanasia movement rolls on in many Western countries, those who combat the "Culture of Death" must learn from those who have made grievous mistakes regarding the value of human life. We *must* learn one lesson from the German, Dutch, American and Australian euthanasia experiences: that all euthanasia begins with an "infinitely small, wedged-in lever."

Dr. Leo Alexander, instructor in psychiatry at Tufts College Medical College, who served as a consultant to the Secretary of War and who was on the staff of the Chief Counsel for War Crimes at Nuremberg, originated this term. He warned:

Whatever proportions these crimes finally assumed, it became evident to all who investigated that they had started from small beginnings. The beginnings at first were merely a subtle shift in emphasis in the basic attitude of the physicians. It started with the acceptance of the attitude, basic in the euthanasia movement, that there is such a thing as life not worthy to be lived.

This attitude in its early stages concerned itself merely with the severely and chronically sick. Gradually, the sphere of those to be included in this category was enlarged to encompass the socially unproductive, the ideologically unwanted, the racially unwanted, and, finally, all non-Germans. But it is important to realize that the infinitely small, wedged-in lever from which this entire trend of mind received its emphasis was the attitude toward the non-rehabilitable sick.[9]

1 Derek Humphry, quoted in Leslie Bond. "Hemlock Society Forms New Organization to Push Assisted Suicide Initiative." *National Right to Life News*, 18 December 1986, pp. 1 and 10.

2 "Medicide: The Goodness of Planned Death. An Interview with Dr. Jack Kevorkian." *Free Inquiry* ["An International Secular Humanist Magazine"], Fall 1991, pp. 14 to 18.

3 From the transcript of a speech by Dr. Julius Hackethal, titled "Medical Help By Suicide—As a Method of Voluntary Euthanasia," presented at the Second National Voluntary Euthanasia Conference of the Hemlock Society on 9 February 1985, in Los Angeles, California.

4 Dr. George Crile, Jr., Head of Surgery at the Cleveland Clinic, Cleveland, Ohio, quoted by Cal Thomas of the *Los Angeles Times* Syndicate, September, 1984.

5 Dr. Mark Siegler, Director, Center of Clinical Ethics, University of Chicago. *Time* Magazine, 31 March 1986.

6 Dr. William Gaylin, professor of psychiatry and law at Columbia University, addressing the American Association of University Women (AAUW), 10 June 1984.

7 Dr. John Goundry. *The Philadelphia Evening Bulletin*, 13 August 1977.

8 World Trends and Forecasts. "Recycling Human Bodies to Save Lives." *The Futurist*, April, 1976, p. 108.

9 Leo Alexander, M.D. "Medical Science Under Dictatorship." *The New England Journal of Medicine*, 14 July 1949, pp. 39-47.

72. Can There Be a Purpose to Human Suffering?

Modern society places great emphasis on convenience, comfort and the avoidance of inevitable trials and pain. When things go disastrously wrong with our jobs, our families or our health, we tend to rage at God or curse our bad luck instead of learning from our experiences and gaining wisdom, strength and insights into life.

Even more fundamentally, we seem to have forgotten that we possess immortal souls made in the image of God—and the possession of a soul, *not* our higher intelligence, is the fundamental difference between ourselves and the lower animals. Pope Pius XII asked a half-century ago: "Is it not such false pity which claims to justify euthanasia and to remove from man purifying and meritorious suffering, not by a charitable and praiseworthy help but by death, as if one were dealing with an irrational animal without immortality?"[1]

In this passage, Pope Pius highlighted the two great intangible purposes of pain: purification and gaining merit.

Anyone who has suffered significant pain for a period of time will find, upon proper introspection, that he has been strengthened by the experience. He realizes that pain is not destructive if suffered for a while, but instead makes him realize that he has the strength to overcome obstacles and fears that may have seemed insurmountable before. This is true for everyone, be they Christian, Jew, Hindu, or atheist.

Of course, severe pain suffered for too long can destroy the strongest of people. This is why the Catholic Church teaches that it is not proper to expect heroic virtue from all people, and that pain-killers may be used, even if they lead to semi-lucidity or quicker death in some cases (see Question 65 for elaboration on the use of pain-killers).

The second great purpose of human pain is the gain of merit. The very first sentence of Pope John Paul II's Apostolic Letter *Salvifici Doloris* ("On the Christian Meaning of Human Suffering") highlights the constant teaching of the Church in this matter: "Declaring the power of salvific suffering, the Apostle Paul says: In my flesh I 'complete what is lacking in Christ's afflictions for the sake of his body, that is, the church'."

As the Vatican's *Declaration on Euthanasia* teaches:

According to Christian teaching, however, suffering, especially suffering during the last moments of life, has a special place in God's saving plan; it is in fact a sharing in Christ's passion and a union with the redeeming sacrifice which He offered in obedience to the Father's will. Therefore, one must not be surprised if some Christians prefer to moderate their use of pain-killers, in order to accept voluntarily at least a part of their sufferings and thus associate themselves in a conscious way with the sufferings of Christ crucified (cf. Mt. 27:34).[2]

A certain degree of pain at the end of life allows us to follow Christ all the way to the Cross. In a way, it seems inconsistent for Christians to be willing to suffer various indignities and inconveniences in the name of Christ over a period of decades during their lives, and then shy away from complete participation in the ultimate suffering of Our Lord at the point of death.

This certainly does not mean that we have to linger in agony until the very last moment of life, because pain itself can be a terrible distraction. However, we must be able to strike a proper balance in our last hours between full consciousness of what is happening to us as we tread the road to Calvary and the degree of pain that we can bear.

We put dumb animals to sleep because there is no purpose to their suffering; they writhe in misery, ignorant and bewildered, and there can be no learning, no enrichment, no redeeming quality to their ordeals. They cannot face the end of their lives with courage and steadfastness. Our only possible response to their tribulations is to end their suffering as soon as possible.

We must treat dumb animals *humanely*; but we must treat persons *humanly*.

What animals need in their last days is mercy; what human beings need is bravery and companionship. Neither is possible if the needle stands ready to "put them down," if real or imagined trials become too much for them.

1 Allocution of Pope Pius XII to the Congress of the International Union of Catholic Women's Leagues, Rome, Italy, 11 September 1947.

2 Sacred Congregation for the Doctrine of the Faith. *Declaration on Euthanasia*, 5 May 1980. Section III, "The Meaning of Suffering for Christians and the Use of Pain-Killers."

••

73. What Does the Catholic Church Teach Regarding Euthanasia?

The Teachings of the Catholic Church

For years, the anti-life group 'Catholics' for a Free Choice (CFFC) has deliberately misrepresented Church teachings on abortion in order to confuse Catholic clergy and lay people.

Various pro-euthanasia individuals and organizations are now using this tactic by misquoting and twisting Church teachings in order to "show" that She supports the withdrawal of food and water, assisted suicide, and even the starvation of handicapped newborn babies.

The Catholic Church has always condemned both abortion and euthanasia, regardless of what dissenting propagandists have to say.[1] Pope Pius XII declared:

> Therefore, medical law can never permit either the physician or the patient to practice direct euthanasia, and the physician can never practice it either on himself or on others. This is equally true for the direct suppression of the fetus and for medical actions which go counter to the law of God clearly manifested. In all this, medical law has no authority and the doctor is not obliged to obey it. On the contrary, he is obliged not to take it into consideration; all formal assistance is forbidden him, while material assistance falls under the general norms of *cooperatio materialis*.[2]

The clearest and most definitive statement on euthanasia recently issued by the Catholic Church is the 1980 *Declaration on Euthanasia*, which says:

> No one is permitted to ask for this act of killing, either for himself or herself or for another person entrusted to his or her care; nor can he or she consent to it, either explicitly or implicitly. Nor can any authority legitimately recommend or permit such an action. For it is a question of the violation of the divine law, an offense against the dignity of the human person, a crime against life, and an attack on humanity.... It is necessary to state firmly once more that nothing and no one can in any way permit the killing of an innocent human being, whether a fetus or an embryo, an infant or an adult, an old person, or one suffering from an incurable disease, or a person who is dying.[3]

Finally, the statement of the Bishops of Ireland shows that the Church recognizes that euthanasia is *intrinsically evil*:

> What must always be remembered is that certain actions are good or evil in themselves already, apart from the motive or intention for which they are done. Deliberately to take one's own life is suicide and is gravely wrong in all circumstances. To cooperate with another in taking his own life is to share in the guilt of suicide. Deliberately to terminate the innocent life of another is murder, no matter how merciful the motives, no matter how seemingly desirable the result.[4]

---

1   The Catholic Church has recently referred to euthanasia as an "infamy," *Gaudium et Spes* 26 (7 December 1965) and *Dominum et Vivificantem* 43 (18 May 1986); "gravely immoral," *National Catechetical Directory for Catholics of the United States* 167 (30 October 1978); "criminal," *Christifideles Laici* 38 (30 December 1988); a "disgrace," *Veritatis Splendor* 80 (6 August 1993); "never morally acceptable," NCCB *Ethical and Religious Directives for Catholic Health Care Services* Introduction, Part 5 (1 December 1994); a "tragedy" and a "grave violation of the law of God," *Evangelium Vitae* 64-65 (25 March 1995); and "murder," *The Catechism of the Catholic Church*, ¶ 2324.

2   Pope Pius XII, in his 11 September 1956 radio message to the International Congress of Catholic Physicians. Reprinted in *Matrimony*, Papal Teachings. Boston: St. Paul Editions, 1963.

3   Sacred Congregation for the Doctrine of the Faith. *Declaration on Euthanasia*, 5 May 1980.

4 The Bishops of Ireland. Joint Pastoral Letter "Human Life is Sacred," 1 March 1975. Reprinted in the
   22 May 1975 English edition of *L'Osservatore Romano*.

• •

74. Why Is Euthanasia Wrong from a Secular Viewpoint?

Introduction

It is one thing to speak of the sanctity of life and of human life being created in
the image and likeness of God—but what does the anti-euthanasia activist say
when he confronts a pro-euthanasia person who does not believe in God, or who
believes in a permissive "god" who allows anything the person wants?

Anti-euthanasia activists must be able to speak in terms of the negative consequences that assisted suicide and euthanasia have on society at large (i.e., personal
insecurity, escalating violence and fraud), and they must be able to explain these
ideas in very specific and relevant terms.

The following paragraphs list some of the reasons that euthanasia is illogical and
wrong from a purely secular viewpoint.

Euthanasia Is Forever

In Question 61, we saw that there are literally hundreds of cases on record where
doctors have judged people to be "irreversibly comatose," and then they have
awakened to lead perfectly normal lives. These individuals include Teisa Franklin,
Scott and Jeff Mueller, Jacqueline Cole, Carrie Coons, Harold Cybulski and Barbie
Blodgett.

In every one of these cases—and in hundreds of other cases that are reported or
unreported *every year*—doctors condemn to a painful death people that they are
"absolutely certain" will never recover.

And, in about 50 percent of these cases, the patient *did* recover, either partially or
completely.

In light of this dismal record, it is obvious that, when predicting the futures of
patients who are deemed to be in so-called "persistent vegetative states," *there is no
such thing as a "sure thing."* It is also obvious that the main motives of many health
professionals are the saving of medical resources and cost control, not the saving or
betterment of human life.

It is the height of irony that our society spends literally millions of dollars on
multiple legal appeals to make absolutely certain that every person executed by the
State is truly guilty as charged—but is so reluctant to take the same kind of care
with people whose only "crime" is being deemed a "life not worthy of life" by the
medical profession.

Capital punishment is forever. And so is euthanasia.

So, to be consistent, those who oppose capital punishment must also oppose
euthanasia.

Euthanasia Promotes Suicide

Whether we like it or not, one of our most important roles as adults in society is
to set the example for younger and less experienced people. After all, what we

teach young people will largely determine how they run the world after they inherit it—and what kind of world our *grandchildren* will inherit.

What we teach young people will also determine how they treat *us* when *we* are elderly and infirm.

The teen suicide rate in the United States has tripled in the last 15 years to more than 2,500 deaths per year. We read about suicide pacts and teen murder/suicides almost on a weekly basis. Experts in the demographics of suicide (suicidologists) already call this situation "epidemic."

What kind of an example does an adult give to teenagers when he kills himself because he is afraid of pain or losing "dignity?" Or because he *may* experience some unknown degree of pain years down the road—pain that could probably be alleviated?

If our society accepts euthanasia, how will we tell a despondent teenager he has no right to kill himself if the cheerleader he adores spurns him? How about the young girl whose pet dies? Or who loses self-respect through fornication? Or the boy who doesn't make the baseball team? Or who flunks out of college?

Teenagers don't respond to a double standard. They don't accept the command, "Do as I say, not as I do." If euthanasia becomes legal and accepted by society, we must expect our "epidemic" of teen suicide to become a "pandemic," with perhaps 10,000 to 20,000 additional cases per year. How will we react to 25,000 cases of teen suicide annually without appearing to be grossly hypocritical?

The Euthanasia Mentality Is Myopic and Lazy

Pro-euthanasia activists are extremely clever and skillful at manipulating public opinion through emotional appeals such as the "hard cases" and through appeals to self-interest. They believe everyone should be able to do away with themselves, and they also believe society should not be concerned about such self-destructive acts.

This philosophy is not only irresponsible, it is extremely dangerous. Everyone in a society develops, throughout his life, a complex web of relationships. Every person significantly affects many other members of society every year, often without realizing it.

Euthanasia is a strain of aggressively malignant societal cancer, which has a small beginning but spreads rapidly.

No human body can live with an acute case of cancer, and no society can endure if its people destroy themselves at a high enough rate.

All of a healthy body's cells work together to promote the common good of the body. Similarly, individuals work together to advance the common good of society. Each of us plays a vital part in this complex *corpus*.

Euthanasia Is Despair Personified

What deeper expression of despair is there than to kill oneself?

Many people have, at one time or another, experienced despair so deep that they may even have considered how easy it would be to just "let go" and die.

This kind of despair can easily lead to one of the more than 25,000 suicides the United States suffers annually.

Perhaps the saddest sight in life is a person totally without hope. This is because, as long as there is a means to overcome one's troubles, hope remains. When a person has lost all hope, he has lost all faith that he has any control over his situation.

Our society's emphasis on "choice" and "control" has aggravated this problem terribly. The anti-lifers, the government, and the media tell us that we cannot have control if we cannot have a wide range of choices or avenues of action. So, we have become conditioned to think that, if we lose options, we have lost control of our lives. And, if we lose control of our lives, we think that those lives are not worth living. We perceive ourselves as less than "fully human" if we cannot have total control all of the time.

This is nonsense. As long as we are living, we can seek to improve our situation. We can actually generate choices ourselves if we have learned to possess initiative and imagination. What's more, there are always people, churches, groups and agencies available to help, whatever our problems may be.

To kill oneself, of course, is to *really* lose control of the situation.

After all—*dead people don't choose!*

1   U.S. Department of Commerce, Bureau of the Census. Reference Data Book and Guide to Sources, *Statistical Abstract of the United States*, 1995. Washington, D.C.: U.S. Government Printing Office. Table 128, "Death Rates, by Selected Causes and Age: 1980 to 1992."

75. How Can I Contact Groups that Actively Oppose Euthanasia?

No matter how talented, imaginative and experienced a person is, he will almost always accomplish more if he joins forces with other people who share his goals.

If you would like to help fight euthanasia, your first step should be to contact a national anti-euthanasia group to see whether it has a branch in your area. If there is no local group that is *specifically* anti-euthanasia, local generalist-type pro-life organizations may be involved in combatting the killing of the sick and elderly.

Appendix A lists organizations that oppose euthanasia in the United States and other English-speaking countries, which have resources and experience that anti-euthanasia activists all over the world will find useful.

Chapter 6

The Nature of the Preborn Child

···

76. What Evidence Do We Have that Preborn Children Are Alive?

The Definition of Life

The Three Categories of Being. All dictionaries define "alive" as "having life." *Blakiston's Pocket Medical Dictionary* defines life as "the sum of properties by which an organism grows, reproduces, and adapts itself to its environment; the quality by which an organism differs from inorganic or dead organic bodies." *The American Heritage Dictionary* defines life as "the property or quality by which living organisms are distinguished from dead organisms or from inanimate matter."

These definitions classify all entities into three categories: (1) alive, (2) dead (formerly alive) and (3) inanimate/inorganic. There are no other possible categories. The term "potential life" is a completely artificial construct with absolutely no scientific evidence to back it up.

Besides this simple demonstration of logic, there are two ways to prove that preborn children are alive by using the above information: (1) directly or (2) by the process of elimination.

Direct Proof. The simplest way to prove that preborn children are alive is simply by observing that the woman's ovum and the man's spermatozoa are living cells. These two living cells then fuse, reorganize, grow and continue to have all of the properties of a live cell.

Naturally, everyone acknowledges that the child, once born, is alive. So a pro-abortionist who denies a preborn baby is alive would have us believe the baby comes from living cells and is living when born, but is either dead or inanimate during the intermediate gestation phase.

Any other attempt to directly prove that preborns are alive will lead to an endless round of quibbling by pro-abortionists. It is much simpler to show that preborn babies are alive by using the process of elimination.

The Facts of Life

Process of Elimination. Preborn babies are not inanimate or inorganic. Obviously, they are comprised of organic matter because they *come from* organic matter, and they swim and move about in their mother's uterus. Additionally, they experience a very high rate of cell division (41 of the 45 total cell divisions in an individual's life take place before birth). Cell division does not take place in a dead or inanimate being.

Secondly, they are certainly not "dead" (formerly alive), or they would be naturally miscarried or reabsorbed by the mother's body, and no abortion would be needed.

This leaves only one possibility: that preborn babies are alive.

Pro-Abortion Absurdities

Pro-abortionists repeatedly prove that intelligence and book learning do not always produce wisdom.

This is most evident when pro-abortionists perform breathtaking feats of semantic contortions concerning the status of preborn babies, in complete disregard of all biological and physical facts.

A famous passage that appeared in 1970 in the journal *California Medicine* described exactly what the pro-abortion strategists had to do in order to achieve abortion on demand:

> Since the old ethic has not yet been fully displaced, it has been necessary to separate the idea of abortion from the idea of killing, which continues to be socially abhorrent. The result has been a curious avoidance of the scientific fact, which everyone really knows, that human life begins at conception and is continuous, whether intra- or extra-uterine, until death. The very considerable semantic gymnastics which are required to rationalize abortion as anything but taking a human life would be ludicrous if they were not often put forth under socially impeccable auspices.[1]

Examples of such verbal engineering abound, but a significant recent example is the pro-abortion brief that 167 pro-abortion scientists and doctors, including 11 Nobel Prize winners, submitted to the U.S. Supreme Court for the July 1989 *Webster* decision. They produced a masterpiece of techno-babble alleging:

> There is no scientific consensus that a human life begins at conception, at a given stage of fetal development, or at birth. The question of "when a human life begins" cannot be answered by reference to scientific principles like those with which we predict planetary movement. The answer to that question will depend on each individual's social, religious, philosophical, ethical and moral beliefs and values.... The only "consensus" that may be said to exist among scientists on the question of when a human life begins is that science alone cannot answer that question.... Science cannot define the essential attributes of human life any more than science can define such concepts as love, faith or trust.

Let us examine several of the fundamental logical absurdities contained in this passage:

- The "scientists" are essentially saying: "we admit our ignorance and incompetence on this subject, but we want the Court to decide in our favor anyhow."

- Note that, in the first sentence, the "scientists" assert that life may not even begin at *birth*. Such statements are cropping up more often as infanticide becomes more common (and must therefore be justified), and as the euthanasia debate heats up. These "scientists" are laying the groundwork for a definition of life that ultimately depends on a person's capabilities and social status.

- Using the "logic" of these allegedly learned men and women, it would be possible for a misguided person, consulting his "social, religious, philosophical, ethical and moral beliefs and values," to decide that an abortionist is not alive. Of course, this type of erroneous logic, if used to murder an abortionist, would not stand up as a defense in court for an instant. However, the U.S. court system uses this logic to enable the killing of tens of millions of preborn baby humans.

- Finally, we must ask ourselves: if 11 Nobel Prize winners thinking together cannot define human life, how can they assert that every woman in the country can? Pro-abortionists claim that preborn children are not alive until the mother accepts them. In other words, it is the mother who decides whether or not her preborn child is living, dead or inanimate. This is, to put it politely, illogical in the extreme. Who has ever heard of anyone outside of a mental institution reclassifying a stone as "alive" or a living animal as "inanimate?"

One other example of this type of self-serving illogic is amusing due to its sheer crassness.

Until recently, Rocky Mountain Planned Parenthood distributed to its customers a booklet comically titled "Let's Tell the Truth About Abortion." It asks, "Is the fetus alive? Is it alive? Algae is alive, and earthworms, and your appendix. Mold on the bread in the refrigerator is alive. People are not agreed on what a life is.... If you look at pictures of human, chicken, pig, and turtle embryos at the same stage of development, it is difficult to tell them apart."[2]

Notice that the pamphlet flatly declares, "mold on the bread in the refrigerator is alive," then states baldly that nobody knows what life is. Since mold is alive and preborn babies are only "potential life," Planned Parenthood therefore assigns a higher status to mold than it does to a nine-month preborn baby. Notice also the blatant dehumanizing of preborn babies by likening them to mold and worms. Finally, it is true that all embryos do look similar at an early stage of development. This is irrelevant, since any competent scientist can identify the species of an embryo by examining it microscopically.

The Consensus on When Life Begins

Pro-abortionists repeat *ad nauseam* the slogan "there is no consensus about when life begins."

They are wrong.

Most dictionaries define "consensus" as "general agreement" or "the judgment arrived at by most of those concerned."[3]

The Nobel Prize Committee for Physiology and Medicine stated decisively in 1991 that "the Nobel Committee noted that life begins with the activation of ion channels as the sperm merges with the egg in fertilization. All cells have electrical charges within and outside the cell and the difference is known as the membrane potential. Fertilization changes the potential to prevent other sperm from joining the fertilized egg."[4]

Virtually every medical school textbook used in every country says human life begins at fertilization. Note this definition from *The Developing Human: Clinically Oriented Embryology*: "*Zygote*. This cell results from fertilization of an oocyte by a sperm and is the beginning of a human being.... Development begins at fertilization, when a sperm unites with an oocyte to form a zygote. Each of us started life as a cell called a zygote."

Biological Principles and Modern Practice of Obstetrics says: "The term conception refers to the union of the male and female pronuclear elements of procreation from which a new living being develops. It is synonymous with the terms fecundation, impregnation, and fertilization.... The zygote thus formed represents the beginning of a new life."

Pathology of the Fetus and the Infant states, "every time a sperm cell and ovum unite, a new being is created which is alive and will continue to live unless its death is brought about by some specific condition."

Foundations of Embryology concludes: "It is the penetration of the ovum by a spermatozoa and the resulting mingling of the chromosomal material each brings to the union that culminates the process of fertilization and initiates the life of a new individual. Every one of the higher animals starts life as a single cell—the fertilized ovum. The union of two such sex cells to form a zygote constitutes the process of fertilization and initiates the life of a new individual."[5]

In recent years, some revised editions of certain medical textbooks have begun to shy away from such definitive statements. The motives of the publishers have nothing to do with new medical discoveries, and everything to do with "going along to get along" and being acceptable to medical school faculties.

Note that, in the long run, there *is indeed* a consensus among scientists about when life begins. No reputable scientist has ever stated that life does *not* begin at conception. They either say that it does, or that they simply don't know. Even when treating this question like a public opinion poll and discounting the fainthearted "don't knows," we have virtually unanimous consent among scientists that, if compelled to name a point at which life begins, it begins at *fertilization*.

Erring on the Side of Human Life

In matters of public safety, we *always* err on the side of human life.

Our society does not allow behavior that *may* take life, even if the chance is small. People are not allowed to shoot firearms in the direction of a freeway just because life might *not* be taken. People are not allowed to poison Halloween treats on a supermarket shelf, just because life might *not* be taken. And we have many local laws that forbid smoking in crowded areas, because second-hand smoke *may* injure others.

Yet pro-abortionists say abortion should be allowed, just because we might not be taking human life (since they *really* don't know when life begins, after all).

1 "A New Ethic for Medicine and Society," 113 *California Medicine* 67, 68 (1970).

2 "Let's Tell the Truth About Abortion." Pamphlet distributed by Rocky Mountain Planned Parenthood. Denver: Fight Back Press, 1985, pp. 3-4.

3 *Webster's New Collegiate Dictionary*. Springfield, Massachusetts: G&C Merriam Company, 1974, p. 241.

4 *New York Times*, 8 October 1991.

5 K.L. Moore. *The Developing Human: Clinically Oriented Embryology* (2nd Edition). Philadelphia: W.B. Saunders Publishers, 1977, pp. 1 and 12. J.P. Greenhill and E.A. Freidman. *Biological Principles and Modern Practice of Obstetrics*. Philadelphia: W.B. Saunders Publishers, pp. 17 and 23. E.L. Potter, M.D., and J.M. Craig, M.D. *Pathology of the Fetus and the Infant* (3rd Edition). Chicago: Year Book Medical Publishers, 1975, p. vii. Bradley M. Patten, M.D. *Foundations of Embryology* (3rd Edition), New York City: McGraw-Hill, 1968.

77. What Evidence Do We Have that Preborn Children Are Human Beings?

The Definition of "Humanity"

A rigorous analysis of the exact biological and social status of preborn babies can only be performed in three steps.

The first level of analysis must answer the most basic question: "Are preborn babies alive?" Question 76 established that they are, without a doubt, living beings.

Since we have answered this strictly biological question in the affirmative, we must further classify this living being as either *human* or *non-human* (there is no other possible classification). If this analysis shows us that preborn babies are human, then we must answer the third and most complex question: "Is this living human being a *person*?"

The American Heritage Dictionary defines "humanity" as "the condition, quality, or fact of being human." It defines "human" as "having or manifesting the form, nature, or qualities characteristic of man .. pertaining to or being a man as distinguished from a lower animal ... [or] from a divine entity or infinite intelligence."

The Fundamental Conflict

Ethicist Hans Tiefel clearly identified the fundamental divergence of philosophy between pro-lifers and pro-abortionists when he observed: "Our continuing disagreements on fetal research, abortion or the nontreatment of seriously handicapped newborns result not from a lack of facts or want of shared principles, but from diverging visions of what it means to be human and of the nature and purpose of human life."

The exterminators of any group of people dehumanize them to the extent that they perceive a threat to themselves. After all, it's *so* much easier to kill or exploit if you have been brainwashed into believing you're not killing a human being.

The Facts of Life

Consider the language used to justify slavery, the Holocaust and any armed conflict.

Pro-abortionists often go to absurd lengths to dehumanize preborn children. Lana Phelan writes: "Yearly, millions of women, driven in fear of the state—not of man's ancient gods—submit themselves to crude abortions at the hands of quacks, or attempt surgery on their own bodies to rid their agonized wombs of endoparasitic growths, which if unchecked, threaten their lives, their sanity, their existing families, their incomes and social futures."

Abortionist Warren Hern states: "The relationship between the gravid female and the fetoplacental unit can be understood best as one of host and parasite."[1] Among the hundreds of dehumanizing terms pro-abortionists apply to living preborn children are "abortus;" "blob of tissue;" "communicable disease;" "defective life;" "embryonic debris;" "genetic garbage;" "gobbet of meat;" "hateful, vile plague;" "marmalade;" "mass of protoplasm;" "product of conception" (POC); "protoplasmic rubbish;" "sub-human non-personhood;" and "unwanted fetal tissue."

The Beginnings of Humanity

There are many differences between a sperm and an ovum and the zygote that they combine to create. The primary difference is in information content. The haploid gametes in the sperm and ovum have exactly half of the information that a zygote has, and therefore cannot constitute a person.

However, after the germ cells of any mammalian species have combined to form a blastocyst, any competent microbiologist can examine the organism to determine exactly which species it is. The egg and sperm are living cells, and they are human (just as human eye and hand cells are), but they must combine in order to produce a *human being*.

Pro-lifers should emphasize that the U.S. government officially acknowledges that every animal is a full-fledged member of its own species from fertilization—with the sole exception of preborn human beings. Court decisions have recognized that embryonic turtles, eagles, cattle, deer and even *lobsters* have a status equal to born members of their species.[2] It is obvious that the courts have exempted preborn humans from protection not due to medical, philosophical or legal proof of any kind, but for sheer convenience.

Some anti-lifers try to dodge the issue by speaking of the "progressive humanization of the fetus." However, this is illogical. After all, we never hear anyone talk about the "progressive chimpanzification of chimpanzees" or the "progressive eaglization of eagles," because nobody is trying to push an illogical and lethal social agenda involving chimpanzees or eagles.

For Some, Even Humanity Isn't Enough ...

The Fallback Position. Ironically, the fact that pro-abortionists heavily favor one area of "science" involving preborn children provides the evidence needed to undermine their own position that the preborn are not human: The "science" of fetal organ harvesting, where researchers use the tissue from aborted preborn babies in attempts to treat the symptoms of Parkinson's Disease, Alzheimer's Disease, diabetes and other illnesses.

Dr. Ralph DeGeorgio neatly sums up the point that pro-lifers must make: "We must recognize why the use of human fetal tissue is being advocated in the first place: precisely because it *is* human."[3]

But even if scientists can prove the biological or genetic humanity of preborn babies, will it stop their wholesale killing? Bioethicist Robert S. Morison plaintively asks: "As gradually improving techniques permit fetal growth to later and more mature stages, then the issue of disposal will be met head-on in the form of the following presently unresolved questions: When do fetuses acquire the status of protectable humanity?... If brought to term, will they finally be admitted into the human community or will they still be considered material appropriate for further experimentation?"[4]

Some of the more extreme anti-lifers say even a healthy *newborn baby* might not be human *because of environmental or economic conditions alone.* Hastings Center "bioethicist" Mary Anne Warren writes:

If we are to make a reasoned judgment about the moral status of fetuses, *and of nonhuman animals, alien life forms, intelligent machines and other problematic entities,* we must develop a criterion of moral rights that is species-neutral. That is, it will not do to make "genetic humanity," or mere genetic affiliation to the human species, either a necessary or a sufficient condition for the possession of full moral rights. [The criteria for personhood is] an entity that has the actual, not merely potential capacity for consciousness, complex, sophisticated perception, rationality, self-awareness and self-motivated behavior ... when an unwanted or defective infant is born into a society which cannot afford and/or is not willing to care for it, then its destruction is permissible.[5]

Dr. Peter Bond is another of the "new utilitarians" who go so far as to tie a person's humanity to the quality of his environment: "A woman can produce a baby in the most squalid circumstances of being homeless, poor, mentally defective and physically ill. The products of conception when they are born at term are then only potentially human."[6]

According to Bond's frightening criteria, population controllers could declare *the whole populations of crowded or poor cities and even entire developing countries to be sub-human or non-human.* It would also mean that, if the children of one race are generally born into conditions more "squalid" than a second race, then pro-abortion utilitarians could accord the second race greater human status than the first.

It is obvious that, when pro-abortionists allege that preborn babies are not human, they are not referring to *genetic* humanity; they are equating "humanhood" with "personhood." A pro-lifer should point this out when debating the humanity of preborn babies.

Humanity Is Really Irrelevant to Pro-Abortionists. Even if pro-lifers could *prove* beyond doubt that preborn babies are living human persons, does anyone really believe the pro-abortionists would suddenly stop the killing?

The "status of the unborn" argument is nothing more than a convenient distraction that lets the abortionists continue to wipe out preborn babies by the millions, while their supporters debate the issues. Alfred Moran, former Executive Vice President of Planned Parenthood of New York, proved this when he asserted:

> ... it seems to me that there are clearly increasing concerns out there that we need to address ourselves to if we ultimately want to come down with the reality that in spite of all those concerns, in spite of all those changes in viability, in spite of those capacities to intercede in fetal developments, that the ultimate choice about carrying a pregnancy to term can only be made by the woman who is pregnant, we will lose it [the 'right' to abortion].[7]

1 Warren M. Hern. *Abortion Practice*. Philadelphia: J.B. Lippincott Company, 1990, p. 14.

2 "Government Says Calves Become Calves at Conception." American Family Association *Journal*, February, 1989, p. 9.

3 *Tissue and Organ Donation By Aborted Preborn and Anencephalic Infants: Medical Aspects of Human Fetal Transplantation.* University of Southern California School of Medicine, 1990, p. 226.

4 Robert S. Morison. "The Human Fetus as Useful Research Material." *Hastings Center Report*, April 1973, pp. 8-11.

5 Mary Anne Warren. "Can the Fetus be an Organ Farm?" *Hastings Center Report*, October 1978.

6 Letter from Dr. Peter Bond. *Journal of Medical Ethics*, 1976, Volume II, Number 45.

7 *National Right to Life News*. "Technical Advances to Make Pro-Abortion Position Tougher." 26 May 1983, p. 12.

....

78. What Evidence Do We Have that Preborn Children Are Persons?

The Definition of "Personhood"

The American Heritage Dictionary defines "person" as "a living human being, especially as distinguished from an animal or thing."

As we saw in the previous two Questions, a rigorous analysis of the exact biological and social status of preborn children can only be performed in three steps.

The first, and most basic, level of analysis must answer the question: "Are preborn children *alive*?"

Question 76 has answered this strictly biological question in the affirmative.

The second step of the analysis is to further classify this living being as either *human* or *non-human* (there is no other possible classification—there is no entity that is "partially" or "potentially" human).

Question 77 shows conclusively that *this* second strictly biological question results in classifying preborn children as human.

If the debate over the status of preborn children were a strictly logical one, it would be simple to show they are persons. After all, Questions 76 and 77 have proven that they meet the qualifications for "a living human being."

But the final step of the analysis is the most difficult and slippery of all, because it deals with a *social*, not *biological*, classification. Are preborn, living humans *persons*, endowed with the same rights as all other persons? Or are they sub-persons, subject to whatever abuse and genocide we may decide to inflict upon their entire "subspecies?"

This Question examines the ideological question: "Should society confer upon these preborn, living human beings the status of person?"

Frightening Concessions

Non-Personhood = the Core of All Oppression. Pro-abortionists in general will concede that preborn children are living human beings, but not that they are *persons*. The National Abortion and Reproductive Rights Action League (NARRAL) says:

> Back to the central issue of personhood and rights; other non-persons (pigs, cows) have toenails, heartbeats, and the capacity to feel pain (some say a fetus can only feel pressure, not pain, but we're not sure), yet these factors alone do not prevent the destruction of such entities. It is a fact that the fetus is human life, but when do we accept that developing human life as a fellow human being? That question can only be answered according to our individual beliefs.[1]

The anti-life front group 'Catholics' for a Free Choice (CFFC) echoed this attitude when it asserted:

> It is important to understand that while abortion does involve the taking of a human life—because all life that is in and of a human being is human life—in order to call it murder we would have to believe that prenatal life in the early stages of pregnancy is a human person and that there were absolutely *no* reasons that justified the taking of that life ... [However], you may feel you have reasons that justify abortion regardless of your beliefs about personhood.[2]

These quotes reveal the very core of oppressionist thinking: that we can somehow classify right out of existence those who are less able to defend themselves. This is precisely what the slavers did to Blacks, exactly what the Nazis did to Jews—and what some men used to do to women. The oppressors *always* say, "the question can only be answered according to one's individual beliefs."

They are completely wrong, of course. The Catholic Bishops of Ireland wrote:

> But the point is that we are not free to refuse to recognize another human being as a person. Refusal to recognize another human being as a person is in fact the essence of all immorality in human relations. It is the basis of all oppression, torture, denial of civil rights, religious and racial discrimination, exploitation, all forms of inhumanity of man to man. All of these are simply ways of refusing to recognize other human beings as human. Once human life exists, we are *morally bound* to respect its right to life, to development, to human dignity. Otherwise, the very basis of morality is undermined.[3]

Kill 'Em Anyway. Unlike those in NARRAL and CFFC, many pro-abortionists have reached the inescapable conclusion that preborn babies are persons. However, as pro-lifers have predicted for years, the debate over the status of preborn children is just a blind, because pro-abortionists will use any excuse to hang on to their precious abortion "right."

Many anti-lifers admit the personhood of preborn children—*and even concede that abortion is murder*—yet see this as no obstacle whatever. Magda Denes, for example, has written:

I *do* think abortion is murder—of a very special and necessary sort. What else would one call the deliberate stilling of a life? And no physician involved with the procedure ever kids himself about that ... legalistic distinctions among "homicide," "justified homicide," "self-defense," and "murder" appear to me a semantic game. What difference does it make what we call it? Those who do it and those who witness its doing know that abortion is the stilling of a life.[4]

Figure 16

I KNOW HOW YOU FEEL! WHEN I WAS A SLAVE DOWN THERE, THE COURTS DIDN'T THINK I WAS FULLY HUMAN EITHER!

It is necessary to first dehumanize a class of human beings before you can exploit or kill them.

Norman Mailer is certainly honest in his attitude toward the preborn; "Let me say something that's shocking. I am perfectly willing to grant that life starts at conception. If a woman doesn't want to have a child, then I think it's her right to say no. But let's not pretend that it isn't a form of killing."[5]

And Virginia Ramey Mollenkott stated in a 'Religious' Coalition for Abortion Rights (RCAR) propaganda pamphlet ludicrously titled "Respecting the Moral Agency of Women":

> Even if we were to concede the highly controversial and recent supposition that an embryo is a human person from the moment of conception, we would still be looking at only *one* very important value that has to be weighed against *many other* very important values, such as the quality of life that the unborn could look forward to after birth; the probable impact of that birth on the welfare of the already existing family; the mental health, well being, and conscience of the potential mother; and the impact on society of laws that repress obedience to the dictates of conscience and remove a woman's control over her own destiny.[6]

This kind of thinking goes one step beyond situational ethics: it admits to the monstrous crime of killing an innocent human being, but accepts the killing as necessary. This means that if pro-eugenics thinkers gain enough power to decree that personhood actually only begins at, say, the age of four (after the child has passed an intensive battery of physical and mental tests), there are plenty of abortion mill staffers out there who would be perfectly willing to kill trusting toddlers.

Does this sound far-fetched? Consider this recent exchange with an abortuary worker:

Interviewer:	"Oh, so as long as you make money, it doesn't matter?"
Clinic Employee:	"As long as it's food in my stomach, no, it doesn't matter. It is legal ... It is legal ... It is legal!"

Interviewer: "So if they legalized killing four-year-old children, you would have no problem?"

Clinic Employee: "No, I would not have a problem.... My conscience is very clear...."[7]

This philosophy is incalculably dangerous. As the above quotes show, many pro-abortionists now concede preborn babies are both alive and human, but say that we can leave the determination of "personhood" to each individual. And others go even further; they are willing to concede the personhood of preborn babies, but reserve the right to kill them anyway.

And it is not only rabid anti-lifers who think this way. Many judges have accepted this "reasoning." In a 1986 abortion mill trespass case, *The State of Virginia v. Christyanne Collins and Harry F. Hand*, Judge Bruce Bach of Fairfax, Virginia, stated in his opinion:

> I will find as a matter of fact that unborn human lives were being terminated in the clinic that morning because that's what the evidence in this particular case is. All of the evidence is that first trimester fetuses are human beings.... I reject the defense of necessity because we have in our society many instances of, I'll call it, State-sanctioned killing of human beings. And while the evidence is that human lives are being terminated, the Virginia statutes clearly allow the termination of human lives ... people at that clinic have a right under our law as it is today to do what they were doing and to do it without interference from people, well-meaning or otherwise.... So I do find them [the defendants] guilty and those are my reasons.[8]

Expanding the Pool of "Non-Persons"

The American Heritage Dictionary defines "non-person" as, "a person whose expunction from the attention and memory of the public is sought, esp. by governmental action and *usually for reasons of ideological or political deviation*" [emphasis added].

Once anti-life groups define the first group of people out of existence, and the public does not respond with outrage, the subsequent steps are much easier and smoother to achieve.

In the United States, the first difficult step in the revocation of the personhood of groups of helpless people came in 1973, when the Supreme Court, in its absurd *Roe v. Wade* decision, revoked not only the *personhood* of preborn babies, but their very status as living beings as well, by labeling them "potential life."

The following two decades saw subsequent steps come at smaller and smaller intervals until they melded into a smooth headlong sprint down the "slippery slope."

Since 1973, the "non-personhood" and privacy doctrines imposed by *Roe v. Wade* and *Griswold v. Connecticut* have justified all of the following, as more and more human beings have had their personhood revoked:

- a Kentucky court ruled that a man who killed his estranged wife's 34-week preborn baby by forcing his hand into her uterus and strangling the *wanted* child could not be convicted of a crime because *Roe v. Wade* does not confer personhood on preborn babies (*Hollis v. Commonwealth*, 652 S.W.2d 61 (Ky. 1983));

■ wrongful birth suits, which are filed by parents who allege that a baby should have been aborted instead of born (*Beaman v. Allen*, 80 N.J. 421, 404 A.2d 8 (1979));

■ letting handicapped newborn babies die a horrible death from starvation and thirst (*American Academy of Pediatrics v. Heckler*, 561 F.Supp.395 (D.D.C. 1983));

■ denying heart surgery to a mentally handicapped toddler (*Bothman v. Warren*, 445 U.S. 949 (1980));

■ stopping cancer treatment for an elderly person (*Supt. of Belchertown v. Saikewicz*, 373 Mass. 728,370); and

■ stopping respiratory aid for a comatose teenager (N.E.2d 417(1977), *in re Quinlan*, 70 N.J., 355/A.2d 647 (1976)).

Let's Highlight Glaring Pro-Abortion Hypocrisy

The hypocrisy and inconsistency of the pro-death position is absolutely astonishing, and pro-lifers should highlight it at every opportunity.

Pro-abortionists will join others to fight for more handicapped parking slots at supermarkets, but stand silently by while nursery staff starve handicapped newborn babies to death all over the country.

They set up shelters for battered and abused women, but oppose laws against sex-selection abortions aimed almost exclusively at those preborn children whose sole birth defect is that they happen to be female.

And they will have sign-language experts translate speeches at pro-abortion rallies for deaf people, while fighting for the "right" to kill all preborn babies who are handicapped in the slightest.

Conclusion

Questions 76 and 77 have shown that preborn children are undeniably "alive" and "human beings." Using the dictionary definition of "personhood" shown at the beginning of this Question, it follows that they are *persons* as well.

The insurmountable difficulty with this simple definition is that pro-abortionists have hijacked it from the arena of biological science to that of metaphysics. So, debates on the status of preborn children will always end in a standoff between opposing opinions, because neither side can employ hard facts.

Pro-lifers should always move the debate from the metaphysical to the practical arena. If this is not possible, then an appeal to conscience is the only recourse: the primary reason for granting personhood to *everyone* is that, when one group is disenfranchised, others will inevitably follow.

1 Looseleaf booklet, "Organizing for Action." Prepared by Vicki Z. Kaplan for the National Abortion Rights Action League, 250 West 57th Street, New York, N.Y. 10019. 51 pp., no date.

2   Marjorie Reiley Maguire and Daniel C. Maguire. "Abortion: A Guide to Making Ethical Decisions." 'Catholics' for a Free Choice, September 1983.

3   The Bishops of Ireland. Pastoral Letter titled "Human Life is Sacred," 1 March 1975, reprinted in the 22 May 1975 English edition of L'Osservatore Romano.

4   Magda Denes. "Performing Abortions." Commentary Magazine, October 1976, pp. 33-37. Also see the "Letters" sections in the December, 1976 and February, 1977 issues of Commentary Magazine.

5   Norman Mailer on the David Frost Show. Quoted in "Norman Mailer Speaks Out on Sex and AIDS." American Family Association Journal, March 1992, p. 3.

6   Virginia Ramey Mollenkott. "Respecting the Moral Agency of Women." "Educational Pamphlet" by the 'Religious' Coalition for Abortion Rights.

7   "Abortion Clinic Staff Worker Gives Her Excuses." Life Advocate (publication of Advocates for Life Ministries, Portland, Oregon), April 1992, p. 21.

8   "Judge in Virginia Trespass Case Acknowledges "State-Sanctioned Killing."" ALL News, 25 April 1986, p. 3.

79. What Are the Primary Milestones in Fetal Development?

"Biography" of the Preborn Child

The biography of the preborn child from beginning until birth is shown in Table 7, counting from the day of fertilization. See also the Color Pull-Out Section depicting the development of the preborn child at the end of this Chapter.

Question 47 describes the differences between fetal (fertilization) age and gestational (menstrual) age.

Question 38 describes the critical difference between fertilization and implantation (nidation), and discusses why pro-abortionists are redefining conception from the traditional union of sperm and egg to implantation instead.

"Embryo," "Fetus" and "Contents of the Uterus"

Traditionally, medicine has called the preborn child, from fertilization until about eight weeks, an "embryo," and thereafter, until birth, a "fetus." The embryo or fetus, when taken together with the placenta and umbilical cord, is referred to as the "contents of the uterus."

Until the mid-1960's, "embryo" and "fetus" were purely medical terms, which most physicians used interchangeably with "unborn child." However, since about 1965, the medical profession and pro-abortionists have studiously used only the terms "embryo," "fetus," and "contents of the uterus," not in the interest of scientific accuracy, but in order to dehumanize the preborn child.

"Pre-Embryo"

The term "pre-embryo" simply did not exist until the mid-1980's. In 1986, the Ethics Committee of the American Fertility Society (AFS) chose "pre-embryo" to cover the 14-day period beginning at fertilization. Their rationale was that, at about 14 days, the preborn child develops a "primitive streak," the precursor to a completed spinal column.[1]

The term "pre-embryo" has absolutely no grounding in medical science. It is nothing more than an attempt to downgrade very early preborn children to an infe-

Table 7

Milestones
in the Development of the Preborn Child

Fertilization The father's sperm penetrates the mother's egg. Genetic instructions from both combine to form a unique new individual life, barely visible to the human eye.

1-4 Days *Taber's Cyclopedic Medical Dictionary* gives us the terminology of the first few days of the new human being's development: **"Following fertilization, cells multiply (cleavage) which results in formation of a morula, which in turn develops into a blastocyst consisting of a trophoblast and inner cell mass. Two cavities (amniotic cavity and yolk sac) arise within the inner cell mass. These are separated by the embryonic disk which gives rise to the three germ layers (ectoderm, mesoderm, and endoderm), these developing into the embryo proper. The blastocyst wall or trophoblast gives rise to auxiliary structures. The zygote enters the uterus and implantation occurs."[2]**

5-9 Days Implantation in the uterus. Of the 45 total generations of cell replication that will take place by mature adulthood, eight have already taken place. The blastocyst now consists of about 256 cells.

14 Days Chemical signals emitted by her own child suppress the mother's menstrual period. The baby's first completed brain cells appear.

20 Days The baby's heart is in the advanced stages of formation. His eyes begin to form, and his brain, spinal column, and nervous system are virtually complete.

24 Days THE BABY'S HEART BEGINS TO BEAT.

28 Days The baby's muscles are developing, and his arm and leg buds are visible. The baby's first neocortal cells appear. The child has grown in size by a factor of 10,000. Blood flows in the baby's veins, separate from the mother's blood.

35 Days The baby's pituitary gland is forming, and his mouth, ears, and nose are taking shape.

42 Days The baby's cartilage skeleton is completely formed and ossification begins. His umbilical cord has developed. The baby's brain coordinates movement of muscles and the involuntary movement of organs. Reflex responses are present.

43 Days THE BABY'S BRAIN WAVES CAN BE RECORDED.

45 Days Spontaneous, voluntary body movements have begun. Milk teeth buds present.

7 Weeks The baby's lips are sensitive to touch, and his ears resemble his family's pattern. The first fully developed neurons (nerve cells) appear on the top of the spinal cord, beginning construction of the brain stem. This portion of the brain regulates vital functions such as breathing, the heartbeat, and blood pressure.

Table 7 (continued)

8 Weeks Baby is well-proportioned, about $1^1/_2$ inches long and 1/25 of an ounce in weight. All organs are present, complete and functioning (except the lungs). Heart beats sturdily. Stomach produces digestive juices. Liver makes blood cells. Kidneys are functioning. The stomach secretes gastric juices. Taste buds are forming. Fingerprints have been engraved. Eyelids and the palms of the hands are sensitive to touch. A tapping stimulus on the amniotic sac leads the baby to move his arms. Of the 45 total generations of cell replication that will take place by mature adulthood, fully two-thirds (30) have already taken place. The baby now has about one billion cells. He also contains more genetic information than every word communicated by every human being who has ever lived since the beginning of the race.

9 Weeks The child will bend his fingers around an object placed in his palm. His fingernails are forming, and he sucks his thumbs.

10 Weeks All sections of the baby's body are sensitive to touch. He swallows, squints, frowns and puckers up his brow. If his palm is stroked, he will make a tight fist.

11 Weeks Baby urinates and makes all facial expressions, including smiling. He is now breathing amniotic fluid steadily and will do so until birth. Fingernails and toenails are now present. Taste buds are now working. The baby will drink more amniotic fluid if it is sweetened, and less if it is given a bitter taste.

12 Weeks: Vigorous activity shows the baby's distinct personality; baby's sleep patterns differ, some hiccup constantly, others cry. Baby can kick, turn over, curl and fan toes, make a fist, move thumbs, open mouth and press lips tightly together. Baby practices breathing.

13 Weeks: Facial expressions resemble those of parents. Movements are vigorous and graceful. Vocal chords are present, and, in rare cases when air enters the uterus temporarily, people have heard the baby crying. External sex organs are present, and the baby's sex can be determined. Auditory sense is now present.

4 Months: Baby can grasp with hands, swim and turn somersaults. Mother may first feel baby's movements. Rapid eye movements (REM), which indicate dreaming, can now be recorded. A very bright light shined on the mother's abdomen will cause the baby to slowly move his arms to cover his eyes. Very loud music will cause him to cover his ears with his hands. Connections between the neocortex and the muscles they control are beginning to appear.

5 Months: A loud sound such as a slammed door may startle the child. Baby responds to sounds that are of frequencies that exceed adult's range in both directions. Baby may be soothed to sleep by gentle music.

6 Months: Most babies are viable at this point (26 weeks—about 60 percent of full gestation). Fine hair grows on head and eyebrows. Tiny eyelashes appear.

Table 7 (continued)	
7 Months:	The baby's weight increases to more than one kilogram (2.2 pounds). The baby's eyeteeth are now present. His eyes open and close and explore his surroundings. His hands can support his entire weight at this time. Baby recognizes his or her mother's voice. Of the 45 total generations of cell replication that will take place by mature adulthood, 38 have already taken place. The baby now has about 300 billion cells.
8 Months:	The baby's weight increases to more than two kilograms (4.4 pounds), and his quarters become cramped. If born now, the baby has more than a 90 percent chance of surviving and being entirely healthy.
9 Months:	In the final six weeks of gestation, the baby gains about an ounce of weight per day. Hormones released by the child trigger labor. The lightest baby ever born to survive healthily weighed 10 ounces. Of the 45 total generations of cell replication that will take place by mature adulthood, 41 have already taken place. At birth, the baby has about two trillion (2,000,000,000,000) cells. The remaining four generations of cell replication will occupy all of the person's childhood and young adulthood. This means that, in developmental terms, we spend **90 percent** of our lives *in utero*.

rior class. Pro-abortionists see this as necessary for several reasons: (1) they may experiment upon "pre-embryos" with impunity; (2) they may dispose of "pre-embryos" after unsuccessful attempts at *in-vitro* fertilization (IVF) or other types of assisted reproduction; (3) they may kill "pre-embryos" with abortifacients such as intrauterine devices (IUDs), oral contraceptives, Depo-Provera, Norplant, and so-called "emergency contraceptives;" and (4) they can use "pre-embryo" as another rationalization to further protect and promote abortion.

1 Bernard Nathanson, M.D. "Of Pre-Embryos and Bourbon Kings." *ALL about Issues*, August-September 1991, pp. 19-21.

2 *Taber's Cyclopedic Medical Dictionary*. New York: Eliot Books, 1983.

··

80. At What Point Does the Preborn Child Begin to Feel Pain?

Fetal Pain: An Irrelevant Question to Pro-Abortionists

The subject of fetal pain often comes up in debates on abortion.

Pro-life debaters must remember one essential point: the topic of fetal pain is *absolutely irrelevant* to pro-abortionists.

Like discussions about fetal humanity, personhood and ensoulment and whether or not abortion is condemned in Scripture, arguments over fetal pain are simply a distraction from the fundamental points. Does anyone really believe that, if someone conclusively proved that preborn babies felt pain during abortions, that pro-

Table 8

Average Fetal Weight and Length
by Gestational Age[a]

Week of Gestation	Fetal Weight Grams	Fetal Weight Lbs-Oz	Fetal Length, Inches	Week of Gestation	Fetal Weight Grams	Fetal Weight Lbs-Oz	Fetal Length, Inches
8	1	0-1/25	1-1/2	25	700	1-9	12-1/2
9	2	0-1/12	2-0	26	800	1-12	13-0
10	4	0-1/6	2-1/2	27	900	2-0	13-1/2
11	7	0-1/3	3-0	28	1,000	2-3	14-0
12	14	0-1/2	3-1/2	29	1,175	2-9	14-1/2
13	25	0-1	4-1/4	30	1,350	3-0	15-0
14	45	0-2	5-0	31	1,500	3-5	15-1/2
15	70	0-3	5-3/4	32	1,675	3-11	16-0
16	100	0-4	6-1/2	33	1,825	4-0	16-1/2
17	140	0-5	7-1/4	34	2,000	4-6	17-0
18	190	0-7	8-0	35	2,160	4-12	17-1/2
19	240	0-8	9-0	36	2,340	5-3	18-0
20	300	0-11	10-0	37	2,500	5-8	18-1/2
21	360	0-13	10-1/2	38	2,775	6-2	19-0
22	430	0-15	11-0	39	3,000	6-10	19-1/2
23	500	1-2	11-1/2	40	3,250	7-3	20-0
24	600	1-5	12-0				

a   Enfamil reference disc, "Fetal Dimensions."

abortionists would suddenly change their minds?

Of course not! They would simply move the focus of their abortion rationalization to some obscure metaphysical point. One abortionist demonstrated this tactic when he said: "This [fetal pain] is a big concern. After all, it *is* a dismembered body. In all of the choice movement, there is a balance between the fetus and the woman. And between my experience with a saline abortion where I suffered, vs. the option of a D&E where yes, the fetus may suffer, I always choose the woman."[1]

Another abortionist, when asked, "Doctor, what does the aborted baby feel while it's dying?," answered "Oh, I think that depends on your philosophy."[2]

The pro-abortionist's usual response to the issue of fetal pain is identical to his approach to the question of whether the baby is alive: "We really don't *know* when pain begins!" What he is actually saying about the agony of preborn children is this: "We really don't *care* when pain begins!"

This typical view is held by Anne-Marie Keary, head of Britain's National Abortion Campaign, who said: "Pain is a factor in life; could an element of pain be a justification for no more abortions? I don't think so."[3]

Mercy for All but the Preborn Child

It is curious indeed that our society goes to extraordinary lengths to spare *animals* unnecessary pain, but can't be bothered to give preborn babies even the mercy of a painless death.

Perhaps this is understandable in light of abortion's status as a "super-right" that overpowers all other rights by brute force, including the rights to life, due process and free speech.

All states have laws meant to protect animals from unnecessary pain, discomfort and fear. For example, the 1967 California Agricultural Code mandates that cattle be rendered insensible by any "rapid and effective" means before being "cut, shackled, hoisted, thrown or cast." Animals being slaughtered must be rendered unconscious by "the simultaneous and instantaneous severance of the carotid arteries with a sharp instrument."

The California Penal Code requires painless means of euthanasia for stray and other animals. If a carbon monoxide or nitrogen chamber is used, the animal's death, which must not take more than 60 seconds, must be carefully monitored. No newborn cat or dog may be killed by any method other than painless drugs, chloroform, gasses or decompression.[4] Yet people force handicapped newborn *humans*, such as Baby Doe of Bloomington, Indiana, to die an agonizing death over a period of days or even *weeks* from starvation and thirst.

In 1982, Congress voted 260-140 to prohibit the National Institutes of Health (NIH) from funding experimentation on preborn or aborted babies. Extremist proabortion Congressman Henry Waxman (D.-Ca.) opposed this amendment bitterly, calling it an "ideological statement," even though he had earlier championed an amendment to protect *laboratory animals* from, "... more than momentary minor pain or discomfort."[5]

When Does Fetal Pain Begin?

The Experts Speak. The world's leading authorities on fetal pain have voiced opinions on the point at which fetal pain begins.

Dr. Vincent J. Collins, professor of anesthesiology at Northwestern University and the University of Illinois Medical Center, is a recognized world authority on pain. In his opinion, fetal pain responses begin by $13^1/_2$ weeks gestation *at the latest*, and probably as early as eight weeks, based upon the development of the preborn baby's nervous system.

Myelinization (development of nerve-sheath insulation) occurs long before birth. These myelinized fibers can transmit pain impulses to the spinal cord and from there to the brain, and nerve tracts *do not* have to be complete in order to function competently.

Several other studies have confirmed Dr. Collins' findings.[6]

Biologists have known since 1968 that the preborn child's sensory pain transmitters are complete by 14 weeks. By then, the cerebral cortex is about 30% to 40% complete, sufficient to allow the child's pain transmitters and receptors to function quite efficiently.[7]

It is interesting to follow the development of those sensory entities that transmit pain in the preborn child. The pro-abortion assumption that pain cannot occur until the nervous system is *complete* is obviously fallacious.

By **Day 56 (8 weeks)**, the preborn child uses his nervous system to move and float freely in the uterus. He would have no reason to move other than to make himself more comfortable.

By **Day 60 (9 weeks)**, the preborn child has spinal reflexes. This means that tactile (touching-type) stimulation will cause a response.

By **Day 77 (11 weeks)**, the preborn child is sensitive to touch in the genital region. The baby begins to swallow, and the rate of fluid intake will vary depending upon the sweetness of the amniotic fluid (which can be harmlessly manipulated by injection). His palms and footpads are extremely sensitive to touch. His eyelids will squint in order to exclude bright light. The cerebral cortex is 30 to 40 percent developed by 12 to 16 weeks. A. William Liley, the "Father of Modern Fetology," and a U.S. researcher, Mortimer Rosen, have confirmed that the baby's response to pain is at least proportional to this amount.[8]

By **Day 100 (14 weeks)**, the "general sense organs" begin to differentiate. These organs are described as "free nerve terminations [which respond to pain, temperature and chemicals], lamelated corpuscles [responding to pointed pressure], tactile corpuscles, neuromuscular spindles, and neurotendinous end organs [which respond to light and pointed pressure]."[9]

Reinis and Goldman, in their authoritative textbook *The Development of the Brain*, state: "[Preborn] lip tactile response may be evoked by the end of the seventh week. By 10.5 weeks, the palms of the hands are responsive to light stroking with a hair, and at 11 weeks, the face and all parts of the upper and lower extremities are sensitive to touch. By 13.5 to 14.5 weeks, the entire body surface, except for the back and the top of the head, are sensitive to pain."[10]

In summary, there is no known "triggering process" that causes the nervous system to start up at birth. The nervous system is functioning long before birth. A statement signed by 26 physicians, including two past presidents of the American College of Obstetrics and Gynecology (ACOG), wrote:

> Over the last 18 years, real time ultrasonography, fetoscopy, study of the fetal EKG and EEG have demonstrated the remarkable responsiveness of the human fetus to pain, touch and sound ... The ability to feel pain and respond to it is clearly not a phenomenon that develops *de facto* at birth. Indeed, much of enlightened modern obstetrical practice and procedure seeks to minimize sensory deprivation of and sensory insult to the fetus during, at, and after birth.[11]

The Abortionists Speak. Perhaps the most chilling philosophy of all is that of those people who can accurately and very eloquently describe the agony of preborn children in their death throes—and then continue to kill them and support their killing.

Abortionist John Szenes shows us what happens during a "salting-out" abortion: "All of a sudden one noticed that at the time of the saline infusion there was a lot of activity in the uterus. That's not fluid currents. That's obviously the fetus being distressed by swallowing the concentrated salt solution and kicking violently and that's, to all intents and purposes, the death trauma."[12]

And Magda Denes, who supports prenatal killing, seems to have completely separated herself emotionally from her poignant description of one of the victims:

> I look inside the bucket in front of me. There is a small naked person in there floating in a bloody liquid—plainly the tragic victim of a drowning accident. But then perhaps this was no accident, because the body is purple with bruises and the face has the agonized tautness of one forced to die too soon. I have seen this face before, on a Russian soldier lying on a frozen snow-covered hill, stiff with death and cold....[13]

If a pro-life activist gets into a debate about fetal pain with a pro-abortionist, he should quote some of the statements above by recognized experts in fetal physiology, then challenge his opponent to produce statements by *other* experts stating that preborn babies *cannot* feel pain.

1   Massachusetts abortion mill employee, quoted in Diane M. Gianelli. "Abortion Providers Share Inner Conflicts." *American Medical News*, 12 July 1993, pp. 5-7.

2   Interview of abortionist Michael Ballard by Mike Levy. *Triumph* Magazine, March 1972, pp. 20-23 and 44. Quoted in Donald DeMarco. *Abortion in Perspective*. Hayes Publishing Company, 1974.

3   Sue Brattle. "Can a Foetus Feel Pain?" London *Daily Express*, 6 August 1996, pp. 25-26.

4   California Penal Code. 597v (kittens), 597w (cats), and 19501 (cattle).

5   Henry Waxman, quoted by Paul Fisher. "House Bans Fetal Experimentation." *The Wanderer*, 14 October 1982, p. 1.

6   Mortimer G. Rosen, Professor of Reproductive Biology at Case Western Reserve University. "The Secret Brain: Learning Before Birth." *Harpers* Magazine, April, 1978, p. 46.

7   Geoffrey S. Dawes. *Fetal and Neonatal Physiology*. Chicago: Yearbook Medical Publishers, 1968, p. 126.

8   A. William Liley. "Experiments with Uterine and Fetal Experimentation." *Australia and New Zealand Journal of Psychiatry*, 6:99, 1972. Also see Mortimer Rosen. "The Secret Brain: Learning Before Birth." *Harper's*, April 1978, p. 46.

9   John T. Noonan, Jr. "The Experience of Pain By the Unborn." *Human Life Review*, Fall 1981, pp. 7-19, and Spring 1984, pp. 105-115.

10   S. Reinis and J.M. Goldman, *The Development of the Brain*. Springfield, Illinois: Charles C. Thomas Publishers, 1980, p. 12.

11   Response to attacks on President Ronald Reagan's address on fetal pain to the National Religious Broadcasters Convention on 30 January 1984.

12   Magda Denes. "Performing Abortions." *Commentary*, October, 1976, pp. 33-37.

....

81. When Do Preborn Babies Become Viable?

The Definition of Viability

Viability means "being able to maintain an independent existence; able to live after birth."[1] *Roe v. Wade* defined viability as when a baby is "... potentially able to live outside the mother's womb, albeit with artificial help." The Court then set an arbitrary viability limit of 30 weeks. The justices were already outdated in their thinking, because the median fetal age of viability in the United States (i.e., a 50 percent survival rate) was 33.7 weeks in 1950, 30.4 weeks in 1960, 28.5 weeks in 1970, 27.1 weeks in 1980, and 25.5 weeks in 1990.[2] In light of this evidence, the Supreme Court's *Planned Parenthood v. Danforth* decision redefined viability as "... that state of fetal development when the life of the unborn child may be continued indefinitely outside of the womb by natural or life-support systems."

Lowering the Limits on Viability

In 1950, a baby born at 30 weeks' gestation had only a slim chance of living. The birth and survival of a "kilogram kid" (a premature baby born at 2.2 pounds) was big news indeed. Now, however, the limits have come down dramatically; researchers estimate that *more than 300* children weighing *less than one pound* have been born in this country, and most of them are living perfectly healthy and normal lives.

The smallest baby on record who has ever survived is Katy Masner, born at 11 ounces and 22 weeks' gestation in July 1991.[3]

What Does It Matter?

Pro-life activists should know by now that the status of preborn babies as living beings, as human, as persons or as developed babies is utterly irrelevant to pro-abortionists. All that matters to them is being allowed to continue to commit their baby killings undisturbed by anyone else.

The following pro-abortion quotes show that viability is not important to those who kill the babies—only the ability to divert attention is.

Writer Nancy Rhoden says: "The compromise forged in *Roe v. Wade* was, and can remain, an acceptable one. But it can do so only if the Court recognizes, when it becomes necessary, the limited ethical relevance of fetal viability."[4]

Janet Benshoof of the American Civil Liberties Union (ACLU) wrote:

The increasing tendency to view the fetus as an independent patient or person occurs at the cost of reducing the woman to the status of little more than a maternal environment.... We need to refocus the right to abortion as one not defined by the fetus or by technological advances, but rather one that is tied to women's constitutional right to privacy, autonomy and bodily integrity.[4]

Another ACLU writer stated: "... the moral premise of abortion remains unchanged. The 'issue of abortion' remains the issue of the right of the woman to choose whether or not to carry something in her own body. No technological advances can rob her of her right to choose whether or not to keep it there."[5]

Judith Hole and Ellen Levine's book *Rebirth of Feminism* neatly summarizes the radical feminist's attitude towards third-trimester abortions:

... any woman who wishes to terminate a late pregnancy undoubtedly has a very good reason and should have the right to do so. In addition, they argue that the concepts of "quickening" and "viability" are based on religious doctrine and ancient myths about when "life" begins. Any woman who believes in them will not seek an abortion beyond the time dictated by her beliefs. All women, however, should not be required to follow one doctrine.[6]

Note carefully that pro-abortionists baldly state that viability is irrelevant, and they even write off the very *concept* of viability (a hard medical definition) as an "ancient myth."

The greatest weapon in the pro-life arsenal is not the photographs of mangled, aborted, late-term preborn babies—although these are still very powerful and necessary.

Figure 17

Abortion is legal in the United States right up until the moment of birth. Gianna Jessen is a rare survivor of one of the thousands of third-trimester abortions committed in the United States every year.

The greatest persuaders the pro-life movement has are the beautiful, full-color photos of preborn babies floating peacefully in their mothers' wombs.

The abortionists know this. They snivel about "shocking anti-choice propaganda featuring aborted fetuses," but they also fanatically oppose the public display of any image of *living* preborn babies.

There is a very good reason for this apparent hypocrisy: pro-abortionists so fear the public seeing the truth about fetal development that they will go to almost any length to obscure or censor the truth.

For example, a debating manual issued by the National Abortion and Reproductive Rights Action League (NARRAL), "Organizing for Action," states: "Another set of questions involves the opposition. Has your audience seen anti-abortion propaganda? Are you debating a Right-to-Lifer? Is the opposition bringing slides or pictures? Try to insist that they not be allowed to.... Find out if your opposition is bringing audio-visuals. Try to insist that you will only speak if they do not."[7]

This is a common theme in pro-abortion publications. Another example of this attempt to dodge plain fact is in abortionist Warren Hern's book *Abortion Practice*:

Television interviews, in particular, should focus on the public issue involved (right to confidential and professional medical care, freedom of choice, and so forth) and not on the specific details of the abortion procedures.... In Colorado, the pro-choice community has decided after some period of disagreement and discussion to refuse all invitations to debate ... we respond to all requests from schools for educational presentations concerning abortion. If the sponsors want both sides presented, however, the presentations must be made on different occasions. We insist that visual aid materials not be presented by either side.[8]

1   Miller and Keane. *Encyclopedia and Dictionary of Medicine, Nursing and Allied Health* (Third Edition). Philadelphia: W.B. Saunders Company, 1983.

2   B. Ferrera, R. Hoekstra, E. Graziano, G. Knox, R. Couser, and J. Fangman. "Changing Outcome of Extremely Premature Infants (<26 Weeks Gestation and <750 Grams: Survival and Follow-Up at a Tertiary Center." *American Journal of Obstetrics and Gynecology*, 1989:161, pp. 1114-1118. This article is analyzed in the January 1990 issue of the *Bernadell Technical Bulletin*, p. 5.

3   *The Kansas City Star*, 5 November 1991.

4   "Late Abortion and Technological Advances in Fetal Viability." Nancy K. Rhoden, "Some Legal Considerations," and Janet Benshoof, "Reasserting Women's Rights." *Family Planning Perspectives*, July/August 1985, pp. 160-163.

5   "Worth Quoting." *National Right to Life News*, 3 February 1983, p. 19.

6   Abortionist Howard I. Diamond of Beth Israel Medical Center. Quoted in Norma Rosen. "Between Guilt and Gratification: Abortion Doctors Reveal Their Feelings." *New York Times Magazine*, 17 April 1977, p. 78.

7   Looseleaf booklet titled "Organizing for Action." Prepared by Vicki Z. Kaplan for the National Abortion Rights Action League (now NARRAL), no date.

8   Warren Hern, M.D. *Abortion Practice*. New York: J.B. Lippincott Company, 1984, p. 323.

The Facts of Life

The Miracle of Life

**Drawings and Photos
Showing the Development
of the Preborn Child**

Chapter 7

Are There "Exceptions" for Abortion?

82. What Are the Advantages and Disadvantages of the "Realistic" and "Full Protection" Pro-Life Views of Abortion Law Exceptions?

The Overall Strategies

Overview. Pro-life groups and individuals advocate two overall strategies: the "pragmatic" (also called "practical" or "realistic") and the "full protection" (also called "absolutist," "purist" or "no exceptions") approaches.

The "Pragmatic" Strategy. Currently, the more popular of these two strategies is the "pragmatic" approach, which asserts that pro-life activists should work for whatever protective laws they can get passed in light of prevailing local conditions. In a liberal state, the best that pro-lifers think they can do is pass a parental notification law, work for stricter state regulation of abortion mills, end public abortion funding, or enact humane fetal disposal laws. This strategy assumes all abortions are bad, but that it may be possible to save *some* babies with a partial abortion ban or with stricter clinic regulations.

The main advantage of the "pragmatic" strategy is obvious. The abortion industry can only work at peak efficiency if there are absolutely no restrictions on it. *Any* restriction or regulation of abortion centers by the State will increase costs and decrease profits. In the short run, since most abortionists are motivated by money, this saves preborn children.

Another important advantage of "pragmatic" activism is that it is more likely to bring short-term victories that keep individuals and organizations motivated. Unfortunately, many pro-lifers have been infected with the "win or else" mentality, so they become lax and unmotivated if they cannot immediately see the fruits of their labors. This is why 80 to 90 percent of new pro-life activists "burn out" within one year. It is the rare person who can doggedly carry on for years in the face of a long string of defeats, or who can continue working without actually seeing babies saved as the result of his work. Almost everyone needs an occasional victory to boost morale.

Advocates of the "pragmatic" strategy point out that a total ban on abortions in the United States and most other Western countries is simply out of the question under current conditions. Even if such a law were passed by a legislature or enacted by popular vote, it would inevitably be struck down by the courts. "Pragmatists" assert that it is far more likely that abortion will ultimately be banned by an "incrementalist" strategy that takes one small step at a time.

The main disadvantage of the "pragmatic" strategy is subtle but extremely important. If pro-lifers give the impression that they are simply working with the State to regulate baby-killing, the credibility of the movement will be destroyed or irreparably damaged. Since pro-lifers claim that all babies are equally valuable, they may appear to be hypocritical to try to save some while apparently abandoning others.

This is a misperception that pro-abortion groups emphasize for propaganda purposes. For example, the pro-abortion front group 'Religious' Coalition for Reproductive Choice (formerly RCAR) says: "Opponents of abortion rights walk a fine line within their own movement when they condone any abortion. Based on their own definition, they are guilty of being accessories to 'murder' in certain circumstances by accepting rape and incest exceptions."[1]

Any intelligent person can see the fallacy of this kind of thinking. One useful analogy is the "sinking ocean liner": If hundreds of people are in danger of drowning and all you have is a six-person life raft, the right thing to do is to save a handful of people. RCAR would have the public think this means the rescuers "condoned" the drowning of all of the other people and were therefore accessories to their deaths, which is obviously illogical. RCAR's propaganda is obviously aimed at trying to goad pro-lifers into formulating and supporting legislation that could not possibly stand a court challenge.

The "Full Protection" Strategy

The second strategy is the "full protection" approach, which works toward a complete ban on all abortions without compromise. "Full protection" pro-life activists refuse to willingly yield any preborn children to the abortionist's knife.

The most crucial advantage to this strategy is that it is consistent in holding that every preborn life is equally precious. In the long run, the public will perceive the pro-life movement as having greater integrity. This steadfast and absolute adherence to the sanctity of life in all cases may indeed lead to ultimate victory.

However, the strategy's main disadvantage is that its adherents must be willing to suffer a long string of defeats, with few preborn children being saved in the interim.

Another point is central to the debate between "pragmatic" and "full protection" pro-lifers. Even if a Paramount Human Life Amendment (HLA) were passed by Congress and withstood court challenges, abortions would continue by the hundreds of thousands each year. As described in Question 13, feminists have vowed to set up "underground railroads" and "menstrual extraction" clinics in order to bypass any law that protects preborn children. History has also shown us that illegal abortionists operated in plush offices with the full knowledge of police for decades before *Roe v. Wade*. All over the world, police, district attorneys, judges and juries allow "illegal" abortion mills to operate with impunity. What evidence do we have that the situation would be different after abortion is criminalized?

What Is the Answer?

Both "realistic" and "full protection" pro-lifers see every baby as equally precious in the sight of God. Contrary to what pro-abortionists say, trying to save some babies does not imply abandoning others.

Evangelium Vitae (73,90) teaches:

> ... when it is not possible to overturn or completely abrogate a pro-abortion law, an elected official, whose absolute personal opposition to procured abortion was well known, could licitly support proposals aimed at *limiting the harm done* by such a law and at lessening its negative consequences at the level of general opinion and public morality. This does not in fact represent an illicit cooperation with an unjust law, but rather a legitimate and proper attempt to limit its evil aspects ... the Church encourages political leaders, starting with those who are Christians, not to give in, but to make those choices which, taking into account what is realistically attainable, will lead to the re-establishment of a just order in the defense and promotion of the value of life.... Here it must be noted that it is not enough to remove unjust laws. The underlying causes of attacks on life have to be eliminated, especially by ensuring proper support for families and motherhood. A family policy must be the basis and driving force of all social policies.

This passage strongly implies that it is not immoral to work for laws that limit or regulate abortion, *as long as pro-lifers make it perfectly clear that they value every human life and that they will never stop working until every last abortion is stopped.*

The Bottom Line

Evangelium Vitae recognizes that it will be impossible to ban abortion by either the absolutist or the realistic strategy until the family has been strengthened and has regained its proper place as the "sanctuary of life" in society.

As long as a society accepts the anti-life mentality, trying to ban abortion is like trying to empty the ocean with a child's plastic bucket. Pro-abortionists are correct in only one aspect of their thinking: no one can legislate morality. Changing the laws may help greatly, but is not the final answer to the slaughter of preborn children.

The ultimate answer to the killing is to convert the hearts and minds of each person in society. By working to strengthen church and family, pro-lifers will eventually rise up and gain control of the courts, the legislatures, the media, the professions and the schools.

Only then will every preborn child be safe.

Until this happens, every pro-life activist should memorize 1 Corinthians 15:58, which tells us: "Never give in then, my dear brothers, never admit defeat; keep on working at the Lord's work always, knowing that, in the Lord, you cannot be laboring in vain."

Just as importantly, "pragmatic" and "full protection" pro-lifers should not impugn each other's motives, but should instead work together for life and support each other's efforts. Pro-lifers who squabble over technique and theory waste precious energy and time. The answer to the abortion holocaust is for "pragmatic" pro-lifers to work at saving preborn babies who are in danger *now*, and for "full protection" pro-lifers to work at saving preborn babies who have not yet been conceived.

1 'Religious' Coalition for Abortion Rights. Booklet entitled "Words of Choice." 1991, Washington, D.C., p. 24.

....

83. What Are the Basic Arguments Against "Hard-Case" Abortions?

Introduction
We can make three fundamental logical arguments against all "hard-case" abortions.

(1) The first is purely practical: the true "hard-cases" (life of the mother, rape and incest and fetal defects) are extremely rare, as described below.

(2) Pro-abortionists use *any* law that allows hard-case abortions to gain and maintain abortion on demand.

(3) Finally, handicapped preborn babies, and those conceived through rape and incest, are just as worthy of protection as all other preborn babies.

The following paragraphs expand upon these arguments.

(1) The Rarity of the "Hard-Cases"
People commonly overestimate the probabilities of very rare catastrophic events such as earthquakes and airplane crashes. People also tend to grossly overestimate the number of abortions committed for the classic "hard-cases" of rape and incest, eugenics and the life and health of the mother.

Table 9 shows that all "hard-cases" *combined* make up only about 0.68 percent of all abortions committed in the United States today (about one out of every 150 abortions). This means 99.32 percent of all abortions are committed basically because the mothers think that a child would adversely impact their lifestyles (see Chapter 13 for the detailed references and calculations that back up these statistics).

According to the pro-abortion publication, *Family Planning Perspectives*, the 10 most common reasons that women have abortions are: concerns about how a baby would change their lives; financial considerations; relationship problems; a desire to avoid single parenthood; a desire to conceal fornication; a feeling of not being ready for the responsibility; feelings of immaturity; a feeling that they have enough children already; pressure from husband or boyfriend; and potential genetic problems for the baby.[1]

Table 9

Numerical Summary
of "Hard-Case" Abortions

	Number	Percent
Average Annual Abortions, 1980-1996	1,558,000	100.00%
The "Hard-Cases"		
To save the mother's life or health	5,610	0.36%
For rape and incest	1,270	0.08%
For fetal birth defects	3,750	0.24%
Total "hard-cases"	10,630	0.68%
"Preservation of Lifestyle" Abortions	1,547,370	99.32%

(2) "Hard-Cases": Wedge for Abortion on Demand

In *every one* of the 56 countries that now have abortion on demand, the first step the pro-abortion forces took was intense lobbying for abortion in the so-called "hard-cases"—the mother's life and health, fetal deformity (eugenics) and/or rape and incest.

Any lawyer will tell you "hard-cases make bad law," but this principle has not stopped pro-abortionists all over the world from using the classic "hard-cases" to introduce first contraception and sterilization, then abortion, then infanticide, and finally euthanasia.

Once the pro-abortionists secure abortion for the any of the "hard-cases," they point out the "inconsistency" in the laws in order to justify abortion on demand.

As Question 84 describes, abortionists expand even a life-of-the-mother exception to mean abortion-on-demand in practice since, according to the pro-abortion mentality, *all* "unwanted pregnancies" threaten the life of the mother.

(3) A Preborn Child Is Created in the Image of God

According to Jeremiah 1:5, God tells us: "Before I formed you in the womb I knew you; before you came to birth I consecrated you." The Psalmist (139) tells us: "It was You who created my inmost self, and put me together in my mother's womb; for all these mysteries I thank You: for the wonder of myself, for the wonder of Your works."

A child conceived by incest or rape, or a child with a birth defect, is still a child—no matter how violent the crime that led to his existence or how serious his disability. We poor human beings, with our limited intelligence and vision, cannot even *begin* to perceive the intricacies of God's plans for our *own* lives, let alone His intentions for a child who has not even been *born* yet.

It is God Himself, and God alone, who confers value upon a human being. People often say we are created in His image—and misunderstand this phrase to mean His *physical* image. But our chief similarities to God lie not in our physical resemblance to Him, but in our *spiritual* likeness to Him.[2] In this way and no other are we all truly equal in the sight of God. And because we are created in His *spiritual* image, abortion, in a very real sense, amounts to an attack on God Himself.

The Great Commandment is to love one another as God has loved us. Abortion is never an act committed in love, despite what some pro-abortion propagandists tell us. As described above, the main motivations behind abortion are shame, guilt and a desire for a more comfortable lifestyle.

Figure 18

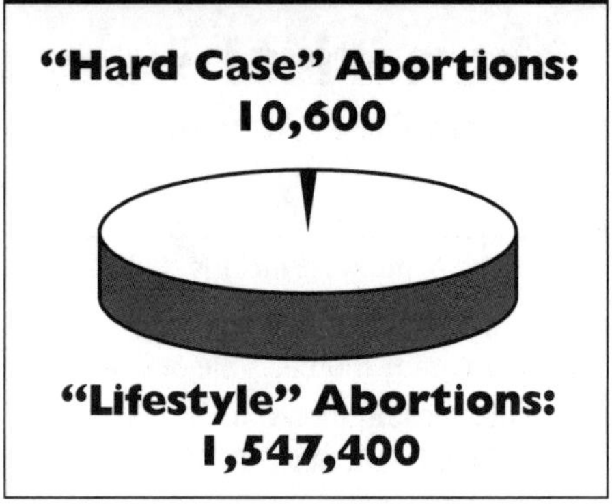

"Hard Case" Abortions: 10,600

"Lifestyle" Abortions: 1,547,400

This pie chart shows the relative numbers of "hard-case" and "lifestyle" abortions committed in the United States each year.

Handicapped children and those conceived by rape and incest present us with a difficult problem. Society's answer to this problem will decide whether we truly reflect the glory of God in our spiritual selves. If we welcome the child who is "less than perfect," in either his appearance or his abilities or the circumstances of his beginning, then we are truly a human—and godly—people. If we reject the child in our midst, we are rejecting God's gift to us, and therefore God Himself.

1 Aida Torres and Jacqueline Darroch Forrest. "Why Do Women Have Abortions?" *Family Planning Perspectives*, July/August, 1988, pp. 169-176.

2 Father Thomas L. Kinkead. *Baltimore Catechism* No. 4, 1891. Chapter 1, "On the End of Man," Question 4.

84. How Common Are Abortions Committed in Order to Preserve the Life or Health of the Mother?

The Two-Step Strategy

Throughout the past 30 years, pro-abortionists have used a time-tested two-step strategy for imposing abortion on demand in nearly 60 countries all over the world.

The first step in the grand scheme is to legalize abortion for the "hard-cases" of the life of the mother, fetal abnormalities, rape and incest. Once a country legalizes abortion for *any* reason, pro-abortionists find that it is always much easier to impose abortion-on-demand. So, the second step is usually to legalize abortion "for the mother's health"—which, in practice, is exactly the same as abortion-on-demand.

Pro-Lifers Must Oppose "Health-of-the-Mother" Exceptions

Introduction. At first glance, it may seem callous for anyone to oppose abortions committed in order to preserve the physical or mental health of women. However, we must remember that abortionists will interpret *any* loophole—even a "life-of-the-mother" exception—to mean abortion-on-demand.

The Practical Applications. Abortionists all over the world use the definition of "maternal health" set by the World Health Organization (WHO): "A state of complete physical, mental, and social well being and not merely the absence of disease or infirmity."[1]

The U.S. Supreme Court defined maternal health to include "mental health" in its *United States v. Vuitch* decision (402 U.S. 62, 71-72 (1971)), and expanded this to say that virtually *all* factors of any type are relevant to the mother's health, including "physical, emotional, psychological, familial, and the woman's age" (*Doe v. Bolton*, 410 U.S. 179, 192 [1973]).

Most abortionists take these definitions at face value. Abortionist Warren Hern states: "It appears that 'unwantedness' may be regarded as a major complication of pregnancy, with surgical intervention in the form of abortion as the indicated treatment.... In fact, a woman seeking an abortion is making a circumstantial self-definition of pregnancy as an illness for which she considers the appropriate treatment to be abortion."[2]

Abortionist Lise Fortier asserts: "Each and every pregnancy threatens a woman's life. From a strict medical viewpoint, every pregnancy should be aborted."[3]

And abortionist Jane Hodgson testified under oath:

> In my medical judgment, every pregnancy that is not wanted by the patient, I feel there is a medical indication to abort a pregnancy where it is not wanted. In good faith, I would recommend on a medical basis, you understand, that it would be 100% ... I think they are all medically necessary.... Occasionally we will advise these women to carry their pregnancy to term, but most of these are medically necessary because I am considering the woman's physical, mental, emotional and social and welfare and family and environment and all that ... I am concerned with the quality of life, not physical existence.[4]

Hodgson also stated, "A medically necessary abortion is any abortion a woman asks for."[5]

Playing the System to Get Abortions. It does no good whatsoever to strictly define "health-of-the-mother" exceptions in the law, because abortionists and unscrupulous women will lie as aggressively as they can to commit abortions. After all, what is a little rationalization and lying to women determined to kill their own preborn children and to people committed to earning money by killing them?

Dr. E. James Lieberman said this about those states that had already legalized abortion for the mother's "health" before *Roe v. Wade*: "In recent years, 90 percent of all legal abortions performed in the United States were justified on psychiatric grounds, since there are few physical conditions which stand in the way of normal gestation and parturition."[6]

Dr. Benjamin N. Branch confirmed this when he revealed, "until June, 1970, almost 90 percent of abortions in New York were in fact certified as necessary to protect emotional health."[6]

The Facts of Life

This kind of dishonesty still occurs on a vast scale. A comprehensive review of the reasons given for abortions in Louisiana during 1975-1988 found that abortionists committed 99.1 percent of all abortions for "mental health" reasons.[7]

Pro-abortionists have written books describing how to "play the system" by faking physical or mental symptoms in order to get an abortion. One example of how to lie during an abortion interview appeared in *The Abortion Handbook* and later in *A Woman's Book of Choices*:

> During the interview, weep, show anger, fear, disgust, outright destructiveness of your clothing or small objects, say, the ashtray on his desk which can be broken on the floor or against a wall. Don't overdo this. You will be billed for the broken things later! Don't break the doctor's head. This is a "no-no" ... How's your attention span?... You can't seem to concentrate on anything for more than a couple of minutes.... Drop sly hints that you are "attracted" to many strange men sexually. Be dull and very sad. Cry a bit. Just sit in silence, and make him repeat questions as though you hadn't heard a word.... And now for the Manic Scene: Just like the opera, ladies! Brighten up, beam like a sunrise ... let your thoughts gallop wildly ... your speech flows like the Danube in flood time ... you might try taking off your shoes, kicking them all the way across his office, wriggling your toes. Then say, "That feels so good, I think I'll take *everything* off ... (musingly)."[8]

The authors of *A Woman's Book of Choices* also admit, "Another pre-*Roe* standby that many women employed successfully was threatening or feigning suicide."[8]

The Reality

Concessions by the Abortionists. Pro-abortionists find it necessary to grossly overestimate the alleged "dangers" of pregnancy and childbirth in order to frighten people into supporting and paying for abortions. So, they define a threat to the life of the mother in the same terms as a threat to her *health*.

However, before pro-abortionists finalized their strategy to legalize abortion all over the world, they were much more honest in their assessments of the "threats" that pregnancy posed to women.

Alan Guttmacher of Planned Parenthood did more to promote and spread abortion on demand throughout the world than any other individual. Yet in 1967 he commented: "Today it is possible for almost any patient to be brought through pregnancy alive, unless she suffers from a fatal disease such as cancer or leukemia, and if so, abortion would be unlikely to prolong, much less save the life."[9] Certainly, with all of the advances in medicine since then, cases in which a woman's pregnancy threatens her health are still rarer today.[10]

Former abortionist Bernard Nathanson said in 1990: "The situation where the mother's life is at stake were she to continue a pregnancy is no longer a clinical reality. Given the state of modern medicine, we can now manage any pregnant woman with any medical affliction successfully, to the natural conclusion of the pregnancy: the birth of a healthy child."[11]

Results of the Studies. Reporting the reasons for abortions is largely voluntary in countries where abortion has been legal for a long time. However, the few studies that *do* include reasons for abortions surveyed more than half a million women obtaining abortions. They show that abortions for genuine health threats to the mother account for 0.36 percent, *or about one-third of one percent of all abortions!*[12]

Dr. Irving Cushner, Professor of Obstetrics at the UCLA School of Medicine, testified before the Senate Judiciary Committee's subcommittee on the Constitution of the United States on 14 October 1981. When one of the Senators asked him how often abortions are necessary to save the life of the mother or to ensure her physical health, Dr. Cushner, who is strongly pro-abortion, answered: "In this country, about one percent."[13]

Medicaid Abortion Funding. Aside from exhaustive studies, changes in both federal and state Medicaid abortion funding standards and the resulting changes in numbers of abortions funded is the best indicator of the number of abortions actually committed for health reasons.

Until 1 October 1977, the federal government funded abortions for the life of the mother, for rape and incest, and for the "health of the mother." After this date, the Hyde Amendment let the government drop funding for the "health" exception, while retaining it for the other exceptions.

The results were truly dramatic. In Fiscal Year 1977, before the Hyde Amendment took effect, the federal taxpayer funded 294,600 abortions. After the Amendment, the federal government paid for only 2,100 abortions in Fiscal Year 1978—a decrease of 99.3 percent!

In other words, abortionists used phony "health" reasons to obtain payment for all but a tiny percentage of federally-funded abortions before the Hyde Amendment took effect.

On the state level, Illinois provided the best example of such a huge drop in taxpayer-funded abortion. The state paid for 23,209 abortions in 1976, mostly for the "health of the mother." After courts upheld a 1977 state law banning the use of state money for abortions unless medically necessary to save the woman's life, the state paid for exactly 12 abortions in 1983.[14] This means 99.95 percent of all abortions committed in Illinois before the funding cutoff were for reasons *not* related to maternal health!

1 Jodi L. Jacobson. "Coming to Grips With Abortion," Worldwatch Institute's *State of the World 1991 Report.* W.W. Norton Publishers, London, 1991, pp. 114-131. Also issued as Worldwatch Paper #97, *The Global Politics of Abortion.*

2 Warren H. Hern. *Abortion Practice.* Philadelphia: J.B. Lippincott Company, 1990, pp. 8-9.

3 Andrew Scholberg. "The Abortionists and Planned Parenthood: Familiar Bedfellows." *International Review of Natural Family Planning,* Winter 1980, p. 308.

4 Transcript, 3 August 1977. at 99-101, *McRae v. Califano,* 491 F. Supp. 630 (E.D.N.Y. 1980), *rev'd sub nom. Harris v. McRae.* 100 S. Ct. 2671 (1980).

5 Human Life International's *Special Report* Number 83, August 1991, pp. 6-7.

6 E. James Lieberman, M.D. "Abortion Counseling," and Benjamin N. Branch, M.D. "Counseling in Abortion Services." Sarah Lewit (Editor). *Abortion Techniques and Services: Proceedings of the Conference, New York, N.Y., June 3-5, 1971.* Amsterdam: *Excerpta Medica,* 1972.

7   Office of Public Health of the Louisiana Department of Health and Hospitals compilation of Louisiana State "Report of Induced Termination of Pregnancy" forms (#PHS 16-ab), Item 9d, "Reason for Pregnancy Termination," 1975 to 1988.

8   Lana Phelan and Pat Maginnis. *The Abortion Handbook*. North Hollywood, California: Contact Books, 1969, pp. 111-115. Also quoted in Rebecca Chalker and Carol Downer. *A Woman's Book of Choices: Abortion, Menstrual Extraction, RU-486*. Four Walls Eight Windows Press, Post Office 548, Village Station, New York, New York 10014. 1992, p. 43.

9   Alan Guttmacher. "Abortion Yesterday, Today, and Tomorrow." *The Case for Legalized Abortion Now*. Berkeley: Diablo Books, 1967, p. 3.

10 The following diseases are among those *not* considered to be indications for abortion today: anemia, blood clotting disorders, hemoglobinopathies, myeloproliferative diseases, thrombocytopenic purpura, all bacterial, viral, spirochetal and protozoal infections, cancers of the breast, central nervous system, thyroid, and gastrointestinal tract, melanomas, leukemia, lymphoma, acute renal failure, acute or chronic glomerulonephy, ectopic kidney, nephrosis, urinary tract infections or calculi, cerebral vascular accidents, chorea gravidarum, epilepsy, multiple sclerosis (MS), myasthenia gravis, obstetrical paralysis, peripheral neuropathies, tetany, Marfan's syndrome, periarteritis nodosa, rheumatoid arthritis, scleroderma, systemic lupus erythematosus, diabetes mellitus, adrenal, parathyroid, pituitary and thyroid diseases, asthma, bronchiectasis, cystic fibrosis, sarcoidosis, tuberculosis, all liver disorders, pancreatitis, regional enteritis, chondrodystrophy, osteogenesis imperfecta, all skin diseases, arterial aneurysms, aerial coarctation, essential hypertension, thromboembolis disease, varicose veins, cardiac arrhythmias, congenital heart disease, coronary artery disease, hypertensive heart disease, and rheumatic heart disease. Denis Cavanagh, M.D., Professor of Obstetrics and Gynecology, University of South Florida College of Medicine. "Medical Treatment for Pregnant Women." *Restoring the Right to Life: The Human Life Amendment*. 1984: Brigham Young University Press, Table 3, pp. 139-141.

11 Bernard Nathanson, M.D. Written statement to the Idaho House of Representatives' State Affairs Committee, 16 February 1990. Also quoted in "Exceptions: Abandoning "The Least of These My Brethren."" American Life League booklet, 1991, p. 22.

12 (1) Office of Public Health of the Louisiana Department of Health and Hospitals compilation of Louisiana State "Report of Induced Termination of Pregnancy" forms (#PHS 16-ab), Item 9d, "Reason for Pregnancy Termination," 1975 to 1988. 114,231 of 115,243 abortions (99.1%) for mental health and 863 (0.75%) for physical health. (2) D.B. Paintin, M.D., Department of Obstetrics and Gynecology, St. Mary's Hospital Medical School, London, England. "Late Abortions." *The Lancet*, 11 November 1989, p. 1158. This study found that 966 of 358,074 abortions reported in the United Kingdom for the years 1987 and 1988 were for a "specified medical disorder." (3) J.J. Rovinsky and S.B. Gusberg. *American Journal of Obstetrics and Gynecology*, 98:11-17 (1967). There were a total of 57,228 deliveries at New York's Mount Sinai Hospital from 1953 to 1964. During the same time period, 69 abortions were committed for physical health reasons. Totals are 1,898/529,533 = 0.36 percent.

13 Dr. Irving Cushner, quoted in *Village Voice*, 16 July 1985.

14 Frontline Updates. "Illinois State-Paid Abortions Drop to Twelve." *National Right to Life News*, 16 August 1984, p. 4.

85. How Does the Principle of the "Double Effect" Apply to Abortion?

The Catholic Church and most other religions recognize the moral principle of the "double effect."

As applied to abortion, this means that any treatment done to save a woman's life that *also* results in the death of a preborn child is not a true abortion, since the primary purpose of the treatment was to *save* a life, not *take* one. Even if the death of the baby is a foregone conclusion, such an action is not an abortion, because the death was an *indirect* effect of the surgical procedure.

Two examples illustrate this principle. If a doctor treats a woman's high blood pressure by aborting her child, he has committed a direct abortion. He is guilty of killing the child in order to treat the condition of the mother. However, if he has to perform a hysterectomy in order to remove a cancerous uterus, he is focusing on the organ itself in an attempt to heal the mother. If the mother was pregnant at the time, this is an indirect abortion—the purpose of the operation was removing the uterus, not the preborn child.

In other words, the *purpose* of the second procedure was not to kill the child in order to preserve the mother's life, but to save the mother's life by removing the organ, not the child. If possible, the doctor must delay treatment as long as possible in order to save both the mother and the child. In some cases, such as with ectopic pregnancies, this is not possible.

Pope Pius XII clearly described the principle of the "double effect:"

> It has been our intention here to use always the expressions "*direct* attempt on the life of the innocent person" [and] "*direct* killing." The reason is that if, for example, the safety of the life of the future mother, independently of her state of pregnancy, might call for an urgent surgical operation, or any other therapeutic application, which would have as an accessory consequence, in no way desired nor intended, but *inevitable*, the death of the fetus, such an act could not be called a *direct* attempt on the innocent life. In these conditions the operation can be lawful, as can other similar medical interventions, provided that it be a matter of great importance, such as life, and that it is not possible to postpone it till the birth of the child, or to have recourse to any other efficacious remedy.... Both for the one and the other, the demand cannot be but this: to use every means to save the life of both the mother and the child.[1]

Some of the treatments that may indirectly kill a preborn child include certain cancer treatments; hysterectomy (removal) of a cancerous or severely traumatized uterus; and salpingectomy (the removal of a Fallopian tube), which is the most common application of the "double effect" as applied to abortion.[2]

Some pro-abortionists assert that the double effect applies in the case of *all* abortions, because they say *all* pregnancies threaten the life of the mother or are more dangerous than abortion (see Question 84 for examples of quotes to this effect). This position is due to a ridiculously broad definition of threats to the life and health of the mother, and is completely illicit. The "double effect" applies *only* in the case of an *actual* and *proximate* threat to the life of the mother. Such instances are rare indeed, as described in Question 84.

1 Pope Pius XII, Address to the Family Front Congress on 27 November 1951. Published in *Matrimony*, Papal Teachings. Boston: St. Paul Editions, 1963, pp. 437-440. See also Pope Pius XII, *Allocution to Midwives*, 29 October 1951, *Acta Apostilicae Sedis*, 43(1951), p. 855.

2 Bernard M. Nathanson and Richard N. Ostling. *Aborting America*. Garden City, N.Y: Doubleday & Company, Inc., 1979, pp. 244-247.

···

86. How Common Are Pregnancies Resulting from Rape and Incest?

Introduction

From an ethical and logical standpoint, the number of pregnancies from rape and incest in most countries is simply irrelevant to the moral case against these exceptions. A baby conceived through violence is as blameless and innocent as one conceived in marriage, and is therefore deserving of the same protection.

However, it is very useful to be able to show just how rare rape- and incest-caused pregnancies really are, because pro-abortionists have persuaded the public that the number is huge. A 1990 national Wirthlin poll found that the average respondent's guess at the number of abortions committed for rape and incest was 21% of the total number of abortions in the United States.[1]

The Frequency of Rape-Caused Pregnancies

Pro-abortion writer N. Lee wrote in 1969: "A pregnancy conceived by forcible rape would probably head the list as the most often unwanted, but it is such an unlikely event that it is not really relevant to an understanding of the reasons why women define certain pregnancies as unwanted."[2]

Six major studies have backed up Lee's statement regarding the frequency of rape-induced pregnancy. These studies, done over the last 30 years, carefully examined the outcomes of more than 155,000 forcible rapes. The combined results of these studies show that one out of 1,238 rapes results in pregnancy, or about 0.08 percent (or one-twelfth of one percent).[3]

A comprehensive review of the reasons given for abortions in Louisiana over the period 1975-1988 confirmed the combined results of these studies. Forty-six of 115,243 abortions were committed for rape, or a rate of 0.04 percent (one twenty-fifth of one percent).[4]

This may seem like an improbably low rate of rape-caused pregnancies and abortions. There are several reasons that rape-induced pregnancy is so rare:

■ About one-third of all rape victims are postmenopausal or have not yet reached menarche (first menstruation). Of those victims who are of childbearing age, 32.1% are *permanently* sterile because of elective surgery or environmental effects. Finally, 34.3 percent of all non-sterile women of childbearing age are *temporarily* sterile due to use of contraception. This means that only (100.0% - 33.3%) x (100% - 32.1% - 34.3%) = 22.4% of all rape victims can become pregnant at the time of the crime.[5]

■ A woman can become pregnant during only about five days out of a typical 28-day cycle, due to survival times of sperm and egg. What's more, even if all conditions are ideal and both man and woman are fertile, and intercourse takes place on *every fertile day*, it will take an average of *five months* (or a total of 25 fertile days out of five 28-day cycles) to achieve pregnancy.[6]

■ Rapists, as a class, have a high degree of erective or ejaculatory dysfunction serious enough to render them sterile—about 57 percent.[7]

■ The legal definition of rape is penetration only; ejaculation need not occur. Of those *nonsterile* rapists who penetrate their victims, only about half deposit sperm.[7]

If we take these factors into account, we see that the rate of rape-caused pregnancies in the United States is about 22.4% x (25/140) x (100% - 57%) x 50% = 0.86%, or less than one percent. This low percentage confirms the results of the six studies mentioned above.

The average number of rapes in the United States each year over the period 1980-1996 inclusive was about 147,755, taking into account under-reporting.[8] This means that about (147,755 x 0.86%) = 1,271 pregnancies are caused by rape in the United States each year. It follows that, if *all* rape-caused pregnancies are aborted, they account for a *maximum* of (1,271/1,558,000) = 0.082%, or less than *one thousandth* of all of the abortions performed in the United States each year.

The Rate of Incest-Caused Pregnancies

The Pro-Abortion View. Abortion for incest is the despicable twin of abortion for rape. Pro-abortionists believe that a woman or girl can "erase" the child conceived of incest just as easily as she can "erase" a child of rape.

Pro-abortionists are notoriously short-sighted and always look for the quick and easy solution. They believe an abortion closes the matter, and then everyone can get on with their lives. However, there is one aspect of incest that is different from the crime of rape: an abortion removes the preborn child, but the predator remains. In fact, it is often the assailant who insists upon the abortion to cover up his own crimes.

Incest-Caused Pregnancies. Incest results in a very low probability of pregnancy—less than one percent. This is due to several factors.

Most cases of incest today involve one to three acts of intercourse, and are promptly reported or uncovered.

According to Robert Carroll of the Santa Clara County Child Sexual Abuse Treatment Program in San Jose, California and Dr. George E. Maloof, a psychiatrist at the Community Mental Health Center in Daly City, California, the pregnancy rate *per victim* (not per incident of felonious intercourse) is "less than one percent."[9]

The Christopher Street program in Minneapolis reported four cases of pregnancy in 400 cases of incest, or about one percent. Santa Clara County's incest treatment program, run by Henry Giaretto, reported slightly less than one percent pregnancies (12 instances) in 1,500 cases of incest. And Washington State's incest treatment program reported *no* pregnancies in more than 600 cases.

If these studies are combined, we see that the probability of pregnancy due to incest (per girl, *not* per case of intercourse), is 16 out of 2,500 cases (one out of 156, or 0.64%).

Abortion as a Cover-up for Incest. Abortion is the most effective cover-up for incest. It is common for Planned Parenthood and similar groups to use "hard-case" stories in their literature, debates, and presentations. They often speak of 12 and 13-

year-old pregnant girls (and sometimes, nine and 10-year-old girls) who are forni-cating or pregnant. Planned Parenthood, of course, supplies abortion, contracep-tives and, *above all*, secrecy ("confidentiality") to these young girls.

We might ask Planned Parenthood whom it thinks the male parties to such sex acts are. Certainly they are not nine or 10-year-old boys! These girls are almost always the victims of (step)father/daughter or big brother/little sister incest. Planned Parenthood and other pro-abortion and pro-homosexual organizations, by promot-ing abortion, are *directly* helping many predatory incestuous situations to continue.

Abortion is just as inept a solution for incest as it is for rape or any other rea-son—especially from the psychological point of view. Incest expert R. Bruce Sloan, M.D., states: "The psychiatric basis for terminating the life of an unborn baby inces-tuously conceived has absolutely no scientific merit and derives from a blind adherence to a legal formulation espoused by abortion promoters now including organized psychiatry."[10]

Georgia Early went to the heart of the matter when she said:

When incest is involved, allowing abortion in pregnancy cases of minors tends to compound the exploitation of the innocent victim and protect the perpetrator from exposure so that he may continue his illegal and immoral acts without fear of discovery.

To rehabilitate child abusers, it is necessary to work on their feelings of self-esteem, their memories of themselves being abused as children, and to get them to see their own children in a new way. Abortion sidesteps this very involved process because the child incestuously pregnant is taken for an abor-tion and then returned to the home where the abuse occurred. Abortion also perpetuates the generational violence where the abused child becomes the child abuser.[11]

Conclusions

Abortion for rape or incest can never be justified for several reasons.

A child conceived in violence is himself innocent and created in the image of God. He has done nothing to deserve the death sentence, any more than a child conceived within the bounds of a loving marriage.

Abortion wreaks more violence, causes no genuine healing, and may lead oth-ers to believe that the "problem" caused by a rape or incest has largely been solved. In cases of incest, abortion can actually help cover up evidence of incest. The solu-tion to rape and incest is not abortion, but prosecution of the rapist so he does not commit more crimes and loving care for his victims so that they experience true physical and emotional healing.

Finally, abortion for the "hard-cases" such as rape and incest is *always* used by pro-abortionists as a wedge to obtain abortion-on-demand. This has occurred in almost all of the developed nations and is now happening in many developing countries. If pro-lifers allow a law with a rape and incest exception to be passed, they will soon be facing abortion on a massive scale.

1 Results of a 1990 Wirthlin poll described in "The Week." *National Review*, 3 December 1990, p. 12.

2 N. Lee. *The Search for an Abortionist*. University of Chicago Press, 1969, p. 149.

3   Registrar General's "Statistical Review of England and Wales for 1969." London: 1971, H.M.S.O. Cited in R. Gardner, *Abortion, the Personal Dilemma* (Eerdmans, 1972), p. 169. Eighty pregnancies out of 54,000 rapes. Study cited in Jack and Barbara Willke. *Handbook on Abortion*. Hayes Publishing Company, 1979, p. 40. Twenty-two pregnancies out of 86,000 rapes. "Illinois State Medical Society Symposium on Medical Implications of the Current Abortion Law in Illinois." *Illinois Medical Journal*, May 1967, pp. 677-680. Zero pregnancies in 14,400 rapes. C.R. Hayman, W.F. Stewart, F.R. Lewis, and M. Rant. "Rape in the District of Columbia." *American Journal of Obstetrics and Gynecology*, 1972; 113:91-97. Twenty-one pregnancies out of 914 rapes. R. Everett and G. Jimerson. "The Rape Victim: A Review of 117 Consecutive Cases." *Obstetrics and Gynecology*, 1977; 50:88-90. Zero pregnancies in 117 rapes. H. Fujita and W. Wagner. "Referendum 20—Abortion Reform in Washington State." In J. Osofsky and D. Osofsky. *The Abortion Experience: Psychological and Medical Impacts*. Harper & Row, 1973. Three pregnancies in 524 rapes.

4   Office of Public Health of the Louisiana Department of Health and Hospitals compilation of Louisiana State "Report of Induced Termination of Pregnancy" forms (#PHS 16-ab), Item 9d, "Reason for Pregnancy Termination," 1975-1988. This study is used under the assumption that pregnancies that end in abortion have the same statistical characteristics as those that are carried to term—a reasonable assumption, given the large numbers involved.

5   R.B. Everett and G.K. Jemerson. "The Rape Victim." *Obstetrics and Gynecology*. 50, 1977, p. 88. Also data based upon telephone communications with Dr. Charles Pratt, Survey of Family Growth Division, National Center for Health Statistics, 4 April 1978, and Planned Parenthood-World Population on 4 April 1978. Summarized in testimony by Rep. Thomas J. Bliley, Jr., (R-Va.) on 25 July 1983, and reprinted in the next day's *Congressional Record*. Also see U.S. Bureau of the Census. Reference Data Book and Guide to Sources, *Statistical Abstract of the United States*. 1990, U.S. Government Printing Office. Table 99, "Contraceptive Use by Women, 15-44 Years Old, by Age, Race, Marital Status, and Method of Contraception: 1982."

6   R. Pearl. *The Natural History of Population*. New York: Oxford University Press, 1939. pp. 72-79. V. Seltzer. "Medical Management of the Rape Victim." *Journal of the American Medical Women's Association*. 32, 1977, p. 141.

7   C. Groth, A. Nicholas, and Ann Wolbert Burgess. "Sexual Dysfunction During Rape." *New England Journal of Medicine*, 6 October 1977, pp. 764-766. M. Dahlke, et al. "Identification of Semen in 500 Patients Seen Because of Rape." *American Journal of Clinical Pathology*. 68, 1977, p. 740.

8   Bureau of the Census, U.S. Department of Commerce. National Data Book and Guide to Sources, *Statistical Abstract of the United States*, 1990. Table 289, "Forcible Rape—Number and Rate, by Selected Characteristics: 1970 to 1988." Also see unnumbered table, "Police Reporting Rates for Personal and Household Crimes: 1975 to 1987," p. 168.

9   Telephone conversation with Robert Carroll on 5 April 1978, quoted by Rep. Thomas J. Bliley (R-Va.) in 25 July 1983 testimony printed in the *Congressional Record*. Also see the report on the presentation made at the Symposium on the Psychological Aspects of Abortion at the Loyola University School of Medicine, 1 November 1978.

10   R. Bruce Sloan, M.D. *New England Journal of Medicine*. Quoted in G. Maloof, M.D., "The Consequences of Incest." *The Psychological Aspects of Abortion*. University Publications of America, 1979, p. 74.

11   Georgia Early. "Incest, Sexual Child Abuse and Abortion." *Life Advocate*, May/June 1980.

Table 10

Risks of Fetal Genetic Abnormalities
Related to Maternal Age

Mother's Age	PERCENT		
	Risk of Down's Syndrome[1]	Total Risk of Any Genetic Abnormality[2]	Healthy Babies
15	0.03% (1 in 3,333)	0.22% (1 in 455)	99.78%
16	0.04% (1 in 2,500)	0.24% (1 in 410)	99.76%
17	0.04% (1 in 2,324)	0.26% (1 in 381)	99.74%
18	0.05% (1 in 2,161)	0.28% (1 in 354)	99.72%
19	0.05% (1 in 2,008)	0.30% (1 in 329)	99.70%
20	0.05% (1 in 1,867)	0.33% (1 in 306)	99.67%
21	0.06% (1 in 1,736)	0.35% (1 in 285)	99.65%
22	0.06% (1 in 1,614)	0.38% (1 in 265)	99.62%
23	0.07% (1 in 1,500)	0.41% (1 in 246)	99.59%
24	0.07% (1 in 1,395)	0.44% (1 in 229)	99.56%
25	0.08% (1 in 1,296)	0.47% (1 in 213)	99.53%
26	0.08% (1 in 1,205)	0.51% (1 in 198)	99.49%
27	0.09% (1 in 1,120)	0.54% (1 in 184)	99.46%
28	0.10% (1 in 1,042)	0.59% (1 in 171)	99.41%
29	0.10% (1 in 968)	0.63% (1 in 159)	99.37%
30	0.11% (1 in 900)	0.68% (1 in 148)	99.32%
31	0.13% (1 in 749)	0.81% (1 in 123)	99.19%
32	0.16% (1 in 624)	0.98% (1 in 102)	99.02%
33	0.19% (1 in 519)	1.17% (1 in 85)	98.83%
34	0.23% (1 in 432)	1.41% (1 in 71)	98.59%
35	0.28% (1 in 360)	1.69% (1 in 59)	98.31%
36	0.35% (1 in 285)	2.14% (1 in 47)	97.86%
37	0.44% (1 in 225)	2.71% (1 in 37)	97.29%
38	0.57% (1 in 176)	3.47% (1 in 29)	96.53%
39	0.73% (1 in 138)	4.43% (1 in 23)	95.57%
40	0.92% (1 in 109)	5.61% (1 in 18)	94.39%
41	0.95% (1 in 105)	5.82% (1 in 17)	94.18%
42	0.99% (1 in 101)	6.03% (1 in 17)	93.97%
43	1.02% (1 in 98)	6.25% (1 in 16)	93.75%
44	1.06% (1 in 94)	6.47% (1 in 15)	93.53%
45	1.10% (1 in 91)	6.71% (1 in 15)	93.29%

87. How Common Are Major Birth Defects? (Table 10)

1 *Hippocrates* Magazine, May/June, 1988, pp. 68-69, and letter dated 21 March 1980 from Hymie Gordon, M.D., Chairman, Department of Medical Genetics at the Mayo Clinic, to Nona Aguilar.

2 Includes incidence of Down's Syndrome, Alpha anti-trypsin enzyme deficiency, alpha thalassemia, beta thalassemia (Cooley's anemia), cystic fibrosis, Duchenne's muscular dystrophy, fragile "X" syndrome, hemophilia, anencephaly, spina bifida, polycystic kidney disease, sex chromosome abnormalities, sickle cell anemia, Tay-Sachs disease, trisomy 13 (Patau Syndrome) and trisomy 18 (Edwards Syndrome).

88. How Common Are Eugenic Abortions?

No Heart Leads to No Soul

The birth defects argument is perhaps the most loathsome of all of the rationalizations for prenatal killing used by pro-abortionists.

While they fight for handicapped parking spaces for those who cannot walk, and while they make sure they have sign language interpreters at their conferences, pro-abortionists see no hypocrisy in advocating abortion for babies whose only crime is that they are less than perfect.

This is pure and simple *discrimination*.

People do not abort a handicapped baby because he would be unhappy. Handicapped people usually are just as happy as those who have no handicaps. People commit eugenic abortions for selfish reasons, regardless of what they say—because the child would make *them* unhappy.

What is particularly distressing about eugenic abortions is the fact that no child, no matter how severely handicapped, is unwanted. None of the more than 100 organizations consisting of the parents of handicapped children has *ever* endorsed abortion. In fact, many of these organizations have standing offers to adopt any child with handicaps.[1]

This means that no eugenic abortion is truly necessary—but many are undoubtedly carried out because genetic counselors and abortion clinic staff do not tell parents about these organizations.

Abortion as the Eugenicist's Tool

The elimination of human beings solely because they have mental and physical limitations is the dream of the pseudoscientific worldview known and universally condemned as eugenics, which is the systematic destruction of "life devoid of value." Today, of course, we use the politically correct term "insufficient quality of life."

The *Decree of the Sacred Congregation of the Holy Office on Eugenics* of 18 March 1931 answered a question about the legitimacy of a practice that was beginning to flourish in the United States:

Question: "What is thought of the theory called 'eugenics,' whether positive or negative, and of the means indicated by it to improve the human race without taking into consideration either natural or divine or ecclesiastical laws relative to marriage and individual rights?"

Answer: "The theory of 'eugenics' is to be held entirely blameable, false and condemned, in accordance with the Encyclical on Christian Marriage, *Casti Connubii*, December 31, 1930."

Margaret Sanger, the founder of Planned Parenthood and a serious disciple of the eugenics philosophy, longed for "a race of thoroughbreds" through positive eugenics—the breeding of "good stock." Now abortionists would like to improve the gene pool through negative eugenics, the "weeding out" of those human beings they consider unsatisfactory.

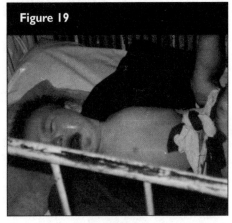

Figure 19

As pro-lifers have predicted from the beginning, "hard-case" abortions lead to "hard-case" infanticides. This little girl, wrapped only in a filthy rag, died within one week of being taken into one of China's "dying room" orphanages.

Marjorie Reilly Maguire and Daniel C. Maguire of the fake religious front group 'Catholics' for a Free Choice, say heartlessly, "while you are making your [abortion] decision, do not let yourself be a victim of romantic thinking about the beauty and value of handicapped children ... such children place extreme demands upon a family."[2]

And Kenneth Vaux, Professor of Ethics at Baylor College of Medicine, shows that such thinking will inevitably lead to *abortion on command*:

> I am told by a reliable scholar that a major private health insurance company is contemplating the policy of requiring amniocentesis or other acceptable forms of antenatal diagnosis for all pregnant women holding a policy with the company. If a diagnosis of congenital defect is made, insurance will be dropped on the potential child. In other words, *abortion will be required*.... We have a legal obligation to protect the unborn from the cruel and unusual punishment of genetic disease. Surely we need ponder whether the abnormal merit our protection, even *in utero*. We now have the possibility, *which means the responsibility*, of deciding whom we will admit to the human community.[3]

Frequency of Birth Defects

There are about 4.2 million births per year in the United States, and about 1.6 million abortions, for a total of 5.8 million pregnancies not concluding in miscarriage. The average age of pregnant women is 26.[4] Considering the data given in Question 87 and the distribution of pregnancies by age not ending in miscarriage, there are about 6,700 cases of Down's Syndrome and about 36,000 cases of other serious fetal genetic defects per year.

1 John and Barbara Willke. *Handbook on Abortion* (Cincinnati: Hayes Publishing Company, Inc., 1979, p. 177. A literature survey was performed on many of the organizations listed in *Reaching Out:*

A Directory of Voluntary Organizations in Maternal and Child Health, 1985. National Center for Education in Maternal and Child Health, 8201 Greensborough Drive, Suite 600, McLean, Virginia 22102, and no endorsements of abortion were found.

2 "Abortion: A Guide to Making Ethical Decisions." 'Catholics' for a Free Choice pamphlet dated September, 1983.

3 Kenneth Vaux. *Biomedical Ethics.* New York: Harper & Row, 1974, pp. 51, 58-59.

4 U.S. Department of Commerce, Bureau of the Census. *Statistical Abstract of the United States 1993.* Washington, D.C.: U.S. Government Printing Office, 1993. Table 93, "Births and Birth Rates: 1970 to 1990."

89. What Are the Various Kinds of Prenatal Genetic Testing?

The Procedures

Amniocentesis. Amniocentesis is usually performed after the 16th week of pregnancy on the preborn babies of mothers who have abnormal alpha-fetoprotein (AFP) concentrations, whose families have a history of birth defects, or who are more than 35 years old.[1]

Guided by ultrasound, the doctor inserts a needle through the abdominal wall into the uterus and withdraws about an ounce of amniotic fluid. Labs grow fetal cells in the fluid for three to four weeks, and examine the cell for chromosomal abnormalities (karyotyping). Abortions are committed about 32 to 45 days following the test. The risks to the baby from the "amnio" range from 0.5 to 2.0 percent fatalities by miscarriage.[1]

In the October, 1986, issue of *Ob-Gyn News,* Dr. Ann Tabor reported that her randomized study of 2,264 women in the 25 to 34 age group showed that 23 women—or one percent—had miscarriages directly caused by amniocentesis. The test detected abnormalities in only one percent of the babies, meaning the amnio killed as many *healthy* babies as it detected babies with abnormalities.

The vast majority of mothers who have eugenic abortions do so at 20 weeks or more, when their babies weigh about a pound. If abortion is the "treatment of choice," the babies die either by being cut apart (D&E abortion) or, less frequently, by one of the other grisly late-term abortion techniques such as dilation and extraction (D&X). Chapter 1 describes these procedures.

The major risks of amniocentesis include maternal hemorrhage and infection, fetal puncture wounds, pneumothorax (injection of gas into the mother's pleural cavity), laceration of the baby's spleen, damage to the placenta and/or umbilical cord and the baby's death from exsanguination (loss of blood).

Chorionic Villus Sampling (CVS). This procedure is physically similar to amniocentesis, but can be done about eight weeks earlier. A doctor uses a plastic catheter to clip villi (hairlike structures) from the placenta, and the results of chromosomal tests are available within a week. The risks of fatality to the baby are greater than with "amnio," however: from one to five percent miscarriages.[1]

Maternal Serum Alpha-Fetoprotein (AFP). AFP is a maternal blood test performed from the 13th to 20th weeks of pregnancy. Neural tube defects (such as anencephaly or spina bifida) in a baby may cause his kidneys to release elevated levels of AFP into the mother's bloodstream, and lower levels signal the possibility of Down's Syndrome. The blood test must be confirmed by ultrasound and/or amniocentesis. The risk to the baby or mother is nil for the blood test by itself.[1]

Ultrasonography. Ultrasound uses high-frequency sound waves that reflect off a preborn child's internal organs and appear on a sonography screen. At the 20th week, ultrasound can spot various defects in the spine, kidney, heart and skeleton. The test can also determine the position of the placenta.[1] Abortionists sometimes use sonograms to position a baby for the kill.

The effects of sonograms on preborn babies are unknown. It is possible that delayed-onset effects of ultrasonography may be significant, and research into this area continues.

Prenatal Testing = The Eugenicist's Ultimate Tool

Eugenics Yet Again. As the medical profession accepts the various gene-selection technologies, and as they become more and more accurate, interest will inevitably turn to cost containment, and the degree of coercion will certainly become greater.

Some insurance plans already refuse to pay for deliveries *or* care of infants with genetic defects if the parents do not accept amniocentesis and abortion to "select out" the "defectives" who have serious birth defects.

In 1975, Anthony Smith wrote: "Medical opinion is generally firm. It recommends that amniocentesis should be offered to the patient only on the clear understanding that if the fetus is found to be affected, the pregnancy *will* be terminated. Abortion laws were unthinkable a dozen years ago. Amniocentesis laws, currently unthinkable, may also be with us before so very long. There will be eugenic strides...."[2]

Kenneth Vaux, Professor of Ethics at Baylor College of Medicine, reports, "Marjorie Shaw, one of the world's most outstanding geneticists, argues that genetic disease is the same as communicable disease, and therefore should be isolated and quarantined as a public health measure—not allowed to transmit itself."[3]

And, on 4 April 1976, the *New York Times* editorialized, "In the far future a subsidy—by insurance companies or the government—might be available if the procedure [amniocentesis] could be shown to save money. Researchers at Columbia University School of Public Health have proposed a voluntary program of screening all pregnant women 40 and over and eventually [a mandatory program to screen] *all* pregnant women to prevent 90 percent of Down's Syndrome."

The crushing weight of godlike "professional opinion" already acts to compel parents to abort preborn babies who are diagnosed as being handicapped. The National Institutes of Health found that parents aborted more than 95 percent of all preborn babies who were found "defective" by prenatal genetic tests.[4]

It seems that we no longer have room for handicapped people on this perfect earth of ours.

1 American College of Obstetrics and Gynecology. Patient Education Pamphlets "Ultrasound Exams in Ob/Gyn," "High-Risk Pregnancy" and "Amniocentesis for Prenatal Diagnosis of Genetic Disorders."

2 Anthony Smith. *The Human Pedigree.* New York: J.B. Lippincott Co., 1975, p. 275.

3   Kenneth Vaux, Professor of Ethics at Baylor College of Medicine. *Biomedical Ethics*. New York: Harper & Row, 1974, pp. 51, 58 and 59.

4   Sorenson, "Some Social and Psychological Issues in Genetic Screening." *Symposium on Intrauterine Diagnosis* (D. Bergsma, editor). 1971, p. 177.

90. Can We Ever Morally Justify Prenatal Testing?

In the realm of prenatal testing, motive determines permissibility.

Most prenatal testing is done in order to find and kill preborn children who fail to "measure up" to parents' and physicians' high standards. Prenatal testing for this purpose is illicit. However, tests for the purpose of healing preborn children are allowable.

The Vatican's *Donum Vitae* answers all the fundamental moral questions about prenatal diagnosis succinctly and completely:

Is Prenatal Diagnosis Morally Licit?

If prenatal diagnosis respects the life and integrity of the embryo and the human fetus and is directed towards its safeguarding or healing as an individual, then the answer is affirmative.

For prenatal diagnosis makes it possible to know the condition of the embryo and of the fetus when still in the mother's womb. It permits, or makes it possible to anticipate earlier and more effectively, certain therapeutic, medical or surgical procedures.

Such diagnosis is permissible, with the consent of the parents after they have been adequately informed, if the methods employed safeguard the life and integrity of the embryo and the mother, without subjecting them to disproportionate risks. But this diagnosis is gravely opposed to the moral law when it is done with the thought of possibly inducing an abortion depending upon the results: a diagnosis which shows the existence of a malformation or a hereditary illness must not be the equivalent of a death-sentence. Thus a woman would be committing a gravely illicit act if she were to request such a diagnosis with the deliberate intention of having an abortion should the results confirm the existence of a malformation or abnormality. The spouse or relatives or anyone else would similarly be acting in a manner contrary to the moral law if they were to counsel or impose such a diagnostic procedure on the expectant mother with the same intention of possibly proceeding to an abortion. So too the specialist would be guilty of illicit collaboration if, in conducting the diagnosis and in communicating its results, he were deliberately to contribute to establishing or favoring a link between prenatal diagnosis and abortion.

In conclusion, any directive or program of the civil and health authorities or of scientific organizations which in any way were to favor a link between prenatal diagnosis and abortion, or which were to go as far as directly to induce expectant mothers to submit to prenatal diagnosis planned for the purpose of eliminating fetuses which are affected by malformations or which are carriers of hereditary illness, is to be condemned as a violation of the unborn child's right to life and as an abuse of the prior rights and duties of the spouses.[1]

Some specific areas in which prenatal testing is licit include:

- testing in the last trimester of pregnancy in order to help assemble properly-trained personnel and equipment needed for a difficult birth due to abnormalities;

- to prepare for *in utero* and post-birth corrective measures, including dietary control for a newborn baby with phenylketonuria or galactosemia; and

- to prepare the parents psychologically, emotionally and financially for the birth of a handicapped child.

1 Sacred Congregation for the Doctrine of the Faith. *Instruction on Respect for Human Life in its Origin and the Dignity of Procreation: Replies to Certain Questions of the Day*, 2 February 1987.

Chapter 8

Church Teachings on Abortion

....

91. What Does the Bible Say About Abortion?

Another Pro-Abortion "Red Herring"

Does anyone *really* believe that if Scripture specifically prohibited abortion, so-called "religious" pro-abortionists would give up their advocacy of it?

The "Scripture and abortion" debate is just like the fetal pain, fetal personhood and viability arguments—a deliberate pro-abortion diversion.

We know this because Scripture clearly, repeatedly and forcefully condemns *other* sex-related sins such as sodomy, divorce, fornication and adultery,[1] yet pro-abortionists tolerate and even embrace all of these as fundamental human rights.

Abortion is no different. Even if all of the Gospels specifically banned abortion, pro-abortionists would simply find another rationale for supporting and promoting prenatal child-killing as yet another "basic human right."

Yes, It's True ...

It is absolutely true that the Bible does not mention the word "abortion."

However, just because the Bible does not contain the word "abortion" does not mean that it does not *condemn* it indirectly. The Bible does not specifically mention other grave sins such as euthanasia, viewing pornography, carjacking, bank robbing, terrorism and torture to name a few. However, all of these acts are condemned by the Commandments as varieties of serious sins such as killing, stealing and adultery.

Table 11 summarizes the major Scripture passages that pertain to abortion directly or indirectly.

Any competent Bible scholar who studies these verses must make several conclusions:

(1)God creates us, body and soul, in His own image.

(2)God has known us *as persons* since before we were even conceived.[2]

(3)God has a plan for each one of us and values everyone.

(4)It is a sin to interfere with the plans of God.

(5)Children are a gift from God.

(6)Children are the most innocent among us.

(7)It is a heinous sin to slay the innocent.

When you consider them as a body, these conclusions can mean only one thing: that abortion is murder, and that authentic Christians must both avoid and condemn it.

It is obvious that pro-abortionists have little regard for Scripture, since they support various acts that it explicitly condemns. When pro-abortionists try to use the Bible to defend abortion, pro-lifers should show them some of the verses in Table 11 and demand that they produce a few that *support* it.

1   **Sodomy:** Deuteronomy 23:17; 1 Kings 14:24, 15:12, 22:46; 2 Kings 23:7. **Divorce:** Matthew 5:31-32, 19:3-9; Luke 16:18; 1 Corinthians 7:10-15. **Fornication:** 2 Chronicles 21:11; Isaiah 23:17; Ezekiel 16:26,29; Matthew 5:32, 19:9; John 8:41; Acts 15:20,29, 21:25; Romans 1:29; 1 Corinthians 5:1, 6:13,18, 7:2, 10:8; 2 Corinthians 12:21; Galatians 5:19; Ephesians 5:3; Colossians 3:5; 1 Thessalonians 4:3; Jude 1:7; Revelation 2:14,20-21, 9:21, 14:8, 17:2,4, 18:3,9, 19:2. **Adultery:** Exodus 20:14; Leviticus 18:20, 19:20, 20:10-12; Deuteronomy 5:18, 22:13-29, 27:20, 27:23; Proverbs 6:26, 6:29, 6:32; Matthew 5:27,28,32, 15:19, 19:9,18; Mark 7:21, 10:11-12, 19; Luke 16:18, 18:20; John 8:4-11; Romans 7:3, 13:9; 1 Colossians 6:9; Galatians 5:19; Ephesians 5:5; Hebrews 13:4.

2   In Scripture, *God personally names* six men before they were even born: (1) Ishmael (Genesis 16:11); (2) Isaac (Genesis 17:19); (3) Josiah (1 Kings 13:2); (4) Solomon (1 Chronicles 22:9); (5) John the Baptist (Luke 1:13); and (6) *Jesus Himself* (Matthew 1:21).

92. When Does Ensoulment Take Place?

Many pro-abortionists (particularly those who belong to "religious pro-choice" groups) assert that preborn life does not begin until the baby gets his soul—and, in their collective opinion, this "ensoulment" occurs only at birth.

What pro-abortionists are doing with this argument is falling back to yet another trench in the moral warfare over abortion: they cannot deny that preborn babies are alive and human, so they are deliberately basing their support of abortion on a question that science will *never* be able to answer. This is a classic use of "mystagoguery": An attempt to render a question so complicated or indefinable that no one can ever answer it.

This is one of the many red herrings the pro-abortion movement throws out. They assert that preborn children are not alive, not human, not persons, do not feel pain, are not viable, are not mentioned in the Bible, are not ensouled, and on and on. Of course, it really doesn't matter to pro-abortionists *when* ensoulment occurs. If, through some metaphysical/scientific breakthrough, we could *prove* preborn babies received their souls at the instant of fertilization, is anyone naive enough to expect pro-abortionists to immediately give up their precious abortion "right?"

Table 11

Summary of Scripture References Concerning Abortion

Human Life Begins in the Womb.
Genesis 16:11 and 25:21-26
   (with Hosea 12:2-3 and
   Romans 9:10-13)
Exodus 21:22-15
   (see also Numbers 35)
Jeremiah 1:5
Isaiah 7:14; 44:2,24; 46:3; 49:1,2; 53:6
Job 3:11-16; 10:8-12; 31:15
Psalm 22:9-10; 139:13-16
Ecclesiastes 5:15 and 11:5
Luke 1:13-15 and 1:39-44

Human Life Begins at Fertilization.
Psalms 51:5
Luke 1:35-36 (also Matthew 1:18-20)

God Knows Us Even before We Are Conceived.
Judges 13:3-7   Jeremiah 1:4-5
Ephesians 1:4 (also Matthew 25:34
   and Revelation 13:8 and 17:8)

Punishment for Causing a Spontaneous Abortion.
Exodus 21:22-25
Numbers 35:22-34

The Slaying of the Innocent Is a Heinous Crime.
Deuteronomy 27:25
Luke 17:2
Jeremiah 7:6 and 22:17
Psalms 106:37-38
Proverbs 6:16-19
Matthew 18:10-14

Abortion for Rape and Incest Is Never Allowed.
Genesis 19:36-38 and 50:20
Romans 8:28
Genesis 38 (see also Ruth 4:18-22,
   Matthew 1:3 and Luke 3:33)

Abortion for Birth Defects Is Never Allowed.
John 9:1-3
Acts 17:25-29
Psalms 94:9
Romans 8:28
Leviticus 19:14
Isaiah 45:9-12

Abortion for the Mother's Mental Health Is Never Allowed.
Genesis 50:20; Romans 8:28

Abortion to Conceal Fornication or Adultery Is Never Allowed.
Genesis 16:2-4 and 21:1-18
Genesis 38 (see also Ruth 4:12)

Children Must not Be Sacrificed for Any Reason.
Ezekiel 16:20-21
Jeremiah 32:35
Exodus 1:15-17
Psalms 106:37-42
II Kings 16:3, 17:17, and 21:6
Deuteronomy 12:31 and 18:10-13
Leviticus 18:21, 24, and 30

Children Are a Gift from God.
Genesis 30:1-2; Psalms 127:3-5

Table II (Continued)

Summary of Scripture References Concerning Abortion

....

Our Response

We Will be Judged on Our Response.
Genesis 9:5-6
Jeremiah 7:5-6
Matthew 25:34-40
Galatians 6:9-10

We Must Not Follow the Master of This World.
Numbers 35:33
Romans 12:1-2
Leviticus 18:21, 24,
    and 29-30

We Must Protect the Fatherless.
James 1:27
Zachariah 7:9-10
Isaiah 1:23 and 10:1-2

We Must Care for Pregnant Women in Need.
James 2:14-26
Matthew 23:3-4, 11, 12, and 25:31-46

Rescue Those Being Dragged to the Slaughter!
Proverbs 24:11-12
Isaiah 1:10-17 and 29:13

When Does Ensoulment Take Place?

Three Possible Times. There are only three possible times when a preborn child could receive his soul: at conception (fertilization), at birth, or at some time in between.

At Birth? Most pro-abortionists assert that ensoulment happens at birth. We must ask a few pointed questions about this argument. To begin with, there is no scientific method for measuring the presence of a "soul," because the very *concept* is metaphysical in nature. How, then, can they be so sure the soul enters the body at birth?

At birth, the only change in the child's status is that he moves from the inside of his mother to the outside, and begins breathing on his own. Some people argue that a baby becomes a separate entity at birth and therefore must receive his soul at this time. However, this assertion makes no sense whatever. Under this kind of "logic," Jonah would have been "desouled" when the whale swallowed him, and would have been ensouled again when the whale spat him up on the beach. Any comatose person who relies on machinery for nutrition and hydration is a part of the machinery, by this definition. And any astronaut is part of the spacecraft that provides him or her with oxygen and other necessities of life, by the pro-abortionists' "logic."

Medical science recognizes the preborn child as a patient because he is an entity separate from his own mother, possessing his own brain, heart and circulatory system. In fact, the placenta, umbilical chord, amniotic sac and amniotic fluid are generated from the fertilized egg and are also distinct from the mother. Does it not make more sense to relate the presence of a soul to the presence of a brain or heart rather than mere location?

Pro-abortionists may equate being inside the mother with being part of her, but they will not extend this nonsensical argument to any other situation.

Are we a part of a car when we drive it? Are we a part of the building we work in? Are we a part of the clothing we wear? Of course not! And neither is the preborn child a part of his mother. After all, if any *actual* part of the mother is removed, depending upon its importance, she will either die or be mutilated. This is certainly not the case if an abortionist removes her preborn child.

Between Fertilization and Birth? Another bizarre pro-abortion assertion holds that God does not create the soul, the *mother* does. The anti-baby group 'Catholics' for a Free Choice (CFFC) denied the procreative ability of *God Himself* when it asserted, "Personhood begins when the bearer of life, the mother, makes a covenant of love with the developing life within her to bring it to birth. It is in the nature of things that woman creates the "soul" just as much as she nourishes the body of developing human life."[1] In other words, the preborn baby is not a person until the mother *decides* he is.

Is this not the *defining statement* of all oppression? What would CFFC say if a group of men asserted that *women* were not persons until *men* decided they were?

There is only one "position" on abortion that really counts: "Before I formed you in the womb I knew you; before you came to birth I consecrated you; I have appointed you as a prophet to the nations" (Jeremiah 1:5)

[Cartoon courtesy of Colorado Springs Sun].

CFFC and other pro-abortion "Catholics" allege that abortion must not be banned because it is impossible to scientifically prove when ensoulment takes place. In its *Declaration on Procured Abortion*, the Vatican decreed: "From a moral point of view this is certain: Even if a doubt existed concerning whether the fruit of conception is already a human person, it is objectively a grave sin to dare to risk murder." In other words, when there is doubt, we must always err on the side of life and safety.

It is illogical to argue that ensoulment takes place progressively over a period of time between fertilization and birth. It is impossible for progressive ensoulment to take place, just as it is impossible for a woman to be "semi-pregnant." Either an entity has a soul or it does not. Nobody can possess one-half or two-thirds of a soul. Instantaneous ensoulment during pregnancy is also an irrational premise, because the development of a human being is an unbroken, smooth continuum that proceeds from fertilization to birth and beyond. In other words, there is no specific point at which the child could become "eligible" to receive a soul—except at fertilization.

At Fertilization! As discussed above, the location of the preborn child changes at birth, and this is not a sufficiently significant event to merit the acquisition of a soul. However, at *fertilization*, a much more profound event takes place. Where before there was only a pair of living, human gametes—the ovum and the spermatozoon—afterwards there is a living, human *person* who did not exist before. As described in Question 78, the definition of "person" is "a living human being, especially as distinguished from an animal or thing."

Individual human sperm cells do not possess souls. Neither do human ova, animals or things. But after fertilization, there is a *unique, living preborn person* in existence who did not exist beforehand. This status does not change at birth, and does not change until the person's death.

Therefore, the only logical time when ensoulment could possibly take place is at fertilization.

1   Mary Meehan. "The Maguires Bring Abortion Issue to a Turbulent Boil." *National Catholic Register*, 27 May 1984, pp. 1 and 7.

....

93. Has the Roman Catholic Church Always Opposed Abortion?

The Assertions

Misinformation about *current* authentic Catholic teaching on abortion abounds because dissenters and other pro-abortionists are deliberately aggravating the situation. The situation is even more confused regarding *historical* Catholic opposition to abortion.

Pro-abortionists frequently make several false statements about ancient Catholic teachings on abortion in order to confuse the faithful, priests and religious.

The most common of these falsehoods are these: "[Prior to 1869], the Church had officially accepted the theory of delayed animation for 500 years.... Abortion before ensoulment was tolerated by the Catholic Church."[1] "The Catholic Church is not consistent in its teaching. From 1211 to 1869, it recognized two types of foetus. It taught that the male foetus became animated at 40 days, and the female at 80 days. Furthermore, until 1869 the Church allowed abortion until quickening."[2]

Illegal abortionist Ruth Barnett revealed the reasoning behind this pro-abortion historical revisionism: "I believe that a case can be made that the church's attitudes towards abortion have varied in past history, are not always consistent and can, like other elements of Catholic dogma, be changed to meet man's increased enlightenment and changing social conditions."[3]

The Truth

The pro-abortion assertion that the Catholic Church *ever* sanctioned or allowed abortion is completely false, as actual Church documents show. No Pope, Council, Saint or early Church Father has ever written or said anything that could be interpreted as support for abortion.[4]

The *Catechism of the Catholic Church* (¶2271) teaches, "since the first century the Church has affirmed the moral evil of every procured abortion. This teaching has not changed and remains unchangeable. Direct abortion, that is to say, abortion willed either as an end or a means, is gravely contrary to the moral law.... Abortion and infanticide are abominable crimes."

The Vatican's *Declaration on Procured Abortion* (¶7) gives the most comprehensive answer to the pro-abortionists' charges that the Church ever permitted abortion:

In the course of history, the Fathers of the Church, her Pastors and her Doctors have taught the same doctrine—the various opinions on the infusion of the spiritual soul did not introduce any doubt about the illicitness of abortion. It is true that in the Middle Ages, when the opinion was generally held that the spiritual soul was not present until after the first few weeks, a distinction was made in the evaluation of the sin and the gravity of penal sanctions. Excellent authors allowed for the first period more lenient case solutions which they rejected for following periods. But it was never denied at that time that procured abortion, even during the first days, was objectively a grave fault. This condemnation was in fact unanimous.

Among the many documents it is sufficient to recall certain ones. The first Council of Mainz in 847 reconsidered the penalties against abortion which had been established by preceding Councils. It decided that the most rigorous penance would be imposed "on women who procure the elimination of the fruit conceived in their womb."[5] The Decree of Gratian reported the following words of Pope Stephen V: "That person is a murderer who causes to perish by abortion what has been conceived."[6] St. Thomas, the Common Doctor of the Church, teaches that abortion is a grave sin against the natural law.[7] At the time of the Renaissance, Pope Sixtus V condemned abortion with the greatest severity.[8] A century later, Innocent XI rejected the propositions of certain lax canonists who sought to excuse an abortion procured before the moment accepted by some as the moment of the spiritual animation of the new being.[9]

Challenge Attacks upon the Faith!

Table 12 cites just a few of the Church's condemnations of abortion during the first few centuries of Her existence.

When a pro-abortionist alleges the Church ever permitted abortion, Catholics must challenge him or her to provide documentation—*not* mere references to other pro-abortionists who make the same spurious charge.

1 Canadian psychiatrist Wendell W. Watters. *Compulsory Pregnancy: The Truth about Abortion*. Toronto: McLelland & Steward, 1976, p. 90.

2   Diane Munday of the British pro-abortion group "Association for the Reform of the Abortion Law." Quoted in Colin Francome. *Abortion Freedom: A Worldwide Movement.* London: George Allen & Unwin Publishers, 1984, pp. 89-90.

3   Ruth Barnett. *They Weep on My Doorstep.* Beaverton, Oregon: Halo Publishers, 1969, pp. 106-107.

4   The early Church Fathers were unanimous in their condemnation of abortion. Among those documents still extant are the *Apocalypse* of Peter; Tertullian, theologian (150-225), *Treatise on the Soul*, pp. 25 and 27; Hippolytus, Bishop of Pontius and theologian (died 236), *Refutation of All Heresies*, 9.7; Origen, theologian of Alexandria (185-254), *Against Heresies*, p. 9; Cyprian, Bishop of Carthage (c. 200-258), *Letters*, p. 48; Methodius, Bishop of Olympus (died 311); Council of Elvira in Granada, Spain (305), *Canons*, 63 and 68; Council of Ancyra in Galatia, Asia Minor (314), *Canon*, 21; Ephraem the Syrian, theologian (306-373), *De Timore Dei*, p. 10; Ephipanius, Bishop of Salamis (c. 315-403); St. Basil the Great, priest (c. 329-379),

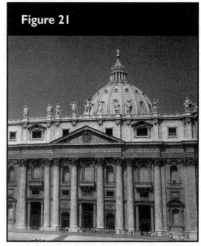

Figure 21

"Since the first century the Church has affirmed the moral evil of every procured abortion. This teaching has not changed and remains unchangeable."
—The Catechism of the Catholic Church (¶2271)

Letters, 188.2, 8; St. Ambrose, Bishop of Milan (c. 339-397), *Hexameron*, 5.18.58; *Apostolic Constitutions* (late Fourth Century); St. Augustine, Bishop of Hippo (354-430), *Enchiridion*, p. 86; St. John Chrysostom, Bishop of Constantinople (c. 347-407), *Homily* 24 ("On The Book of Romans"); St. Jerome (died in 420); Council of Chalcedon (451); Caesarius, Bishop of Arles (470-543), *Sermons*, 1.12; Council of Lerida (524); Second Council of Braga (527), *Canons*, 77; St. Martin of Braga (580); and *Consillium Quinisextum* (692).

5   Canon 21 (Mansi, 14, p. 909), Council of Elvira, Canon 63 (Mansi, 2, p. 16), and the Council of Ancyra, Canon 21 (*ibid*, p. 519).

6   Gratian, *Concordiantia Discordantium Canonum*, c. 20, C 2, q.2.

7   *Commentary on the Sentences*, book IV, dist. 31, exposition of the text.

8   Constitutio *Effraenatum* in 1588 (*Bullarium Romanum*, V, I, pp. 25-27); *Fontes Iuris Canonici*, I, no. 165, pp. 308-311.

9   The Constitution *Apostolicae Sedis* of Pius XI (*Acta Pii* XI, V, pp. 55-72).

···

94. Didn't St. Jerome and St. Thomas Aquinas Say Ensoulment Didn't Occur Until Quickening?

The Claims

Pro-abortion propagandists often point out that St. Thomas Aquinas and St. Jerome speculated as to when God infuses the soul. They then make a stupendous leap in "logic" and assert that this uncertainty constitutes some sort of approval of abortion. For example, the 'Religious' Coalition for Abortion Rights (now RCRC) alleges:

Catholic theology, which now regards the early fetus as a person, did not always do so. The Church first adopted the belief of Aristotle, St. Jerome, St. Augustine, and St. Thomas Aquinas that ensoulment occurs several weeks after conception. Pope Innocent III, who ruled at the turn of the 13th Century, made that belief part of Church doctrine, allowing abortion until fetal animation. It was not until 1869 that the Church prohibited abortion at any time and for any reason.[1]

This is just one in a galaxy of misleading statements that pro-abortionists use to support prenatal child-killing. An even more bizarre statement came from Marjorie Reilly Maguire, who said with a straight face that the Annunciation "proves" that ensoulment does not take place until the mother consents to "the pregnancy that is within her."[2]

Table 12

Early Teachings of the Catholic Church against Abortion

• •

"You shall not kill an unborn child or murder a newborn infant."
—*The Didache*, II, 2.

"You shall love your neighbor more than your own life. You shall not slay the child by abortion."
—Barnabas (c. 70-138), *Epistles*, Volume II, p. 19.

"For us [Christians], murder is once and for all forbidden; so even the child in the womb, while yet the mother's blood is still being drawn on to form the human being, it is not lawful for us to destroy. To forbid birth is only quicker murder.... He is a man, who is to be a man; the fruit is always present in the seed."
—Tertullian, 197, *Apologeticus*, p. 9.

"Those women who use drugs to bring about an abortion commit murder and will have to give an account to God for their abortion."
—Athenagoras of Athens, letter to Marcus Aurelius in 177, *Legatio pro Christianis* ("Supplication for the Christians"), p. 35.

"... there are women who, by the use of medicinal potions, destroy the unborn life in their wombs, and murder the child before they bring it forth. These practices undoubtedly are derived from a custom established by your gods; Saturn, though he did not expose his sons, certainly devoured them."
—Minucius Felix, theologian (c. 200-225), *Octavius*, p. 30.

Table 12 (Continued)

"... if we would not kill off the human race born and developing according to God's plan, then our whole lives would be lived according to nature. Women who make use of some sort of deadly abortion drug kill not only the embryo but, together with it, all human kindness."
— Clement of Alexandria, priest and the "Father of Theologians" (c. 150-220), *Christ the Educator*, Volume II, p. 10.

"Sometimes this lustful cruelty or cruel lust goes so far as to seek to procure a baneful sterility, and if this fails the fetus conceived in the womb is in one way or another smothered or evacuated, in the desire to destroy the offspring before it has life, or if it already lives in the womb, to kill it before it is born."
— St. Augustine, Bishop of Hippo (354-430), *De Nuptius et Concupiscus* ("On Marriage and Concupiscence"), 1.17.

"Some virgins [unmarried women], when they learn they are with child through sin, practice abortion by the use of drugs. Frequently they die themselves and are brought before the ruler of the lower world guilty of three crimes; suicide, adultery against Christ, and murder of an unborn child."
— St. Jerome (c. 340-420), *Letter to Eustochium*, 22.13.

"The hairsplitting difference between formed and unformed makes no difference to us. Whoever deliberately commits abortion is subject to the penalty for homicide."
— St. Basil the Great (c. 329-379), "First Canonical Letter." *Three Canonical Letters*. Loeb Classical Library, Volume III, pp. 20-23.

"Those who give drugs for procuring abortion, and those who receive poisons to kill the foetus, are subjected to the penalty for murder."
— Trullian (Quinisext) Council (692), *Canons*, 91.

Of course, the Gospels record the Virgin Mary consented just *before* the moment of conception. Maguire also conveniently neglected to mention that, during the Visitation, the unborn St. John the Baptist leapt with joy in his mother's womb at the presence of another unborn child—Jesus.

The Truth

Such quibbling is designed to distract and confuse the faithful. Both Sts. Thomas and Jerome knew that ensoulment and abortion were two separate issues. Although they were not sure when ensoulment took place, they saw that this very uncertainty meant abortion must be sinful, because it was impermissible to *risk* killing a being that might have a soul, even if no one could prove its presence. St. Jerome warned, "some virgins [unmarried women], when they learn they are with child through sin, practice abortion by the use of drugs. Frequently they die themselves and are brought before the ruler of the lower world guilty of three crimes;

suicide, adultery against Christ, and murder of an unborn child."[3]

In any case, the matter of when the body is "ensouled" has historically made no difference to the Catholic Church, as explained by St. Basil the Great, who had obviously dealt with pro-abortionists, judging from his language: "The hairsplitting difference between formed and unformed [unsouled and ensouled] makes no difference to us. Whoever deliberately commits abortion is subject to the penalty for homicide."[4]

In summary, Sts. Thomas and Jerome were offering a theory based upon the best medical knowledge of their times, which Aristotle had set forth centuries before. Aristotle taught that preborn children did not become human until 40 days after conception.[5] This notion was discarded only in 1621, as a result of the work of Paulo Zacchia in his *Quaestiones Medico-Legales*. Zacchia, Physician-General of the Vatican State, argued that ensoulment takes place at conception and that the preborn child's physical development is a continuum.[6]

It is quite certain that Sts. Thomas and Jerome, if they had had access to current medical technology, would have declared that life begins at fertilization.

1 'Religious' Coalition for Abortion Rights. "ABORTION: Why Religious Organizations in the United States Want to Keep it Legal." Pamphlet dated June, 1978.

2 D.J. Dooley. "The Cuomo Syndrome." *Fidelity* Magazine, December, 1987, pp. 8-11.

3 St. Jerome (c. 340-420), *Letter to Eustochium*, 22.13.

4 St. Basil the Great (c. 329-379), *First Canonical Letter*, from the work *Three Canonical Letters*. Loeb Classical Library, Volume III, pp. 20-23.

5 Aristotle consulted a number of the most distinguished thinkers of his time, including Democritus, Anaxagoras, Thales, Diogenes, Heraclitis and Alcmaeon, and concluded the soul is a "motive force;" therefore, the preborn only receive them when they begin moving. He concluded, "All, then, it may be said, characterize the soul by three marks, Movement, Sensation, Incorporeality." See A.J. Smith's translation of Aristotle's *On the Soul* (Book I, 2-3).

6 Paolo Zacchia. *Quaestiones Medico-Legales*. Lyons: 1620. Library 6, Title 1, Questions 7 and 16.

··

95. Didn't Pope Pius IX Declare Abortion to Be Murder Only in 1869?

The Assertion

For at least a century, pro-abortionists have tried to confuse the faithful with a flawed, three-step logical analysis:

(1) the Church has not always taught that ensoulment begins at conception;

(2) therefore, the Church has not always opposed abortion;

(3) therefore, the Church can change its teachings on abortion *again* if it wants to.

There are countless examples of this kind of deceit. Michael Carrera says: "Although Catholic teaching on abortion has shifted through the centuries, the current position is clear: abortion is murder. This position has been fixed since 1869, when Pope Pius IX reinstituted the doctrine that the soul enters the body at the moment of conception."[1]

The Truth

As we saw in Question 93, the Catholic Church has *always* taught that abortion constitutes the killing of a human being. However, some confusion exists because the Church has changed the *penalties* for the killing of a preborn child several times in Her history.

In 1588, Pope Sixtus V tried to discourage abortion by reserving confession and absolution to the Holy See alone, a practice enforced only for a handful of the most egregious sins. It soon became evident that this arrangement was impractical, so just three years later Pope Gregory XIV returned the power of absolution for abortion to the local bishops.[2] Today, of course, any priest with faculties can hear a confession for the sin of abortion.

In 1679, Pope Innocent XI condemned the writings and teachings of two theologians, Thomas Sanchez and Joannis Marcus, who believed abortion was lawful if the fetus was not yet animated or ensouled.[3] This proved that the Church did not tolerate abortion, and would prosecute those who spread error about it.

The French Jesuit Theophile Raynaud (1582-1663) believed indirect abortion of a viable baby to save the mother's life was allowable. This was notable because he was the *first* theologian to hold this view and his teachings were unique in the Church until about 1850. They were an early statement of the "double effect," described in Question 85.

In 1869, Pope Pius IX took the action that "Catholic" pro-abortionists deliberately misrepresent in order to buttress their heretical views. The abortophiles allege that, in this year, the Pope condemned abortion for the very first time.

In reality, the Pope merely removed the distinction between the animated and unanimated fetus from the Code of Canon Law.[4] This action dealt not with theology, but with *discipline*, and merely made the punishment for abortion at any stage uniform. The Pope took this action in light of recent medical discoveries, and after prolonged discussion with his theologians.

1   Michael Carrera. *Sex: The Facts, The Acts, and Your Feelings.* New York: Crown Books, 1981, p. 290.

2   Lucius Farraris, *Bibliotheca Iuridica Moralis Theologica.* Roma: 1885, Volume I, pp. 36-38.

3   Denzinger-Schoenmetzer. *Enchiridion Symbolorum.* Rome: Herder, 1965, pp. 2134-2135.

4   *Codicus Iuris Canonici Fontes.* Rome, 1923 to 1939, specification number 552.

••

96. Didn't Vatican II Allow Greater Freedom of Conscience in Making Moral Decisions?

The Claims

Some dissenting "Catholics" say the only teachings of the Church that its members are bound to follow are those solemnly declared infallible.

Conversely, they allege that any teaching of the Church that has *not* specifically been declared infallible is open to individual interpretation. This interpretation, of course, is based upon the dictates of one's "conscience," no matter how poorly formed. In other words, they say that any action is excusable as long as the person can assert, "I was only following my conscience."

This principle is very handy for dissenters, of course, because they can then follow their vestigial consciences and feel free to commit acts such as sodomy, masturbation, fornication, adultery, abortion, divorce, sterilization, using pornography and contracepted sex.

The Truth: Natural Law

In order to answer the fundamental question of how to balance conscience and authority, we must first define "natural law."

Romans 2:12-16 and Jeremiah 31:33 tell us that God imprints His natural law on the heart and soul of man, and this lets him recognize innately whether an act is good or evil. In other words, "natural law" is man's instinctual knowledge of right and wrong—his "conscience."

St. Thomas Aquinas explains, "the light of natural reason, whereby we discern what is good and what is evil, which is the function of the natural law, is nothing else than an imprint on us of the Divine light."[1]

The nature of God never changes. Because the natural law is an "imprint on us of the Divine light," it, too, can never be changed. This means that Church teachings on faith and morals made according to natural law can never be changed—not even by the Pope and all of his assembled cardinals and bishops. And *certainly* not by disgruntled lay people and dissident priests!

The Truth: On Conscience

However, 'Catholics' for a Free Choice (CFFC) and other dissenters never tire of telling us we can choose abortion *if* we do so with a clear conscience. The kind of "conscience" CFFC is talking about is the kind that lets us do whatever we *want* to do. CFFC says: "If you carefully examine your conscience and then decide that an abortion is the most moral act you can do at this time, you're not committing a sin. Therefore, you're not excommunicated. Nor need you tell it in confession since, in your case, abortion is not a sin."[2]

Under this kind of "logic," of course, a man could easily justify rape if he felt victimized by women. And a person who thought he did not have all of the material possessions that he was entitled to could justify stealing. In other words, CFFC is implying that there is no sin in the world, because everyone tries to justify the evil he commits.

Sometimes these pro-abortion "Catholics" quote a Vatican II document, *Declaration on Religious Freedom*, to support their notion that we should be able to do anything our consciences don't object to. For example, CFFC's pamphlet "Did You Know that Most Catholics Believe in Reproductive Freedom?" claims that, "according to Vatican II, 'Declaration on Religious Liberty': 'the Christian faithful have the civil right of freedom from interference in leading their lives according to their conscience.'"

However, Fr. John Courtney Murray, S.J., principal author of the *Declaration*, foresaw this kind of dishonesty. In a footnote to the Abbott-Gallagher edition of the Council texts, he cautioned:

The *Declaration* does not base the right to the free exercise of religion on "freedom of conscience." *Nowhere does this phrase occur.* And the *Declaration* nowhere lends its authority to the theory for which the phrase frequently stands, namely, that I have the right to do what my conscience tells me to do, simply because my conscience tells me to do it. This is a perilous theory. Its particular peril is subjectivism—the notion that, in the end, it is my conscience, and not the objective truth, which determines what is right and wrong, true or false.[3]

The point that pro-abortionists invariably miss is that we must act according to a *properly formed* and *informed* conscience. As Pope Pius XII explained, "Conscience is a pupil, not a teacher." It is not enough that an action "feels right;" a person must know what the Church teaches about it and honestly assess the situation, after sufficient prayer and reflection. And, of course, no one in any instance may commit acts that are *intrinsically evil*—such as contraception, abortion, sterilization, adultery or sodomy—*regardless* of what his "conscience" tells him.

On the Infallibility of *Humanae Vitae*

Ex Cathedra Pronouncements. After defining "natural law" and "conscience," we must turn our attention to the related issue of *ex cathedra* ("from the chair") pronouncements of the Pope.

There are two ways Catholics may know that a teaching of the Church is infallible and, therefore, must obey it *in order to remain Catholic.*

The first, of course, is a formal *ex cathedra* pronouncement. Popes rarely make this kind of solemn declaration, and then only to address absolute fundamentals of Catholic faith. Only once since 1870 has a pontiff spoken *ex cathedra*: On 1 November 1950, when Pope Pius XII declared the doctrine of the Assumption of the Blessed Virgin Mary necessary for all Catholics to believe.

Many pro-life theologians have debated the wisdom of a pope declaring the Church's teachings on contraception and abortion infallible, and have decided this would not be prudent. The reason is, such a pronouncement in an area of morals (as opposed to fundamental beliefs) would imply all other moral teachings of the Church were optional. This might lead to disbelief running rampant in the areas not specifically addressed *ex cathedra*, and demands for such pronouncements in almost every area of Church teaching.

The Ordinary [Universal] Magisterium. The second way Catholics can know a Church teaching is infallible is by studying the ordinary or universal Magisterium—the day-to-day expression of the Church's ordinary teaching authority.

The Canon of St. Vincent of Lorenz declares that any doctrine taught *semper ubique omnes*—always, everywhere, and by everyone—makes it part of the ordinary and universal Magisterial teaching.[4]

We saw in the quotes from ancient Catholic theologians in Question 93 that the prohibition against abortion has indeed been taught *semper ubique omnes*. This means that Pope Paul VI's 1968 encyclical *Humanae Vitae* does not declare or create some new doctrine or dogma. It simply reiterates and summarizes the *infallible doctrine* that human life is sacred from conception to natural death.

The Catechism of the Catholic Church (¶892) restates the authority of the ordinary Magisterium:

Divine assistance is also given to the successors of the apostles, teaching in communion with the successor of Peter, and, in a particular way, to the bishop of Rome, pastor of the whole Church, when, without arriving at an infallible definition and without pronouncing in a "definitive manner," they propose in the exercise of the ordinary Magisterium a teaching that leads to better understanding of Revelation in matters of faith and morals. To this ordinary teaching the faithful "are to adhere to it with religious assent" which, though distinct from the assent of faith, is nonetheless an extension of it.

So, we may state with certainty that the Catholic Church's teaching on abortion is, indeed, an infallible doctrine.

The Fundamental Question

Before concluding this discussion of infallibility, we must pause for a moment to consider this: do we really believe that "Catholic" abortophiles would suddenly stop advocating prenatal child-killing if the Pope issued an *ex cathedra* decree against abortion?

Obviously, they would not. Just as with the question of ensoulment, the pro-abortionists couldn't care less about the degree of solemnity of Catholic condemnation of abortion. This is another red herring they use to distract attention from the real issue—the killing.

1 St. Thomas Aquinas, *Summa Theologica*, First Part of the Second Part, Question 91, Answer 2, Para. 1/1. Translation of the Dominican Fathers of the English Province.

2 'Catholics' for a Free Choice undated brochure titled "You Are Not Alone."

3 Russell Shaw. "Answers." *National Catholic Register*, 13 September 1992, p. 4.

4 As described in Msgr. William Smith, "*Humanae Vitae*, Dissent, and Infallibility," a presentation at Human Life International's World Conference on Love, Life, and the Family, held in Santa Clara, California in March, 1991. St. Vincent stated, "Moreover, in the Catholic Church itself, all possible care must be taken, that we hold that faith which has been believed everywhere, always, by all. For that is truly and in the strictest sense 'Catholic,' which, as the name itself and the reason of the thing declare, comprehends all universally. This rule we shall observe if we follow universality, antiquity, consent. We shall follow universality if we confess that one faith to be true, which the whole Church throughout the world confesses; antiquity, if we in no wise depart from those interpretations which it is manifest were notoriously held by our holy ancestors and fathers; consent, in like manner, if in antiquity itself we adhere to the consistent definitions and determinations of all, or at the least of almost all priests and doctors" (*The Commonitory* of St. Vincent of Lerins, Chapter II [6], "A General Rule for Distinguishing the Truth of the Catholic Faith from the Falsehood of Heretical Pravity," 434 A.D.).

··

97. What Penalty Does the Church Impose for Any Degree of Participation in an Abortion?

Excommunication for Abortion

The teaching of the Catholic Church on abortion could not be clearer. Only a person who is willfully blinding himself or herself to the facts could make the ridiculous claim that there is "room for a diversity of opinion" in the Church on abortion.

The Church not only does not *want* to change its teaching on abortion, it *absolutely cannot*, because this crucial issue deals with fundamental questions that derive from the natural law.

The Canon and Its Requirements

Canon 2350 states that all who procure abortion shall be automatically excommunicated.

Canon Law Number 1398 states, quite simply, in Latin and English:

Qui abortum procurat, effectu secuto, in excommunicationem, latae sententiae, incurrat—'Those who successfully abort [a living human fetus] bring on themselves instant excommunication.'

Abortum procurat means anyone who provides aid without which the abortion could not have been committed. This may be the boyfriend, husband, father or mother who drives the pregnant woman or girl to the abortion mill, pays for the abortion in full or in part, or even advises that abortion may be an option. Section 2 of Canon Law 1329 states, "accomplices, even though not mentioned in the law or precept, incur the same penalty [*latae sententiae* excommunication] if, without their assistance, the crime would not have been committed ... otherwise, they can be punished with *ferendae sententiae* [inflicted by clergy] penalties."

Latae sententiae means the person brings instant excommunication upon himself or herself with his act. No solemn pronouncement need be made by the Church or a bishop or priest, and no one else need even know about the abortion. For automatic excommunication to take place, the woman (and those who cooperate in the abortion) must meet three conditions:

(1) They must *know* abortion is a mortal sin. Most Catholics have probably never heard this preached from the pulpit. However, if a person reads about or hears of the Church's teachings on abortion from any source, he or she has been informed. Even if a person does not agree with or *accept* the teachings, he or she knows the Church teaches abortion is a mortal sin.

(2) The woman and those who cooperate in the abortion must *know* or *suspect* she is pregnant. Many women use abortifacients, including oral contraceptives, Norplant, mini-pills, Depo-Provera, and intrauterine devices (IUDs), and may be aborting several babies a year. It is important to note that the woman must have full knowledge of her act. Most people (even many doctors) are completely unaware of the abortifacient effects of these devices and drugs, and therefore generally would not be liable to excommunication. However, if a woman knows a method is abortifacient and uses it anyway, she risks excommunication.

(3) The woman must *freely choose* abortion. This does not mean she can interpret a boyfriend's, husband's or parent's disapproval of her pregnancy as coercion; she must make a vigorous and positive attempt to avoid abortion, no matter how much pressure she feels. If she believes that she is in danger of physical harm, she should turn to other family members or social service or law enforcement agencies for assistance. In protecting her preborn child, she must exert the same degree of effort she would if the child were an infant or toddler.

Effectu secuto means the excommunication takes place only if the abortion is completed. At the moment the woman's child dies, she is cut off completely from all the Sacraments, and cannot return unless she sincerely repents and makes a good confession.

Excommunication for People Taking Part in Abortion

The sanction of excommunication also applies to the abortionist, nurse or counselor, and anyone else who aids or assists in an abortion. This is why a bishop publicly excommunicated Mary Ann Sorrentino, a "Catholic" who ran a Planned Parenthood abortuary in Rhode Island.

No Catholic health worker may take part in committing abortions, sterilizations or distribution of abortifacients, even if his or her employer or job description demands it. *Evangelium Vitae* (¶89) insists:

Absolute respect for every innocent human life also requires the exercise of *conscientious objection* in relation to procured abortion and euthanasia. 'Causing death' can never be considered a form of medical treatment, even when the intention is solely to comply with the patient's request. Rather, it runs completely counter to the health-care profession, which is meant to be an impassioned and unflinching affirmation of life.

On Dissenters

The U.S. Catholic Bishops have stated clearly that one cannot be Catholic and even support the *general concept* of abortion: "At this particular time abortion has become the fundamental human rights issue for all men and women of good will.... No Catholic can responsibly take a "pro-choice" stand when the "choice" in question involves the taking of innocent life."[1]

In other words, the term "pro-choice Catholic" is the ultimate oxymoron.

However, this does not stop various self-proclaimed "Catholics" from imagining that they can pick and choose among Church teachings. For example, Pamela Maraldo, former President of Planned Parenthood Federation of America (PPFA), said: "I go to church on Sunday but do not subscribe to many of the basic tenets of the Church. That does not mean I am any less a Catholic."[2]

To appreciate the absurdity of this and similar statements, imagine what would happen if a PPFA board member announced, "I come to all of Planned Parenthood's meetings but do not subscribe to many of its basic beliefs. I believe fetuses are persons, I do not believe in convenience abortions, I do not believe tax dollars should pay for abortions and I do not believe we have any business handing out contraceptives in school. That does not mean I am any less 'pro-choice' than anyone else."

Planned Parenthood, 'Catholics' for a Free Choice and other pro-abortion groups demand that the Catholic Church tolerate dissent in its ranks—yet no pro-abortion group tolerates any dissent *whatsoever*, no matter how mild. If a person does not rigidly support the entire pro-abortion agenda *without exception*, their "pro-choice" organization denounces them as "anti-choice fanatics" and expels them. As just one example, Planned Parenthood of Southwestern Indiana fired its longtime Medical Director, Dr. Roger Newton, when it learned of his support for a bill requiring "humane disposal of fetal remains." Newton observed accurately, "Unless you are willing to be absolutely pro-abortion, then evidently you are not welcome."[3]

1 *Resolution on Abortion* at the Annual Meeting of the Catholic Bishops of the United States on 16 November 1989.

2 "More on Maraldo." *National STOPP News*, 20 January 1993, p. 1.

3 "PPFA Official Fired for Supporting "Humane Disposal" of Aborted Babies." *National Right to Life News*, 16 May 1985, p. 4.

98. Who Are 'Catholics' For a Free Choice?

CFFC's Missions

'Catholics' for a Free Choice (CFFC) is to the abortion movement what the North American Man-Boy Love Association (NAMBLA) is to the homosexual movement: such an obviously disreputable and spurious group that not even the ultra-liberal *National Catholic Reporter* will accept its advertisements.

CFFC began its disreputable existence in PPFA headquarters in Washington, D.C.[1] CFFC's leadership consists of such people as Frances Kissling (rhymes with "quisling"), whom her friends call the "Cardinal of Choice," former priest Daniel Maguire, and several ex-nuns who were expelled from their orders.

CFFC has three main goals.

The first goal is to create confusion among the faithful about what the Church teaches on abortion. CFFC strategists know that if they can plant a seed of doubt in people's minds about the traditional Catholic response to abortion by asserting that the Church did not *always* oppose prenatal baby-killing, then the Church will appear inconsistent and punitive when it *does* oppose abortion.

CFFC's second goal is to persuade people that abortion is fundamentally linked with religious freedom. CFFC asserts that, if abortion is restricted in any way, then somehow religious freedom is also restricted. CFFC says that if abortion is criminalized, a particular religious belief about when life begins is being forced upon the nation. Of course, CFFC never mentions that the particular religious belief that life begins at *birth* is being enforced by the government now.

CFFC's third goal is to persuade people that they can be good Catholics and still kill their preborn children with clear consciences. In fact, CFFC insists people cannot be good Catholics *unless* they support abortion! This is in line with its insistence that *every* Catholic hospital must commit abortions and every insurance plan must pay for them, even if the hospital or insurance plan is operated by a church to whom baby-killing is morally repugnant.[2]

CFFC dissenters gnaw away at the structure of the Catholic Church like termites. They need its structure, power and resources. If CFFC would simply be honest and admit that it was not truly Catholic, its platform would disappear, the news media would forget it, and it would soon vanish into the void as a forgotten, shrill fringe group. CFFC is a spiritual vampire, greedily feeding on its host while actively sucking away its vitality.

CFFC's Membership and Funding

Before being embarrassed into admitting it was a non-membership group, CFFC "boasted" about 3,500 members, or less than 1/10,000 of the total Catholic Church membership of 55 million.

It is very interesting that CFFC derives only about $5,000 per year from its $15 dues. This means it has an actual paying membership of only about 300 people. The vast majority of its multi-million dollar worldwide budget comes from organizations with philosophies hostile to the teachings of the Catholic Church.[3]

For example, CFFC's biggest source of funds is the Sunnen Foundation, which makes Emko contraceptive foam and which poured money into funding the lawsuit that led to the *Roe v. Wade* decision. Sunnen's director has called the Catholic Church "detrimental to the world," and has demanded that She be *forced by law* to change Her teachings on abortion.[4]

Figure 22

People of all faiths who wish to be citizens of the "Culture of Life" would do well to emulate the examples of one of the greatest pro-life activists of all time—Pope John Paul II, author of Evangelium Vitae.

CFFC also gets much money from the Brush Foundation, founded by a eugenicist friend of Margaret Sanger, and the Ford Foundation, which gives more than $10 million annually to pro-abortion and population control groups.

Most interestingly, the Playboy Foundation has poured tens of thousands of dollars into CFFC's coffers.

Joseph O'Rourke, an early CFFC activist, revealed the real reason the group even exists: "CFFC really was just kept alive for years because the mainline pro-choice movement wanted a Catholic voice."[5]

Catholics or Witches?

CFFC has never in the slightest way resembled anything truly Catholic. The group chants, "If men could become pregnant, abortion would be a sacrament." However, CFFC has already made abortion into a witchcraft-style "sacrament!" A CFFC brochure, "You Are Not Alone" includes two "liturgies" for mothers who have decided to kill their preborn children:[6]

■ The first "liturgy" is supposed to make a mother feel good about the inevitable decision to abort (and there IS no question that she will abort, none whatsoever). She should play some soothing background music and "light a candle, absorb its power, and pray." Then she must imagine herself 10 years from now (a) with a child and (b) without a child. Next, she talks with a helper about her feelings and sings a song, "i found god in myself." Then she does something "nice for herself" after the exhausting ordeal of deciding to abort.

■ Of course, there is a "liturgy" for all of those Good Catholic Women who decide that abortion is the Most Moral Thing For Them To Do. The "liturgy" "affirms that a woman has made a good and holy decision [to abort]." The "celebrant" and her friends chant the following blasphemous and self-indulgent prayer: "Praised be you, Mother and Father God, that you have given your people the power of choice. We are saddened that the life circumstances of [aborting woman's name] are such that she has had to choose to terminate her pregnancy. We affirm her and support her in her decision."

It is significant that CFFC doesn't include a "liturgy" for mothers who choose to keep their babies. This, after all, is the essence of "pro-choice": there is really only one choice that pro-abortionists celebrate, and that is the choice to *kill*.

Frances Kissling: "Cardinal of Death"

Frances Kissling is the longtime director of 'Catholics' for a Free Choice, and this position suits her morality and theology perfectly. There is no more ideal person to run CFFC.

Kissling likes to mention her background as a nun (conveniently not mentioning that she quit the Sisters of St. Joseph after only six months). She boasts about shacking up with men, says that she would have an abortion if she got pregnant, and says she was sterilized in 1978 (the Catholic Church also teaches that sterilization is a mortal sin).[7]

She co-founded the National Abortion Federation (NAF), the abortionists' trade association, and worked as a highly-placed official of the International Projects Assistant Services (IPAS), which specializes in subverting the law in foreign countries and setting up illegal abortion centers in contravention to local beliefs and customs.[7]

Kissling also helped set up illegal abortion mills in Mexico and Italy, and ran two New York aborturaries: the Eastern Women's Center and the Pelham Medical Group, which, she boasts, killed 13,000 preborn babies every year during 1970-1973.[8]

Kissling's wide range of pro-abortion acts represents enough grave sin to excommunicate her a thousand times. She revealed her totally pro-abortion worldview and her stark hatred of the Church she claims as her own when she raved, "The Catholic religion makes the fetus into an icon, a figure of religious veneration, which I think is sick, really sick."[7]

Despite Scripture mentioning sexual behavior more than any other kind of behavior, Kissling blandly asserts, "I don't think God cares very much about our sexual activity."[8]

Human Life International publishes a detailed report on the activities and background of CFFC entitled "'Catholics for a Free Choice' Exposed: Dirty Ideas, Dirty Money." Send $4.95 (this includes shipping and handling) to HLI, 4 Family Life, Front Royal, VA 22630, or telephone (540) 635-7884.

1 William McGurn. "Catholics & 'Free Choice.'" *National Catholic Register*, 14 February 1982, pp. 2 and 6.

2 Janet B. Carroll. "Catholic Colleges, Hospitals Should Fund Abortions, Says RCAR." *National Right to Life News*, 30 April 1987, p. 13.

3 Mary Meehan. "CFFC Membership Is Nil." *National Catholic Register*, 4 May 1986, p. 1.

4 1979 letter to Michael Schwartz of the Catholic League for Religious and Civil Rights.

5 Mary Meehan. "Foundation Power." *Human Life Review*, Fall, 1984, pp. 42-60.

6 Mary Meehan. "How Can They Be Called Catholic?" *National Catholic Register*, 19 November 1989, p. 5.

7 Ron Brackin. "'Sister' Frances Kissling: Cardinal of Death." *Liberty Report*, January, 1987.

8 Mary Meehan. "Kissling Speaks Frankly about Past Activism." *National Catholic Register*, 7 September 1986, p. 1.

99. What Are the Traditional Teachings of the Jewish Faith on Abortion?

The Major Jewish Beliefs

Non-Jews can better understand Jewish religious beliefs by recognizing that religious Jews generally follow one of four different spiritual paths, which may overlap to a considerable degree in some areas:[1]

■ **Orthodox Jews** maintain strict adherence to traditional customs, including the Biblical laws on family purity. About 10 percent of U.S. Jews count themselves as members of this group.

■ **Reform or Liberal Jews** are essentially Humanistic, but apply nominally Jewish customs to contemporary life. About 41 percent of U.S. Jews call themselves members.

■ **Conservative Jews** try to maintain a strong Jewish identity while combining important elements of both Orthodox and Reform Judaism. About 40 percent of U.S. Jews are Conservative.

■ **Hasidic Jews** may be seen as even more conservative than Orthodox Jews because they follow a uniquely mystical path.

There are more than a dozen major branches of Judaism in the United States.

Those branches that have adhered to the original teachings of Judaism are invariably pro-life. Groups representing these branches include the Rabbinical Alliance of America, the Rabbinical Council of America, United Orthodox Rabbis of the United States and Canada and the Union of Orthodox Jewish Congregations of America.

Organizations representing totally pro-abortion Jews include: the American Jewish Committee, the American Jewish Congress, B'nai B'rith Women, the Central Conference of American Rabbis [Reform], the Federation of Reconstructionist Congregations, Hadassah Women, the Jewish Labor Committee, Na'amat USA, the National Federation of Temple Sisterhoods [Reform], the National Council of Jewish Women, New Jewish Agenda, North American Temple Youth, Rabbinical Assembly, the Union of American Hebrew Congregations [Reform], United Synagogues of America [Conservative] and Women's League for Conservative Judaism.

The Facts of Life

Traditional Jewish Teachings on Abortion

To what can the child be compared inside his mother's womb ... as with a candle perched on his head he perceives the world from one end to the other? ... [W]ho shall replace me in those former months, the days when the Lord watched over me? ... and he is taught the entire *Torah* ...

—*The Talmud*, Nidah 30b

Introduction. Why do various Jewish factions disagree so radically about abortion?

Basically because the Jewish faith has suffered the same catastrophic ethical schism that Christendom has endured: most of its adherents have discarded the inspired Word of God and now see themselves as their own masters. Meanwhile, Orthodox Jews struggle to pass on their beliefs and practices to their children in an ever more anti-religious world. The original faith has splintered into a patchwork of sects embracing the complete range of beliefs on every imaginable social issue. There is a great chasm between religious Jews and cultural Jews.

To understand this conflict and the resulting range of views on abortion, we must review the basics of traditional Jewish religious law.

Summary of the Seven Noahide Laws. First and foremost, the Jewish faith is based upon a body of Commandments that include the seven Noahide Laws and 613 parochial commandments.

These laws are interpreted (but *not* altered) by a vast body of rabbinic opinions and case law called *Halakhah* (*The Talmud*), which is based upon divine revelation.[2]

The seven Noahide Laws are universal: They apply to *everyone*, Jew or Gentile. Bereshis 9:6 contains the seven commandments of B'nei Noach, as follows;

(1) Thou shalt not engage in idol worship.

(2) Thou shalt not blaspheme God.

(3) Thou shalt not kill.

(4) Thou shalt not engage in incestuous, adulterous, or homosexual relations, nor commit the act of rape.

(5) Thou shalt not steal.

(6) Thou shalt establish laws and courts of law to administer these laws.

(7) Thou shalt not be cruel to animals.

The main purpose of the 613 parochial commandments in the *Torah* (The Five Books of Moses) is to support and preserve the seven indispensable Noahide laws. Therefore, they are not applicable to all people.

Some examples of these parochial commandments are;

■ Do not randomly cut down trees (Deuteronomy 20:19);

■ Do not randomly castrate animals (Leviticus 22:24); and

■ Jewish men who sterilize themselves are cast out of the community (Deuteronomy 23:2).

Interpretation of the Third Noahide Law. The Old Testament contains the seven Noahide Laws in Genesis 9:6. The third law includes the admonition, "He who spills the blood of a man in a man, his blood will be spilt." *The Talmud* (Sanhedrin 57b) defines "a man in a man" as a preborn baby in his mother's womb. This passage specifically says abortion is a capital crime, a view supported by one of the leading sages of *The Talmud*, Rabbi Yishmael.[3]

Maimonides, the great 12th Century interpreter and codifier of Jewish law, stated that "Six commandments were commanded by God to Abraham and the commandment of cruelty to animals was added to Noah ... When Abraham came he was commanded to circumcise ... and Moses was given the *Torah*."[2]

In his interpretation of the Third Noahide Law, Maimonides writes in his *Mishneh Torah* that abortion is a capital crime for Jews: "A descendant of Noah who kills any human being, even a fetus in its mother's womb, is to be put to death."

On "Hard Travail." Maimonides ruled abortion allowable only if the pregnancy definitely *and without question* endangered the life of the mother (*Hilkhot Rozeah* 1:9 and *Shulhan Arukh Hoshen Mishpat* 425:2): "This also is a negative precept: Not to have compassion on the life of a pursuer. Therefore, the Sages' rules [regarding] a pregnant woman in hard travail that it is permitted to dismember the fetus in her womb, whether by chemical means or by hand, for it [the fetus] is as one pursuing her in order to kill her."[3]

This passage refers to "hard travail," a delivery complicated by the size or position of the baby, so that a normal birth was impossible. At the time this commentary was written (before the development of obstetrical forceps and, later, safe surgical techniques for a Cesarean section), this kind of problem often resulted in the deaths of both mother and baby. The only way to remove a baby who was "stuck" was to dismember him. In most cases, the mother would have been in labor literally for days, and the baby would have died from anoxia.

In summary, *The Talmud* rules abortion permissible only in extreme cases: specifically when a woman's "hard travail" places her life in unquestionable danger (*Oholoth* 7:6). This is a codification of Maimonides' concept of the *rodef*, or "pursuer."

So, traditional Jewish law holds that the preborn child has a right to life equal to the mother's—*except* when he poses an *imminent* and *actual* danger to her life.

The Catholic parallel to the "hard travail" exception is called the "double effect," as described in Question 85.

The Chief Justice of the Supreme Rabbinical Court of America and the U.S. coordinator of the Jewish Survival Legion, Rabbi Marvin S. Antelman, clearly stated the position of Jewish Noahide law on abortion when he said, in 1978, "All major religions have their parochial and their universal aspects, and the problem of abortion is *NOT* a parochial one. It is of universal morality, and it is neither a Catholic problem, nor a Jewish problem, nor a Protestant problem. It involves the killing of a human being, an act forbidden by *universal* commandment."[4]

Chief Rabbi of England Dr. Immanuel Jakabovits outlined the basis for the reasoning behind this statement when he explained, "Jewish law sees every human life as having the sanctity of intrinsic and infinite worth. One life has as much value as one hundred or one thousand; you cannot multiply infinity and you cannot divide it. So every human being has an identical worth and is identically worth saving."[5]

Exceptions to the Third Noahide Law. It is interesting to compare the thinking of scholars from the various branches of Judaism on permissible exceptions for abortion.

Jewish law, although not specifically granting full personhood (*nefesh*) status to preborn children, modified strict obligations in order to accommodate pregnant women while protecting the interests of the preborn child. The Sanhedrin allowed people to violate the Sabbath for the sake of a preborn child, and no pregnant woman could be tried for a capital offense until she had given birth.[6]

The Talmud held that the preborn baby was "one of the living limbs of the mother." This might sound like support for the pro-abortion "woman's body, woman's choice" slogan, but note that *The Talmud* also forbade any form of amputation or self-mutilation. Protection for the preborn child—except in the case of "hard travail"—was absolute.

Orthodoxy permits abortion to save the life of the mother only in "grave necessity." This might include aggravation of a serious heart condition or if the mother's physical health would suffer drastically as the direct result of fetal deformity, a very rare occurrence.[6]

Relying upon this and related rulings, in certain extraordinary cases, Orthodox rabbis have, for *specific individuals* and in *extreme circumstances*, allowed abortions in cases of *documented* pathologic mental anguish.

These few specific exceptions (numbering no more than six) have led pro-abortion propagandists to say Jewish law allows abortion for any physical or mental indication whatever. Pro-abortion activists used the very same ploy in secular courts to expand the "physical-and-mental-health-of-the-mother" exception until it could "justify" abortion on demand.

Mirroring this strategy, Conservative and Reform scholars require only that the mother show "severe anguish" before an abortion, which, of course, leaves no protection whatsoever for the preborn child. Any mother can say she will suffer "severe anguish" if she is "forced" to continue her pregnancy. Any mother facing a crisis pregnancy can legitimately claim "severe anguish"—and that, of course, has absolutely no bearing on the value of the preborn child's life.

Conservative and Reform scholars say the Sinaitic Laws referring specifically to the Jewish people do not treat abortion as a capital crime in Exodus 21:22-23. But the Hebrew word for a miscarried baby in Exodus 21:22 is *y'ladeha*, or "child," not *u'bar* or *v'lad*, meaning "embryo" and "fetus." So, this passage implies that the preborn child has already attained full humanity, and to deliberately cause his death would be a form of homicide.

Exodus 21:12 speaks of capital punishment specifically for killing a man, so many liberal scholars conclude that the passages in Chapter 21 of Exodus mean the death penalty is imposed for killing a man but not a preborn baby.

But the Conservative and Reform scholars seem to avoid the fundamental point in all of this. *The Talmud*, in Nidah 31a, states that there are three partners in the creation of a child: The father, the mother, and *Hashem*. According to Chazal, this means the creation of a child is the direct will of the Creator Himself. Does it make any sense to obstruct the will of the Almighty by killing one of His human creations for any reason less important than to save *another* of His human creations—a mother in "hard travail?"

Rabbis Get to the Essential Point. A number of Orthodox Rabbis clearly see the dangers that abortion poses, not only to morality in general, but to the Jewish people in particular.

Chief Rabbi Dr. Immanuel Jakabovits, the world's foremost authority on Jewish medical ethics, laments, "these self-inflicted [abortion] losses are proving far more catastrophic than anything we've experienced in our history."[7]

Rabbi Doctor Chaim U. Lipschitz, editor of *The Jewish Press*, states:

Certainly on the issue of abortion we, as the true practitioners of the total and complete law of our immutable Holy *Torah*, are not represented by those Jewish secularists who advocate open and legalized abortion. Again I say it: *We consider abortion to be murder, plain and simple.* We do permit it only to save the life of the mother, as the saving of a sure life is of greater priority to us than killing an existing one in order to complete a life in formation. Every case is judged individually. Other than that, we oppose abortion in every way and for every reason. This is the Jewish point of view, and it is important to let our non-Jewish friends know that.[8]

Rabbi Doctor Bernard Poupko, Chairman of the Rabbinical Board of Greater Pittsburgh, and National President of the Religious Zionists of America, explains:

Judaism has been the moral mentor of Western civilization, and no code of morality surpasses our Bible's concern for human life. Our holiest days and every religious precept must be set aside in order to save a human life. A sensitivity to social injustice is embedded within our tradition. And it is Judaism which resists a blanket allowance to abortion except under controlled circumstances as prescribed by competent rabbinic authority. Living in a time as we do when divinely revealed, universally binding and time-proven moral principles and ethical values which are divinely revealed are being challenged by a new and ruthless onslaught of secularism and nihilism, when some priests in the 'Temple of Science' are relegating the sanctity of human life into the confines of a test tube, we who are committed to the notion of the divine image of man must speak up and act, vigorously and courageously, for the preservation of human life, *both born and unborn.*

Finally, the Union of Orthodox Jewish Congregations of America declared at its 78th National Convention in 1976, "Judaism regards all life—including fetal life—as inviolate. Abortion is not a private matter between a woman and her physician. It infringes upon the most fundamental right of a third party—that of the unborn child."

1 Seymour P. Lachman and Barry A. Kosmin. "What Is Happening to American Jewry?" *The New York Times*, 4 June 1990.

2 J. David Bleich. "Abortion and Jewish Law." *New Perspectives on Human Abortion*. Edited by Thomas W. Hilgers, M.D., Dennis J. Horan, and David Mall. Frederick, Maryland: Aletheia Books, University Publications of America, 1981, pp. 405-419.

3 Gabriel Meyer. "Israel and Abortion." *National Catholic Register*, Volume LXIII, Number 47, p. 5. Also see Rabbi Aryeh Spero. "Therefore Choose Life: How the Great Faiths View Abortion." *Policy Review*, Spring, 1989, pp. 38-45.

4 Rabbi Marvin S. Antelman, Chief Justice of the Supreme Rabbinical Court of America. "Why Jews Oppose Abortion." *The Review of The News*, 1 May 1974, pp. 1-6.

5 Bill Moloney, "Jewish View." *National Right to Life News*, June, 1979, p. 6.

6 Gabriel Meyer. "Israel and Abortion." *National Catholic Register*, Volume LXIII, Number 47, p. 5. Also see Rabbi Aryeh Spero. "Therefore Choose Life: How the Great Faiths View Abortion." *Policy Review*, Spring 1989, pp. 38-45.

7 Bill Moloney. "News Briefs." *National Right to Life News*, June 1979, p. 6.

8 "A Rabbi Looks at Abortion." Supplement to the Catholic League for Religious and Civil Rights newsletter of June, 1977.

100. What Pro-Life Groups Are Available for Activists of Specific Denominations?

A pro-life activist who belongs to a pro-abortion (or indifferent) church or congregation is a lonely person indeed. In order to be the most effective "light in the darkness" he can be, he must draw strength from other pro-lifers who share his faith.

A number of pro-life groups that have resources tailored to the needs of individual denominations are always willing to share advice and materials that help pro-life activists in their work.

You will find addresses and telephone numbers of these pro-life groups, which include Baptist, Episcopal, Evangelical, Jewish, Lutheran, Methodist, Orthodox, Presbyterian and United Church of Christ organizations, in Appendix A.

Chapter 9

Assisted Reproduction

101. What Are Some of the Most Common Assisted Reproductive Techniques?

Artificial Insemination (AI)

Artificial insemination (AI) is the most basic assisted reproductive technique. The sperm donor typically masturbates to collect sperm, which is then introduced into the woman's vagina by a catheter.

AI is usually classified as AI-H (artificial insemination-husband, or "homologous" insemination) or AI-D (artificial insemination-donor or "heterologous" insemination).

In Vitro Fertilization (IVF)

The IVF Procedure. *In vitro* (literally, "in glass") fertilization (IVF) is the beginning of a new human being outside the mother's body. The main difference between AI and IVF is that, in AI, only the biological father's gametes are isolated from his body. In IVF, both the father's and the mother's gametes are isolated.

The first step in an IVF procedure is to obtain a healthy egg from the woman. A doctor does this during a laparoscopy, under general anesthesia. He inserts a laparoscope (a camera with a miniature flashlight on its head) into an incision near the woman's navel. He locates a ripe egg that is about to be released from the follicle and extracts it with an aspirating tube. Doctors using more advanced techniques use ultrasound, and make a "band-aid" incision under local anesthesia.

A technician places the retrieved egg in a Petri dish filled with a nutrient solution and exposes it for half a day to a few drops of semen. If the egg is fertilized, he monitors it for proper growth. At the third or fourth day, (approximately the 8 or 16-cell stage), the doctor inserts the embryo into the woman's uterus with a catheter or tube which he passes through the cervix.[1]

Baby Louise. On 25 July 1978, Louise Brown, the first baby conceived in a Petri dish, was born. Since then, more than 75,000 such babies have been born, about one-third of them in the United States. Other leading IVF centers are in England, France, Germany, Austria, Belgium and Australia.[2]

Doctors Edwards and Steptoe, who produced Louise Brown, discarded 99.5% of the ova fertilized in their lab over a period of 12 years. This means they had failed in their first 200 attempts at transferring the embryo to the uterus.[3]

Steptoe's very lucrative abortion practice wholly financed his IVF research.[4] He required the parents to agree to abort Louise if there was the slightest hint of an abnormality in her, so that the reputation of his new "science" would be protected. It would be interesting to know how Louise would react to knowing the doctors would have disposed of her if she had been less than perfect—or to knowing 200 embryos before her had a chance at life but were discarded.

The first child conceived through IVF, then frozen, thawed, implanted and born is Zoe Leyland of Melbourne, Australia, who was born on 28 March 1984. Her mother was "superovulated" and produced 11 eggs which were then fertilized. Ten of these were deliberately destroyed through selective abortion or died naturally.[5]

Zoe was very lucky indeed to survive.

IVF Procedure Efficiency. The chances of a single transplanted embryo surviving the entire IVF process are quite slim. So, the donor woman routinely receives fertility drugs to make her produce several eggs during ovulation (a process known as "superovulation"). Doctors fertilize these multiple eggs with sperm, then transfer them to the receiving woman's uterus.

Despite using multiple eggs, the average probability of pregnancy per *in vitro* cycle is only about 10-15 percent.[6]

Pro-life activists object to IVF mainly because it requires the intentional killing of many human embryos. For example, only 4% of 14,585 human embryos survived to birth, according to a 1984 European study, and a 1987 study in the United States' largest IVF center in Norfolk, Virginia, concluded that only 5% of 4,500 embryos survived to birth.[6]

Embryos that appear to be defective in any way are simply discarded as biological waste. If a woman becomes pregnant with multiple embryos, an abortionist often commits a "pregnancy reduction," a fancy name for selective abortion. The unwanted children are killed with a shot of potassium chloride to the heart, and they are simply reabsorbed by the mother's body.

IVF and Pregnancy Reduction. One of the many ugly ethical problems that fertility drugs and IVF have created is an alleged "need" for "pregnancy reduction" abortions. Doctors tell a woman that she is carrying too many preborn babies, and an abortionist selectively kills one or more of them. Question 14 describes the "pregnancy reduction" (selective abortion) procedure.

The U.S. Congress' Committee on Small Business found that many unregulated IVF enterprises deliberately implant too many embryos just to increase their chances of success:

IVF success rates are so discouraging that there are some centers trying to do better in terms of creating babies by using multiple [embryo] implants. It shows at the forty-one [leading] centers there were an average of three embryos used. Some centers use more than that. When they do, they sometimes create multiple pregnancies, three, four, five or six babies. Then they use fetal reduction, which is killing some fetuses to preserve the health of the mother and to help the other fetuses survive. That is a serious procedure. But because of the lack of pressure to standardize, routinize and assure quality in the centers out there, we have this kind of dubious activity going on out there.[6]

The usual scenario is that a doctor claims a woman is carrying so many babies that her life or theirs may be endangered.

IVF doctors are often wrong. One told a woman her five babies would all die, but she chose to carry them all to term. They were all born healthy, and the entire family appeared in a 1991 *People* Magazine cover story.

As always, abortionists lean on the "hard case" argument. Some women seem to think *twins* are too many kids, and abortionists agree with them. So the "mother's health" argument, in general, does not hold up when twins can be "reduced" to one child with a sort of abominable reverse "Sophie's choice." In other words, the mother is not choosing which of two children will *live*, but which will *die*. Actually, people can "justify" *all* abortions with the same flimsy arguments used to rationalize "pregnancy reduction." After all, most abortions are just the "reduction" of one preborn baby to none.

In fact, abortionists commit most "pregnancy reductions" to kill one of a set of twins. Even in such apparently simple cases, "pregnancy reduction" is an abysmal failure at delivering its intended result. A recent medical journal admitted:

> The first six twin pregnancies to undergo selective termination at Mount Sinai Hospital "worked out very badly," with the unintended miscarriage of four unaffected fetuses as well as the six targeted for abortion. These first attempts involved the use of exsanguination [draining all of the blood from the preborn babies] or injection of saline or an air embolism [to cause heart attacks], Dr. Berkowitz said.[7]

As with all immoral acts, "doctors" and "mothers" need Newspeak to insulate themselves from the reality of what they are doing. The term "pregnancy reduction" is an example. Others take self-deceptive language even further: Dr. Seymour Romney suggests we call the "roulette killing" of some of the babies in a multiple pregnancy "enhanced survival of multifetal pregnancies," or ESMP for short.[8]

Embryo Transfer

The standard embryo transfer procedure involves impregnating a volunteer (or paid) woman by artificial insemination with sperm from an infertile wife's husband. Five days after conception, the embryo is flushed out ("lavaged") and transferred to the infertile woman's uterus. The embryo may also be the result of IVF.

In artificial insemination, the precursor to IVF, only the male gamete is isolated from the body. In the IVF procedure, both male and female gametes are isolated.

Embryo transfer takes this process one step farther: an embryo that is conceived (usually by AI-D) is removed and transferred to another woman.

As reproductive technology "progresses," motherhood and fatherhood are divided into successively smaller "pieces." One or more men may donate sperm, one woman the egg, another the womb, and maybe a third the actual raising of the child. In embryo transfer procedures, a child has at least two mothers and one father, and may have up to three mothers and two fathers: a genetic mother, a gestational mother, an adoptive mother, a genetic father and an adoptive father.

This kind of technology certainly lends new meaning to the term "extended family." At the rate we're going, it won't be too long before it takes a village to *conceive* a child.

"Surrogate motherhood" usually involves the artificial insemination of a woman with a husband's sperm if his wife is infertile or does not want to carry a pregnancy to term for a variety of reasons. In some cases, the surrogate is implanted with the couple's embryo after IVF. The surrogate receives anywhere from $10,000 to $30,000 for carrying the child, and she relinquishes him to the contracting couple immediately after birth. This practice is sometimes called "Rent-a-Womb" or "mercenary motherhood."

Interestingly, most contracts between the surrogate and the husband and wife insist the surrogate abort the child if genetic tests show abnormalities unacceptable to the husband and wife—in direct conflict with the surrogate woman's alleged "right to choose."[9] Proponents of "surrogate motherhood" deny any infringement of rights, of course, because they say that the baby in question is mere property under contract.

In response to a question about whether "surrogate motherhood" is morally licit, the Sacred Congregation for the Doctrine of the Faith replied:

> No, for the same reasons which lead one to reject artificial fertilization: For it is contrary to the unity of marriage and to the dignity of the procreation of the human person. Surrogate motherhood represents an objective failure to meet the obligations of maternal love, of conjugal fidelity and of responsible motherhood; it offends the dignity and the right of the child to be conceived, carried in the womb, brought into the world and brought up by his own parents; it sets up, to the detriment of families, a division between the physical, psychological and moral elements which constitute those families.[10]

Gamete Intra-Fallopian Transfer (GIFT)

IVF mixes human sperm and eggs in a glass dish, and the embryo(s) are then implanted into the uterus. By contrast, a GIFT procedure fertilizes a woman's egg inside her body.

Doctors incise the Fallopian tube at a point past any blockage and, using a laparoscope, remove the woman's ripe egg from the follicle and place it and the man's sperm inside the tube. The sperm was previously collected by a method such as use of a perforated condom. If conception does occur, the pregnancy will proceed in the usual way—the embryo will travel down the tube and implant in the uterus.

At this writing, the Catholic Church and most Bible-believing Protestant churches have not voiced objections to GIFT, because it does not involve sins such as masturbation to obtain the sperm, or the discarding of "excess" embryos. As long as GIFT does not involve masturbation or gametes from persons other than the husband or wife, Catholics, after rightly forming their consciences, may choose either to use it or reject it.[11]

GIFT has a 20% to 30% success rate, compared to IVF's 5% to 15% overall success rate, and a single GIFT procedure costs about the same as one IVF cycle—$3,000 to $4,000.

Other Reproductive Technologies

Low Tube Ovum Transfer (LTOT) is also acceptable to the Catholic Church and many other faiths. This procedure relocates the woman's egg past the damaged portion of her Fallopian tube so that *in vivo* (in the body) fertilization takes place after normal intercourse.[12] Two other procedures acceptable to almost all faiths include "assisted semination" (not artificial insemination) and sperm intra-fallopian transfer (SIFT).[13]

There are many other assisted reproductive procedures that are basically variations and enhancements of AI, IVF and ovum and embryo transfer.[14]

Infertile Couples Should Look into Microsurgery

Many couples who are considering resorting to IVF and other procedures should first look into the rapidly-growing field of alternative procedures that can actually restore fertility in many or even most cases.

According to the executive director of Resolve, the national infertility-counseling organization, various micro-surgery techniques can restore fertility to about 70 percent of all infertile women.[15] Dr. Joseph Ballina, Director of the Laser Research Institute of New Orleans, has reported an 80% success rate in repairing blocked or cut Fallopian tubes. After surgery, 80% of these women later become pregnant.[16]

The repair of damaged Fallopian tubes is an example of using medicine to repair an injury or pathological condition, after which natural conception and pregnancy can take place. By contrast, IVF and certain other assisted reproductive procedures *replace* natural intercourse.

1   Albert S. Moraczewski., O.P. "*In Vitro* Fertilization and Christian Marriage." Also Eugene Diamond, M.D. "A Call for Moratorium on *In Vitro* Fertilization." Both articles are in the November 1979, issue of *Linacre Quarterly*.

2   *Parade* Magazine, 2 July 1989, p. 19.

3   Eugene Diamond, M.D. "A Call for Moratorium on *In Vitro* Fertilization." *Linacre Quarterly*, November 1979.

4   *Time* Magazine, 31 July 1978.

5   Claudia Wallis. "The New Origins of Life." *Time* Magazine, 10 September 1984, p. 40. Also Jo Wiles. "The Gift of Life." *Star World*, 24 April 1986, pp. 24-26.

6   U.S. Congress, Committee on Small Business. *Consumer Protection Issues Involved in* In Vitro *Fertilization Clinics*. Washington, D.C.: U.S. Government Printing Office, 1988, pp. 26-27.

7   "Selective Abortion in Multiple Gestation." *Obstetrics and Gynecology News*, 1-14 August 1989.

8   Debra Evans. *Without Moral Limits: Women, Reproduction, and the New Medical Technology*. Westchester, Illinois: Crossway Books, 1989, p. 116.

9 Donald DeMarco. *In My Mother's Womb: The Catholic Church's Defense of Natural Life.* Manassas, Virginia: Trinity Communications, 1987, p. 181.

10 Sacred Congregation for the Doctrine of the Faith. *Donum Vitae* ("Instruction on Respect for Human Life in its Origin and the Dignity of Procreation: Replies to Certain Questions of the Day"), 2 February 1987, II,A,3.

11 31 July 1996 letter from Fr. Germain Kopaczynski, OFMConv., Director of Education, Pope John Center for the Study of Ethics in Health Care.

12 David Q. Liptak. "Catholic Hospital Begins '*In Vivo*' Ovum Transfers." *The Catholic Standard and Times*, 22 September 1983, p. 14. Also David Q. Liptak. "New 'Infertility Bypass (LTOT)' Assessed." *Catholic Transcript*, 6 January 1984.

13 Orville N. Griese. "Promising Approaches to Human Infertility." *International Review of Natural Family Planning*, Fall 1986, pp. 243-255.

14 These procedures include Fallopian tube sperm perfusion (FSP), intrauterine insemination (IUI), pronuclear stage tubal transfer (PROST), sub-zonal insemination (SUZI), transvaginal intratubal embryo transfer (TIET), transvaginal-transmyometrial embryo transfer (TTET), transvaginal tubal embryo stage transfer (TV-TEST), tubal embryo stage transfer (TEST), tubo-ovarian transplantation (TOT), vaginal intratubal insemination (VITI), *zona pellucida* drilling and cutting, and zygote intra-fallopian transfer (ZIFT).

15 Claudia Wallis. "The New Origins of Life." *Time* Magazine, 10 September 1984, p. 40.

16 "*In Vitro* Lab Approved." *National Right to Life News*, January 1980, p. 23.

102. What Are the Ethical and Moral Implications of Reproductive Technologies?

Introduction

It seems that bioethicists, technocrats, "family planners" and "sex educators" no longer glorify the way human reproduction *should* be (sex resulting in babies). Instead, they extol sex *not* resulting in babies (by means of contraception, abortifacients, sterilization and abortion) and babies resulting without *sex* (by means of artificial insemination, embryo transfer and IVF).

Among reproductive scientists, there has been a fundamental shift in philosophy from assisting the begetting of children in a loving family environment to manufacturing a product—and the "manufacturers" can dispose of the "product" if it does not meet their rigid specifications.

Teaching of the Catholic Church

The Catechism of the Catholic Church (¶2376-2377) describes the major moral problems of most of the assisted reproductive technologies in use today—corruptions of both the unitive and procreative functions of marriage between husband and wife:

> Techniques that entail the dissociation of husband and wife, by the intrusion of a person other than the couple (donation of sperm or ovum, surrogate uterus) are gravely immoral. These techniques (heterologous artificial insemination and fertilization) infringe the child's right to be born of a father and mother known to him and bound to each other by marriage. They betray the spouses' "right to become a father and a mother only through each other."

Techniques involving only the married couple (homologous artificial insemination and fertilization) are perhaps less reprehensible, yet remain morally unacceptable. They dissociate the sexual act from the procreative act. The act which brings the child into existence is no longer an act by which two persons give themselves to one another ....

How to Determine Whether a Procedure Is Licit

There are currently more than 100 different assisted reproductive techniques available to couples who are suffering from infertility. Couples may be unsure whether the procedure(s) they are considering are morally acceptable.

According to the Vatican Instruction *Donum Vitae*, the liceity of assisted reproductive procedures revolves around their relationship to natural intercourse: "If the technical means facilitates the conjugal act or helps it to reach its natural objectives, it can be morally acceptable. If, on the other hand, the procedure were to replace the conjugal act, it is morally illicit" (II, B, 6).

Donum Vitae states that an assisted reproductive procedure must meet these five specific criteria in order to maintain the procreative and unitive aspects of the marital act, as well as to avoid other grave sins:

(1) All assisted reproductive procedures should be performed upon married couples only. "Respect for the unity of marriage and for conjugal fidelity demands that the child be conceived in marriage; the bond existing between husband and wife accords the spouses, in an objective and inalienable manner, the exclusive right to become father and mother solely through each other" (II, A, 2).

(2) The wife must contribute the egg and the husband must contribute the sperm. No other person must be involved, as this constitutes "technological adultery." "Recourse to the gametes of a third person, in order to have sperm or ovum available, constitutes a violation of the reciprocal commitment of the spouses and a grave lack in regard to the essential property of marriage which is its unity" (II, A, 2).

(3) Masturbation must not be required. "Masturbation, through which the sperm is normally obtained, is another sign of this dissociation: Even when it is done for the purpose of procreation, the act remains deprived of its unitive meaning ...." (II, B, 6). See also the *Catechism of the Catholic Church*, ¶2352. Note that sperm collection can licitly be accomplished through "home collection," which consists of the use of a perforated condom during natural intercourse.

(4) Fertilization must take place inside the woman's body. "The origin of the human being thus follows from a procreation that is "linked to the union, not only biological but also spiritual, of the parents, made one by the bond of marriage." Fertilization achieved outside the bodies of the couple remains by this very fact deprived of the meanings and the values which are expressed in the language of the body and in the union of human persons" (II, B, 4, c).

(5)"Spare" embryos must not be discarded, frozen, or experimented upon, and procedures such as "selective abortion" (pregnancy reduction) must not be used. "... those embryos which are not transferred into the body of the mother and are called "spare" are exposed to an absurd fate, with no possibility of their being offered safe means of survival which can be licitly pursued" (I, 5).

103. Shouldn't Pro-Lifers Favor Any Procedure That Generates New Human Life?

Pro-abortionists and others who do not understand the pro-life position (or pretend not to understand it) often take the label "pro-life" at face value. They believe pro-lifers advocate generating as many people as possible, by any available means. So, these people say, it follows that pro-lifers should favor any method of producing babies for infertile couples, no matter how outlandish.

This viewpoint grossly oversimplifies the pro-life position and completely disregards the inherent dignity of human life.

Pro-lifers have several objections to certain assisted reproductive procedures:

(1) Some procedures, such as IVF and heterologous artificial insemination, involve external acts that are clearly sinful. These include the destruction or disposal of embryos that are imperfect or "spare," which is morally the same as abortion; the act of masturbation, which is intrinsically disordered; and "technological adultery," the introduction of the gametes of a person outside the marriage. All of these acts seriously degrade the unitive aspect of marriage.

(2) Many reproductive scientists see a baby not as the supreme gift of God, but as a commodity to be produced. A sign in one IVF center's waiting room boasts, "They say babies are made in heaven, but we know better."[1] This attitude has led to widespread acceptance of practices such as the production of embryos for the sole purpose of experimentation. The overall effect is the same as that of widespread abortion and contraception: a loss of respect for the precious gifts of fertility and life.

(3) Not only do these procedures degrade the sacredness of God's gift of children, but they weaken the sacramental aspect of the marriage bond. Many procedures commonly used today bypass God's will for us (even if it includes infertility). In this fundamental sense, some assisted reproductive procedures, which thwart God's plan for our *infertility*, are identical to abortion, which thwarts God's plan for our *fertility*.

These points seem obscure to those with a utilitarian worldview. However, a sure sign of accepted evil is that more and greater evil follows it. We have already seen an incredible number of evils linked to certain assisted reproductive techniques. These include the creation of embryos purely for experimentation and subsequent disposal; selective and eugenic abortion on a wide scale; unethical practices by doctors, including impregnation of women with their own sperm; and proposals to clone human beings and to create chimeras and other bizarre creatures, as described in Question 105.

1 Michael Gold. "The Baby Makers." *Science* Magazine, April 1985, pp. 26-38.

....

104. Don't Infertile Couples Have the Right to a Child?

Of all people, pro-life activists can empathize with the yearning for a child that an infertile couple experiences. Crisis pregnancy center workers and sidewalk counselors, especially, are struck by the irony of abortionists killing thousands of perfectly healthy children each day—while thousands of couples undergo the stress and pain of a complicated and expensive series of tests and procedures so they can have what others are contemptuously disposing of as "biological waste."

People who know infertile couples wish that they could somehow miraculously present them with the infant they long for.

This kind response is commendable, but unfortunately it defines children as a "right" and intrinsically and unconsciously reduces their status from a supreme "gift of the Lord" (Psalm 127:3) to an acquisition or a possession.

Donum Vitae explains,

Figure 23

Many couples are faced with infertility, a particularly difficult cross to bear. They must always resist the temptation to see a child as a "right."

A true and proper right to a child would be contrary to the child's dignity and nature. The child is not an object to which one has a right, nor can he be considered as an object of ownership: rather, a child is a gift, "the supreme gift" and the most gratuitous gift of marriage, and is a living testimony of the mutual giving of his parents. For this reason, the child has the right, as already mentioned, to be the fruit of the specific act of the conjugal love of his parents; and he also has the right to be respected as a person from the moment of his conception."[1]

Our Lord gives every one of us crosses to bear. Some of these involve losses close to us and are much more difficult to carry than others—such as the death of a child, the inability to conceive or the inability to find a spouse.

We can respond to these severe trials in one of two ways. We can struggle against them with all of our energy and strength, and, whether we conquer them or not, find ourselves afflicted with a strange emptiness of soul. Or we can use licit technology to a moderate extent in an attempt to bypass our infertility, while acknowledging God's mastery over our lives, knowing that our ultimate happiness is His concern.

Donum Vitae offers hope to infertile couples:

Spouses who find themselves in this sad situation are called to find in it an opportunity for sharing in a particular way in the Lord's Cross, the source of spiritual fruitfulness. Sterile couples must not forget that even when procreation is not possible, conjugal life does not for this reason lose its value. Physical sterility in fact can be for spouses the occasion for other important services to the life of the human person, for example, adoption, various forms of educational work, and assistance to other families and to poor or handicapped children.[1]

1 Sacred Congregation for the Doctrine of the Faith. *Donum Vitae* ("Instruction on Respect for Human Life in Its Origin and the Dignity of Procreation: Replies to Certain Questions of the Day"), 2 February 1987 (II, B, 8).

105. What May the Future Hold for Assisted Reproductive Technologies?

A Straight and Predictable Path

Assisted reproductive technology is following a fairly straightforward and predictable path.

A century ago scientists invented artificial insemination, which isolated the male gamete from the body. Then came IVF, which isolated both the male and female gametes. And next came embryo transfer, which removes the developing human being from the body entirely for a short time.

It is easy to project this line of technology to its logical conclusion: extracorporeal gestation (EG), where technicians conceive a child in a dish (or generate him by parthenogenesis, without sperm) and gestate him entirely outside the mother in an artificial uterus.

This is not science-fiction fantasy: intensive research into EG has been ongoing since 1975. Late-term aborted babies have already been kept alive for days in pressurized vessels: the Italian embryologist Daniele Petrucci has kept a female embryo alive for 59 days in an artificial uterus.[1]

Many scientists and doctors, including Dr. Bernard Nathanson, believe an artificial womb will soon be perfected.[2] According to bioethicist Joseph Fletcher, "The womb is a dark and dangerous place, a hazardous environment. We should want our potential children to be where they can be watched and protected as much as possible."[3] Isaac Asimov revealed the anti-life thinking behind this technology when he wrote, "if a woman could extrude the fertilized ovum for development outside the body, she would then be no more the victim of pregnancy than a man is."[4]

A growing number of prominent pro-abortion scientists have already proposed the ultimate scenario that will be achieved by this line of research. In their ideal society, pregnancy will be abolished and everyone will be surgically sterilized by age 18. Before the sterilization process, however, girls will be superovulated and their eggs "harvested." Boys will masturbate to produce sperm samples. Scientists will carefully gene-map the sperm and eggs (enabled by the Human Genome Project, now in progress), and will discard any samples that are subnormal in any way. When there is a projected need for a scientist 20 years down the road, technicians will conceive and grow one in an artificial uterus. When there is a projected need for a negotiator, they will grow one. When talented prostitutes are required, scientists will grow them too.[5]

When reading about these predictions, we must remember that they are not the imaginings of some crackpot conspiracy theorist—they have been outlined in black and white by scientists, feminists and thinkers in the forefront of the pro-abortion and assisted reproduction movements.

Fantasies Without Limit

Although still a minority, a growing number of reproductive scientists and other opinion-molders are setting forth visions of what they might "accomplish" using today's technology as a base. These visions are amusing because of their science-fiction quality, and frightening because they are *desired* by influential people.

These notions may seem far-fetched and improbable, and therefore harmless. However, it is important for pro-life activists to know the ultimate goals of the anti-life movements. Showing these goals to others can be a "wake-up call" that helps motivate them to fight all the anti-life proposals that could eventually lead to the Brave New World.

Time Magazine begins by dispensing with the family:

It is reasonable to ask whether there will be a family at all. Given the propensity for divorce, the growing number of adults who choose to remain single, the declining popularity of having children and the evaporation of the time families spend together, another way may eventually evolve. It may be quicker and more efficient to dispense with family-based reproduction. Society could then produce its future generations in institutions that might resemble state-sponsored baby hatcheries....[6]

A team of scientists outlines one of the most treasured goals of the anti-life movements—the elimination of all genetic defects through "positive" eugenics:

"Preimplantation diagnosis" holds staggering implications for the use of the gene discoveries that are destined to come out of the mapping of the human genome.... It appears highly likely that young couples, possibly those in the next generation, will be able to make choices about the genetic traits of their children that would astonish today's generation. As the genetic secrets of stature are uncovered, for example, couples would be able, if they desired, to select the height of their children within certain limits. As the gene mapping proceeds, other traits affecting intelligence, athletic or musical ability, even personality could become matters of parental *choice*.[7]

Many other "bioethicists" have let their imaginations run rampant with the possibilities posed by assisted reproductive techniques, eugenics, and bio-engineering, all of which have absolutely no moral limits.

Joseph Fletcher dreams:

It would be justifiable to bio-engineer or bio-design para-humans or "modified men"—as chimeras (part animal) or cyborg-androids (part prostheses). I would vote for cloning top-grade soldiers and scientists, or for supplying them through other genetic means, if they were needed to offset an elitist or tyrannical power plot by other cloners—a truly science-fiction situation, but imaginable. I suspect I would favor making and using man-machine hybrids rather than genetically designed people for dull, unrewarding or dangerous roles needed nonetheless for the community's welfare—perhaps the testing of suspected pollution areas or the investigation of threatening volcanos or snow-slides.

Coital reproduction is, therefore, less human than laboratory reproduction—more fun, to be sure, but with our separation of baby making from lovemaking, both become more human because they are matters of choice, and not chance. This is, of course, essentially the case for planned parenthood. I cannot see how either humanity or morality are served by genetic roulette.

To be men we must be in *control*. That is the first and the last ethical word. For when there is no choice, there is no possibility of ethical action. Whatever we are compelled to do is a-moral.... It is human need that validates rights, not the other way around.[8]

Fletcher is not alone in his fantasies. British geneticist George Haldane predicted we might breed a race of legless humanoid mutants with prehensile tails or feet for space travel. Other scientists would like to see women laying eggs that could be hatched or even *eaten* (i.e., we would cannibalize our own pre-hatched children); human beings with gills for underwater travel; and people with two sets of arms and hands—one for heavy work, and the other for lighter tasks.[9]

These typify the horrible visions being dreamed up for humanity by powerful people with no moral limits. These nightmares are the logical destination of a society that has fully succumbed to situational ethics: where the limits are set by technology and not by morality, by man and not by God.

This is the future for all mankind if Fletcher's "planned parenthood" movement triumphs.

1 Donald DeMarco, Ph.D. *In My Mother's Womb: The Catholic Church's Defense of Natural Life*. Manassas, Virginia: Trinity Communications, 1987.

2 Tom Paskal. "Tampering with the Machinery of God." *Weekend* Magazine, 18 September 1971, p. 7. Also see Bernard Nathanson, M.D. *Aborting America*. Garden City, New Jersey: Doubleday Press, 1979, p. 282.

3 Joseph Fletcher. *The Ethics of Genetic Control*. Garden City, New Jersey: Doubleday Press, 1979, p. 103.

4 Isaac Asimov. "On Designing a Woman." *Viva* Magazine, November 1973, p. 8.

5 Edward Grossman. "The Obsolescent Mother: A Scenario." *Atlantic* Magazine, May 1971, p. 49. Shulasmith Firestone. *The Dialectic of Sex: The Case for Feminist Revolution*. New York: William Morrow, 1972, p. 238. See also the proposed public law entitled "Reversible Fertility Immunization" in Edgar R. Chasteen. *The Case for Compulsory Birth Control*. Englewood Cliffs, New Jersey: Prentice-Hall, 1971.

6 *Time* Magazine Fall 1992 Special Issue "Beyond the Year 2000: What to Expect in the New Millennium."

7 Jerry E. Bishop and Michael Waldholz. *Genome*. New York: Simon and Schuster, 1990, pp. 17-20, 278, 308.

8 Joseph Fletcher. "Ethical Aspects of Genetic Controls." *New England Journal of Medicine* (285:776-783, 1971).

9 Paul Ramsey, Ph.D. "On *In Vitro* Fertilization." *Human Life Review*, Winter 1979, pp. 17-30.

Chapter 10

Fetal Experimentation and Tissue Transplantation

....

106. What Are the Basic Moral Objections to Fetal Experimentation and Fetal Tissue Transplantation?

Proponents of fetal experimentation say their studies will eventually lead to great strides in medical knowledge that will vastly benefit the human race. Among many possibilities, they cite the growing of organs for transplantation into adult human beings, the elimination of birth defects that cause misery for both the children and their parents, and perhaps even the "mapping" and ultimate "improvement" of the genetic "maps" of all human beings, leading to a jump in evolution that staggers the imagination.

All of these assertions divert attention from the central problem with fetal experimentation: the reduction of preborn children from human beings created in the image of God to mere biological scrap—useful *material* for others to manipulate and dispose of as they see fit.

Pro-abortionists never tire of telling the world no one can determine the moral status of preborn children, because questions of life, personhood and humanity are theoretical and theological in nature and therefore can be answered only by each person for himself. Fr. Bernard Häring answered, "The very probability that we may be faced with a human person in the full sense constitutes, in my opinion, an absolute veto against any type of [*in-vitro*] experimentation."[1]

We find specific guidelines on fetal experimentation in the Vatican's Instruction *Donum Vitae*, which answers the question "How is one to evaluate morally research and experimentation on human embryos and fetuses?" as follows:

Medical research must refrain from operations on live embryos, unless there is a moral certainty of not causing harm to the life or integrity of the unborn child and the mother, and on condition that the parents have given their free and informed consent to the procedure. It follows that all research, even when limited to the simple observation of the embryo, would become illicit were it to involve risk to the embryo's physical integrity or life by reason of the methods used or the effects induced.

As regards experimentation, and presupposing the general distinction between experimentation for purposes which are not directly therapeutic and experimentation which is clearly therapeutic for the subject himself, in the case in point one must also distinguish between experimentation carried out on embryos which are still alive and experimentation carried out on embryos which are dead. If the embryos are living, whether viable or not, they must be respected just like any other human person; experimentation on embryos which is not directly therapeutic is illicit.

No objective, even though noble in itself, such as a foreseeable advantage to science, to other human beings or to society, can in any way justify experimentation on living human embryos or fetuses, whether viable or not, either inside or outside the mother's womb.... To use human embryos or fetuses as the object or instrument of experimentation constitutes a crime against their dignity as human beings having a right to the same respect that is due to the child already born and to every human person....

Figure 24

Since preborn children were declared expendable by Roe v. Wade, *researchers have committed inhumane experiments on babies like this perfectly-formed six-week-old preborn.*

In the case of experimentation that is clearly therapeutic, namely, when it is a matter of experimental forms of therapy used for the benefit of the embryo itself in a final attempt to save its life, and in the absence of other reliable forms of therapy, recourse to drugs or procedures not yet fully tested can be licit.[2]

1 Fr. Bernard Häring. *Ethics of Manipulation.* New York: Seabury Press, 1975, pp. 198-199.

2 Sacred Congregation for the Doctrine of the Faith. *Donum Vitae* ("Instruction on Respect for Human Life in Its Origin and the Dignity of Procreation: Replies to Certain Questions of the Day"), 2 February 1987, II,B,8.

107. What Are Some Examples of Experiments Committed upon Aborted Preborn Babies?

Overview

Fetal experiments generally fall into two classes: experimentation on early and on late preborn children. The first category usually involves research on embryos resulting from *in-vitro* fertilization (IVF), up to about 14 days after fertilization. The second class involves preborn babies aborted alive, from eight weeks after fertilization up until the moment of birth.

Early Embryo Experiments

Introduction. All embryo experiments are committed with specific goals in mind. These include analyses meant to gain knowledge of early fetal development so researchers can produce new abortifacients, and genetic studies identifying and eliminating "undesirable" genes (negative eugenics).

Birth Control Research. Scientists all over the world are studying every aspect of human reproduction, with emphasis on the incredibly complex events that transpire immediately after fertilization. Much of this research involves IVF and the growing of early human embryos for a period of days for various purposes.

The International Population Union Conference on the Scientific Study of Population, held in London in 1969, was funded by the governments of the United Kingdom, Denmark, Finland, West Germany, Norway, Sweden and the United States. It neatly summed up its vision for IVF research in the chairman's opening speech: "There are grounds for hoping that the use of IVF embryos for research will lead to the discovery of efficient new methods of population control. This is the real justification for the promotion and funding of IVF by governments and organizations involved in population planning."[1]

The research proposed and funded at this conference (and all those held ever since) has been searching for a pill that would destroy the *corpus luteum* whether fertilization had taken place or not (the *corpus luteum* secretes progesterone, which maintains the embryo and prepares the uterine lining to accept the new life). Researchers need a very large and continuous supply of human embryos for this purpose, and government-funded IVF programs supply most of these for destruction in tests of abortifacient drugs. In other words, human life is being created *for the express purpose of destroying it.*

Genetics and Eugenics. From late in the 19th century to about 1950, eugenics was a very popular cause in Western nations, and counted among its devotees thousands of influential people, including Henry Ford, Margaret Sanger, Madison Grant, Lothrop Stoddard, H. L. Mencken, Charles Davenport, George Bernard Shaw, William Shockley, Friedreich Nietzsche and Charles Darwin.

The faces of the eugenicists have changed. So has their technology. But their fundamental dream remains the same: the creation of a "race of thoroughbreds." And fetal experimentation (especially in the first week after fertilization) promises to place undreamed-of tools in the hands of eugenicists.

The most efficient (and aesthetic) way for eugenicists to "cull" imperfect human beings from the population is through the testing of embryos and the elimination of all but the "very best."

The most efficient negative eugenics method currently consists of subjecting preborn children to CVS (chorionic villi sampling), AFP (maternal alphafetoprotein), amniocentesis, or some other test past ten weeks' gestation, and aborting those deemed "unfit." This is a messy, emotional and expensive project that the eugenicists would like to streamline.

The Human Genome Project is a multi-billion dollar effort funded primarily by the U.S. government. Its goal is to identify and "map" all human genes.

This huge undertaking is already bearing fruit that eugenicists see as beautiful. But we may find this fruit is deadly poison—especially to preborn human beings.

Jerry E. Bishop and Michael Waldholz have given us a "progress" report on the Human Genome Project, and commented on some of the possible uses of its findings:

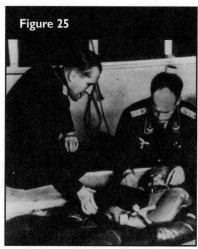

Figure 25

The list of common diseases that have roots in this kind of genetic soil is growing almost daily. As of this writing [in 1990], it includes colon and breast cancer, Alzheimer's Disease, multiple sclerosis, diabetes, schizophrenia, depression, at least one form of alcoholism, and even some types of criminal behavior ... [S]ome contend that almost every disorder compromising a full and healthy four score and ten years of life can be traced in one way or another to a genetic vulnerability.

Dr. Sigmund Rascher and another Luftwaffe physician examine a prisoner of war who was immersed in ice water for three hours in order to see what the effects of hypothermia would be. Even worse experiments are being performed on living preborn babies now, as described in Question 107. [Yad Vashem Photo Archives, courtesy of USHMM Photo Archives].

Indeed, among geneticists involved in Huntington's Disease, there is a quiet, but intense debate over the ethics of aborting any fetus whose disease won't erupt until later in life. Perhaps by then there will be a cure, or at least treatments to mute the disease's symptoms, some say. Others argue, however, that abortion for even the slightest of risks is justified.

"I've had several conversations with people who say, 'Well, with prenatal tests we can wipe out the gene in a generation or two merely by *not allowing any fetus at risk to be born*'," says [geneticist] Hayden.

"Preimplantation diagnosis of genetic disease provides an alternative to the therapeutic abortion offered to couples at risk of producing children with severe inherited disorders," Holding and Monk [two other geneticists] asserted. "Preimplantation diagnosis could allow identification of normal and mutant embryos and the replacement in the mother of only those embryos shown to be free of the defect. The experiment introduces an entirely new dimension into the concept of prenatal genetic diagnosis, that of making a genetic diagnosis *before* pregnancy, thereby circumventing the question of abortion."

Such "preimplantation diagnosis" holds staggering implications for the use of the gene discoveries that are destined to come out of the mapping of the human genome. As prenatal genetic diagnosis becomes simpler and easier, the temptation will arise to use it for less severe genetic aberrations. It appears highly likely that young couples, possibly those in the next gener-ation, will be able to make choices about the genetic traits of their children that would astonish today's generation. As the genetic secrets of nature are uncovered, for example, couples would be able, if they desired, to select the height of their children within certain limits. As the gene mapping pro-ceeds, other traits affecting intelligence, athletic or musical ability, even per-sonality could become matters of parental *choice*.[2]

We might be tempted to dismiss as improbable these musings by leading Human Genome Project scientists. However, pro-life activists must realize that, whenever researchers develop anti-fertility technology, it *will* eventually be used on a vast scale. As one leading genetic researcher boasted, "[Scientists] have the right to exercise their professional activities to the limit ... as lay attitudes struggle to catch up with what scientists can do."[3]

This has already happened with contraception. What almost everyone thought intrinsically evil 50 years ago, people now accept as the norm. This also happened with abortion. What people almost universally perceived as the murder of preborn children only 40 years ago is now commonplace and a "woman's right." And now this is happening with euthanasia. Assisted suicide was not even a topic that peo-ple could discuss in polite company a decade ago; now polls say more than half of all Americans believe there is a "right to suicide."

What reason is there to think pre- and post-implantation eugenics will follow a different course?

None whatsoever, as the eugenicists themselves have informed us!

Authors Madeleine Simms and Keith Hindell have revealed the reasoning behind prenatal eugenics: "An abnormal foetus is not aborted because it would die, but on the contrary because it would be healthy enough to live a sub-human exis-tence. Essentially it is for social, ethical and *aesthetic* reasons that some people recoil from the survival of such sub-humans and prefer to see them aborted."[4]

Simms, Research Fellow of the Eugenics Society, takes her reasoning one step further and pushes for actual coercion: "Has she [the woman] the right to choose to inflict this burden on the state?"[5]

The eugenics philosophy, as it becomes entrenched in the public mind, expands inevitably and inexorably. Dr. Julius Adlam expanded the demand for mandatory eugenic abortion to cases of women whose income and possessions are not up to his lofty standards: "I am not afraid to stick by my belief that only those couples who have the necessary material possessions and sources of income to ensure an eco-nomically secure and safe cradle should allow a pregnancy to progress to term."[6]

Humanity has yet to learn the stern lesson that every evil must be dressed up in the pretty robes of "rights" and "compassion" in order to gain a foothold, and then inevitably is forced upon people under the banners of "progress," "realism" and "social necessity." Nowhere is this more evident than in the rush to eliminate birth defects.

Two-time Nobel Prize winner Dr. Linus Pauling suggested that those who carry "dysfunctional genes" have information on their disabilities tattooed on their foreheads.[7]

The Facts of Life

Dr. Cecil B. Jacobson, Chief of the Reproductive Genetics Unit of George Washington University Hospital, asserts, "I can't imagine any reasonably responsible person arguing against the abortion of mongols.... If we could tell what fetuses are going to be affected with cancer in their 40s and 50s, I would be for aborting them now."[8]

And, in a 1979 symposium sponsored by the March of Dimes, Joseph Fletcher argued: "People who carry genetic disease should be prevented from having children. We ought, in conscience, to have a humane minimum standard of reproduction, not blindly accepting the outcome of every conception. And we ought to act on our genetic information to prevent the birth of children below that minimum."[9]

Later Fetal Experiments

While certain scientists tinker with complicated genetic mechanisms immediately after fertilization, others commit repulsive and inhumane experiments on preborn children anywhere from eight weeks old to near-term.

They do these studies allegedly to gather information on fetal physiology, with a special emphasis on the brain and heart. These experiments are so brutal as to seem almost satanic, and we must ask ourselves why the authorities have let them continue.

The answer is simple: because we do not learn the lessons of history. At the Nuremberg Trials, Nazi doctor Julius Hallervorden said, in his own "defense," that he told the death camp soldiers, "I heard that they were going to do that and so I went up to them and said: 'Look here now boys, if you are going to kill all these [Jewish] people, at least take the brains out so that the material may be utilized.'"[10] Nearly half a century later, the U.S. National Institutes of Health said exactly the same thing (only in more flowery language) in their October 1988 *Draft Report of the Human Fetal Tissue Transplant Panel:* "Inasmuch as it is cadaver tissue [from abortions] we are concerned with, and inasmuch as it would ordinarily be disposed of; and inasmuch as research on this tissue holds the promise of saving countless lives and alleviating the suffering of countless others, we find the use of such tissues acceptable."

Of course, fetal tissue "ethics panels" are mere rubber stamps whose only purpose is to lend a veneer of respectability to inhumane experimentation. "Bioethicists" have never found any use of fetal tissues *un*acceptable, as the following cases show:

- An anesthetist at Pittsburgh's Magee Women's Hospital described how third-trimester babies were deliberately aborted alive and then packed in ice for shipment to laboratories. She said that "it was repulsive to watch live fetuses being packed in ice while still moving and trying to breathe, then being rushed to a laboratory."[12]

- Viable third-trimester preborn babies who are aborted are, of course, the most valuable for research because they are the most highly developed. In one experiment, several viable third-trimester preborn babies were delivered alive by hysterotomy abortion. Researchers then punctured their heads and drained blood from them in order to "gain information about intrauterine malnutrition."[13]

■ The *American Journal of Obstetrics and Gynecology* published the details of an experiment involving cutting the beating hearts out of aborted babies and placing them in a nutrient solution where their contraction rates could be examined: "The hearts were dissected from the fetuses and were mounted in a thermostatically controlled bath ... the hearts survived for many hours without any significant change in their spontaneous contraction rate.... Electrograms were displayed on a polygraph and served as a basis for determination of the spontaneous heart rate."[14]

■ At the University of Helsinki in Finland, Dr. Peter Adam of Case Western Reserve University took part in experiments on preborn babies of up to 21 weeks' gestation who were aborted by hysterotomy. The experimenters cut their heads off (the researchers used the classic euphemism "isolating surgically from the other organs").[15] The alleged purpose of this "research," explained in the June, 1973, issue of *Medical World News*, was to find out the chemical-processing capability of live fetal brain cells. Researchers kept the brains alive for up to 30 minutes by pumping fluids through them.

The 8 August 1975 *Federal Register* noted the details of this particularly ghastly experiment, which echoed very strongly those committed by Nazi doctors: "To learn whether the human fetal brain could metabolize ketone bodies [an organic compound] as an alternative to glucose, brain metabolism was isolated in 8 human fetuses (12-17 weeks gestation) after hysterotomy abortion by perfusing the head separated from the rest of the body. This study, conducted in Finland, demonstrated that the human fetus, like previously studied animal fetuses, could modify metabolic processes to utilize ketone bodies."[15]

When colleagues criticized him for his grisly experiments, Adam replied, "once society's declared the fetus dead, and abrogated its rights, I don't see any ethical problem.... Whose rights are we going to protect once we've decided the fetus won't live?"[15]

■ Researchers at the University of Rochester Medical Center removed the brains from preborn babies as old as 19 weeks and kept the entire brains or parts of them alive for up to five months, subjecting them to comprehensive testing.[16]

■ A certain Dr. Kekomaki took late-term aborted babies and, while they were still alive, sliced them open and ransacked their organs without even giving them an anesthetic. A nurse described one case: "They took the fetus and cut its belly open. They said they wanted its liver. They carried the baby out of the incubator and it was still alive. It was a boy. It had a complete body, with hands, feet, mouth and ears. It was even secreting urine." Asked to explain the reasons for this atrocious "experiment," Kekomaki replied, "an aborted baby is just garbage."[17]

Such monstrosities seem inspired by "B"-grade Hollywood horror movies. But the horror is real, and is displayed proudly not in shabby movie theaters, but in prestigious medical journals.

If researchers are exhibiting *these* repulsive experiments for all the world to see, we can only imagine what hideous things they are doing in secret.

1 Gary Potter. *"Intra Urbem Extraque."* *The Wanderer*, 18 May 1989, p. 3.

2 Jerry E. Bishop and Michael Waldholz. *Genome.* New York: Simon and Schuster, 1990, pp. 17-20, 278, 308.

3 Dr. George Haldane, quoted in Paul Ramsey, Ph.D. "On *In Vitro* Fertilization." *The Human Life Review*, Winter 1979, pp. 17-30.

4 M. Simms and Keith Hindell. *Abortion Law Reformed.* London. Described in Nancy B. Spannaus, Molly Hammett Kronberg, and Linda Everett (eds). *How to Stop the Resurgence of Nazi Euthanasia Today.* Transcripts of the International Club of Life Conference, Munich, West Germany, 11-12 June 1988. *Executive Intelligence Review* Special Report, September, 1988. EIR, Post Office Box 17390, Washington, D.C. 20041-0390.

5 Debra Sanders. "Amniocentesis—Risks." *Women for Life* Newsletter. London, 1980. Described in Spannaus, *op.cit.*

6 Letter from Dr. Julius Adlam. *Medical News*, 6 April 1977. Described in Spannaus, *op.cit.*

7 Linus Pauling. Foreword to "Reflections on the New Biology." *UCLA Law Review*, February, 1968, p. 269.

8 Cecil B. Jacobson, Chief, Reproductive Genetics Unit, George Washington University Hospital, Washington, D.C. *Psychology Today*, September, 1975, p. 22.

9 *Proceedings* of the Second National Symposium on Genetics and Law, held in Boston in May, 1979, sponsored by the March of Dimes.

10 William Brennan. *The Abortion Holocaust: Today's Final Solution.* Life Issues Bookshelf, Sun Life, Thaxton, Virginia 24174, 1983.

11 James J. Kilpatrick. "Fetal Tissue Issue Will Haunt Bush." *The Oregonian*, 26 April 1992, p. B4.

12 Nick Thimmesch. "Bizarre Cases of Abortions Gone Awry." St. Louis *Globe-Democrat*, June 19-20, 1982, p. 5.

13 Maurice Mahoney, M.D. "The Nature and Extent of Research Involving Living Human Fetuses." Appendix to *Research on the Fetus*, Department of Health, Education and Welfare National Commission for the Protection of Human Subjects of Biomedical and Behavioral Research. Washington, D.C.: U.S. Government Printing Office. 1976, pp. 1-23 to 1-25.

14 Bela A. Resch, *et.al.* "Comparison of Spontaneous Contraction Rates of *In Situ* and Isolated Fetal Hearts in Early Pregnancy." *American Journal of Obstetrics and Gynecology*, 1 January 1974, pp. 73-74.

15 "Post-Abortion Fetal Study Stirs Storm." *Medical World News*, June 8, 1973, page 21. Also see Peter A.J. Adam, N. Ratha, E. Rohiala, *et al.* "Cerebral Oxidation of Glucose and D-Beta Hydroxy, Butyrate in the Isolated Perfused Human Head." *Transactions of the American Pediatric Society*, 309:81, 1973.

16 Lowell W. Lapham and William Markesbery. "Human Fetal Cerebellar Cortex: Organization and Maturation of Cells *In Vitro*." *Science*, 27 August 1971, p. 829.

17 *Our Sunday Visitor.* "Cardinal Relates Horror Story about Human Fetuses." 29 March 1987, p. 23.

108. Why Is Fetal Tissue Attractive to Some Researchers?

About 20 million people in the United States suffer from diseases and injuries that doctors allegedly could treat, to various degrees, with fetal tissue transplants. These maladies include Parkinson's Disease, Alzheimer's Disease, diabetes, head injuries, strokes and paralysis. These are the conditions that pro-harvesting researchers focus on when they say that fetal transplants can be of help.

So, some "bioethicists" and hospital researchers have become almost giddy over the prospect of having access to an abundant source of useful "fetal material" produced by millions of abortions.

As Dr. Abraham Lieberman of the New York University Medical Center put it, "This [fetal tissue techniques] is to medicine what superconductivity is to physics."[1]

Fetal cells can be used for transplantation because they are "immunologically naive," meaning they have not yet developed all of the antigens that allow a transplant recipient's immune system to identify and reject them. Also, fetal nerve cells regenerate and grow, unlike adult nerve cells.

Despite these remarkable qualities, fetal tissue transplants have not lived up to their advanced billing, as the next Question explains.

1   Richard John Neuhaus. "The Return of Eugenics." *Commentary*, April 1988, pp. 15-26.

....

109. Have Fetal Tissue Transplants Helped Relieve the Symptoms of Various Diseases?

Selective Indifference

One common tactic that all anti-lifers use is aggressive publicizing of scientific studies that support their viewpoints and a stony indifference to a larger body of evidence that supports the opposing view.

For example, the very few articles supporting the idea that homosexuality is genetic have become centerpieces for the pro-homosexual campaign, even though they were based on studies that were shoddily done, flawed in execution, and obviously the products of extreme conflict-of-interest. Anti-lifers recognize the propaganda value of "scientific" support for their positions.

The same scenario is unfolding in the fetal tissue debate. More than three-fourths of all studies in this area have concluded that fetal tissue transplants benefit only a very few people: the scientists who get the grants for the studies. Only a very few articles have described measurable improvement in symptoms related to neurological and other disorders, and most of these describe studies that are incomplete or fatally flawed.

Verdict from Scientists on Fetal Tissue Transplants

The most comprehensive study to date on the potential of fetal tissue transplantation was the University of Minnesota's 1990 *The Use of Fetal Tissue: Scientific, Ethical and Policy Concerns*. This report, written by 25 doctors and health professionals from a wide range of medical and biomedical ethics disciplines, concluded:

The results in humans of fetal tissue transplant ... have been less encouraging ... [than] research in animals. The lack of knowledge about how fetal tissue grafts work, the immunobiology of these grafts, the reliability of inferences based on currently available animal models of human diseases, and about the methods necessary for assuring the identity and quality of the tissue being transplanted raises important questions about whether transplants in human subjects should have been attempted or ought to be tried again in the near future. Some [researchers] believe that fetal tissue will be replaced by genetically engineered cell lines in the next several years.[1]

Dr. Robert J. White of Case Western Reserve Medical School reviewed studies specifically oriented towards the "promising" field of fetal brain tissue transplantation, and concluded: "The clinical studies so far conducted in transplanting human fetal brain tissue into the cerebral hemisphere of patients with Parkinsonism have demonstrated little evidence of measurable, lasting improvement in neurological dysfunction.... Many neurologists are extremely doubtful that the transplant surgeries have had any therapeutic benefit whatsoever."[2]

Dr. Linda Gourash, a professor of pediatrics at the University of Pittsburgh, confirms this negative judgment:

No evidence of a reduction of Parkinson's Disease symptoms due to implanted fetal cells has been demonstrated from animal model work or from patients undergoing this drastic procedure.... There is a scientific controversy about whether or not fetal tissue transplantation is effective. This ... is being downplayed in the lay media, who are presenting fetal tissue transplantation as a proven effective treatment, which it is not. The lay media also fail to report on other approaches to effective treatment now being funded by the NIH, and these approaches do not use fetal tissue.[3]

Professor Janice Raymond, an outspoken supporter of abortion "rights," has testified before Congress:

No one really knows whether fetal cells can live up to their promise. It has been difficult for critics to raise objections to fetal tissue research because that research has been promoted as a cure for the most debilitating of diseases such as Alzheimer's. Thus opposing the use of fetal tissue is portrayed as opposing medical treatment that not only could benefit a large number of people but cure the worst kind of disease the people suffer.[4]

Researchers the world over have experimented with fetal tissue transplantation for treating a variety of conditions. To date, it has proven *ineffective* at curing or lessening the symptoms of radiation sickness, leukemia and Parkinson's Disease, three areas in which it allegedly held the greatest promise.[1] And in no other area have scientists proven fetal tissue transplantation to be consistently effective.

1 Center for Biomedical Ethics, University of Minnesota. *The Use of Human Fetal Tissue: Scientific, Ethical and Policy Concerns*, January, 1990, pp. 1-2, 4. Results of experimentation on radiation sickness, leukemia and Parkinson's Disease victims is found on pp. 36-37, 39, 94, 109-110, and 115.

2 Robert J. White, M.D. "Data Mostly From Rats." Letter to *The New York Times*, 8 May 1991, p. A22.

3 Philip C. Weber. "Fetal Tissue Research Is a Dead End." *HLI Reports*, April 1993, p. 1.

4 Janice G. Raymond, professor of women's studies and medical ethics, University of Massachusetts, Amhurst, Congressional Testimony on HR 1532, "Research on Transplantation of Fetal Tissue," 20 March 1991.

110. What Is the Status of the "Harvesting" of Organs from Preborn Babies?

I Need a Brain, Igor—A *Small* Brain

The History of "Harvesting." The first fetal organ transplant took place in December, 1985, in Denver. Researchers Everett Spees and Kevin Lafferty transplanted fetal pancreatic tissue into the body of a 51-year-old diabetic. These cells soon began to produce insulin that the patient needed.[1]

In late 1988, researchers went one step further. They transferred brain cells from an aborted seven-week-old baby to an adult patient for the first time. The cells were implanted in an unnamed 55-year-old male Parkinson's Disease victim by a surgical team under Dr. Curt Freed and Dr. Robert Breeze at the University of Colorado Health Sciences Center. The experimental procedure was financed by private donors and was approved by the University of Colorado human subjects committee.[2]

Later, researchers set their sights on late-term aborted babies, who are more desirable for organ "harvesting" purposes because their body systems are larger, more mature, and generally freer of genetic defects.

Eight Swedish researchers did a study that was revealing because it indirectly showed how desirable late-term babies are for "harvesting" purposes: "Pancreatic glands of human fetuses obtained from 31 consecutive legal abortions were used. The abortions were induced by prostaglandin and carried out over a period of three months. The crown-heel lengths of the fetuses ... ranged from 12 to 34 cm [28 weeks gestation]."[3]

Going All the Way. The experiments described above use dead aborted babies as organ donors. Repulsive though these practices are, many people see no moral obstacle to using *live, unanesthetized* preborn babies for "harvesting" purposes as well!

It is inevitable that aborted babies will become transplant donors, because babies who are the result of miscarriages and ectopic pregnancies are generally not suitable for this purpose. This was shown by Frederick Bieber, a geneticist in the pathology department of the Brigham Women's Hospital, who examined 1,025 miscarriages over a period of one year. He found that only 39 (3.8 percent) of them produced a genetically normal baby who had not died two or three weeks before. Of these 39 babies, most had some infection and so were also unusable. During this same year, almost all the babies who died as a result of 125 ectopic pregnancies that Bieber studied were also very tiny or were unusable for transplant purposes.[4]

In the February 1987 issue of the *Hastings Center Report*, "ethicist" Mary Mahowald and researchers Jerry Silver and Richard Ratcheson of the Case Western Reserve School of Medicine stated that cannibalizing of *live* babies "... is morally defensible if dead fetuses are not available or are not conducive to successful transplants."

This, of course, is no limitation at all, because everyone knows *live* fetuses are more "conducive to successful transplants" than *dead* ones.[5]

This type of cannibalization already occurs on an almost routine basis in some Mideastern countries. In one case, an impotent Lebanese man had a testicle transplant from a near-viable preborn baby aborted at 25 weeks.[6]

The Facts of Life

The state legislatures of California, New Jersey, and Ohio have attempted to go one step farther by trying to pass bills allowing the *"harvesting" of all organs from live handicapped newborn babies!*

Among others, "bioethicist" Mary Anne Warren recommends that women become pregnant *specifically and intentionally to grow babies for the sole purpose of harvesting their organs.* One of the examples she gives is deliberate conception and then abortion of a baby at six months' gestation (or even later) for the purpose of taking both his kidneys to make a genetic match for the baby's father.[7]

The Death Dealers

Where There Is Money to Be Made ... Whenever a morally dubious medical "advance" comes along, medical professionals of equally dubious character flock around the new technology like vultures around a ripe carcass.

Since the profit potential of fetal organ "harvesting" is almost unlimited, it was inevitable that certain doctors and others with no particular regard for human life—or medical ethics—would seize the opportunity to milk the babies for all the money they are worth.

And sometimes they are caught with their hands in the bloody cookie jar.

From the Women of Developing Nations. Flow Labs of Rockville, Maryland, is one of at least a dozen fetal organ tissue traffickers in the United States. It gets its tissue from more than 250 suppliers in 12 different countries, mostly in the Third World. These nations include Haiti, Brazil and South Korea. Just three years after *Roe v. Wade*, at least 100,000 domestic and foreign preborn babies were "used" in the United States each year for research purposes.[8]

One South Korean abortionist, Lee Myung Bok of Seoul University's Medical Department, paid doctors to cut the kidneys out of more than 12,000 freshly killed preborn babies, then pack them in ice and ship them to the United States. He grossed $180,000. The doctors and nurses who committed the abortions were paid with whisky, nylon stockings and chewing gum.[8]

In July, 1988, authorities arrested six Paraguayan men for plotting to sell seven male *newborn infants* in the United States for the purpose of organ "harvesting." The men had already "collected" the infants from various sources. They testified that they had been doing this for years, and that the practice was "common."

These men merely sold the babies to middlemen, who transported them to the United States in the arms of women hired to act as their mothers (the babies flew free of charge), and then delivered them to unnamed firms in the United States. According to the men, there was no shortage of demand in the United States for healthy babies whose ultimate fate was to be killed and then cut up for parts.[9]

From Poor Women in the United States. Of course, it is the poor women of all nations whom medical people with no scruples exploit. Besides ransacking the organs of the preborn children of developing nations, the abortionists and others target the babies of poor women in the United States as well.

In 1976, *The Washington Post* revealed that the District of Columbia's General Hospital had received more than $68,000 for the organs of babies its abortionists had killed. The 21 March 1977 *Village Voice* reported these abortionists had encouraged welfare mothers to wait and have late-term abortions because these preborn babies yielded more and better-developed organs.[8] This practice directly contradicts the standards of the National Abortion Federation (NAF), which say babies should be aborted as soon as possible, because maternal risk increases with each week of gestation.

Perhaps the General Hospital abortionists thought the lives of welfare mothers were worth risking for the greater "good" of selling their babies' bodies.

1 "Aborted Baby's Brain Cells Implanted in Parkinson's Victim." *The Wanderer*, 24 November 1988, p. 1.

2 J.C. Willke, M.D. "Loma Linda's Lethal Transplants." *National Right to Life News*, 10 March 1988, p. 3.

3 Sandler, Andersson, Swenne, Petersson, Hellerstrom, Bjorken, Christensen and Groth. "Structure and Function of Human Fetal Endocrine Pancreas before and after Cryopreservation." *Cryopreservation of Human Fetal Pancreas*. Huddings, Sweden, 1982. p. 230.

4 Richard Saltus of *The Boston Globe*. "Brain Implants of Fetal Tissue Show Promise." *The Oregonian*, 13 June 1992, p. A5.

5 Leslie Bond and Dave Andrusko. "More Medical Facilities Preparing to Make Jump into Fetal Brain Transplants." *National Right to Life News*, 7 April 1988, p. 1. See also Leslie Bond and Dave Andrusko. "Harvesting Anencephalic Babies: Controversy Grows in Intensity." *National Right to Life News*, 25 February 1988, p. 1.

6 Nick Thimmesch. "Strange Tales of Fetal Life and Death." *Human Life Issues*, January, 1983, p. 4. Also see Bettina Conner. "World Trade in Human Embryos." *Elements*, May 1976, p. 4.

7 Mary Anne Warren. "Can the Fetus Be an Organ Farm?" *Hastings Center Report*, October 1978.

8 World Trends and Forecasts. "Recycling Human Bodies to Save Lives." *The Futurist*, April 1976, p. 108.

9 *Il Tempo* (Rome, Italy), 9 August 1988, and *America* magazine, 10 December 1988.

I I I. What Is the Status of the "Harvesting" of Organs from Newborn Babies?

Definitions

Before we can discuss fetal and newborn baby tissue "harvesting" and experimentation, we must be familiar with the body systems most affected by the diseases that fetal tissue transplants allegedly ameliorate in patients.

Here are some pertinent definitions.

Brain Stem: The lower portion of the brain, at the upper end of the spinal column, that mainly handles involuntary bodily functions, including breathing, swallowing, circulation, digestion and reaction to pain.

Cerebellum: A portion of the brain forward of and above the medulla, consisting of two lateral lobes and a median lobe. The cerebellum coordinates the muscles and maintains balance.

Anencephaly: Total lack of the cortex (upper brain), with lack of skull closure. Usually, the hypothalamus is malformed and the cerebellum is rudimentary or absent. This condition exposes the cranial matter to air and is almost always fatal within hours or days (about 75 percent are stillborn, with mortality of birth survivors being 90 percent in the first week), although some anencephalic babies live several years. This condition occurs in about one out of 1,000 pregnancies in the United States, and parents with an anencephalic baby have a 5% chance of having another such baby. The AFP test or amniocentesis can detect this condition.

Hydranencephaly: A purely descriptive term, not related to any particular disease, which means spinal fluid entirely replaces the cortex (upper brain). There is total or near-total hemispherical destruction, with great ventricular (brain cavity) enlargement with little or no cerebral mantle. The brain stem, cerebellum, and basal ganglia are present but may be abnormal. The brain stem usually remains functional.

Hydrocephalus: The obstruction of the normal accumulation or drainage of cerebrospinal fluid from its sources to its areas of absorption. The baby's head will have an increased quantity of this fluid under persistent or intermittent increased pressure.

Microcephaly: Abnormally small head size, usually (but not always) associated with brain disease and/or mental retardation. The baby's head circumference is more than two standard deviations (about the smallest 5%) below normal for all babies. The baby has a small or missing front fontanel (soft spot) and a recessed and/or sloping forehead. This condition usually occurs in babies with Trisomy 13-15 and Trisomy 17-18.

Megalencephaly: The baby's head is enlarged due to abnormal enlargement of the brain. This condition is often accompanied by convulsions, retardation and hypotonia (localized low osmotic pressure). It is usually present in the later stages of Tay-Sachs Disease and Alexander's Disease.

Why Should We Stop at the Unborn?

"Little Monsters." As always, the anti-life ethic "progresses" along its corpse-strewn trail one inevitable step at a time. If we do not want to "waste" the valuable tissue from dead aborted babies and from *living* aborted babies, we certainly do not want to "waste" the tissue from newborn babies who are "going to die anyhow"— especially anencephalic babies, those children heartlessly called "monsters" by anti-lifers. Dr. Leonard Bailey, who gained fame for transplanting a baboon's heart into a newborn baby, commented, "It's absolutely absurd that I have a legal right to abort that baby out of the mother within a week of delivery and throw it out, but because it's delivered, I have no access to it [for its organs]."[1]

Tiny Organ Farms. As anencephalic babies slowly die, so do all their organs. By the time doctors declare them "brain dead," their organs are not suitable for transplantation.

California's Loma Linda Hospital saw these little ones as a gold mine of opportunity for research and transplantation. At one point, this research center was actually keeping these babies alive so that their organs would be fresh for removal when a suitable recipient was found. Doctors would then kill them and cut the required organs out of their little bodies.[2]

Just One Little Problem ... Of course, there is one troublesome little detail (nothing really major, actually): the babies are still alive.

How can we get around this irritating little obstacle?

Why, we can just redefine "death," and then classify anencephalic newborns as "dead!"

And why not? We have already done this with preborn babies, so why not "stretch the envelope" just a little more?

At the 1990 annual meeting of the National Medical Association in Las Vegas, Dr. Mark Evans seriously proposed the "... possibility of creating a new legal definition to permit physicians to declare anencephalic neonates [newborn babies] "brain absent" and therefore legally dead, so their organs might be harvested for transplantation."[3]

State legislatures are getting into the act, too. The first attempt to reclassify anencephalic babies out of human existence occurred in February, 1986, as California State Senator Milton Marks introduced Senate Bill 2018, which stated baldly, "An individual born with the condition of anencephaly is dead."

After the "harvesters" have free rein to pillage the little bodies of anencephalic babies, they will inevitably target other groups of newborn children. Other likely unwilling "donors" will include newborn babies with Tay-Sachs disease, Werdnig-Hoffman disease, hydranencephaly, grade IV intracranial hemorrhage, and Trisomy 13, 18 and 21.

1   David H. Andrusko. "A Time to Stop." *National Right to Life News*, 10 March 1988, pp. 2, 10.

2   J.C. Willke, M.D. "Loma Linda's Lethal Transplants." *National Right to Life News*, 10 March 1988, p. 3.

3   This proposal also appeared in the 1-14 October 1990 issue of *Obstetrics and Gynecology News*.

The Facts of Life

Chapter 11

Sex Education and School-Based Clinics

···

112. What Are the Three Kinds of Sex Education?

Introduction

Most parents, whether religious or not, believe that everyone needs education in sexuality, even people who remain celibate all their lives. Christians believe that God would not have given us the marvelous gifts of sexuality and reproduction if He had not wanted us to know about them and use them wisely for His greater glory.

Committed Christians and secularists agree on very little beyond this basic point.

The *content* of the sex-related information that schools present is the main point of disagreement between Christian parents and secular school authorities.

The Three Types of Sex Education

There are basically only three types of sex education, regardless of the titles applied to them.

(1) Chastity Education. This kind gives children the moral and practical instruction they need to resist the pressures and temptations of the world and the inclinations of our fallen nature, and helps them understand God's precious gift of human sexuality. To be effective, this kind of instruction cannot stand alone. It must be part of a *lifestyle* taught by people who live moral lives, and who present it as a part of an integrated program on Christian living throughout all 12 years of grade and high school. The Vatican's 1995 document *The Truth and Meaning of Human Sexuality: Guidelines for Education Within the Family* (¶3) explains, " ... sexuality is not something purely biological, rather it concerns the intimate nucleus of the person."

We do not need detailed instruction in the functioning of the reproductive system to live our lives any more than we need detailed knowledge of the gastrointestinal system in order to digest our food.

The Facts of Life

Chastity education requires the most preparation of any kind of sexuality instruction. This is because it is the most difficult to teach, it is countercultural and works against man's fallen nature and, in order to be most effective, it must be carefully tailored to the needs and personality of each child. For these reasons, the parents of each child are the most appropriate chastity educators.

The Truth and Meaning of Human Sexuality provides four general guidelines for education in chastity. Parents who want to teach and form their children in chastity should carefully study the following paragraphs from this document:

(1) Each child is a unique and unrepeatable person and must receive individualized formation (¶65-67).

(2) The moral dimension of sexuality must always be part of the parent's explanations (¶68-69).

(3) Formation in chastity and timely information regarding sexuality must be provided in the broadest context of education for love (¶70-74).

(4) Parents should provide this information with great delicacy, but clearly and at the appropriate time (¶75-76).

Some may allege that education in chastity is "oppressive." These people have the situation backwards. Which is more "oppressive": to control one's sexual drive, or be controlled by *it*? *The Truth and Meaning of Human Sexuality* describes the crippling nature of addiction to endless fornication:

If the person is not master of self—through the virtues and, in a concrete way, through chastity—he or she lacks that self-possession which makes self-giving possible. Chastity is the spiritual power which *frees* love from selfishness and aggression.... Chastity is the joyous affirmation of someone who knows how to live self-giving, free from any form of self-centered slavery ... either man governs his passions and finds peace, or he lets himself be dominated by them and becomes unhappy (¶16,17,18).

The document continues:

In the light of the Redemption and how adolescents and young people are formed, the virtue of chastity is found within temperance—a cardinal virtue elevated and enriched by grace in baptism. So chastity is not to be understood as a repressive attitude. On the contrary, chastity should be understood rather as the purity and temporary stewardship of a precious and rich gift of love, in view of the self-giving realized in each person's specific vocation. Chastity is thus that "spiritual energy capable of defending love from the perils of selfishness and aggressiveness, and able to advance it towards its full realization" (¶4).

Finally, *The Truth and Meaning of Human Sexuality* says that the three main goals of chastity education should be:

(a) to maintain in the family a positive atmosphere of love, virtue and respect for the gifts of God, in particular the gift of life;

(b) to help children understand the value of sexuality and chastity in stages, sustaining their growth through enlightening word, example and prayer; and

(c) to help them understand and discover their own vocation to marriage or to consecrated virginity for the sake of the Kingdom of Heaven in harmony with and respecting their attitudes and inclinations and the gifts of the Holy Spirit (¶22).

(2) Biological Sex Education. This kind, sometimes called an "organ recital," limits itself to information on the functioning of the reproductive system. Such programs are billed as "value-free" or "reality-based" because their backers say it is literally impossible to attach values to purely biological instruction. Sadly, the *reverse* is true: it is impossible to present such teaching without *implied* values, in any setting, whether at home or in school.

The primary drawback of such instruction is that it neglects the spiritual aspect of human beings and treats them as purely physical beings. Additionally, it is virtually impossible to avoid violating the latency period and innocence of young children with any type of sex education.

(3) Comprehensive Sex Education. This type of sex education teaches children not only about the biological facets of sex, but also about birth control, abortion, masturbation, homosexual behavior and other evils. This type of sex education, too, is supposedly "value-free," but this is, of course, impossible. When an authority figure such as a teacher tells children that no sex act is immoral, and that we should not judge others who have "different sexual lifestyles" than ourselves, this, *by definition*, teaches a completely amoral set of values.

The Planned Parenthood Federation of America (PPFA), the United States' leading proponent of comprehensive sex education, defines sex education as a course of instruction that includes at least four of the following six topics:[1]

(1) Biological facts about human reproduction;

(2) Information on sexual development;

(3) Information on preventing sexual abuse;

(4) Comprehensive birth control information;

(5) Information on abortion and how to obtain one; and

(6) Information on contraceptives and how to obtain them.

By Planned Parenthood's definition, comprehensive sex education *must* at least contain information on contraceptives and abortifacients and how to obtain them. Strictly biological sex education would contain only points (1) and (2), above.

Note that Planned Parenthood's definition of comprehensive sex education does not mention interpersonal relationships or chastity skills at all—not surprising in a program that assumes teenagers are animals having "needs" they cannot control and therefore must satisfy.[2]

Gandhi Speaks

Mahatma Gandhi, India's "Great Soul," often spoke on sexual morality, and frequently emphasized the importance of sex education. He defined the fundamental difference between comprehensive sex education and chastity education as follows:

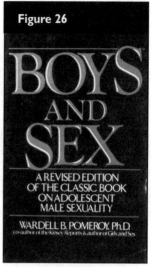

Figure 26

> Sexual science is of two kinds, that which is used for controlling or overcoming the sexual passion, and that which is used to stimulate and feed it. Instruction in the former is as necessary a part of a child's education, as the latter is harmful and dangerous, and fit, therefore, only to be shunned.
>
> The sex education that I stand for must have for its object the conquest and sublimation of the sex passion. Such education should automatically serve to bring home to children the essential distinction between man and brute, to make them realize that it is man's special privilege and pride to be gifted with the faculties of head and heart both, that he is a thinking no less than a feeling animal, and to renounce the sovereignty of reason over the blind instincts is, therefore, to renounce a man's estate. In man, reason quickens and guides the feeling; in brutes, the soul lies ever dormant.[3]

"Any of the farm animals may become a sexual object—ponies, calves, sheep, pigs, even chickens or ducks. Dogs are commonly used, but cats rarely."
—Wardell Pomeroy's sex education text Boys and Sex.

1 "American Teens Speak: Sex, Myths, TV and Birth Control." Poll conducted for PPFA by Louis Harris and Associates, September-October 1986.

2 Among the more than 100 organizations that support or promote comprehensive sex education and school-based clinics are the Alan Guttmacher Institute (AGI), the American Academy of Pediatrics (AAP), American Association of Marriage Counselors (AAMC), American Association of Sex Educators, Counselors and Therapists (AASECT), American Civil Liberties Union (ACLU), American College of Obstetricians and Gynecologists (ACOG), American Eugenics Society, American Humanist Association (AHA), American Medical Association (AMA), American Public Health Association (APHA), Association for Voluntary Surgical Contraception (AVSC), 'Catholics' for a Free Choice (CFFC), Center for Population Options (CPO), Children's Defense Fund (CDF), Concern for Dying, Council of Churches of Christ in the United States, Dignity, Euthanasia Educational Council, Euthanasia Society of America, Ford Foundation, Kinsey Institute for Research on Sex, Gender, and Reproduction, Metropolitan Community Churches, National Abortion and Reproductive Rights Action League (NARRAL), National Education Association (NEA), National Family Planning and Reproductive Health Association (NFPRHA), National Organization for Women (NOW), National Support Center for School-Based Clinics, Negative Population Growth (NPG), North American Man/Boy Love Association (NAMBLA), Pathfinder Fund, Parent-Teacher Association (PTA), Planned Parenthood Federation of America (PPFA), Playboy Foundation, Population Council (PC), Population Crisis Committee (PCC), 'Religious' Coalition for Abortion Rights (RCAR), Robert Wood Johnson Foundation, Rockefeller Foundation, Sex Information and Education Council of the United States (SIECUS), Unitarian Universalist Association, United Nations International Children's Emergency Fund (UNICEF), United Methodist Church, United Nations

Educational, Scientific, and Cultural Organization (UNESCO), United States Agency for International Development (USAID), World Health Organization, World League for Sexual Reform, Young Women's Christian Association (YWCA) and Zero Population Growth (ZPG).

3   Fr. A.S. Antonisamy. *Wisdom for All Times: Mahatma Gandhi and Pope Paul VI on Birth Regulation.* Family Life Service Centre, Archbishop's House, Pondicherry 605001 India, June 1978.

···

113. What Are Some Examples of the Material Used in Comprehensive Sex Education?

Overview

Most school-aged children in the United States spend more than one-third of their waking hours in the public school system. So, the schools inevitably exert a profound influence upon their morals and attitudes.

These children are exposed to an indirect erosion of Christian values through systematic censorship and deliberate omission of Christian viewpoints. Situation ethics—the absolute antithesis to the teachings of Christ—defines student behavior. School systems have officially banned the Bible and school prayer. Despite repeated Supreme Court rulings to the contrary, public school systems systematically suppress Bible clubs and other Christian groups. To avoid controversy, history texts omit entirely the roles of God, religion and the family in the formation and development of the country.

Purging Religion from Textbooks

Researchers funded by the National Institute of Education examined 60 standard social studies textbooks used by the majority of children in grades one through 12 in U.S. public schools. The central conclusion of the study was dramatic: religion, traditional family values, and conservative positions on every known moral issue have been expunged *completely* from the curricula of all public school students. Not *one word* of the more than 1.5 million total words in the 60 volumes mentioned *any* religious activity in contemporary American life. The only role models given were Democrats, minorities or women. Not one word mentioned the influence on society of a prominent preacher or clergyman, such as Billy Graham, Bishop Fulton Sheen or Norman Vincent Peale. The words "marriage," "wedding," "husband," and "wife" did not appear *once* in any of the 60 textbooks.[1]

Such censorship *indirectly* erodes Christian values, but one area of instruction is organized so that it *directly* attacks Christian values. This area is sex education.

Whereas Christianity emphasizes virginity before marriage and faithfulness to God and spouse afterward, public schools have diligently banned God, and tell kids that contraception, sterilization, abortion, fornication, adultery, sodomy, masturbation and even *sex with animals* are value-free and therefore involve *human rights* that no one can tamper with—*especially* parents.

Examples of Sex Education Curricula

The following paragraphs describe the contents of some of the most common sex education books and curricula used by public schools in the United States today. *All of these texts* emphasize the "rights" to birth control, abortion, free sex, adultery and homosexual behavior; all are objectionable throughout. The quotes below typify their entire contents.

Guide for Young Adults

Dr. Patricia Shiller, founder of the American Association of Sex Educators, Counselors, and Therapists (AASECT), says Gary F. Kelly's *Learning about Sex: The Contemporary Guide for Young Adults* is "A must for all young people." It includes the following statements:

> Sado-masochism [inflicting pain for sexual purposes] may be very acceptable and safe for sexual partners who know each other's needs and have established agreements for what they want from each other.... Some people are now saying that partnerships—married or unmarried—should not be exclusive. They believe that while a primary relationship is maintained with one person, the freedom for both partners to love and share sex with others should also be present.... A fair percentage of people probably have some sort of sexual contact with an animal during their lifetime, particularly boys who live on farms. There are no indications that such animal contacts are harmful, except for the obvious dangers of poor hygiene, injury by the animal, or guilt on the part of the human.[2]

Changing Bodies

Changing Bodies, Changing Lives: A Book for Teens on Sex and Relationships is probably the most popular sex education text in the United States and has been in continuous use in thousands of high schools since it appeared in 1980. It includes the statement: "Bisexuality is an openness to loving, sexual relationships with both sexes—*our true nature*.... Gay men, too, have many ways of making love. One may caress the other's penis with his hand or his mouth. Or one may put his penis in the other's anus."[3]

Boys and Girls and Sex

Wardell Pomeroy's companion books *Boys and Sex* and *Girls and Sex* are so extreme that they are the number-one target of Christian parents who oppose immoral school sex education.

These books assert:

> Premarital intercourse does have its definite values as a training ground for marriage or some other committed relationship. ... to make everyday comparisons again, it's like taking a car out for a test run before you buy it. ... I have known cases of farm boys who have had a loving sexual relationship with an animal and who felt good about their behavior until they got to college, where they learned for the first time that what they had done was 'abnormal.' Then they were upset.... Any of the farm animals may become a sexual object—ponies, calves, sheep, pigs, even chickens or ducks. Dogs are also commonly used, but cats rarely.[4]

Enhancing Skills

The extremely popular (and misleadingly-named) program *Enhancing Skills to Prevent Pregnancy* tells teachers how to break down their student's inhibitions with the formidable weapon of peer pressure:

> Some teachers are able to combine humor with demonstration by bringing cucumbers or zucchini to class and showing how to apply and remove condoms. Open the packages and unroll condoms for students to inspect. Pass them around. If you are using cucumbers, have one student hold the cucumber while the other student puts the condom on the cucumber. Expect students to laugh at first and be embarrassed! This is healthy....[5]

One Washington State parent testified about the coercive nature of many sex education programs. These programs use peer pressure to forcibly destroy the natural modesty of young people:

> There is one teacher in Bellevue who has all the boys say 'vagina'; he calls them individually, and they all have to say it out loud in class. The boys say 'vagina' and the girls say 'penis.' One girl told me that she was so embarrassed that she could hardly bring out the word 'penis' because all these boys were sitting in the class. It just embarrassed her so. So he made her get up in front of the class and very loudly say it ten times.[6]

Homosexual Recruitment

Most Christian parents would be shocked and outraged to learn that most sex education curricula in U.S. public schools today teach children not only about contraception and abortion, but about a wide range of homosexual acts as well.

Many public school sex education "experts" blandly promise parents that they may take part in teaching their children about sex. However, most parents who have tried to get their hands on a copy of the sex ed materials find it is almost impossible to do so. Even when parents *do* get a look at the material presented to their children, they do not realize the teacher's editions are usually far more explicit.

This is not surprising, because these materials tell the users to keep parents out of the teaching process entirely.

For example, homosexual activist Cooper Thompson, a key figure in the "Homophobia Task Force," prepared a $161,000 federally-funded program titled "Mutual Caring/Mutual Sharing." Thompson knew parents would strongly object to his program, so its instructions state, "It is unrealistic and even undesirable to include parents in this program."[7]

The main goal of the program, according to the literature, is "to foster an acceptance of the various sexual preferences and orientations of their peers, and an acceptance of their own preference or orientation."[7]

Another homosexual sex ed propaganda program warns teachers not to let parents know what they are teaching their children in class: "Caution: Participants should not be given extra copies of the form to show to their parents or friends. Many of the materials of this program shown to people outside the context of the program itself, can evoke misunderstanding and difficulties."[8]

The Facts of Life

This program, which more than 1,000 public high schools use, features color slides of sodomy and X-rated pornographic audiotapes of a wide variety of sexual perverts talking about the many rewards of their bizarre "orientations."

The purpose of this program is, "To make clear that sexual relationships with the same sex during youth are normal."[8]

One of several textbooks that push the homosexual agenda under the guise of "AIDS education" is *One Teenager in Ten*. It peddles the now-discredited line that 10% of all people are prone to homosexuality.

One Teenager in Ten is filled with fabricated "case histories" that are nothing more than a pornographic come-on to the homosexual deathstyle. The book's purpose is to lure any child who has the slightest inclination toward or curiosity about perversions (and even many who do not) into homosexual activity.[6]

One of the many "case studies" involves "Amy," a 13-year-old girl, who describes various perversions inflicted upon her by a 23-year-old lesbian who seduced her. She gushes, "I became a lesbian and a woman that weekend!"

Another phony "case study" centers on "Rick," who, at 15, was sodomized by a drifter: "He came back with a tube of KY [lubricant] stuck in his towel.... I felt like a bride on her honeymoon.... I was in love."[6]

The fact that such activities are felonies is not mentioned.

Nor is there any mention of the depression, the loneliness, the dozens of diseases and addictions that homosexuals suffer, the shortened lifespans, or the overtly exploitative nature of homosexual "love." Not a syllable.

All secular sex ed books paint the homosexual "community" experience as nothing but sweetness, light, flowers and KY lubricant.

Expanding the Program

Parents who demand to see the textbooks and teaching aids for a particular sex education program may be shown material that seems perfectly innocuous.

However, nothing restricts teachers to teaching only what their study guides outline. The messages that adults *actually transmit* to children are what count—not what the study materials contain. As mentioned before, the material in the teacher's edition is usually far more explicit than in the student's edition.

Sol Gordon, whose teachings have been ruled pornographic by the courts, describes how sex ed teachers may flatly lie to get around any limitations, merely by feigning ignorance of the rules: "Young people are not paying any attention to us because we have these dumb messages ... and the dumbest one is 'just say no!' ... Don't you [teachers] dare try to implement anything I say unless you have job security and tenure.... If a supervisor says to you, 'But you're not supposed to do this stuff,' always say, 'Oh, I didn't know.'"[9]

In practice, sex educators can say *anything they want to* in class. Many conservative organizations have reported that Gordon's type of instruction in deception and outright lying is *common* in comprehensive sex education programs.

And, when you think about it, this is only logical: what is the purpose of secular sex education except to prepare teenagers to fornicate?

Other Gateways

Religious parents should never assume secular sex education programs are the only tools available for corrupting their children. The evil intentions of the "sexperts" are matched only by their almost limitless imaginations.

Planned Parenthood Federation of America (PPFA) workers, of course, have the most active imaginations of all. They have spawned literally hundreds of programs designed to 'desensitize' children to sexual acts. Translated, this means the first step to getting kids in bed with each other is getting them used to the idea.

One typical program was Vermont Planned Parenthood's "Safety Dance," in which adults had kids use nametags and placards to arrange the sequence of events involved in putting on a condom. In another skit, kids arranged some 25 "sexual activities" in order of HIV-infection potential.

The instruction manual for the "Safety Dance" suggested making the event part of a homework assignment, so kids would face a coercive choice: take part in the brainwashing or get a failing grade for the day.

The "Safety Dance" is just one of the ways Planned Parenthood (PP) deliberately and systematically undermines parental, familial and religious values. But, like termites, PP does its most dangerous work out of sight—not in public confrontations, but in day-to-day classroom instruction.

For example, in its widely used "Sensitivity Training" program, Planned Parenthood breaks down kids' home training by having mixed groups of students discuss "Virginity, Oral-Genital Sex, Intercourse, Masturbation, Sterility, Group Sex, Homosexuality, Extra-Marital Relations, Abortion and Nudity—with acquaintances, with family, with the opposite sex, with the same sex, and with close friends." Those children who refuse to change their attitudes "are considered non-conformists or deviants." In some schools, not taking part in these classes gets the student suspended from school.[10]

And, in its "Positive Imaging" program, PP tries to plant guided imagery in students' minds. In one scenario, adults tell kids to have fantasies involving "... sexual feelings about people of the same or opposite sex, parents, brothers and sisters, old people, animals, nature, inanimate objects, and almost anything you can imagine."[11]

There can be no possible purpose for these and similar exercises except to break down students' *inhibitions* and lead them to take the first step to an unrestrained and omnisexual lifestyle—by getting them to *imagine* and *talk about* every perverted sex act in the sex educator's books.

Are Catholic Schools Safe?

Many concerned parents have been lulled into believing that children enrolled in Catholic schools are safe from the baleful influence of the sex educators.

Unfortunately, nothing could be further from the truth.

The National Conference of Catholic Bishops (NCCB) has produced a series of deeply flawed documents on sex education, including the 1968 *Human Life in Our Day*, which sanctions "responsible dissent" from *Humanae Vitae*; the 1972 *To Teach as Jesus Did*, which blatantly usurped the fundamental rights of parents; and the November 1990 *Human Sexuality: A Catholic Perspective for Education and Lifelong Learning*, which was seriously confused as to the nature of human sexuality.[12]

The Facts of Life

These documents are partly to blame for the confusion surrounding sex education in Catholic schools today, and for the fact that attitudes among public school students and Catholic school students regarding sexual morality scarcely differ from each other.

Most of the sex education programs used in Catholic schools today are deeply flawed, and their sole effect is to damage the morals and faith of young people. These programs include:

- William C. Brown's *New Creation* series, which seriously violates the latency phase of development with explicit instruction in grades one through four, bases its material on secular humanist rather than Catholic sources and is the subject of more complaints by parents than any other curriculum. It recommends that teachers use Planned Parenthood materials for further information and research into specific topics.

- Benziger's *Family Life Program*, used in the Washington, Miami and Atlanta dioceses, reflects many of the flaws in the NCCB's document *Human Sexuality*. It attempts to redefine the family, contains virtually no mention of sin, includes graphic photographs, treats differences between men and women as purely physical and refers students to "New Age" and radical feminist resources.

- *In God's Image: Male and Female* is promoted as "A Catholic Vision of Human Sexuality." Sadly, this "vision" is distorted and misleading. The 20 videos and accompanying worksheets omit and misrepresent the most critical Church teachings on sexuality, describe acts that severely damage the innocence of the seventh and eighth graders for which it is designed (such as masturbation), incorporates "New Age" philosophy and manipulates children psychologically.[13]

The conclusion that can be drawn from the sex education situation is crystal clear. If parents do not take the time to carefully review the sex education material that their children are exposed to (whether in public or Catholic schools), and aggressively shield them from it if necessary, they will almost certainly experience deep and unceasing heartbreak later in life. Their children will be much more likely to fornicate, become pregnant, abort, "shack up," suffer from venereal diseases and severe guilt, give up the Faith, and be far more likely to divorce and be unhappy later in life.

1 Paul C. Vitz. "Scholars Say Textbooks Censor Out Religion." National Federation for Decency *Journal*, March 1986, p. 6.

2 Gary F. Kelly. *Learning about Sex: The Contemporary Guide for Young Adults*. New York: Barron's, 1968, pp. 61, 136.

3 *Changing Bodies, Changing Lives: A Book for Teens on Sex and Relationships*. Random House: New York, 1980, pp. 117-122.

4 Wardell Pomeroy, Ph.D. *Boys and Sex*. Delacorte Press, New York, 1981, pp. 117, 171, 172.

5 R.P. Barth. *Enhancing Skills to Prevent Pregnancy*. School of Social Welfare, University of California, Berkeley, Network Publications, p. 95.

6 Gene Antonio. "America's XXX-Rated Sex Education Curricula." *New Dimensions* Magazine, September 1990, pp. 72-77.

7   S.G. Philliber and M.L. Tatum. "The Impact of Sex Education on Students, Parents, and Faculty: A Report from Falls Church." November 1979, p. 11.

8   "Public School Sex Education: A Report." Published as an insert in the October 1990 issue of the American Family Association *Journal*. Also available for $2.00 from the American Family Association, Post Office Drawer 2440, Tupelo, Mississippi 38803.

9   Margo Szews. "The Pied Piper of Sex and Sleaze: Dr. Sol Gordon and Friends Tell Kids to "Just Say *Yes* !"" *ALL about Issues*, June-July 1989, pp. 40-42.

10 Eleanor S. Morrison and Miln Underhill Price. *Values in Sexuality*. New York: Hart Publishing Company and A&W Publishers. 1974, p. 100.

11 "What Is Sexual Fantasy?" *What's Happening?* Atlanta: Emory University, Grady Memorial Family Planning Program. 1976, p. 4.

12 The NCCB document *Human Sexuality* reflects in many ways the attitudes of the known dissenters on the committee. The document blesses graphic public school sex education programs; misunderstands the transcendental character of the mystery of human sexuality; confuses what it means to be male and female; treats Christ as a fallen "sexual person" (not Divine); fails to note that human sexuality is fallen and wounded; fails to account for the effects of Original Sin; seems to condone homosexuality; attempts to redefine the family; does not mention purity anywhere; and denies the "latency period" ("years of innocence") in its quest to portray humans as sexual from birth [21 July 1992 analysis of *Human Sexuality* by Catholics United by the Faith].

13 Detailed information on sex education programs being used in Catholic schools can be obtained from Human Life International, 4 Family Life, Front Royal, VA 22630, telephone: (540) 635-7884, FAX (540) 636-7363. An excellent newsletter that deals with sex education is *Mother's Watch*, PO Box 2780, Montgomery Village, MD 20286-2780. Subscription price is $20 per year.

114. Is Comprehensive Sex Education Effective at Preventing Teen Pregnancy and Abortions?

Europe: A Portent of Our Future

Europe is dying. Only two European countries—Ireland and tiny Malta—are replacing their populations. Married couples in Europe once had an average of five children, and now the ideal is only one boy and one girl. As described in Chapter 12, 38 of Europe's 47 nations are currently at or under replacement fertility levels (33 of 35, not counting the former USSR). Twelve European nations have remained below replacement level continuously since 1965.

Why is this happening?

One of the basic reasons is that pervasive and mandatory "value-free" sex education programs have isolated sexual intercourse from the context of marriage, family, procreation and even *love* in the minds of millions of Europeans, leading to the widespread acceptance of contraception, sterilization and abortion. Most people now see sex as having no meaning but pleasure, and pregnancy as a dread disease to avoid at all costs.

In order to control this "disease," abortion and contraception are universally available at taxpayers' expense, with very few exceptions. *The Truth and Meaning of Human Sexuality* explains, "... our society has broken away from the full truth about man, from the truth about what man and woman really are as persons. Thus it cannot adequately comprehend the real meaning of the gift of persons in marriage, responsible love at the service of fatherhood and motherhood, and the true grandeur of procreation and education."[1]

The implications of such sex-ed programs, instituted on a continental scale, are staggering. And they are utterly predictable.

Denmark is one example. Concerned about rising illegitimate births, the Danish government launched compulsory sex education in 1970. The result? The 30 March 1985 *Human Events* reported: "Illegitimate births, which were supposed to drop, instead nearly doubled; abortion rates, which were predicted to fall with the ready availability of condoms and other contraceptives in grocery stores, actually doubled; venereal disease more than doubled; and divorces doubled."

As Alan Guttmacher revealed: "The only avenue the International Planned Parenthood Federation and its allies could travel to win the battle for abortion on demand is through sex education."[2]

The Experts Speak

Leading "sexologists" in the United States have admitted that comprehensive sex education—including contraceptive training—is completely ineffective at stopping teen pregnancy.

Jane Mauldon and Kristin Luker state: "Despite long-standing public support for sex education in the schools, it has been difficult to show concrete effects of sex education on sexual and contraceptive behavior."[3]

Researcher D.A. Dawson found:

It is important to note at the outset that most researchers agree that sex education does not decrease the rate of teenage pregnancies or the incidence of sexual activity.... It is widely believed that providing teenagers with information about pregnancy and birth control is crucial if the incidence of adolescent pregnancy is to be reduced, and that formal sex education programs are an appropriate and important vehicle for providing information.... However, our analyses fail to show any consistent relationship between exposure to contraceptive education and the subsequent initiation of intercourse.... The final result to emerge from the analysis is that neither pregnancy education nor contraceptive education exerts any significant effect on the risk of premarital pregnancy among sexually active teenagers—a finding that calls into question the argument that formal sex education is an effective tool for reducing adolescent pregnancy.[4]

William Marsiglio and Frank Mott reported the results of a large study of high-school teenage girls: "In 1982, 1,888 women (ages 15 to 19) were surveyed and researchers found that 'prior exposure to a sex education course is positively and significantly associated with the initiation of sexual activity at ages 15 and 16'."[5]

A writer for *Forbes* Magazine discovered:

Massive, federally subsidized 'sex education' programs entered the American public school system during the 1970s, often supplemented by clinics located in the schools and offering additional information and referrals on matters of sex, pregnancy and abortion. Before these programs began, teenage pregnancy was already declining, for more than a decade.

This long decline in teenage pregnancy then reversed and teenage pregnancies soared, as "sex education" spread pervasively throughout the public schools. The pregnancy rate among 15 to 19-year-old females was 68 per thousand in 1970 and 96 per thousand by 1980....

Soaring rates of abortion were in fact offsetting soaring rates of pregnancy. Between 1970 and 1987, for example, the number of abortions increased by 250,000, even though the number of teenagers declined by 400,000.[6]

Amazingly, even veteran "sexologist" Sol Gordon admits, "Teenagers need to be reassured that it is normal not to have sex. The best people to learn that from is their parents. There are no substitutes for parental guidance. *Sex education without morals and values is useless.*"[7]

The quotes above are exclusively from sources that are adamantly pro-abortion and pro-comprehensive-sex-ed, so no one can accuse the sources of "pro-life bias."

So Why Continue a Failed Program?

The psychological and monetary investment in comprehensive sex education programs is enormous. To quit or to change direction at this late date would not only mean admitting error, but *liability* as well. Also, the "sexperts" have become locked into their own self-perpetuating bureaucracy; its main purpose (as with *any* bureaucracy) is survival and, if possible, expansion.

And so, as the teenage pregnancy rate rises, the "sexperts" keep prescribing more of the poison that caused the illness in the first place.

Comprehensive sex ed has definitely contributed to an exploding teen pregnancy rate by encouraging increased fornication. In 1970, only 4.6% of all 15-year-old girls in the United States had fornicated. By 1990, this rate had increased more than sevenfold to 33.1%. Of all unmarried girls 15-19, 28.6% had fornicated in 1970. This rate had more than doubled to 61.4% by 1990.[8]

In 1986, Harris and Associates performed a comprehensive poll for Planned Parenthood on teen fornication and the effects of sex education upon it. Here are the results:[9]

Teenagers receiving *comprehensive* sex education—46% had engaged in sexual intercourse.

Teenagers receiving *no* sex education at all—32% had engaged in sexual intercourse.

Teenagers receiving *biological* sex education—26% had engaged in sexual intercourse.

It is obvious from these figures that well-prepared chastity education programs, presented by parents living in marriages as God designed them, would produce a much lower incidence of fornication than any of the three above options.

The Facts of Life

The Long-Term Results of Secular Sex Education

Compulsory sex education has been with us for a long time now. Not surprisingly, Washington, D.C.—the first major city to impose sex ed programs—has the highest teen pregnancy rates and abortion rates in the country.

Without question, values-free and morals-free sex education has had a profound effect upon U.S. society. When authority figures tell an entire generation of children that sex is for recreation and all sex acts (both inside and out of marriage) are good, kids will inevitably turn these ideas into lifestyles. As Dr. Donald McDonald, former administrator of the Alcohol, Drug Abuse, and Mental Health Administration, has said: "Asking schools to teach morally and ethically neutral sex education is asking for failure."[10]

And we most certainly *have* failed. From 1960 to 1991, a span of just three short decades, we have seen the following trends in U.S. society, much of which must be laid at the doorsteps of the sex educators:[11]

- Abortions have increased **800 percent.**
- The illegitimate birthrate has increased **457 percent.**
- Child abuse has increased more than **500 percent.**
- The divorce rate has increased **133 percent.**
- The percentage of single-parent families has increased **214 percent.**
- "Living together" has increased **279 percent.**
- The incidence of venereal diseases has increased **245 percent.**
- The teen suicide rate has increased **214 percent.**
- The juvenile violent crime rate has increased **295 percent.**

It is not at all surprising that the "sexperts" have had such a profound effect on U.S. society. Their combined power and scope is worldwide. Their network is extremely well-organized and richly funded and they rigidly control the sexual mores of the United States.

A Final Note on Marital Chastity

Almost everyone *mis*understands chastity to mean only complete abstinence from sexual intercourse before marriage. In reality, "Married people are called to live conjugal chastity; others practice chastity in continence."[12] This means, simply, abstinence before marriage and faithfulness afterward.

The fruits of fornication are rotten, as we saw above. But those of adultery, abortion and contraception are even more bitter: physical injury and death, divorce, broken homes, widespread poverty for women and children, child abuse and deep-rooted mistrust between spouses.

Chastity between husband and wife bears directly upon the question of sex education, because teenage children are totally aware of their parent's sexuality and how they value it and live with it. Parents who are faithful to each other in thought and deed, who respect the gift of fertility and who value the children it brings will be able to pass on such values to their children. Parents who use contraception, who "stop at two" and then get sterilized, and who use pornography or watch dirty TV shows and movies will find it impossible to teach chastity to their children.

Truly, parents cannot teach chastity unless they *understand* it, and cannot understand it unless they *practice* it.

1   The Pontifical Council for the Family. *The Truth and Meaning of Human Sexuality: Guidelines for Education within the Family*. 21 November 1995, ¶6.

2   *Humanity* Magazine, August/September 1979, p. 11.

3   Jane Mauldon and Kristin Luker. "The Effects of Contraceptive Education on Method Use at First Intercourse." *Family Planning Perspectives*, January-February 1996, pp. 19-24.

4   D.A. Dawson. "The Effects of Sex Education on Adolescent Behavior." *Family Planning Perspectives*, July-August 1986, pp. 162-170.

5   William Marsiglio and Frank Mott. "The Impact of Sex Education on Sexual Activity, Contraceptive Use and Premarital Pregnancy among American Teenagers." *Family Planning Perspectives*, July/August 1986 pp. 151-162.

6   Thomas Sowell. "The Big Lie." *Forbes*, 23 December 1991, p. 52.

7   Sol Gordon and Judith Gordon. *Raising a Child Conservatively in a Sexually Permissive World*. New York: Simon and Schuster, 1983.

8   "The US Family Staggers into the Sexy Secular Future." Family Research *Newsletter,* January-March 1991, p. 1, Table 1, "Percentage of Women Aged 15-19 Who Reported Having Had Premarital Sexual Intercourse, By Race and Age—United States, 1970-1988." Numbers from 1988 to 1992 linearly extrapolated using 1985-1988 rates.

9   "American Teens Speak: Sex, Myths, TV and Birth Control." Poll conducted for the Planned Parenthood Federation of America (PPFA) by Louis Harris and Associates, September-October 1986.

10 "Censorship Is in the Eye of the Beholder." *New Dimensions* Magazine, December 1990, p. 15.

11 U.S. Department of Commerce, Bureau of the Census. Reference Data Book and Guide to Sources, *Statistical Abstract of the United States*. 1990 (110th Edition). (Washington, D.C., U.S. Government Printing Office), 1990. Tables 80, 90, 185, 296, 297. U.S. Department of Justice, Bureau of Justice Statistics, *Sourcebook of Criminal Justice Statistics*, 1992 (Washington, D.C., U.S. Government Printing Office), 1992.

12 *Catechism of the Catholic Church*, ¶2349.

●●●
I I5. What Is a School-Based Clinic?

The General Concept

School-based clinics are merely an extension of graphic sex education curricula. When the sex educators saw that their school-based programs were being exposed as completely ineffective, as we saw in Question 114, they took the easy way out. Instead of admitting their errors and changing direction (perhaps returning to morality and chastity), they merely transformed the concept of sex education from classroom-taught theory into *a concrete and tangible form* by installing school-based clinics.

A school-based clinic is simply an office, which may be manned by a nurse and occasionally a physician, set in a junior or high school under the guise of providing a wide range of health services. The most controversial service of the clinics (giving kids abortion advice and contraceptives) is considered by proponents to be the primary reason why these clinics are proposed in the first place.

The Facts of Life

In April 1985, the Support Center for School-Based Clinics issued a report, "School-Based Clinics: An Emerging Approach to Improving Adolescent Health and Addressing Teenage Pregnancy." It declared, *"by definition,* all of the [school-based] clinics are involved in family planning."

The First School-based Clinics

The first school-based clinic, sponsored by the University of Texas Health Sciences Center, opened in Dallas in 1970. The Maternal and Infant Care Program of the St. Paul Ramsey Hospital opened three years later in St. Paul, Minnesota's Mechanics Arts High School.

By 1995, there were about 500 clinics operating in the United States' 15,500 school districts. The overwhelming majority of these clinics are in minority schools. Ultimately, the clinic pushers want more than 5,000 of them in operation. Faye Wattleton, former President of PPFA, insists, "We must establish many more school-based health clinics that provide contraceptives as part of general health care."[1]

1 *The Humanist,* July / August 1986, p. 7.

··

116. Do School-Based Clinics Refer for Abortions?

The Ineffectiveness of Contraceptives and Abortifacients for Teenagers

We must make it clear from the start that the main goal of school-based clinics is not stopping teenage sex. Clinic proponents do not care whether a nation's teenagers are fornicating.

The only thing that matters to them is reducing the pregnancy, birth, and venereal disease rates. As Dr. David Perkins says: "Stopping teenage sex is *not* our objective. Stopping teen pregnancy *is*."[1] Faye Wattleton stated:

> Too many of us are focused upon stopping teenage sexual activity rather than stopping teenage pregnancy.... Sexuality education must be a fundamental part of the school curricula from kindergarten through twelfth grade in every school district in the country.... Easier access to contraception must be another priority—access without any barriers. We must establish many more school-based health clinics that provide contraceptives as part of general health care.[2]

Clinic backers tell us the only practical way to reduce teen pregnancy rates is by making sure all teens have access to contraceptives. But reproductive technologists universally recognize that contraception often fails, *especially* among teenagers. Abortion statistician Christopher Tietze stated flatly that teens who rely on contraception will inevitably have several "failures" during their reproductive lives: "The safest regimen of control for the unmarried and for married child-spacers is the use of traditional methods [of contraception] backed up by abortion; but if this regimen is commenced early in the child-bearing years, it is likely to involve several abortions in the course of her reproductive career for each woman who chooses it."[3]

We can illustrate this concept by checking the failure rates for the most common birth control devices given out at school-based clinics: condoms and oral contraceptives.

The teenage user failure rates are 14% per year for condoms and 12% per year for oral contraceptives.[4] The teenage failure rates for other common methods of contraception are even worse: 31.6% per year for the diaphragm and 34.5% per year for spermicides.[5]

Consider the above statistics for a moment. The birth control pill is the *most* effective contraceptive weapon commonly used against teenagers' fertility. A girl on the Pill has a one in eight chance of becoming pregnant *each year* (not to mention the times that she will conceive and abort without even knowing it). And a girl who starts using it at 15 and uses it for six full years (till age 21) has a *56% chance of becoming pregnant*. If, instead of her using the Pill, her boyfriend(s) faithfully use condoms, this probability increases to *60%*. If she uses a diaphragm or spermicides, it is *90%*.

The Ultimate Aim: To Increase Teen Abortions

We can summarize the situation as follows.

Clinic proponents say teaching abstinence is "unrealistic" because they believe teenagers are simply a type of emotional animal that has no control over its urges. This attitude, of course, gives the green light to unlimited teenage fornication. As we saw in the quotes above, clinic advocates believe the first step in stopping teenage *pregnancies* is the widespread distribution of contraceptives and abortifacients.

Enter the school-based clinic.

But clinic pushers *also* know that teenagers using contraceptives and abortifacients have a huge number of "failures."

So, they believe, it is *mandatory* that clinics also refer girls for abortions, although of course this aspect is hidden from the public as much as possible.

Because the actual ultimate aim of the clinics is to cut the teen *birth*rate by facilitating abortion, clinic backers have to use ingenious, ruthless methods to deceive and bypass parents and other concerned groups. Most parents simply will not stand for the idea of *public schools* giving their daughters contraceptives or sending them for abortions.

So the clinic pushers accept a variety of restrictions on their abortion activities, knowing full well there is no restriction they cannot easily bypass.

If a teenage girl gets a positive pregnancy test at a school clinic, all the clinic has to do is refer her to an organization not bound by such restrictions—usually a Planned Parenthood clinic or a county health department. In its publication, *School-Based Clinics 1988 Update*, the Center for Population Options (CPO), the major force behind school-based clinics, stated that 89% of reporting clinics did "pregnancy detection," and a full 98% of them did "pregnancy assessment and referral to community health systems," a euphemism for sending kids out for abortions.

How School-Based Clinics Deceive Parents

Once the clinic is in place, its personnel—who are well-trained in standard, unethical pro-abortion procedures—use underhanded tactics to make sure teenagers can get abortions and birth control devices, regardless of parental wishes.

For example, once a parent has given permission for *any* health clinic service (say, a sports physical), the child may then obtain *any other* service (such as birth control pills), *without* parental knowledge or consent.

Virtually no parents know about this sneaky *carte blanche*.

The CPO encourages school-based clinics to distribute parental consent forms worded in such a way that any forms *not* returned to the clinic are taken to signify parental notification and consent. In other words, clinic personnel may simply give a girl who wants the Pill one of these forms, advise her *not* to give it to her parents, and then tell her this "covers" her for permission to use any clinic service whatever.

One Montana clinic worker said her clinic advised teen girls to "bring a note from their parents—*any* note," and promised the staff would not "investigate" or even read it. The girls caught on quickly and forged their own notes.[6]

1 Dr. David Perkins, at the 1987 University of Maine conference, "A Strategy for Preventing Teenage Pregnancy."

2 Faye Wattleton, former president of Planned Parenthood Federation of America (PPFA). *The Humanist*, July/August 1986, p. 7.

3 C. Tietze, J. Bongaarts, and B. Schearer. "Mortality Associated with the Control of Fertility." *Family Planning Perspectives*, January-February 1976, pp. 6-14.

4 Robert A. Hatcher, *et.al. Contraceptive Technology*, 1986-1987 (13th Revised Edition). New York: Irvington Publishers, 1986, p. 139.

5 W. R. Grady, *et.al.* "Contraceptive Failure in the United States: Estimates." *Family Planning Perspectives*, September/October 1986, p. 204.

6 Mary Meehan and Elizabeth Moore. "Forced Abortion Suggested at Clinic Owner's Conference." *NRL News*, 2 June 1980, pp. 1, 13.

117. What Is the Five-Step Strategy for Installing a School-Based Clinic over Student and Parental Objections?

The Overall Strategy

Advocates of school-based clinics have fought to put them into public schools since about 1970. As time has passed and their successes have mounted, they have refined their general strategy until it is now almost an art form. The perfected, step-by-step process for installing clinics follows the five-step plan described below almost without exception.

The details of this plan of attack come directly from how-to manuals issued by the Sex Information and Education Council of the United States (SIECUS). Any parents' group that is serious about fighting school-based clinics or comprehensive sex education should contact SIECUS and get its latest strategy manuals. Only when parents know how the opposition thinks, and what its strategies are, will their resistance to sex ed and school-based clinics succeed.

A few of the ploys used to sugar-coat the clinics in order to enhance public acceptance are:

■ hiding the birth control aspect of the clinics among a plethora of other stated purposes, such as preventing malnutrition, poverty, drug use and dropping out of school;

■ selling the "birth control" aspect by playing on public fears and emphasizing AIDS and pregnancy prevention;

"Messages from our school-based health clinics."

- emphasizing that abortion referrals will not be done by the clinics. This restriction is circumvented easily by referring girls to agencies that do not commit abortions *themselves*, but which immediately give a second referral to an abortion mill; and

- heavily propagandizing students for a long time before proposing the clinic by using"'saturation" sex education classes and other gatherings with speakers and literature emphasizing personal autonomy and freedom. In this way, students become conditioned into desiring the services of the clinic. This is a very important step, because studies have shown that students, before the brainwashing, *do not want clinics in their schools.* Surveys have repeatedly found that seven out of eight teenagers do not want a contraceptive-dispensing clinic in their school. Sixty percent do not want places that give out contraceptives located anywhere *near* their schools. Three out of four teens believe teens should wait until they are adults before engaging in sexual intercourse, and 79% believe most teens start having sex too soon.[1]

Step 1: Lay the Foundation

Laying the foundation for a school-based clinic (or a sex education curriculum) involves three basic, simultaneous tasks: (1) creating the impression that there is a need, (2) making connections and (3) attacking the opposition.

To begin with, get one or more major public officials concerned about the high teen pregnancy rate by using doctored statistics. Preferably, this person or persons will be school district superintendents or the mayor and city council members.

Second, make contacts *only* with pro-clinic groups while ignoring pro-family and conservative groups. A SIECUS publication, *Winning the Battle for Sex Education,* advises networking specifically with the National Abortion and Reproductive Rights Action League (NARRAL), the National Organization for Women (NOW), Planned Parenthood Federation of America (PPFA), the Young Women's Christian Association (YWCA) and the League of Women Voters (LWV). The same book says:

> The key word for successful public relations for a sex education program is *anticipation:* Preparing in advance. Initial contacts should in any case be made at the latest several weeks before you have agreed to "go public" with information/details about the program. Public relations is in certain respects the art of knowing when you want publicity and when you don't.[2]

Finally, launch a series of *confidential* meetings with high-ranking people from friendly media outlets. Supply them with derogatory material about people who might voice any objections to the program. The SIECUS "how-to" publication, *Winning the Battle: Developing Support for Sexuality and HIV/AIDS Education,* shows how to paint any opposition as "fanatics" by ruthlessly stereotyping them and baldly lying about their objectives and beliefs:

> Regardless of their official platform, their goal is often to curtail freedom of expression and academic freedom as well as the right to one's privacy, the right to sexual information, and right to a healthy, sexual life,... They mistakenly believe that telling young people about sexuality causes them to have sexual intercourse, become promiscuous, and get pregnant.[3]

SIECUS targets specific pro-life groups in this publication, including the American Family Association (AFA), American Life League (ALL), Concerned Women for America (CWA), Eagle Forum, Focus on the Family and the National Association for Abstinence Education (NAAE).

The same publication shows how to attack abstinence-based programs such as *Sex Respect,* no matter how effective they are. Instances of forcing schools to drop *Sex Respect* in favor of explicit sex ed are labeled "success stories" in the book, showing that SIECUS does *not* believe in pluralism, and that it thinks its solution is the *only* one.

Expert Richard Weatherley summarized the general strategy for neutralizing opposition to school-based clinics:

> The most common strategy adopted to avoid opposition was to maintain a low profile—generally by keeping programs out of sight, by avoiding potentially controversial preventive services, by staying clear of abortion services, by relying on word of mouth for recruitment and by giving names to programs that obscured their functions (Cyesis, Teen Awareness, Access, Services to Young Parents, Healthworks, and Continuing Education to Young Families are some examples). ... Program advocates and service providers are more or less obligated to exaggerate the potential benefits of services in order to

secure political and material support. One popular ploy revealed an incredible array of problems that allegedly would be solved by the provision of services for pregnant teenagers and adolescent parents. In claims reminiscent of the 19th Century, it was argued that teenage pregnancy services would combat child abuse, infant mortality, mental retardation, birth defects, drug abuse and welfare dependency.[6]

Step 2: Create a Committee
Get the "concerned citizens" to appoint a "Blue Ribbon Committee" to study the problem. Pack this committee with church, political and school leaders who *seem* open-minded, but who in fact sympathize with Planned Parenthood / SIECUS-type goals. Make sure one (and *only* one) committee member is a Catholic priest, a prominent Evangelical pastor, or other such representative of traditional values, but make sure he is not really informed about the life issues. The presence of this one person will deflect criticism that the committee is "loaded," and will give the appearance of fairness. SIECUS reveals, "In Memphis, Tennessee, a Catholic priest who was a member of the [sex education planning] committee effectively neutralized the opposition's charge that religious values were being ignored."[3]

Winning the Battle: Developing Support for Sexuality and HIV/AIDS Education suggests:

> In many communities, opponents are invited to serve on the planning committee for new programs. Although it may seem easier to have only proponents on this committee, it is one way to defuse the opposition at an early stage. According to sexuality educator Mary Lee Tatum, "Listen to them and let them participate on committees; then make committee statements using facts and data, *underscoring the majority opinion.*"[3]

In other words, put one or two of the "opposition" on the 12 to 14-member board for appearance's sake, then act as if they and their viewpoints do not exist by emphasizing *only* the pre-ordained "majority opinion."

Step 3: Prohibit Public Participation
Make certain the committee makes the right recommendations (i.e., in favor of school-based clinics or sex education). These are usually copied almost verbatim from previous committee news releases used in other areas. If possible, make sure *no public meetings are allowed!* The public *may* submit recommendations only by letter; ignore these if they attack the proposed clinic or sex ed program. Always say *at least* 80% of all mail favors the clinic or sex curriculum (it is much easier to lie about mail that only *you* see than about public statements *everyone* sees). SIECUS recommends simply ignoring the opposition: "In fact, if possible, the [responding] statement can ignore the charges entirely and consist of a positive statement about the program and its real or potential accomplishments."[3]

Allow parental involvement in the decision-making process *only* if the parents are "enlightened." This exalted term applies only to parents who share the views of the sex educators and clinic pushers. Of course, in their opinion, the vast majority of parents are by no means "enlightened." This title is only bestowed upon parents who do not care whether their teenagers fornicate, contracept, sodomize and abort, as long as it is *safe* fornication, contraception, sodomy and abortion.

Step 4: Install the Clinic

If intense opposition surfaces against the birth control and abortion referral "services" of the clinic, install it without them. A simple charter amendment can be made when the uproar has died down and people have forgotten about the clinic. It is much easier to add birth control and abortion referral *after* you have opened the doors than it is to include those features in the original plan.

Joy Dryfoos of the CPO advises that clinics "can avoid local controversy by starting with primary health care and then adding family planning services."[4] Kathleen Arnold-Sheeran, founder of the National Association of School-Based Clinics, outlined this step in the strategy, and showed that proponents believe every clinic *must* include contraceptive services: "Be willing to make compromises. Better something than nothing. Do not compromise on being in school. In Kansas City, they met with religious leaders and agreed to leave out birth control. Eight months later, birth-control services were added. Get your foot in the door. Be trusted. Total health care means birth control."[5]

Step 5: Entrench Gains

Using prepackaged media kits, trumpet the fraudulent "fact" that the teen birthrate is down, concealing the rise in pregnancies and abortions. Use this "success" story to get clinics or sex ed into other high schools in the area.

Just in case opposition surfaces again at some future date, entrench sex education by blending it into other subjects. SIECUS observes, "They [the strategists] agree with many experienced sex educators that various facets of sexuality can— and should be—incorporated into biology, physiology, English, history, and other courses in a natural context."[2]

Conclusion

The five-step strategy above makes it clear to everyone that clinic proponents simply cannot be trusted. Their goal is to make contraceptives and abortion available to all teenagers, regardless of their religious or cultural beliefs. The ultimate goal, of course, is to further weaken ties between parents and children exactly when teenagers need more parental guidance, *not* interference from tax-funded anti-family bureaucrats.

Any public-school mother or father who does not vigorously oppose school-based clinics is likely to reap the fruits of his or her inaction: pregnant daughters faced with the awful decision either to abort their babies or face diminished prospects in job-hunting, education and marriage; and guilty sons whose irresponsibility ruins the lives of others and sets the stage for a lifetime of selfishness.

1 *American Teens Speak: Sex, Myths, TV, and Birth Control*, subtitled "The Planned Parenthood Poll," p. 71, conducted for the Planned Parenthood Federation of America, fieldwork done September/October 1986, by Louis Harris and Associates, Inc., 1986.

2 Irving R. Dickman. *Winning the Battle for Sex Education*. Sex Information and Education Council of the

United States (SIECUS), 80 Fifth Avenue, Suite 801, New York, New York 10011. 1982.

3   Debra W. Haffner and Diane de Mauro. *Winning the Battle: Developing Support for Sexuality and HIV/AIDS Education.* SIECUS, March 1991.

4   Joy Dryfoos. "School-Based Health Clinics: A New Approach to Preventing Adolescent Pregnancy?" *Family Planning Perspectives,* March-April 1985, pp. 70-75.

5   Michael Schwartz. "Sex as Apple Pie." *National Review,* 10 June 1988, pp. 39-40, 57.

6   Richard Weatherley, *et.al.* "Comprehensive Programs for Pregnant Teenagers and Teenage Parents: How Successful Have They Been?" *Family Planning Perspectives,* March/April 1986, p. 76.

118. Are School-Based Clinics Effective at Preventing Teen Pregnancy and Abortions?

More Contraception Always Leads to More Abortions

A growing body of evidence amassed by both sides of the clinic debate shows that they *never* reduce the teen pregnancy rate, and only *occasionally* reduce the teen birthrate—but *only* if the "excess" births are prevented by abortions.

As we saw in Question 114, comprehensive sex education and the availability of contraception in schools leads to increased fornication. Because contraceptives and abortifacients often fail when teenagers use them, the teen pregnancy rate invariably soars. So, the only way to cut teen births is through the widespread availability of abortion.

Experienced researchers have compared reducing the teen pregnancy rate by making contraceptives and abortifacients freely available to chasing the pot of gold at the end of the rainbow—or, more accurately, to trying to put out a fire with a bucket of gasoline.

The *Report of the House Select Committee on Children, Youth and Families* of the U.S. Congress concluded that reducing the teen pregnancy rate through contraceptives is not only *morally* impossible, it is *statistically* impossible: "The contraceptive failure rate for teens who always use contraceptives is about 10% (Zelnik and Kantner, 1976 and 1979). Therefore, hypothetically, if sexual activity among teens reached 100% and the constant use of contraceptives 100%, we would still have a pregnancy rate of about 10%."[1]

As we saw in Question 114, a girl who starts using the Pill at 15 and uses it for six full years has a 56% chance of becoming pregnant. If, instead of her using the Pill, her boyfriend(s) faithfully use condoms, this probability increases to 60%. If she uses a diaphragm, it is 65%. And if she uses any other method, she is virtually certain to become pregnant within just six years.

As Edouard Cardinal Gagnon, president of the Pontifical Council for the Family, pointed out in his address to the Bishops of the United States on 10 March 1989: "Planned Parenthood programs of sex education in no way resolve the problem of teen-age pregnancies but rather increase it by encouraging promiscuity."[2]

A Concise Summary of School-Based Clinic Ineffectiveness.

There is one unavoidable reason why school-based clinics will *never* achieve their stated mission. Prof. Kingsley Davis of the fanatically pro-abortion group Zero

Population Growth (ZPG), summed up this prime deficiency in the clinic mentality:

> The current belief that illegitimacy will be reduced if teenage girls are given an effective contraceptive is an extension of the same reasoning that created the problem in the first place. It reflects an unwillingness to face problems of social control and social discipline, while trusting some technological device to extricate society from its difficulties. The irony is that the illegitimacy rise occurred precisely while contraceptive use was becoming *more*, rather than *less*, widespread and respectable.[3]

Prof. Davis is correct. The illegitimacy rate for births among teenage girls hovered around 5 to 7% for decades, until about 1960. Between 1960 and 1970, it doubled as the birth control pill helped usher in the "Sexual Revolution." After 1970, the teen illegitimacy rate literally exploded as comprehensive sex education programs and school-based clinics were introduced. In 1996, the illegitimacy rate among teenage girls is about 40%.[4]

This is not just an ethical or religious concern: it is a profoundly *practical* one. It is common knowledge that children born into one-parent families are more likely to be abused and abusive, to be undereducated and underemployed, to have illegitimate children themselves and to commit crimes.

So, it is obviously in society's best interest for educators to scrap the unworkable school-based clinic program and start again from scratch by teaching basic morality in the schools, or at least leaving such teaching to parents and churches where it belongs.

The birth control pill failed to curb teenage pregnancy.

Coercive comprehensive sex education programs failed to curb teenage pregnancy.

And, finally, the school-based clinics are failing to curb teenage pregnancy.

When will we learn that a return to our original values is the only possible cure for this moral rot?

The Experts Speak

The push to establish thousands of school-based clinics in high schools involves tens of thousands of people in every discipline. So, it is inevitable that the propaganda mask that hides the clinics' ineffectiveness will occasionally slip a little and yield a glimpse of the truth.

Scores of clinic experts *and* proponents have admitted the program's abysmal failure.

Douglas Kirby, director of CPO, the most vigorous promoter of clinics, conceded:

> We find basically that there are *no measurable*—I want to underline that word and put it in boldface—there is *no measurable impact* upon the use of birth control nor upon pregnancy rates or birthrates. This is all based upon the survey data.... School-based clinics have no measurable impact on teen pregnancy rates.... In the absence of knowledge of whether or not young women are getting abortions, we really can't say whether or not the school clinic program is preventing pregnancy. And since abortions are usually underreported in personal interviews, pregnancy rates are difficult to measure.[5]

Researcher Lynn Landma reported in *Family Planning Perspectives*: "More teenagers are using contraceptives and using them more consistently than ever before, yet the number and rate of adolescent pregnancies continue to rise."[6]

Finally, after a thorough review of the literature, Stan Weed and Sam Olson concluded: "Instead of the expected reductions in overall teenage pregnancy rates, greater teenage involvement in family-planning programs appears to be associated with higher, rather than lower, teenage pregnancy rates."[7]

A Phony Clinic Success Story

Because school-based clinics are by their very natures doomed to failure, pro-life activists can expect to meet a fog of evasions and fake statistics from those who try to justify continuing the program.

For example, an incredible success rate for a Baltimore clinic was claimed in the July 1986 issue of the Alan Guttmacher Institute's *Family Planning Perspectives*.

According to the report, the pregnancy rates among inner-city girls at a clinic-equipped school dropped 30.1%, while the pregnancy rate at three other local schools *soared* an incredible 57.6% during the same 28-month test period. The results of this study were uncritically swallowed by *Time* Magazine, *The New York Times* and dozens of other publications, and the Baltimore clinic became a prime propaganda tool for the pro-clinic forces.

However, the researchers refused to reveal their study methodology and supporting statistics. On 5 September 1986, Anne Gribben, a member of the House Select Committee on Children, Youth, and Families, summed up these evasions: "Because reports of this study fail to include some very pertinent information, they leave us with as many questions as when we started."

When some of the study methodology used by the researchers was finally revealed, the degree of dishonesty in the manipulation of the data shocked even clinic proponents. For example, one Planned Parenthood official who examined the Baltimore clinic effectiveness rate did follow-up interviews with only a carefully-selected (not random) 10% of those teenagers who had had contact with her three-year program, and did not count dropouts![8] Also, she arbitrarily *excluded* 12th graders—the oldest and most sexually active group—from her numbers on fornication, but *included* them when calculating the pregnancy rate among the sexually active, thereby skewing her study results in her favor.[9]

It is obvious that any study that has its methodology kept top-secret by its proponents, and its numbers manipulated so dishonestly, is nothing more than a pretty package of lies and should be dismissed out of hand. Any "researchers" who hide their methodology are almost certainly guilty of "cooking the numbers." The United States' premier "sexologist," Alfred Kinsey, also refused to let researchers examine his methods and data—but despite this fatal shortcoming, most of today's sex education programs are based upon Kinsey's work!

1 *Report of the House Select Committee on Children, Youth and Families.* "Teen Pregnancy: What Is Being Done? A State-by-State Look." Washington, D.C., U.S. Government Printing Office, December 1985, pp. 378 and 385.

2 Quoted in *The Oregonian* [Portland], 11 March 1989, p. 7.

3 Professor Kingsley Davis. "The American Family, Relation to Demographic Change." *Research Reports,*

United States Commission on Population Growth and the American Future. Volume I, *Demographic and Social Aspects of Population Growth*, edited by Robert Parke, Jr., and Charles F. Westoff. Washington: U.S. Government Printing Office, 1972, p. 253.

4 Department of Commerce, Bureau of the Census. Reference Data Book and Guide to Sources, *Statistical Abstract of the United States*. 1990 (110th Edition). Washington, D.C.: U.S. Government Printing Office. Table 13, "Total Population, By Age and Sex: 1960 to 1988." Table 90, "Births to Unmarried Women, By Race of Child and Age of Mother: 1970 to 1987."

5 Douglas Kirby, speech given at the 16th annual meeting of the National Family Planning and Reproductive Health Association (NFPRHA), Washington, D.C., 2 March 1988. Quoted in Richard D. Glasow, Ph.D. "SBC Advocate Admits Clinics Fail to Reduce Number of Teen Pregnancies." *NRL News*, 10 March 1988, pp. 4-5.

6 Lynn C. Landma. "Anniversaries." The Alan Guttmacher Institute's *Family Planning Perspectives*. October 1980, p. 2.

7 S.G. Philliber and M.L. Tatum. "The Impact of Sex Education on Students, Parents, and Faculty: A Report from Falls Church." November 1979, p. 11.

8 "Public School Sex Education: A Report." Published in the October 1990 issue of the AFA *Journal*. Also available for $2.00 from the American Family Association, Post Office Drawer 2440, Tupelo, Mississippi 38803. This is an excellent encapsulation of the incredible nonsense being drilled into our children by sex educators posing as teachers. If this is not a powerful incentive to homeschool your children, nothing will be.

9 Gene Antonio. "America's XXX-Rated Sex Education Curricula." *New Dimensions* Magazine, September 1990.

10 Stan Weed and Sam Olson. "Effects of Family Planning Programs for Teenagers on Adolescent Birth and Pregnancy Rates." *Family Perspective*, Vol. 20, No. 3, p. 153.

11 Laurie S. Zabin, *et.al.* "Evaluation of a School and Clinic Based Primary Pregnancy Prevention Program for Inner City Junior and Senior High School Males and Females." Baltimore: The Johns Hopkins University School of Medicine, 1986. Also see Laurie S. Zabin, *et.al.* "Evaluation of a Pregnancy Prevention Program for Urban Teenagers." *Family Planning Perspectives*, May/June 1986, pp. 119-126.

12 Jacqueline R. Kasun. "The Baltimore School Birth Control Study: A Comment." In Robert G. Marshall. *School Birth Control: New Promise or Old Problem?* Stafford, Virginia: American Life League, 1986.

119. What Can Parents Do About Comprehensive Sex Education Programs and School-Based Clinics?

"How Could this Happen to My Child?"

The vast majority of parents do not even know whether their children are getting sex education in school. Those who *do* know usually know nothing about the programs their children are being exposed to. Most parents blindly trust the "sexperts" with their children's health and moral development.

This haze of indifference lasts only until their daughter turns up pregnant. Or injured by a "safe and legal" abortion. Or when their son contracts a venereal disease.

Or when their child contracts AIDS.

Then they begin to care very much.

Only *then* do they ask, "How could this happen to *my* child?"

The brutal truth is evident: parents who do not inform themselves very carefully about the sex education their children are getting are, by default, letting their children adopt the values of strangers. They are letting their children stroll into a sexual minefield without the necessary guidance of moral standards. These parents simply do not love their children as much as they say they do.

They are abandoning their children to a system they simply are not equipped to cope with.

The Results of Promiscuity

The way we conduct ourselves sexually is a sign of how we live the rest of our lives. This is particularly true of teenagers, who are in the process of building the moral framework that will guide the way they think and act for the rest of their lives.

Figure 28

Drs. Donald Orr and Gary Ingersoll of Indiana University Medical School studied thousands of unmarried teenage girls who fornicated and thousands who did not. They found that those who fornicate are five times more likely to be suspended from school for a serious offense, 10 times more likely to have used illegal drugs and six times more likely to have attempted suicide. Boys who fornicate are six times more likely to abuse alcohol and five times more likely to use marijuana.[1]

The best "sex education" is provided by example. Parents who live their lives according to the principles of marital chastity have a much better chance of raising chaste teenagers.

Significantly, girls who fornicate suffer severely diminished self-esteem, whereas boys who fornicate actually experience *increased* self-esteem. The implications are obvious. Dr. Ingersoll states, "Girls with low self-esteem may be using sex as a way to build esteem, but then it only makes them feel worse about themselves. Early experience is still regarded as more deviant for girls."[1]

Those teenagers who fornicate, use illegal drugs, and commit other illegal and/or immoral acts are tortured by their guilt, which builds until it is unbearable. There are only two ways out of this agony: repentance (which becomes more and more difficult as the various addictions take hold) or rationalization and continuation of an immoral lifestyle.

It is far better to avoid this hell on earth by beginning one's independent life with a firm and sound set of morals—but nothing makes this more difficult than permissive sex education.

Take Action!

The sex educators, media pundits and left-wing politicians chuckle condescendingly at Christian parents who worry about their children's morals. Planned Parenthood and similar groups often portray concerned parents as control-oriented, paranoiac, religious fanatics who see a conspiracy around every corner.

Although the "sexperts" do not operate in a conspiracy *per se*, they think in similar ways and use similar tactics to achieve their goals.

The Facts of Life

The only defense against the well-organized sex educators and reformers is to maintain constant and fruitful *communication* with your children. It is also essential to know where they are and what they are being taught in school, and who their companions are both in and out of school. Finally, parents must be their children's *friends*—the first people children will consult when they have questions or problems.

If gaining this knowledge requires parents to do a little overt surveillance in class or to make themselves a royal pain in the neck to the local "sexperts," then so be it. Parents should not apologize for monitoring their children and guiding their development. Despite what the Humanist experts say, bringing up children is a parent's God-given duty—*not theirs!*

Parents should band together to reach their goals. They should demand to know the details of sex education curricula and should study these materials closely. If the materials are immoral, or if they are stonewalled by the bureaucracy, parents should pull their kids out of the class.

If the situation is *really* bad, parents might make the ultimate statement of disgust with the school system by taking their children out of school completely and educating them at home. This may be the only option for truly conscientious parents, because the secular sex educators are tireless and have access to our children for six to eight hours per day for nine months of the year. No parent can realistically monitor the situation at all times, because comprehensive sex education is being integrated into every facet of high school education.

If parents cannot be absolutely sure their children are not being exposed to immoral sex education, it is their *duty* to remove their children from school. The Catholic Church recognizes the paramount importance of chastity education and the irreparable damage to the soul that can be caused by even a fleeting exposure to pornographic or comprehensive sex education programs. For this reason, the Church teaches that *parents* are the only appropriate teachers of sex education.

Vatican II declared, "The role of parents in education is of such importance that it is almost impossible to find an adequate substitute ... The family is therefore the principal school of the social virtues which are necessary to every society."[2]

Familiaris Consortio and *The Truth and Meaning of Human Sexuality* lay out clearly the standards expected of every Christian parent:

> Sex education, which is a basic right and duty of parents, must always be carried out under their attentive guidance, whether at home or in educational centers chosen and controlled by them. In this regard, the Church reaffirms the law of subsidiarity, which the school is bound to observe when it cooperates in sex education, by entering into the same spirit that animates the parents.[3]

Organizations that Help Promote Chastity

It is not enough for concerned parents simply to be against secular sex education programs. Parents need resources in order to answer questions and guide teenagers. Parents must be armed with facts and with the most up-to-date pro-chastity materials in order to be able to handle the delicate and critical question of teen sexuality. Even if children have been exposed to comprehensive sex education at a public or Catholic school, it may be possible to stem *part* of the resulting extensive moral and psychological damage by giving them chastity education at home.

It must be stressed that instruction in chastity must be part of an overall program of teaching and living the cardinal virtues, or else it will be useless. The virtues interlock and support one another; if one or more are neglected, the practice of the others will suffer as well.

The cardinal virtues are *prudence* ("the virtue that disposes practical reason to discern our true good in every circumstance and to choose the right means of achieving it"); *justice* ("the moral virtue that consists in the constant and firm will to give their due to God and neighbor"); *fortitude* ("the moral virtue that ensures firmness in difficulties and constancy in the pursuit of the good"); and *temperance* ("the moral virtue that moderates the attraction of pleasures and provides balance in the use of created goods").[4]

Appendix A lists the major pro-chastity groups in the United States and Canada. They provide information, guidance and materials for educating other parents and children in chastity and Christian sexuality.

1   Marilyn Elias. "Early Teen Sex May Indicate Drugs, Drinking." *USA Today*, 6 February 1991, p. D1.

2   Vatican Council II. *Gravissimum Educationis*, "Declaration on Christian Education," 28 October 1965. ¶3.

3   Apostolic Exhortation *Familiaris Consortio* ("The Role of the Christian Family in the Modern World"), 15 December 1981, ¶37. The Pontifical Council for the Family. *The Truth and Meaning of Human Sexuality: Guidelines for Education within the Family*. 21 November 1995, ¶43.

4   *Catechism of the Catholic Church*, ¶1805-1809, "The Cardinal Virtues."

120. What Are the Benefits of Homeschooling?

The Problems with Public Schools

Question 113 describes some of the sex education curricula used in U.S. high schools today, and Question 116 shows how school-based clinics undermine the relationship between parents and children and help destroy the morals of teenagers.

However, the problems with public schools extend much farther than difficulties with teaching morality.

Among developed nations, the United States ranks third in money spent per pupil, just behind the Netherlands and Sweden.[1] The United States spends the second-largest portion of its gross national product on education of all the countries in the world—7.5%, as compared to Japan's 5.5% and West Germany's 4.5%.[2]

Yet many U.S. children are virtually illiterate when they leave high school. They can hardly read, and they have difficulty doing simple mathematical chores such as balancing a checkbook. Incredibly, one-third of U.S. high school graduates cannot even locate their country on a world globe![2]

This is a tragedy, not only for the individual child and for the nation as a whole, but for the hundreds of thousands of talented and caring teachers who simply cannot overcome the "system" so they can do their jobs well.

What Is Being Taught?

Sooner or later, all children in public schools will be exposed to the following ideas, either by the school itself, by groups that work with the school or by peer groups:

- homosexuality is a perfectly acceptable alternative lifestyle;
- abortion is a matter to be decided not by the church or the state, but solely by a woman and her doctor;
- "overpopulation" threatens the world;
- communism is merely another economic system;
- Christianity has absolutely no place in education, although "New Age" and various Eastern and African practices abound;
- there are no fixed moral or ethical rules, and all problems must be considered on a case-by-case basis ("moral relativism" or "situation ethics");
- there is really no good or evil, and the concept of "sin" is outmoded; and
- above all else, the highest virtues are compassion and tolerance.

The public school environment will probably include most or all of the following:

- "lifeboat exercises," which force children to conclude that some lives are worth living, and some are not;
- secret psychological counseling that ruthlessly undermines parental authority;
- totally immoral comprehensive sex education classes, in which teachers either ignore chastity or ridicule it as "outmoded and quaint'" and demonstrate all manner of birth control devices in lurid detail;
- "death education," in which teachers may force children to write suicide notes, visit mortuaries, lie in coffins, and write essays on topics such as "End of the World—Coming Soon or Not?", "Infanticide—Right or Wrong?" and "Active Euthanasia for Deformed Infants—Right or Wrong?";
- a school environment saturated with gangs, weapons, and drugs; and
- an overall nihilistic atmosphere that tells the child life is really not worth living, except for the moment.

Inventing the Beast

All of these aberrations flourish in an environment where 'good' and 'evil' are abstract terms that have no application to real life.

In 1968 and 1969, the Western Behavioral Sciences Institute in La Jolla, California created the first formal "value-free" curriculum. This effort, which the R.J. Reynolds Tobacco Company funded, took the historic step of replacing the standard for personal decision-making. The original standard was human *reason*; the new standard is human *feelings*.

The fundamental underlying concept of this new "value-free" curriculum is moral relativism, or "situation ethics," which asserts that the only *absolute* rule is that there are no absolute rules—not even laws against murder. Situational ethicists argue that every rule has exceptions, and that people must be free to judge whether society's rules apply to them.

So far, so good. Almost every man-made rule *does indeed* have exceptions. And, of course, people must sometimes judge whether these rules apply to them in particular situations.

But such decisions are properly made only in the most extreme or unusual situations, which occur when you must commit one evil in order to prevent or ameliorate a greater evil. Examples would be trespassing on private property in order to save lives, destroying property in order to save property of much greater value, or even killing someone in order to save others, as in a hostage situation.

Above all, one must never forget that man's laws are frequently flawed and sometimes even immoral, and in all cases must give way to God's law. There are certain acts (such as adultery, abortion, contraception, euthanasia, and homosexual behavior) which are *intrinsically evil* and can never be made good. There are no extenuating circumstances for such acts, even if they are committed to avoid what people may think is an even greater evil.

Shifting the Focus

The principle of situation ethics—which an ordinary person with a properly-formed conscience might need to use once or twice in an entire lifetime—has been extended to everyday living. The situational ethicists have also shifted the focus of the beneficiary of such acts from society to the individual.

In other words, if a person can derive more personal benefit from a possession than someone else, then nobody can say it is wrong to steal it. If a person believes the United States is on a mission of capitalist imperialism in some far-flung land, he is perfectly justified in cheating on his income tax return. If he believes clearcutting a forest will harm the environment, he may destroy logging equipment. If an unborn child interferes with a relationship even in the most trivial way, he or she immediately becomes expendable.

The situational ethicists usually contradict themselves by producing a laundry list of exceptions to *their* exceptions to the rules. In short, all rules may be broken except the rules *they* say may not be broken.

Doin' Bad and Feelin' Good

So, the only possible conclusion is that "situation ethics" courses are simply another fancy tool that Humanists use to control and indoctrinate our children.

Our kids do not object to this covert manipulation, because one goal of Humanist teaching is to make them *feel good* about themselves. And, of course, good little students who are kept psychologically numbed and sated with sex, drugs, freedom (license) and everything else they could possibly want are not likely to rebel against the Humanist system. Even as kids spout drivel about "personal freedom" and "independence," they are becoming embedded in the Humanist ideology as surely as a fly caught in a spiderweb soon becomes part of the spider.

The effects of this brainwashing became evident after a 1989 survey of 100 seventh-graders from six countries. Researchers gave the students a rigorous mathematics test and then asked how they thought they performed against seventh-graders from the other five countries.

The Facts of Life

The Korean children did exceptionally well on the test, followed by the Spanish, British, Irish and Canadian children, in that order. Students from the United States finished dead last, far behind the Canadians.[3]

However, when the children were asked whether they considered themselves to be good at mathematics, the Koreans came in last (23% answering yes) and the Americans first (68% answering yes).

This meant that the children from the United States had an inverted sense of reality regarding their own performance.

In other words, U.S. children are failing abysmally in academics while being indoctrinated into *not caring* that they are failing. All that matters is that they feel good about themselves.

The Decisive Christian Response—Homeschooling!

Many Christian parents are tired of constantly monitoring their school in order to ensure that children escape permanent damage from a score of dangers ranging from head lice to violent students.

Christian parents who know the nature of the public schools and many "Catholic schools" and the tactics of the social engineers also realize it is *theoretically impossible* to protect their children from all of the harmful influences they will encounter there. In other words, no parent can monitor his or her children enough to save them from being indoctrinated. The public schools have a child under their control for more than 10,000 hours and have dozens of ways to indoctrinate them.

U.S. schools have been transformed into obstacles to moral living that our children must endure and survive.

So, more and more Christian parents are rescuing their children from the militantly atheistic U.S. public school system and are educating them properly—*themselves!* In fact, more than *one million* children from kindergarten to twelfth grade are being homeschooled in the United States—and they are loving it!

The Advantages of Homeschooling

There are many reasons for this seemingly radical action. A homeschooled child does not learn about "safe sex." He does not learn that homosexuality is a "perfectly acceptable alternative lifestyle," or that abortion is a private decision between a woman and her doctor. He is not subjected to secret psychological counseling, "lifeboat exercises," Planned Parenthood condom lessons, or value- and God-free education.

What's more, he may proceed at his own learning pace, instead of being held back to accommodate slower students. On the other hand, if the child is slow in some areas, he is not warehoused in a "slow" section and forgotten, and does not suffer ridicule and embarrassment. And he is not exposed to pervasive peer pressure to violate his Christian value system through sex, drugs and violence.

Numerous studies and interviews by a wide variety of organizations (some of them quite left-wing) reveal that homeschooled children score higher on achievement tests, are superior in their breadth and depth of knowledge, and are more adaptable and sociable than public-school children.

The greatest benefit of homeschooling, of course, is that children receive the proper training in Christian values and spirituality.

But What about Socialization?

Parents give several reasons for not homeschooling their children. They think they do not have the time or money. They are wary of taking such a "radical" step. But most of all, they worry that their children will be poorly socialized.

Parents should ask themselves, "What *kind* of socialization do I want for my children?"

Most kids who attend public schools are perfectly normal, if not especially moral. However, socialization in the public schools inevitably includes exposure to classmates who are violent, openly promiscuous, and abusers of alcohol and drugs. Children are exposed to pornographic sex education, immodesty, filthy language, repulsive rock lyrics and trashy video games on a regular basis, all of which have a bad influence on them. They also absorb false values: that the way one dresses is critical, that success in sports is more rewarding than success in academics, that virgins are *not* "cool," and that the "system" was made to be beaten by any available means.

At home, children's socialization is with brothers and sisters, and with parents who love them. If interaction with other children is a concern, parents who are considering homeschooling should contact one of the national support groups listed in Appendix A and get the address of their state or provincial homeschooling group. It can answer their concerns, and put them in contact with homeschooling families in their area. Parents can make sure their kids spend most of their play time with other homeschooled children who share their beliefs.

Homeschooling Resources

Many faiths, from Roman Catholic to Episcopalian to Mennonite, have outstanding homeschooling curricula, proven by the test of time. The groups listed in Appendix A can get parents in touch with the people who organize and distribute these programs, and can also answer any questions they might have.

The Legal Status of Home Schooling

Some U.S. states are very supportive of home schooling, and require only a year-end test for each child to ensure that he is keeping up. In other states, parents who dare to homeschool their children often run into legal troubles and harassment from local school districts.

You can learn the legal status of home schooling in each state and province from:

The Rutherford Institute
1445 East Rio Road
Charlottesville, Virginia 22906-7482
Telephone: (804) 978-3888

Request the *Home Education Reporter* for your state or province. Each *Reporter* is $10 US.

The Facts of Life

The Home School Legal Defense Association (HSLDA) issues a quarterly newsletter, *The Home School Court Report*. Annual dues are $100, but HSLDA provides relatively cheap legal aid if trouble should arise. HSLDA charges anywhere from $100 to respond to threats from a local official to $5,000 for trial appearances and preparation, including appeals. Contact:

Home School Legal Defense Association
Paeonian Springs, Virginia 20129
Telephone: (540) 338-5600

1 U.S. Department of Commerce, Bureau of the Census. Reference Data Book and Guide to Sources, *Statistical Abstract of the United States*. Washington, D.C.: U.S. Government Printing Office. 1990 (110th Edition). Table 1,445, "Public Expenditures for Education and Illiteracy, By Selected Country."

2 John McLaughlin. "Bennett the Bold." *National Review*, 1 November 1985, p. 23.

3 Charles Krauthammer. "Education: Doing Bad and Feeling Good." *Time* Magazine, 5 February 1990.

Chapter 12

The International Population Control Program

....

121. What Is the Origin of the Current Concern About Overpopulation?

The Malthus Manifesto

For two centuries a tremendous battle of minds has raged over the question of world population vs. world resource supply. This struggle, formerly little-noticed by the public, came to the forefront about 1970, when renewed interest developed in the work of the British economist, the Rev. Thomas Malthus, who published his landmark *Essay on the Principle of Population* in 1798.

The heart of Malthus' philosophy, and the cornerstone of the population controllers' credo, is found in his book, which asserted:

> The power of population is indefinitely greater than the power of the earth to produce subsistence for man. Population, when unchecked, increases in a geometrical ratio. Subsistence increases only in an arithmetical ratio.... By that law of our nature which makes food necessary to the life of man, the effects of these two unequal powers must be kept equal. This implies a strong and constantly operating check on population from the difficulty of subsistence.

Absurd Predictions

Great advances in agricultural and food storage and processing technology has rendered Malthus' equation obsolete. Since at least 1900, food production has kept pace with or exceeded population increases, thanks to numerous technological innovations. Nevertheless, the "New Malthusians" seem to delight in painting pictures of mass horrors that will inevitably befall society if all of the nations of the world do not "control" their populations *right now*. The population controller's predictions are invariably wrong—and frequently comical due to their extreme nature.

In 1972, Paul Ehrlich, the dean of the population frightmeisters, warned that 65 million Americans would die of starvation by 1985.[1] In reality, the United States and Canada have tens of thousands of weight-loss clinics, and diet books routinely occupy *The New York Times* bestseller list. In the same year, Planned Parenthood-World Population circulated an article chillingly titled "The Human Race has Thirty-Five Years Left: After that, People will Start Eating Plankton. Or People."

In the 1970s, the mass media, ever ready to hitch a ride on the coattails of a politically correct cause, cautioned that by 1990 we would need to build huge artificial islands in the middle of the ocean to handle the earth's population; that by the year 2000 the world's oil supplies would be totally depleted; and that by the year 1990 the prime motive of all wars would be to seize other nations' food stocks.[1]

Some population controllers project current trends far past the point of physical possibility in order to frighten people unfamiliar with statistical theory or demographics. The vast majority of the population is unschooled in these disciplines, and so accepts the phony mathematics of the population controllers without question.

Population controllers have predicted that, if world population growth continues at a rate of 2% annually for 650 years, there will be standing room only by 2610, with only one square foot of land per person.[2]

In other words, the world population under this absurd scenario would be 1,589 *trillion*, or 270,000 times the world population in 1997.

Even *this* was not the most ridiculous forecast the population controllers have made. Ansley Coale won the prize for the most ludicrous projection when he said we are experiencing," ... a growth process which, within 65 centuries and in the absence of environmental limits, could generate a solid sphere of live bodies expanding with a radial velocity that, neglecting relativity, would equal the velocity of light."[3]

In other words, Coale believes there will eventually be more people than the number of *atoms* in the known universe!

Such statistical extrapolations obviously have no bearing on reality whatsoever and are useless for anything but scaring people and generating contributions.

Opposing Viewpoints

Fifty Billion ... Intellectuals interested in the population "problem" have generally gravitated toward two poles. Some assert that it is indeed possible for the world population to grow almost indefinitely, because we could feed as many as 50 billion people or even more comfortably if we could just remove all the existing barriers to food production and distribution.

This is an unrealistic viewpoint. If the population continued to grow at the current rate, it would indeed exceed the food supply, even if production and distribution operated under ideal conditions. At the rate the world population is currently growing (1.5 percent per year), we would reach this 50 billion (or more) limit by 2141. What would we do then? How would we possibly overcome the momentum of such massive population growth? In such a scenario, any measures to limit population growth would be much more severe than they would be today. And, of course, the human suffering caused by any large-scale population-limiting or reducing disaster such as war, famine or epidemic would be much worse than under current conditions.

But such a course of events is unlikely. The 1997 population of the world is about 5.9 billion, and the growth rate is about 1.5% per year (see Appendix B for details). Historical data show that the world population growth rate slowed steadily at the rate of about 0.02% annually since 1960.[4]

Several factors assure that this trend will continue. First, the spread of medical technology in developing countries has greatly decreased infant mortality rates, so agrarian families no longer feel they need numerous children. Second, the availability of abortion and sterilization has been steadily spreading all over the world, and will continue to do so for a number of years. Third, increased wealth in developing nations has naturally caused the birth rate to decline and the marriage age to rise. Fourth, the global trend toward longer life spans seems to be slowing.

The population fright-meisters have been with us for a long time indeed. This cartoon was featured in the June 1918 issue of Margaret Sanger's Birth Control Review. The caption read: "Hey, you! Can't you realize that we need quality, not quantity?"

Finally, experience shows that the native populations of countries that have embraced the anti-life mentality simply stop growing. Only immigration is increasing the populations of most European countries. If all or most countries accept sterilization and abortion, there will be very few places that immigrants can come *from*, and the total world population will begin to fall.

In light of these trends, it is logical to assume that the long-term, steady drop in the growth rate will continue.

If the historical 1960-1997 continental trends continue, the world's population will be about 6.2 billion by 2000, 10.0 billion by 2048, and will level out at a maximum of 11.9 billion by 2095.

... or One Billion. Another viewpoint of those interested in population questions is much more practical. It is also terrifying.

The primary goal of those who hold this view is limiting population at any cost. They include members of the Rockefeller Foundation, the International Planned Parenthood Federation (IPPF), all of the branches of the United Nations (World Bank, UNICEF, UNFPA, etc.), Zero Population Growth (ZPG), and literally hundreds of other pro-abortion, pro-euthanasia, population-control, animal-rights, and environmental organizations. This extensive, vastly wealthy, and very influential cartel is so bold in its work, and so convinced it is correct in its moral reasoning, that it does not even bother to conceal or package its activities in a more attractive format any more.

Appendix C lists the names of nearly 400 pro-abortion and population control organizations.

People who think this way believe Man has no special status on this earth and is just another animal who must consider all the other animals when making decisions about his own welfare.

This all sounds logical from a Humanistic point of view, but when people start seeing themselves as morally equal to or even inferior to animals, a certain depressive world outlook must inevitably result. After all, if we are not the supreme creation of God, then we are a cancer. If we do not occupy a privileged place on this earth, we occupy the lowest rung of existence because of our unparalleled ability to destroy other species. If we want to escape responsibility in sexual and other matters, we may soothe our consciences by accepting blame for "destroying" our planet—a psychological ploy that lets us take no concrete action other than being politically correct in our speech.

We find this attitude in many statements of animal rights activists such as Ingrid Newkirk, who once raved, "We [humans] have grown like a cancer. We're the biggest blight on the face of the earth."[5] Although not an activist by any means, even U.S. Supreme Court Justice Oliver Wendell Holmes once remarked, "I see no reason for attributing to man a significance different in kind from that which belongs to a baboon or a grain of sand."[6] In his pulp scare book *The Population Bomb*, Paul Ehrlich asserted, "We must cut out the cancer of population growth."[7] The U.S. Department of State was even more direct, calling mankind "the cancer of the planet."[8]

Some environmentalists even wish for death, not only for themselves, but for the entire human race. For them, the world is an unending circus of horrors, to endure and survive until the end of their lives brings them blessed release.

As Bill McKibben wrote in *The End of Nature*:

> We are not interested in the utility of a particular species or free-flowing river, or ecosystem, to mankind. They have intrinsic value, more value to me than another human body, or a billion of them. Human happiness, and certainly human fecundity, are not as important as a wild and healthy planet.... Somewhere along the line—at about a billion years ago, maybe half that—we quit the contract and became a cancer. We have become a plague upon ourselves and upon the earth.... Until such time as *homo sapiens* should decide to rejoin nature, some of us can only hope for the right virus to come along.[9]

Molly Yard, former president of the National Organization for Women (NOW), neatly tied abortion and radical environmentalism together when she said, "The abortion question is not just about women's rights, but about life on the planet—environmental catastrophe awaits the world if the population continues to grow at its present rate."[10]

1   David Wallechinsky and Amy and Irving Wallace. *The Book of Predictions*. New York: William Morrow and Company, 1980.

2   Murray Bookchin. "The Population Myth." *Kick It Over*, Spring, 1992, pp. 8-12. Also see Reverend John A. O'Brien. *Pastoral Life*, July-August 1966.

3   Ansley Coale. "Increases in Expectation of Life and Population Growth." In Louis Henry and Wilhelm Winkler (editors), *Proceedings of the International Population Conference* (Vienna, Austria), p. 36.

4   U.S. Department of Commerce, Bureau of the Census. Reference Data Book and Guide to Sources, *Statistical Abstract of the United States*. 1990 (110th Edition). Washington, D.C.: U.S. Government Printing Office. Table 1,440, "World Population."

5   Ingrid Newkirk of PETA, quoted in Charles Oliver. "Liberation Zoology." *Reason* Magazine, June 1990, pp. 22-27.

6   Supreme Court Justice Oliver Wendell Holmes, quoted in Richard Hertz. *Chance and Symbol*. Chicago: University of Chicago Press, 1948, p. 107.

7   Paul Ehrlich. *The Population Bomb*. New York: Ballantine, 1968.

8   "U.S. Presents Views on Population Growth and Economic Development." *The Department of State Bulletin*, 31 January 1966, p. 176.

9   David M. Graber quoting Bill McKibben's *The End of Nature* in the *Los Angeles Times* book review, as printed in the Orange County (California) *Register*, 28 October 1990.

10 *Proletarian Revolution*, Fall 1989.

122. What Is the Thinking Behind "Contraceptive Imperialism?"

The Plague of "Contraceptive Imperialism"

"It is the *moral obligation* of the developed nations to provide ... birth control techniques to the developing portions of the globe."

—*Humanist Manifesto II*, Article 15

The anti-life philosophy asserts that in order for a nation to advance economically or socially, it must strictly control its reproduction. This goal is paramount, so the elite may use any means necessary to implement it, including widespread coercion. Alan Guttmacher, former medical director of the International Planned Parenthood Federation (IPPF), said: "Each country will have to decide its own form of coercion and determine when and how it should be employed. At present, the means available are compulsory sterilization and compulsory abortion. Perhaps someday a way of enforcing compulsory birth control will be feasible."[1]

The underlying truth is that if developing nations do not control *their* populations, the commercial interests of *the United States* will be at risk.

Senegalese novelist Himidou Kane coined the expression "colonization of the mind." He said there are basically two ways to control a people. The first is through force: but when one nation uses force to subdue others, it must continually restrain its people from resisting. A more permanent solution is to get the people to accept new attitudes through a systematic program of propaganda. They are then under tight control, and the best part is, they think they made their decisions themselves. Of course, such a victory necessarily destroys the *identity* of the defeated; the indigenous population eagerly participates in its own genocide.

Dr. Charles Ravenholt, director of the Population Office, candidly explained:

Population control is needed to maintain the normal operation of United States commercial interests around the world. Without our trying to help those countries with their economic and social development, the world could rebel against the strong United States commercial presence. The self-interest thing is a compelling element. If the population explosion proceeds unchecked, it will cause such terrible economic conditions abroad that revolutions will ensue. And revolutions are scarcely ever beneficial to the interests of the United States.[1]

This condescending attitude is at the heart of the West's "contraceptive imperialism." The nations of North America and Europe have been frightened into accepting the theory of "differential fertility": i.e., if we don't do something fast, people from poor and backward nations will multiply, revolt against U.S. and European commercial control of their economies, and even become financially independent.

Obviously, contraceptive imperialism is, *by its very nature*, racist.

Back in 1971, feminist writer Lynn Phillips recognized the strong link between "population aid" and external coercion and control:

[Birth control] is an international strategy in application throughout the world; in Vietnam, population control of 'uncontrollables' takes the form of outright genocide, but in Latin America, India, here, and in American colonies, birth control is the favored method.... If there is any truth to the idea of a genocide campaign against black and other minority women, our sisterly concern for [illegal] abortion victims begins to look like a blind.[2]

Contemporary author K. Agnes White offers a disturbingly accurate analysis of the *real* reason for the West's meddling in the demographic affairs of other countries:

The willful distribution of such dangerous forms of birth control [i.e., IUDs banned in the United States for health reasons] to Third World women and the restriction of their use in industrialized countries makes it clear that population control is a racist as well as sexist policy. Along with the fear that the poor and hungry will rebel is the fear that the poor and hungry—by and large people of Color—will out-breed Whites.[3]

The Fatal Flaw

Mahatma Gandhi, whose country has been a population control battleground for decades, struck at the heart of the matter when he pointed out to Planned Parenthood foundress Margaret Sanger:

If it is contended that birth control is necessary for the nation because of over population, I dispute the proposition. It has never been proved. In my opinion, by a proper land system, better agriculture, and a supplementary industry, this country [India] is capable of supporting twice as many people as there are in it today.

I am totally opposed to artificial means of controlling the birthrate, and it is not possible for me to congratulate you [Sanger] or your co-workers on having brought into being a league whose activities, if successful, can only do great moral injury to the people. I wish I could convince you and your co-workers to disband the league and devote your energy to a better purpose. You will pardon me for giving my opinion in a decisive manner.[4]

Differential fertility certainly *will* lead to a vastly different world socio-economic picture before very long. Muslims, among others, recognize very clearly that there is more than one way to conquer the world. As Atifa Dawat stated, "The more children we have, the better. When there are enough Moslems in the world, then we will have world victory."[5]

The United States would like to exert control by the opposite means: persuading Third World women to *stop* having babies.

The Process of Emasculation

The story is the same on every continent and in every country subverted by the West's "contraceptive imperialism." The process of corrupting and destroying the morals, traditions and religious beliefs of "less-developed" countries invariably follows the seven-step sequence outlined in Table 13. The steps are usually not distinct because they merge into one another and are often executed simultaneously. However, they generally follow the order shown.

Population control programs in developing countries have been devastatingly effective. Figure 30 shows the impacts of depopulation programs on the world's 20 most populous countries. Eighteen of these countries have suffered a steep drop in fertility over the past 30 years. The People's Republic of China (PRC), the world's most populous country, has suffered a 71% decline in its fertility rate since 1965, from 6.3 to 1.8 children per family, largely as a result of its coercive population program.

Appendix B summarizes the worldwide impact of the population controllers. The world population growth rate has declined from 2.1% per year during 1966-1970 to 1.5% per year during 1996-2000—a 29% decrease.

The population controllers keep very careful track of the trends shown in Appendix B, and have proclaimed that their work has just begun. Even when the population of the planet levels off and starts to decline, they will *always* find more to do.

Case Study: Nigeria

In developing countries with large populations, the Population Council, the International Planned Parenthood Federation, and the U.S. Agency for International Development (USAID, a part of the Department of State) use effective CIA-style tactics to infiltrate government ministries, the media and the entertainment industry, recruit "focus groups" of local people to test their theories on and undermine indigenous values and traditions.

According to Information Project for Africa (IPFA) researcher Elizabeth Sobo, the goal of such intensive programs is to "literally saturate the media with birth-control themes, and at the same time to make it appear that these ideas represent nothing more than a spontaneous change in local customs."

Table 13

The Seven-Step Strategy
for Population Control in Developing Countries

(1) First, international population control organizations target the national legislature. They must persuade it (or force it by economic "disincentives") to accept the equation, SMALL FAMILIES = PROGRESS. The population controllers say this is the one certain road to economic equality with the West.

(2) Once the anti-population forces get contraception approved "for family planning purposes," they flood the country with pills, IUDs, abortifacients such as the injectable Depo-Provera and Norplant, and, deadliest of all, the "family planning" experts, who maintain a hawklike vigilance to make sure the suppression of fertility in the country goes smoothly.

(3) The national government funds and launches a massive propaganda campaign. Its purpose is to implement the "sexual revolution," under the guise of persuading the people to abandon their "backward" and "unsophisticated" lifestyles and embrace the idea that unbridled sex is desirable. The groundwork for State-funded abortion on demand is laid. National customs and culture are progressively undermined and abandoned, to be replaced by the glitzy, glittery allure of Western living. One by one, the ties that hold families together are severed.

(4) Because the ultimate goal of the "popcon" experts is zero (or even negative) population growth, widespread sterilization is next. Governments offer often-coercive "incentives" for male and female neutering and set up camps in some countries to conduct large-scale sterilization programs. Often, doctors involuntarily sterilize women as they are having their second child.

(5) Because contraception very often fails, abortion becomes a "necessary" backup, especially for the "hard cases." The population planners are careful to leave in place plenty of meaningless "restrictions" on abortion, to make it appear they are not really pro-abortion.

(6) After the initial controversy has died down, the abortion "restrictions" are eliminated one by one for "humanitarian" reasons.

(7) Once respect for preborn lives has been sufficiently eroded, the movement to legalize euthanasia can begin—only for the "hard cases," of course.

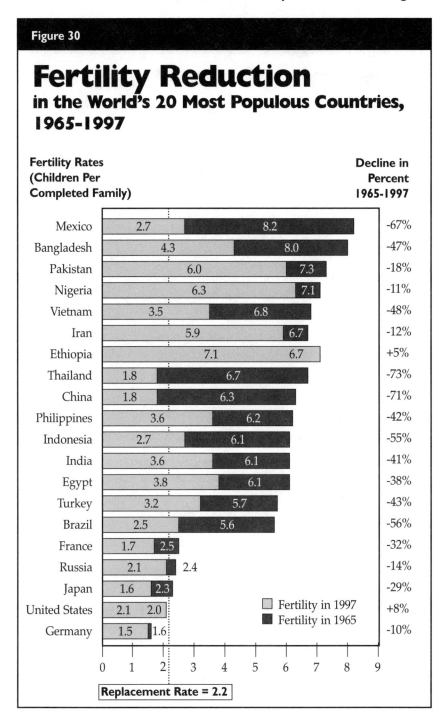

Figure 30

Fertility Reduction
in the World's 20 Most Populous Countries, 1965-1997

Fertility Rates (Children Per Completed Family)

Decline in Percent 1965-1997

Country	Fertility in 1997	Fertility in 1965	Decline
Mexico	2.7	8.2	-67%
Bangladesh	4.3	8.0	-47%
Pakistan	6.0	7.3	-18%
Nigeria	6.3	7.1	-11%
Vietnam	3.5	6.8	-48%
Iran	5.9	6.7	-12%
Ethiopia	7.1	6.7	+5%
Thailand	1.8	6.7	-73%
China	1.8	6.3	-71%
Philippines	3.6	6.2	-42%
Indonesia	2.7	6.1	-55%
India	3.6	6.1	-41%
Egypt	3.8	6.1	-38%
Turkey	3.2	5.7	-43%
Brazil	2.5	5.6	-56%
France	1.7	2.5	-32%
Russia	2.1	2.4	-14%
Japan	1.6	2.3	-29%
United States	2.1	2.0	+8%
Germany	1.5	1.6	-10%

Fertility in 1997
Fertility in 1965

Replacement Rate = 2.2

Table 14

Elements of the USAID
Population Control Program for Nigeria

■ "At least 3,000 television, radio, film and fold [print] media programs and spots, and newspaper and magazine inserts in at least five languages;

■ a music project [to develop] popular songs containing family planning themes [that are] composed and recorded by popular local musicians;

■ integrating family planning messages into existing popular radio and television [entertainment] series;

■ recorded testimonials from traditional and religious leaders;

■ television and radio specials and serials;

■ workshops [and] observation study tours for selected media practitioners;

■ motivational and technical video programs for broadcast, and for transfer onto 16 mm film to be shown through mobile vans;

■ special broadcasts on population issues to enlighten decision-makers;

■ symposia and meetings for traditional and religious leaders [and for] opinion leaders;

■ audience research [and] community analysis;

■ a series of workshops in at least 15 states for a minimum of 200 urban secondary and post-secondary school teachers;

■ [and] a national population quiz show eliciting competition from at least 300 secondary schools throughout Nigeria."

These programs feature not just localized radio and television spot ads, but massive nationwide and even continent-wide media and propaganda saturation campaigns.

As one example out of hundreds, a written contract between USAID and the Nigerian government outlines the various points of the country's proposed "family planning" program as shown in Table 14.[6]

1 Dr. Charles Ravenholt, Director, Population Office. Quoted in "Population Control of Third World Planned: Sterilization Storm in U.S." Dublin, Ireland *Evening Press*, 12 May 1979, p. 9.

2 Lynn Phillips. *Everywoman*. 22 January 1971, pp. 17-18. Reprinted from the 14 December 1970 *Liberated Guardian*.

3   K. Agnes White. "When is a Decision a Choice?" The Portland [Oregon] *Alliance*. April 1989, p. 10.

4   Mahatma Gandhi, in a letter to N.S. Phadke, Esq., The Honourable Secretary, The Bombay Birth Control League, dated 20 March 1924. D.G. Tendulkar (Editor). *The Collected Works of Mahatma Gandhi*, Volumes 2 and 4. Published by the Ministry of Information and Broadcasting, Government of India.

5   Atifa Dawat, an Iranian delegate to the July 1985 conference "Forum '85," in Nairobi, Kenya, quoted in Janie Hampton. "Women at U.N. Conference Stage Heated Fight over Abortion." *The Oregonian*, 21 July 1985.

6   John Cavanaugh-O'Keefe. "Working against Overseas Population Control." *National Catholic Register*, 18 November 1990, p. 12.

123. What Is the Status of Abortion Legislation Worldwide?

The Raw Numbers

A numerical summary of the status of world abortion legislation appears in Table 15. As of 1997, there are 191 countries, sovereignties and dependencies with populations greater than 100,000.

Slightly fewer than half of these countries (93) protect their preborn citizens completely or allow only strictly monitored exceptions such as "life of the mother,"

Table 15

Summary
of World Abortion Legislation

Current Status of Abortion Laws	No. of Countries	1997 Population	% of 1997 World Pop.*	Total Fertility Rates 1965	1997	Decrease	Pop. Growth Rate
Full Protection	51	1,268,619,000	21.50%	6.5	4.3	-35%	2.27%
Strict Exceptions	42	761,797,000	12.91%	6.5	4.3	-34%	1.97%
Many Exceptions	11	108,400,000	1.84%	6.5	3.5	-46%	1.72%
Abortion on Demand	87	3,759,693,000	63.73%	5.0	2.5	-50%	1.20%
World Totals	191	5,898,509,000	99.98%	5.6	3.1	-44%	1.51%

* The total world population as of 1 July 1997 is 5,899,971,000. The 33 countries, sovereignties and dependencies with a 1997 population of fewer than 100,000 people each (1,460,000 people total) are not included in these calculations.

---

rape, incest and eugenics. However, these countries have only about 34 percent of the world's population.

Ninety-eight of the world's nations offer little or no legal protection to their pre-born citizens. Their laws allow either abortion-on-demand or the physical and mental "health of the mother" exceptions, which, in practice, means abortion-on-demand. All of the developed countries of the world force their taxpayers to pay for all abortions for the mother's "physical and mental health," which, of course, means *all* abortions. The sole exception is the United States, which leaves funding decisions up to the 50 states.[1]

The countries that offer little or no protection to preborn babies are home to about 66% of the world's people and two of these countries (India and China) have 37% of the world's population.

There are currently about 55 million surgical abortions being committed in the world each year. This appalling number has steadily increased since 1960, when there were about 40 million surgical abortions worldwide.[1,2]

This means that, during 1960-1997, inclusive, surgical abortionists have killed about *1.8 billion* babies—a number equal to 30% of the world's entire living population.

Frightening Trends

Abortion laws have a profound effect on the total fertility rates (TFRs) and population growth rates of nations, as shown in Table 15. Nations with abortion on demand have a much lower TFR than those that protect their preborn citizens (2.5 children per "completed family" vs. 4.3), and have suffered much steeper declines in TFR since 1965.

Also, nations that provide little or no protection for their preborn citizens have only about half the population growth rate that nations that protect them do (1.20% vs. 2.27%).

1 Stanley K. Henshaw. "Induced Abortion: A World Review, 1990." *Family Planning Perspectives*, March-April, 1990, pp. 76-89.

2 Emily Campbell Moore-Cavar. *International Inventory of Information on Induced Abortion.* International Institute for the Study of Human Reproduction, Columbia University, 1974. Table 6.1, "Legally Induced Abortions: National Registered Incidence from 21 Countries."

···

124. What Is the Status of Abortion Legislation in the Americas?

North America

As of 1 July 1997, the United States and Canada have a total population of 297,711,000 people in a land area of 19,348,753 square kilometers, for an average density of 15 people per square kilometer, about one-third of the world average.

The average weighted total fertility rates (TFRs) of the United States and Canada actually rose from 2.0 children per woman in 1965 to 2.1 in 1997, making this one of only two regions in the world that have increased their TFRs during this time (the other is Central Africa). This is because of two reasons: (1) the "baby boom echo," and (2) the high childbearing rates of immigrant families. Despite these influences, the North American TFR will soon inevitably begin to drop again. The United States and Canada are the only countries in the Western Hemisphere with TFRs that have stayed below replacement level since 1965.

Neither the United States nor Canada give any protection to their preborn citizens. In fact, Canada has absolutely no restrictions on abortion whatsoever in its law; the only other country in the world where preborn babies have no protection at all is the (Communist) People's Republic of China (PRC).

Central America

As of 1 July 1997, the eight nations of Central America have a total population of 131,890,000 people in a land area of 2,481,366 square kilometers, for an average density of 53 people per square kilometer, slightly above the world average.

The average total fertility rates (TFRs) of the Central American nations have plunged from 7.9 children per woman in 1965 to 3.1 in 1997, a total decline of 61%, the second-highest of any region in the world. The highest 1997 TFR for Central America is Guatemala's 5.2 children per woman, and the lowest is Panama's 2.5.

Mexico suffered a two-thirds reduction in TFR during 1965-1997, eighth-highest in the world.

Guatemala, Honduras, Nicaragua and Panama all have laws that fully protect preborn children or allow for only a "life-of-the-mother" exception, although many illegal abortions occur. Belize is the only Central American country with abortion on demand.

The Caribbean

As of 1 July 1997, the 12 nations of the Caribbean have a total population of 35,979,000 people in a land area of 230,500 square kilometers, for an average density of 156 people per square kilometer, three and a half times the world average.

The average total fertility rates (TFRs) of the Caribbean nations have declined from 5.3 children per woman in 1965 to 2.6 in 1997, a total decline of 51 percent. The highest 1997 TFR for the Caribbean is Haiti's 4.6 children per woman, and the lowest is Cuba's 1.6, which is also the lowest in the Americas.

Jamaica suffered a 69% reduction in TFR during 1965-1997, fifth-highest in the world.

Of all of the Caribbean nations, only the Dominican Republic has laws that fully protect preborn children. Six nations—Barbados, Cuba, Jamaica, Puerto Rico, St. Lucia, and St. Vincent and the Grenadines—have abortion on demand.

South America

As of 1 July 1997, the 14 nations of continental South America have a total population of 328,073,000 people in a land area of 17,794,798 square kilometers, for an average density of 18 people per square kilometer, less than half of the world average.

The average total fertility rates (TFRs) of the nations of South America have dropped from 5.6 children per woman in 1965 to 2.6 in 1997, a total decline of 54%,

Figure 31

"Contraceptive imperialism" committed on a vast scale by developed countries has destroyed hundreds of indigenous cultures and is threatening those that remain. The population controllers work by severing the ties between members of extended families, like this one from Ecuador.

fourth-highest of all the regions in the world. The highest 1997 TFR for South America is Bolivia's 4.2 children per woman. Three nations—Guyana, the Netherlands Antilles and Uruguay—have the lowest TFRs, at the replacement level of 2.2. The smallest drop in TFR during 1965-1997 was Argentina's 19%, and the highest was Suriname's 66%.

The most populous countries in South America are Brazil with 164,320,000 people (fifth in the world), with Colombia and Argentina far behind at 37,380,000 and 35,033,000 respectively.

Reflecting its strong Catholic heritage, South America is relatively friendly toward preborn children. The only countries with abortion on demand laws are the small Guyana and the Netherlands Antilles. Brazil, Chile, Colombia, Paraguay and Venezuela (which have three-fourths of South America's population) all have laws that fully protect preborn children or allow for only a "life-of-the-mother" exception—although massive numbers of illegal abortions occur, often supported by international population control organizations.

However, this situation is changing, for several reasons. Anti-population groups have targeted the South American countries with the highest TFR for special attention. Subversive groups such as 'Catholics' for a Free Choice (CFFC) hold huge conferences and peddle vast quantities of propaganda undermining Church teachings on abortion, contraception and sterilization. And numerous Protestant sects, which generally hold permissive or "neutral" positions on divorce, fornication, adultery, contraception and abortion, are growing rapidly in predominantly Catholic countries.

125. What Is the Status of Abortion Legislation in Europe?

Demographic Trends in Europe

As of 1 July 1997, the 47 nations of Eastern and Western Europe and the former USSR have a total population of 814,268,000 people in a land area of 27,150,355 square kilometers, for an average density of 30 people per square kilometer, about two-thirds of the world average. Without the ex-USSR countries, Europe's population density is 103 people per square kilometer, second only to Asia's.

The direct cause of abortion is the separation of sex from procreation. Nowhere is this more obvious than in Europe, which has been in the grip of the anti-life mentality since after World War I.

The demographic effects of anti-life policies are becoming obvious. The average total fertility rates (TFRs) of the nations of Europe (including the former USSR) have dropped from 2.6 children per woman in 1965 to 1.9 in 1997, a total decline of 29% from an already-low figure. The highest 1997 TFR for Europe is Tajikistan's 4.2 children per woman, followed by Kyrgyzstan with 3.8. The highest European TFR outside of the former USSR is 2.4 children per family for Albania and Malta, just barely above replacement level.

Thirty-eight of Europe's 47 nations are currently at or under replacement fertility levels (not counting the former USSR, 33 of 35 are). Twelve European nations have remained below replacement level since 1965. The greatest decrease in TFR during 1965-1997 was Spain's 69%; the only European nation to *increase* its TFR was Finland.

Five of the lowest six national TFRs in the world belong to European countries; Italy's is the lowest on earth at 1.1 children per family, followed by Spain at 1.2, Greece and Portugal at 1.3, and Austria at 1.4.

What all of this means is that, if someone built a fence around Europe and let no one emigrate or immigrate, and if the current rates of population growth kept falling at the same rate as they have since 1965, the last European would die around 2285, followed shortly by the last remaining North American in 2290. Bulgaria has already begun losing population, being one of only two nations in the world that has a smaller population than it did 30 years ago (the other nation is Guyana).

The most populous countries in Europe are Russia with 150,498,000 people (sixth in the world), Germany with 82,068,000, and France, Italy and the United Kingdom, all with about 58 million.

The only European country with laws that fully protect preborn children or allow for only a "life-of-the-mother" exception is tiny Malta, home to just 0.05 percent of Europe's population. Ireland's traditional protection of preborn children is eroding rapidly, with many Irish women and girls travelling legally into England for abortions.

Forty-one European nations (including all of the nations of the former USSR) have actual or practical abortion on demand. These nations represent 88 percent of the total population of Europe.

The Facts of Life

The Effects of European Anti-Life Policies

The nations of Europe are already feeling the profound demographic effects of their longtime anti-life policies. These include:

- significant imbalances in population segments, leading to increased aging of the work force and the population. This, in turn, results in fewer workers supporting more retired people (creating great pressure on social security systems and retirement plans) and greatly increased health care costs, leading to a strong push for euthanasia.

- a great increase in the number of divorces (from 125,000 in 1960 to about 600,000 in 1995); illegitimacy (4.5 percent of all births in 1960 to about 20 percent in 1995); unemployment (from five million in 1977 to 12.7 million in 1988); and a huge increase in abortions, from about 250,000 in 1960 to more than a million today among the EC12 countries alone.[1]

- an influx of up to 50 million Muslims by 2025, mainly from North Africa. Because they are a very religious people, Muslims tend to integrate poorly with secular European society, a situation causing great tension and conflict that will only worsen in the future.[2] This state of affairs is a direct result of falling European birthrates; the last year "native" Europeans replaced themselves was 1973, and since then there has been a shortfall of more than 22 million births required to replace the population.[3]

Some European countries are trying to reverse their plunging birthrates, but with little success. History shows us that once the people of a nation are conditioned to believe they should live for themselves and that children are a burden, it is virtually impossible to persuade them otherwise. The only answer is for pro-life activists to convert the hearts and minds of the people, one by one.

For example, European population alarmists have been exaggerating the high cost of raising kids for decades as a ploy to get people to have fewer children. It is laughable when (for example) the German State of Brandenburg offers to pay its citizens $650 to have a child, and the people remember the propaganda that says it costs $125,000 to raise that child.

No wonder Wolfgang Jahmer, director of a social welfare program in Schwerin, Germany, says, "We have some fears that the tree of life may be falling."[4]

1 Eurostat. *A Social Portrait of Europe*. Luxembourg: Eurostat, 1991. The EC12 countries are Belgium, Denmark, Germany, France, Greece, Ireland, Italy, Luxembourg, Netherlands, Portugal, Spain and the United Kingdom.

2 R. Clarke. "Population Imbalances: The Consequences." *Forum* [Council of Europe], 1986, pp. 5-7.

3 Calculations and extrapolations based on figures from the *Institut National d'Etudes Demographique* (INED). "Short Fall in Births Europe." *Population*, July/September 1983.

4 Stephen Kinzer, *New York Times* News Service. "German State Pays Bounty for Babies." *The Oregonian*, 25 November 1994, p. A13.

126. What Is the Status of Abortion Legislation in Africa?

Demographic Overview

As of 1 July 1997, the 53 nations of Africa have a total population of 760,444,000 people in a land area of 30,308,333 square kilometers, for an average density of 25 people per square kilometer, about half of the world's average.

The average total fertility rates (TFRs) of the nations of Africa have dropped from 7.0 children per woman in 1965 to 5.8 in 1997, a total decline of 17 percent, the lowest of any continent except Asia. In fact, the eight nations of Central Africa have actually *increased* their average weighted TFR; they are one of only two regions in the world to do so (the other is North America).

This means Africa has by far the highest TFR of any region of the world, nearly double that of Asia. This is why Africa is becoming the number-one target of the developed countries' population control efforts.

The highest 1997 TFR in Africa is Rwanda's 8.6 children per woman, which is also the highest national TFR in the world. Cape Verde and Mauritius have the lowest TFRs (1.8), and are the only African nations below the replacement rate.

Eleven African nations—Angola, the Central African Republic, Burkina Faso, Equatorial Guinea, Ethiopia, Gabon, Guinea-Bissau, Malawi, Rwanda, Uganda and Zaire—actually increased their TFRs during 1965-1997, and 14 others held even. Gabon had the distinction of having the highest national increase in TFR in the world during 1965-1997, a whopping 40%.

The highest drop in TFR among African nations during 1965-1997 was Tunisia at 74%, second-highest in the world after North Korea.

The most populous countries in Africa are Nigeria with 107,824,000 people (tenth in the world), followed by Egypt and Ethiopia with about 64 million each.

The only African countries that have abortion-on-demand laws are Gambia, Tunisia and South Africa. In many nations such as Guinea-Bissau, the law states that abortion is only allowed to save the life of the mother. However, the law is not enforced and abortion is largely tolerated. The same law exists in Mozambique, but "official interpretation" allows abortion on all grounds.

The South African Situation

The strong-arm tactics of the African National Congress (ANC) were blatant even by pro-abortion standards when the South African parliament passed its Termination of Pregnancy Bill in 1996, giving South Africa the dubious distinction of having the worst abortion law on earth.

Every South African poll showed that every social and political group overwhelmingly opposed abortion-on-demand, by an average margin of two to one. In fact, the highest degree of opposition was among rank-and-file ANC supporters, at 77%.[1] Yet Nelson Mandela's party, while calling itself "democratic," simply ignored the wishes of its own constituency.

South Africa's Freedom of Choice Bill specifies a fine of 100,000 Rand ($22,000 US) and 10 years' imprisonment on the first offense for anyone obstructing abortion in any way. This includes doctors who refuse to refer for abortions. This means conscientious Catholic (and other) doctors face a brutal three-way choice: take part in procuring abortions (an excommunicable offense), give up practicing medicine, or go to jail for a decade. South African pro-abortionists have promised to use the new laws to prosecute every pro-life doctor in the land, and have vowed to demand long jail terms for any pro-lifers who take part in any kind of civil disobedience or even picketing in front of abortion mills.[2]

1 Brian Stuart. "Row Brews over Bill for Abortion on Demand." *The Citizen* [Johannesburg], 7 April 1996, pp. 1-2.

2 Personal communications with Claude Newbury, M.D., president of Pro-Life South Africa.

127. What Is the Status of Abortion Legislation in Asia?

As of 1 July 1997, the 42 nations of Asia (including the Middle East) have a total population of 3,500,704,000 people in a land area of 27,571,727 square kilometers, for an average density of 127 people per square kilometer, about three times the world average. Asia has 60% of the world's population, living on land with an average population density equal to that of Ohio, Pennsylvania or Florida.[1]

The average total fertility rates (TFRs) of the nations of Asia have dropped from 6.2 children per woman in 1965 to 3.0 in 1997, a total decline of 52%. This steep decline is exceeded only by that of South America.

The highest 1997 TFR for Asia is Yemen's 7.1 children per woman. Hong Kong has the lowest TFR at 1.3 (tied for third-lowest in the world), followed closely by South Korea and Taiwan at 1.5 and Japan and Singapore at 1.6.

The only Asian countries to raise their TFRs during 1965-1997 were Laos and Macau. The largest drop in TFR during 1965-1997 was North Korea at 75% (the largest drop of any country in the world), followed closely by South Korea and Thailand at 73%.

The most populous countries in Asia are China with 1,225,400,000 people (the most in the world), followed by India with 969,963,000 (second) and Indonesia with 210,161,000 (fourth).

Slightly more than half of Asia's nations (22) either provide full protection for their preborn citizens or have narrow exceptions. Sadly, these countries are home to only about one-fourth of the total population of Asia.

1 U.S. Department of Commerce, Bureau of the Census. Reference Data Book and Guide to Sources, *Statistical Abstract of the United States*. 1993 (113th Edition). Washington, D.C.: U.S. Government Printing Office. Table 31, "Resident Population—States: 1970 to 1992."

128. What Is the Status of Abortion Legislation in Oceania?

As of 1 July 1997, the 12 nations of Oceania have a total population of 29,440,000 people in a land area of 8,539,227 square kilometers, for an average density of just three people per square kilometer, by far the lowest population density of any continent in the world.

The average total fertility rates (TFRs) of the nations of Oceania have dropped from 3.6 children per woman in 1965 to 2.4 in 1997, a total decline of 33%.

The highest 1997 TFR in Oceania is the Solomon Islands' 5.0 children per woman. Australia has the lowest

Cartoon courtesy of Colorado Springs Gazette Telegraph.

TFR at 1.8, followed closely by New Zealand at 2.0.

The largest drop in TFR during 1965-1997 was French Polynesia's 61%. The smallest decline in TFR was Western Samoa's 24%.

The most populous countries in Oceania are Australia with 18,772,000 people, followed by Papua New Guinea with 4,492,000 and New Zealand with 3,437,000.

Five of Oceania's nations protect their preborn citizens with laws banning abortion except for narrow exceptions. Six countries and protectorates (Australia, Fiji, Guam, New Zealand, the Solomon Islands and Western Samoa) have abortion on demand.

129. What Are the Details of the Coercive Population Control Program in the People's Republic of China (PRC)?

Origins of the Chinese Population Control Program

Since the mid-1970s, the U.S. government has been deeply committed to both domestic and foreign population control programs. Billions of dollars of U.S. taxpayers' money have financed many immoral programs, including most notably the Chinese forced-abortion atrocity.

The National Security Council (NSC) is the highest U.S. government body charged with planning and directing foreign policy. One of the central aspects of this policy is population control.

The idea behind NSC population control policy is fundamentally racist and elitist. The concept is "differential fertility": If there are too many of "them" (people of foreign races) and too few of "us" (Western races), then the worldwide influence of the West will decline, and if the situation becomes serious enough, Western nations will eventually cease to be "global players" entirely. So, Western countries must use their vast reserves of "foreign assistance" money to cut down on threatening "foreign" populations, while there is still time.

This policy is an altered version of the Nazis' *Lebensraum* concept, the driving force behind the start of World War II and the extermination of millions whom the Nazis deemed inferior.

One highly sensitive NSC document, "Implications of Worldwide Population Growth for U.S. Security and Overseas Interests" (the National Security Study Memorandum (NSSM) 200, also known as the "Kissinger Report"), was written in 1974 and only declassified in late 1990. This document was the foundation for the United States' anti-natalist population philosophy.

The document argues: "Commitment to population stabilization will only take place when leaders of less-developed countries (LDCs) clearly see the negative impact of unrestricted population growth and believe it is possible to deal with this question through governmental action."

The paper goes on to suggest that U.S. food assistance might be made conditional, depending on the LDC's population control performance. More significantly, it says U.S. agencies should be planning on the use of force in the future: "It is important in style as well as substance to avoid the appearance of coercion ... mandatory programs may be needed and that we should be considering these possibilities now."

In 1976, the Interagency Task Force on Population Policy for the Under Secretaries' Committee of the NSC reported: "In some cases, strong direction has involved incentives such as payment to acceptors for sterilization, or disincentives such as giving low priorities in the allocation of housing and schooling to those with larger families. Such direction is the *sine qua non* [essence] of an effective program."

Forced Contraception and Early Abortions in the PRC

There is obviously no "right to privacy" in the People's Republic of China, especially when the subject is human reproduction. The euphemistically-named five-million-member "Women's Federation" is the Gestapo of the Chinese family planning program.

It aggressively "educates" women, detects pregnancies and accompanies mothers to the abortion mills to make sure they do not have a change of heart (thus playing the same role as abortuary "clinic escorts" in the United States). In the factories, the Women's Federation even records and publicly displays a chart of each woman's menstrual cycle and makes sure she uses contraception.

The United States suffers about 1.55 million surgical abortions per year. This is a large number, but pales in comparison to the Chinese. During 1975-1995, the Chinese have killed more than 200 million preborn babies, with an almost incomprehensible high of 14,371,843 in 1983 alone.[1]

Forced Late-Term Abortions in the PRC

China annually commits about half a million third-trimester abortions. Many of these babies are viable when they are killed, and virtually all of these abortions are against the mother's will. Author Steven Mosher has described how the Communists imprison pregnant women in a small room, isolated from their families, and do not even let them leave to change clothes or go to the bathroom. While they sit in misery on hard wooden benches, shifts of professional cadre endlessly berate them, shouting that they must do their "duty to the State and the Party" by aborting their babies.[2]

This barbaric brainwashing endures for weeks, if necessary, until the helpless mothers finally break down and agree to "voluntary" abortions. This is why Chinese "family planning" officials can insist with straight faces that there are no forced abortions or illegitimate children in their country.

After she finally breaks, a mother in her last trimester is usually taken to the local abortion mill and injected with Rivalor (*du zhen*, or "poison shot"), which causes congestive heart failure in the preborn baby. The child usually dies in agony over a period of about a day, and then is delivered dead.[2]

China's Infanticide

As bad as forced abortions are, the most extreme horrors of the Chinese program are reserved for those poor, brave mothers who somehow manage to hold out against the brutal pressure, or who conceal their pregnancies in some remote part of the Provinces. This illegal activity is common enough that the Chinese call it "childbirth on the run."

The Law and Second Children

Couples in rural areas are only allowed one or, at most, two children. Any third child is officially labeled "excess," and the law dictates that these "excess" children be delivered in the commune clinic. Large red placards proclaim, "THE CLINIC WILL NOT BE RESPONSIBLE FOR ANY MISHAPS THAT OCCUR DURING THE BIRTHS OF EXCESS BABIES."[2] This is because the infant mortality rate for third babies in these clinics is a perfect *100%!*

If a mother tries to give birth to a third child, she is led to believe that perhaps an exception will be made in her case. She is soothed and told that all will be well—that she and her child will be taken care of. Everything is, indeed, all right until the baby's head crowns. Then the "barefoot doctor" locates the fontanelle (soft spot) on the baby's head and injects a formaldehyde solution through it into the baby's brain. As the mother watches in horror, her child thrashes in agony as his or her brain slowly disintegrates.[2] Of course, the "doctor" merely shrugs and disavows knowledge of what is happening. The injection site in the fontanelle is so small that the grieving mother cannot detect it.

Michael Weisskopf of *The Washington Post* describes this type of murder:

In the Inner Mongolian capital of Hohot, however, hospital doctors practice what amounts to infanticide by a different name, according to a Hohot surgeon who would not allow his name to be used for fear of reprisal. After inducing labor, he revealed, doctors routinely smash the baby's skull with forceps as it emerges from the womb. In some cases, he added, newborns are killed by injecting formaldehyde into the soft spot of the head. He estimated that hundreds of babies die this way in his hospital every year.[3]

The Facts of Life

Gender Imbalance in the PRC

Because the Chinese value boys more than girls, female infanticide (femicide) is common. The 3 March 1983 *People's Daily* admitted, "The butchering, drowning, and leaving to die of female infants has become a grave social problem."

China's newborn male-to-female sex ratio was about 1.085 boys to 1 girl in 1981, compared to the historical Chinese ratio of 1.06 boys to 1 girl. This means there was a "shortfall" of 232,000 baby girls in 1981. The sex ratio climbed to 1.110 in 1983, for a shortfall of 345,000 baby girls that year.[3] Because amniocentesis, sonography and other means of detecting fetal sex are almost unknown outside the largest Chinese cities, it is obvious that "doctors" kill the vast majority of these "disappearing" girls at birth, when their parents discover their sex.

The 1983 sex ratio stayed about the same until 1987, then rose to 1.125 in 1989 and dropped slightly to 1.113 by May, 1990. The Chinese census also revealed that the sex ratio for first children is about 1.060, and about 1.140 for second and later children.

This means "doctors" killed about 3.5 million baby girls at birth solely because of their gender *in the last decade alone*.

Kang Ling of the Secretariat of the All-China Women's Federation estimates that by 2010, 40 million males of marriageable age will be unable to find wives, as a direct result of this mass femicide.[4]

Beijing's *China News Service* has also announced that 93% of unmarried adults in Beijing are men. Single men outnumber single women by one million in the 29-49 age group in Beijing alone. Men's prospects for marriage, of course, are even bleaker in the rural areas, where female infanticide is most prevalent.

Applause from the United States

Pro-abortion groups like to say that pro-lifers who do not vigorously condemn clinic bombings actually support such actions by their silence. Because no national pro-abortion group in the United States has condemned forced abortions in China, their own logic leads us to the inescapable conclusion that Planned Parenthood, the National Organization for Women (NOW), and all other pro-abortion groups *support forced abortions*.

The proof is in the (non)speaking.

NOW Supports Forced Abortions

However, pro-abortion support for forced abortions is by no means limited to a refusal to attack them. The most vociferous U.S. supporter of China's forced abortion program is Molly Yard, former president of NOW.

In the midst of the Congressional debate over the issue, Yard, during a March 1989 appearance on the Oprah Winfrey Show, continued to offer support, excuses and rationalizations for mandatory abortions: "I consider the Chinese government's [population control] policy among the most intelligent in the world.... It is a policy limited to the heavily overpopulated areas, and it is an attempt to feed the people of China. I find it very intelligent."

Shortly thereafter, in a 7 April 1989 news conference, she said criticism of China's family planning program comes, "from a lot of people who don't know what they're talking about." She also said: "China's population is so enormous that, if they didn't control it, they wouldn't be able to feed their people. The Chinese government doesn't coerce people. They use education. It's very clear when you're there. You can't miss it. Even if you can't read the language, you can't miss it."[5]

Even after viewing the mountain of evidence that persuaded Congress that U.S. tax dollars are supporting coercion in China, Yard continued to ignore the facts and sidestep the central issue. During her keynote address at the 1990 NOW National Convention, she asked: "What is moral about denying family planning funds to China, which is what the United States has done, because the Chinese have a policy of allowing abortions and encouraging a one-child family? What is moral about insisting that our point of view should be adopted by the Chinese when the only responsible policy they can have is to control family planning?"[6]

ZPG Supports Forced Abortions

Incredibly, Zero Population Growth founder and perennial population control hack Paul Ehrlich found a forum in the (formerly) prestigious *National Geographic* magazine. On page 922 of the December 1988 issue (the one with the flashy full-holograph cover), Ehrlich praised China's coercive population-control program as "remarkably vigorous and effective" and applauded her "as a leader in a grand experiment in the management of population and natural resources."

The Worldwatch Institute Supports Forced Abortions

Lester R. Brown, president of the Worldwatch Institute, stated in the 8 May 1985 *New York Times*: "The main difference between China and other densely populated developing countries ... may be that the Chinese have had the foresight to make projections of their population and resources and the courage to translate their findings into policy."[7]

Other Pro-Abortion Support for Forced Abortions

In prefaces to various Chinese family planning manuals, Planned Parenthood darlings William Draper and Andrew O'Meara say: "The methods and techniques used in the People's Republic of China will be of great interest to other nations," and ask, "Why not adopt China's population goals and methods?"[8]

In June 1992, the ubiquitous Garrett Hardin (who has four children) said in *Omni* Magazine: "I give the Chinese credit for officially recognizing that they have a problem and for having the nerve to propose the single-child program ... They have failed, however, by not making this directive universal throughout the country. The one-child policy is only enforced in congested urban areas."[9]

And, of course, in 1983, Ted Turner, owner of Cable News Network (CNN), produced a bogus half-hour "documentary," "A Finite World: China," which praised the forced-abortion-and-sterilization program there. For this enthusiastic endorsement of population coercion, the Population Action Council awarded him the "Media Excellence Award."[10] This revealing episode shows us exactly where the population controllers stand on forced abortions.

Ted's pro-abortion, pro-euthanasia Hollywood stars certainly have not helped the poor women in China exercise *their* "right to choose." In fact, as more Chinese atrocities are revealed one by one, Hollywood seems to endorse the coercion more and more.

Turner's Better World Society demonstrated its wholehearted support of China's forced-abortion program when it gave its 1988 "Envision a Better World" Award to the head of the China Family Planning Association, Wang Wei. Attending the lavish banquet were, among other stars, "New Age" guru Shirley MacLaine, Margot Kidder, Turner, Carl Sagan, Robin Chandler Duke, Jean-Michel Cousteau and Phil Donahue.[11]

As expected, the pro-abortion U.S. media did not hesitate to defend the Chinese population control program.

A particularly virulent supporter of coerced family planning is *The New York Times'* Anthony Lewis, who roundly condemned Jerry Falwell for mixing religion and politics, while praising anti-apartheid Bishop Desmond Tutu of South Africa for getting into politics up to his neck.

The same Anthony Lewis excused the Khmer Rouge's 1975 forced march of three million people out of Pnomh Penh, Cambodia, because it was being done to build "a vision of a new [Communist] society," and branded U.S. objections to the atrocity as "cultural arrogance." In 1987, he admitted the Chinese population control program includes forced abortion and sterilization, but stated: "The propriety of the methods used to discourage children is a fair question. But outsiders should not make ringing statements about it without understanding the reality of the problem China faces."[12]

The Current Situation—and the Future

The Chinese government is still rigorously enforcing the policies of its Draconian "family planning" program. Third or fourth babies are automatically slated for abortion. Second babies are also killed if they are conceived less than a fixed period of time after the first—usually four or five years.

Central Committee Directive Number 7 of 1983 summarizes the one-child policy currently applied: "All state officials, workers and employees, and urban residents, except for special cases which must be approved, may have only one child per couple."[4]

A more detailed statement on the basics of China's inhuman anti-population program is a directive by Shanxi Province Communist Party Chief Zhang Boxing on 10 July 1983: "Those women who have already given birth to one child *must* be fitted with IUDs, couples who already have two children *must* undergo sterilization of either the husband or the wife, and women pregnant outside the Plan *must* abort as soon as possible" [emphasis in original].[13]

This is the essence of "reproductive choice" in the "People's Paradise."

There are no exceptions to the "one-child" policy in the city, but if couples in the countryside have "real difficulty" with their first child—which means the child is a girl—the Party may allow them to have a second. Of course, women have no choice when it comes to being neutered: the official Central Committee policy, handed down in 1983, dictates that women with one child be fitted for an IUD, and women with two children be sterilized, whether they want to be or not.

1 John S. Aird. *Slaughter of the Innocents: Coercive Birth Control in China.* Washington, D.C.: American Enterprise Institute, 1990.

2 Steven W. Mosher. "A Mother's Ordeal." *Reader's Digest,* February 1987, pp. 49-55, and Alex Shoumatoff. "The Silent Killing of Tibet." *Vanity Fair,* May 1991, pp. 76-80.

3 Michael Weisskopf. "China's Birth Control Policy Drives Some to Kill Baby Girls." *The Washington Post,* 8 January 1985, p. A1.

4 "China's Population Policy Is Proving to Be Effective." *Beijing Review* (English Edition), 6-12 November 1989, pp. 42-44.

5 Mary Meehan. "Women as Guinea Pigs." *National Catholic Register,* 30 April 1989, p. 4.

6 Debra J. Saunders, *Los Angeles Daily News.* "NOW's Shrillness Becomes Embarrassment to Feminism." 7 August 1989, p. D4.

7 Jim McFadden's Introduction to the *Human Life Review,* Summer 1985, p. 3.

8 Wenming Su (editor). *Population and Other Problems.* Beijing Review Special Feature Series #1, April 1981.

9 "Interview: Garrett Hardin." *Omni* Magazine, June 1992, pp. 56-63.

10 "Rich Boy Ted Turner Pushing Population Control." *ALL News,* April, 1984, p. 40. Also see *International Dateline,* November 1983.

11 "Honors and Accolades: Third Annual Awards Dinner a Smashing Success." *Better World Letter,* Vol. 4, No. 4.

12 "The Week." *National Review,* 20 September 1985, pp. 12, 14.

13 "The Week." *National Review,* 27 May 1988, p. 15.

130. How Many People Die of Hunger Each Year?

The Assertions

Overpopulationists commonly allege that hunger kills 60,000 people every day worldwide. This figure is repeated *ad nauseam* by virtually every population control group from AID to ZPG, and has become almost a mantra for them.

Of course, neo-Malthusians use this huge figure to imply that the world's population has already outrun the food supply, and that the only solution is not to increase food production, but to cut population.

The Truth

According to the World Bank, there are about 50 million total deaths in the world each year, 39 million of which occur in developing countries.[1]

Table 16 shows that deaths due to hunger rank twelfth among all causes of fatalities in those countries.

A total of 0.6 million deaths per year equals 1,644 deaths from malnutrition each day. This means that the "60,000-per-day" figure is an exaggeration of 3,650%!

This is still an appallingly high figure. However, it lends credence to the belief that deaths caused from hunger could be more easily managed, and that maldistribution (not a shortage) of food is the root cause of most deaths from malnutrition.

Table 16

Causes of Death
in Developing Countries[a]

Rank	Cause of Death	Total Deaths
1	Cardiovascular diseases	9.0 million
2	Respiratory infections, including tuberculosis	8.3 million
3	Malignant neoplasms	3.7 million
4	Injuries	3.4 million
5	Childhood diarrhea	3.0 million
6	Maternal deaths and perinatal causes	2.8 million
7	Measles, tetanus, diabetes, pertussis and meningitis	2.4 million
8	Digestive diseases not caused by hunger or malnutrition	1.4 million
9	Malaria and other tropical diseases	1.2 million
10	Neuropsychiatric causes	0.6 million
11	Congenital abnormalities	0.6 million
12	Nutritional and endocrine deficiencies	0.6 million
13	Genitourinary causes	0.5 million
14	Venereal and related diseases, including HIV/AIDS	0.4 million
—	Other causes of death	1.1 million

Total annual deaths in developing countries: 39.0 million

a World Bank. *Development Report* 1993, "Investing in Health," pp. 224-225.

131. What Does the Catholic Church Teach About Population Control?

The Abuses of "Contraceptive Imperialism"

As described in Question 122, Western-style "contraceptive imperialism" and population control have destroyed countless cultures and millions of lives.

China's brutal "one-child" policy oppresses a fifth of the world's people. Forced sterilization camps brought down Indira Gandhi's government. Western interests test Norplant and other abortifacients on the women of developing countries, many of whom die or are crippled. Eugenicists keep advocating the forcible sterilization of mentally handicapped people and other "undesirables," especially in developing countries. The World Bank and other international organizations refuse to aid needy countries' projects unless their governments accept population control quotas.

Developing nations cannot voice their objections to these and many other atrocities, even at major world conferences, because Western nations threaten them with suspension of vital aid projects, immediate recall of loans or increased interest rates on past debts. This kind of naked manipulation occurs routinely at United Nations conferences. At the June 1996 U.N. Conference on Human Settlements (Habitat II) in Istanbul, for example, a Tanzanian delegate confided that she could not speak out against the anti-family agenda of the West because, "If I don't conform, my people will suffer."[1]

Evangelium Vitae (¶16) noted and condemned this type of naked aggression and abuse:

> They [Western nations] too are haunted by the current demographic growth, and fear that the most prolific and poorest peoples represent a threat for the well-being and peace of their own countries. Consequently, rather than wishing to face and solve these serious problems with respect for the dignity of individuals and families and for every person's inviolable right to life, they prefer to promote and impose by whatever means a massive program of birth control. Even the economic help which they would be ready to give is unjustly made conditional on the acceptance of an anti-birth policy.

What Constitutes True Economic Development?

Western pro-abortionists insist that the number of children a woman has is strictly her own affair, and that one should not interfere with her choices regarding reproduction.

Apparently, this principle only holds true for Western women.

Pro-abortionists and population controllers see little inconsistency in flooding developing countries with abortion machines, abortifacients and contraceptives, and mounting massive propaganda campaigns designed to retool the thinking of women away from national tradition and towards smaller families.

Developing nations suffer terribly because of the West's obsession with population control. In many countries, the shelves of clinics and hospitals are crammed with complete lines of contraceptives and abortifacients, and their doctors and health workers are trained in the very latest abortion and sterilization methods. However, antibiotics, vitamins, anesthetics and other basic health care supplies are in desperately short supply.

This is all in support of the theory that when a country has fewer children, it somehow becomes richer.

This is not true economic development. It is a typical, short-sighted anti-life "solution" to a serious problem that will only bring even worse problems just a few years down the road.

A program of authentic economic development that would make each dollar count the most would instead:

■ provide basic health care and prenatal care to women and children, thereby dramatically reducing infant mortality rates;

■ build road systems and bridges to remote areas, thus promoting regional economic self-sufficiency;

- help break down artificial economic barriers, such as family-run utility monopolies and overly complicated procedures for securing permits in order to start small businesses, thereby stimulating healthy competition;
- improve agricultural production with rural electrification, mechanization and adequate grain storage, thereby improving nutrition;
- provide clean running water to villages, reducing endemic diseases; and
- provide basic education to those who are not receiving it.

Evangelium Vitae (¶91) is the most concise and complete summation of Catholic teaching on population and authentic development, and we should read it in its entirety:

> Today an important part of policies which favor life is the issue of *population growth*. Certainly public authorities have a responsibility to "intervene to orient the demography of the population." But such interventions must always take into account and respect the primary and inalienable responsibility of married couples and families, and cannot employ methods which fail to respect the person and fundamental human rights, beginning with the right to life of every innocent human being. It is therefore morally unacceptable to encourage, let alone impose, the use of methods such as contraception, sterilization and abortion in order to regulate births. The ways of solving the population problem are quite different. Governments and the various international agencies must above all strive to create economic, social, public health and cultural conditions which will enable married couples to make their choices about procreation in full freedom and with genuine responsibility. They must then make efforts to ensure "greater opportunities and a fairer distribution of wealth so that everyone can share equitably in the goods of creation. Solutions must be sought on the global level by establishing a true *economy of communion and sharing of goods*, in both the national and international order." This is the only way to respect the dignity of persons and families, as well as the authentic cultural patrimony of peoples [emphasis in original].

1 Tom McFeely. "The Ugly Canadian." *Western Report* [Western provinces of Canada], 1 July 1996, pp. 28-33.

132. What Are Some of the Foremost Population Control Organizations?

There are more than 500 major pro-abortion and population control groups worldwide. Some of these, like the International Planned Parenthood Federation (IPPF) and various organs of the United Nations, have global influence. Others are national organizations which directly or indirectly support the population control agenda through contributions, propaganda, publicity, letter-writing or political campaigns.

If the annual budgets of these organizations were combined, the resulting figure would be equivalent to or greater than the gross national product of many countries.

It is very important for pro-life organizations, particularly those in developing countries, to be able to identify the opposition quickly and accurately. Appendix C lists the names of about 400 pro-abortion and/or population control groups. A bright red warning flag should go up if any of these groups are involved in any community program or national initiative. If this is the case, pro-lifers should do some very careful background research and observation to ensure that the values of their children and communities are not being undermined.

The Facts of Life

Chapter 13

United States Abortion Statistics

133. Why Are Abortion Statistics Important to Pro-Life Activists?

The Unparalleled Value of Documented Statistics

Anyone who has opposed the "Culture of Death" realizes how heavily anti-lifers rely on emotional appeals to support their arguments.

This is particularly true of pro-abortionists, who strongly dislike using hard facts and statistics, because they do not support the pro-abortion position. Instead, they write and talk endlessly about (usually) fictional stories of anonymous women "brutalized" by illegal abortions, or about the "hard-cases" for abortion—rape, incest and severe fetal deformities.

While acknowledging the tragic nature of such situations, pro-lifers can deflate pro-abortion arguments with statistics that show how rare they truly are.

When you use documented statistics during written or oral attempts to persuade, you elevate yourself above the emotional level and appeal directly to logic and reason. No pro-abortionist can refute documented statistics—especially when they originate with *pro-abortion* sources, which eliminates accusations of "anti-choice bias."

You can use statistics in many areas of activism other than formal debate:

■ When a new pro-lifer asks about the "hard-cases" you can show that they comprise about one-half of one percent of all abortions.

■ When a clinic escort tries to justify her actions by alleging that "5,000 to 10,000" women died from illegal abortions before *Roe v. Wade*, you can prove to her that this is a wild exaggeration.

■ When a school-based clinic advocate says we should give condoms to students because of high teen pregnancy rates, you can show that this is likely to lead to *more* teen pregnancies and abortions due to the high user failure rate of condoms, especially among teenagers.

The Facts of Life

■ When a population control supporter says 60,000 people die of hunger each day and calls for universal contraception for the women of developing countries, you can prove that this figure is overstated by a factor of more than 30.

You can use statistics proactively as well as reactively to show that more than half of the mothers who get abortions in the United States had contraceptive failures; that the abortion rate for minority women is two-and-half times higher than that of White women, thereby revealing the inherent racism of abortion; and that people use abortion mainly to cover up fornication, because more than 80% of all mothers who abort in the United States are unmarried.

Use Word Pictures in Discussions

The old saying that a picture is worth a thousand words is as true as ever. You can modify this adage by painting "word pictures" to illustrate your points during discussions or debates. A debater makes a tremendous impact on listeners by using his imagination to relate the abortion issue to everyday images that people are familiar with.

In other words, we frame the issue in terms that people understand, and will therefore remember.

This is an extremely effective tactic, especially when the pro-lifer's sources are unimpeachable, or when his sources are *pro-abortion* people or groups.

The following paragraphs describe some "word pictures" relating to abortion.

The Vietnam Memorial

You might get your audience thinking by asking how many of them have visited the National Vietnam Memorial in Washington, D.C. You can describe the Memorial as a shiny black wall that stretches 492 feet and lists the names of the 58,022 known Americans killed in that war.

You can then go on to say that, if such a wall listed the names of the 36.5 million babies legally killed by surgical abortions in the United States it would be nearly *60 miles long!*

And a wall that commemorated the *1.8 billion* preborn babies wiped out by surgical abortions worldwide since 1960 would stretch 2,891 miles—from coast to coast, San Francisco to New York City.

Cemeteries for Preborn Babies

Pro-life activists have occasionally set up temporary displays of thousands of crosses representing the number of preborn babies killed by abortions in the United States every day. These crosses make a riveting display of the brutal reality of abortion.

If standard burial plots were allocated to each preborn child killed by surgical abortion in the United States, the resulting cemetery would cover 260 square miles. If there were a cemetery for all of the 1.8 billion preborn babies killed by surgical abortions in the world since 1960, it would cover nearly 13,000 square miles—larger than Vermont and New Hampshire combined. Finally, if all of the 6.5 billion

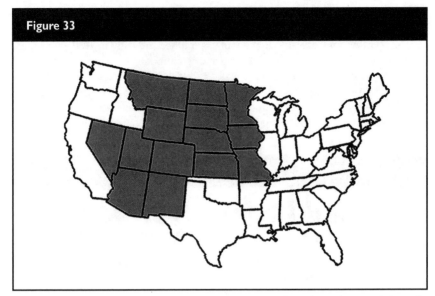

Figure 33

The "dead states." Since California, Colorado and North Carolina liberalized their abortion laws in 1967, 36.5 million preborn children have died—equivalent to the combined populations of the states blacked out on the above map.

babies of the world killed by surgical and chemical abortion since 1960 were properly interred, the resulting cemetery would cover a total land area of 47,000 square miles—larger than Pennsylvania.

But, because of "freedom of choice," all of these hundreds of millions of children will never see the light of day.

The Dead States

Surgical abortionists have killed a number of children equal to the combined populations of 14 states: Montana, Wyoming, North and South Dakota, Colorado, Nebraska, Kansas, Minnesota, Iowa, Missouri, Utah, Nevada, Arizona and New Mexico.[1] Figure 33 is a map of the United States with all of these states blacked out, and is a real attention-getter. This gives an audience some idea of the colossal magnitude of the abortion disaster.

1 U.S. Department of Commerce, Bureau of the Census. Reference Data Book and Guide to Sources, *Statistical Abstract of the United States* (1995, 115th edition). Washington, D.C.: U.S. Government Printing Office. Table 361, "Land and Water Area of States and Other Entities: 1990."

....

134. How Many Abortions Have Been Committed in the United States Since Legalization?

Surgical Abortions

As of 31 December 1996, there had been 36,405,760 legal *surgical* abortions in the United States since the first states legalized prenatal child-killing in 1967.[1] Of these,

1,878,990 were committed before abortion was legalized nationwide by *Roe v. Wade* and *Doe v. Bolton* on 22 January 1973, and 34,526,770 have been committed since.

The abortion rate leveled out at about 1.55 million annually in 1980. Since then, an average of 1,558,000 babies have been aborted annually over the 17-year period 1980-1996 inclusive. The worst year was 1990 with 1,608,600 abortions; since that year, the number of abortions has declined each year, due to the "ripple effect" of having fewer young women who are aborting. This phenomenon is itself a reflection of the sad fact that there are fewer young women because many of their peers

---

Table 17

Annual Legal Abortions
in the United States, 1967-1996

Year	Legal Abortions Committed		Year	Legal Abortions Committed
1967	57,160		1982	1,573,920
1968	114,330		1983	1,575,000
1969	171,490		1984	1,577,180
1970	228,650		1985	1,588,550
1971	574,090		1986	1,574,000
1972	693,380		1987	1,559,110
1973	744,610		1988	1,590,750
1974	898,570		1989	1,566,900
1975	1,034,170		1990	1,608,600
1976	1,179,300		1991	1,556,510
1977	1,316,700		1992	1,528,930
1978	1,409,600		1993	1,522,890*
1979	1,497,670		1994	1,516,860*
1980	1,553,890		1995	1,510,820*
1981	1,577,340		1996	1,504,790*

Total Legal Abortions, 1967-1996: **36,405,760**

* Estimates

Reference: Stanley K. Henshaw and Jennifer Van Vort. "Abortion Services in the United States, 1991 and 1992." *Family Planning Perspectives*, May/June 1994, pp. 100-112, Table 1 (1973-1992 figures). Centers for Disease Control and Prevention, *Surveillance Summaries*, 4 September 1992 (1970-1972 figures). 1967-1969 figures allocated and interpolated by state.

were *themselves* aborted 15 to 20 years ago.

Table 17 shows the number of legal abortions that have been committed in the United States each year since the first states began legalizing it in 1967.

The Planned Parenthood Federation of America (PPFA) owns the largest chain of abortion clinics in the United States. These clinics have committed slightly more than 2.2 million surgical abortions since 1972.[2]

Table 18 shows the total number of abortions committed in each state and the District of Columbia since legalization. Interestingly, states that pay for abortions for poor women (shown in bold letters in Table 18) have abortion rates nearly 50% higher than other states. This shows that women abort more often when abortion is cheap or free and easily available.

The surgical abortion rate drops quickly when a state stops funding abortions. For example, during the last year that Michigan funded abortions (1988), there were 63,410, ending 30.6% of all pregnancies in the state. The number of abortions committed in Michigan has dropped each year to an estimated 51,200 in 1996 (a decrease of 19%), ending about 24.5% of all pregnancies.

Chemical Abortions

Pro-lifers believe a preborn child is equally precious during every stage of its journey from fertilization to birth, and that a deliberate killing at the eight-cell stage is just as tragic as one in the late third trimester. After all, regardless of his or her level of development, a preborn child is still a precious creation of God.

Despite the efforts of abortionists to hide the truth, pro-lifers have sometimes displayed the tragic aftermath of surgical abortions for all the world to see. Sadly, few people will ever see the tiny remains of babies aborted by chemicals. This means their deaths at the hands of women who use abortifacients, including oral contraceptives (OCs), intrauterine devices (IUDs), Norplant and Depo-Provera, are largely ignored.

This is unfortunate, because the number of preborn children killed by abortifacients dwarfs the surgical abortion holocaust.

All abortifacient methods occasionally let a woman ovulate, so they work by preventing implantation. This is why all abortifacients have a method (perfect use) effectiveness rate of less than 100 percent, as we saw in Question 26.

Since 1965, an average of 10.8 million women have used abortifacient methods of birth control in the United States at any given time. If we assume a standard of 13 cycles of use per calendar year, and a low rate of ovulation/fertilization of 12% (2% of which account for "contraceptive failures," or pregnancies proceeding past implantation), a total of 14 *million* chemical abortions are committed in the United States each year, and there have been 450 *million* chemical abortions during 1965-1996, inclusive.[3]

According to the U. N., about 180 million women use abortifacient methods of birth control worldwide.[4] This means a total of 234 *million* chemical abortions are committed worldwide each year. Some 4.5 *billion* chemical abortions were committed during 1965-1996, inclusive. So, more surgical and chemical abortions were committed during 1965-1996 than there are people in the world today.

Table 18

Legal Abortion Statistics
by State, 1967-1996[2]

	Total Legal Abortions 1967-1996	Average Annual Abortions 1980-1996	Percentage of Pregnancies Aborted 1967-1996
Alabama	380,760	18,370	23.38%
Alaska	59,360	2,443	18.54%
Arizona	400,840	20,019	24.86%
Arkansas	150,860	6,531	15.32%
California	7,258,450	297,926	36.97%
Colorado	538,480	21,634	28.46%
Connecticut	452,470	20,965	33.94%
Delaware	118,960	5,163	31.52%
Dist. of Columbia	637,460	23,833	55.83%
Florida	1,725,330	81,381	31.96%
Georgia	957,210	38,967	26.88%
Hawaii	255,930	11,140	35.79%
Idaho	45,870	2,160	11.41%
Illinois	1,576,310	67,661	27.25%
Indiana	343,390	16,154	16.61%
Iowa	183,540	8,141	17.98%
Kansas	343,460	12,620	23.97%
Kentucky	238,990	10,184	16.80%
Louisiana	343,630	16,559	18.25%
Maine	98,820	4,619	22.48%
Maryland	776,140	31,747	32.90%
Massachusetts	943,330	41,441	33.91%
Michigan	1,361,030	60,018	30.73%
Minnesota	396,550	17,372	21.17%
Mississippi	127,980	6,686	12.48%
Missouri	374,050	17,033	19.45
Montana	74,340	3,563	21.77%
Nebraska	136,750	6,140	20.02%
Nevada	227,830	11,765	38.23%
New Mexico	168,230	6,576	20.71%
New Hampshire	99,900	4,853	24.26%
New York	4,964,880	191,618	41.53%
New Jersey	1,254,430	59,119	36.11%

Table 18 (Continued)

	Total Legal Abortions 1967-1996	Average Annual Abortions 1980-1996	Percentage of Pregnancies Aborted 1967-1996
North Carolina	867,610	35,818	27.29%
North Dakota	46,480	2,168	16.79%
Ohio	1,253,180	54,458	25.48%
Oklahoma	232,290	10,649	18.95%
Oregon	414,130	16,153	27.69%
Pennsylvania	1,304,810	55,138	25.45%
Rhode Island	149,040	7,257	33.71%
South Dakota	32,030	1,256	9.38%
South Carolina	275,660	13,020	19.79%
Tennessee	503,540	21,352	23.00%
Texas	2,113,730	99,921	24.71%
Utah	87,600	4,199	10.20%
Vermont	72,690	3,253	30.51%
Virginia	748,510	34,609	28.35%
Washington	812,390	32,937	32.16%
West Virginia	66,710	3,376	12.28%
Wisconsin	393,330	17,341	20.13%
Wyoming	16,470	698	8.96%

Percentage of Pregnancies Aborted, 1967-1996

All States	31.26%
States Funding Abortions (listed in **bold** above)	37.15%
States Not Funding Abortions	25.48%

1 Years in which individual states liberalized their abortion laws before *Roe v. Wade* in 1973: Colorado, California and North Carolina (1967); Georgia and Maryland (1968); Arkansas, Delaware, Kansas, New Mexico and Oregon (1969); and Alaska, Hawaii, New York and Washington (1970).

2 Abortions committed by Planned Parenthood Federation of America by year, beginning with 1973, are 20,000; 29,500; 38,000; 48,500; 58,660; 66,136; 72,112; 77,880; 79,997; 82,916; 85,242; 88,824; 91,065; 98,638; 104,411; 111,189; 122,191; 129,155; 132,314; 130,844; 134,277; 133,289; 135,000; and 136,000. Figures for 1973-1976 and 1995-1996 are estimates. Confirmed figures are from PPFA annual reports.

3 U.S. Department of Commerce, Bureau of the Census. Reference Data Book and Guide to Sources, *Statistical Abstract of the United States* (1965 to 1995 editions). Washington, D.C.: U.S. Government Printing Office. Tables on contraceptive usage by category.

4 U.N. Department for Economics and Social Information and Policy Analysis, Population Division. Wall chart, "World Contraceptive Use 1994."

••

135. How Many Minority Women Have Abortions in the United States?

White vs. Minority Abortions

We can express the number of abortions committed on White and minority women's babies in several ways: by absolute numbers, by percentages and by comparative rates.

Some 24,202,000 White women and 12,203,760 minority women have aborted since the first states legalized prenatal child-killing. Because about 46 million minority people live in the United States, this means more than one-fifth of the country's minority population has been wiped out by surgical abortion.[1]

The average annual number of abortions among White women is 1,031,500 (66.2% of all abortions), and the average annual number among minority women is 526,500 (33.8%).

During 1980-1996, 25.5% of White women's pregnancies have ended in abortions, while 40.1% of minority women's pregnancies have been aborted. This means a pregnant minority woman is 57% more likely to abort her baby than a pregnant White woman.

The average 1980-1996 abortion rate among White women of childbearing age was 22.4 abortions per 1,000; the average rate among minority women was 55.8—two and a half times higher.

Relative Availability of Abortionists

Because of the long-term disparities between the abortion rates of White and minority women, pro-life activists maintain that abortionists target minority women. An examination of the number of abortionists in cities with high and low minority populations verifies this allegation.

Human Life International researchers used U.S. Census Bureau and Alan Guttmacher Institute statistics to analyze the 198 U.S. cities with 1992 populations greater than 100,000 with regard to minority populations and numbers of abortionists. They found that the 11 U.S. cities with more than 70% minority populations (averaging 78% minority) had an average of 52.74 abortionists per million people, whereas the 11 U.S. cities with less than 10% minority populations (averaging 6% minority) had only 15.75 abortionists per million.[2]

This means high-minority cities have more than *three times* the number of abortionists per million citizens than low-minority cities.

We could reasonably argue that this tremendous discrepancy represents nothing less than a systematic pattern of genocide against minorities by abortionists and their supporters. Pro-abortionists may argue that cause and effect are being confused here; but, as we saw above, a pregnant minority woman is 57% more likely to abort than a pregnant White woman. If pure supply and demand principles were at work here, 23 years of steady availability of legal abortion would have led to a stable situation in which the number of abortionists would be roughly proportional to the demand— in other words, there would be about 50-60% more abortionists in minority neighborhoods than in White ones. Instead, there are 235% as many.

In an ambiguous situation in which you may confuse cause and effect, you usually find the "leading" trend by identifying the one that differs the most from the mean or initial conditions. Obviously, in this case, the huge surplus of abortionists in minority areas is the primary factor causing a large disparity in abortion rates between minority and White women.

Abortion Death Rates Among White and Minority Women

Abortionists not only target minority women's preborn children, they kill the mothers themselves at a tremendous rate by providing grossly substandard "care" to them.

Kevin Sherlock's compendium of legal abortion deaths, *Victims of Choice*, documents the case studies of a sample of 126 women who have been killed by so-called "safe and legal" abortion. Sherlock positively identified the races of 72 of these women. The dead included 35 Blacks, 20 Latinas, 2 Asian, and 15 Whites. This means that 79% of these legal abortion deaths have occurred among minority women.

By comparison, as noted above, minority women obtain 33.8% of all abortions. This means that the death rate among minority women who abort is *seven times higher* than that of White women who abort.[3] This number is underestimated by Planned Parenthood, which still admits that the risks of abortion for Black women *are more than three times as high as for White women*. Planned Parenthood says that the death rates for second-trimester abortions for Black and White women respectively are 24.8 and 6.8 deaths per 100,000 abortions.[4]

The death rate among poor minority women may be even higher than this estimate, because such women feel disenfranchised by the "system" and do not trust attorneys or anything to do with litigation, for good reason—and therefore do not press their claims.

Nobody seems to care about this continuing slaughter of minority women, least of all those who hypocritically call themselves "pro-choice." In fact, pro-abortionists puff up with contrived anger and rage whenever anyone suggests that they might be committing or supporting genocide. For example, Helen I. Howe, a spokesperson for the 'Religious' Coalition for Abortion Rights (RCAR), alleged that "RCAR views it as an insult to black women to make the generalized claim that abortions performed on black women are genocide."[5]

What is the truth in this matter?

One mother, Mattie Byrd, recently mourned her dead daughter Belinda in a letter to a friend as she said:

> I cry every day when I think of how horrible her death was. She was slashed by them and then she bled to death.... Where is [the abortionist] now? Has he been stopped? Has anything happened to him because of what he did to my Belinda? ... People tell me nothing has happened, that nothing ever happens to White abortionists who leave young Black women dead.[6]

Stephen Pine of the Inglewood Women's Hospital was the busy abortionist who killed Belinda Byrd. She was his 74th abortion of the day!

Pine perforated Byrd's uterus and she died three days later. As a partial result of this botched abortion, the Inglewood Women's Hospital had its license revoked by the State of California and closed down. However, money is a great motivator, and it opened only two weeks later with a different name: The West Coast Women's Medical Group. It was subsequently bought by mega-abortionist Edward Allred (whose facilities have also had several maternal abortion deaths), and still functions to this day.

1   U.S. Department of Commerce, Bureau of the Census. Reference Data Book and Guide to Sources, *Statistical Abstract of the United States.* Washington, D.C.: U.S. Government Printing Office, 1995. Table 12, "Resident Population—Selected Characteristics, 1790 to 1994, and Projections, 1995 to 2050."

2   City populations and minority population percentages are from the *Statistical Abstract,* Table 46, "Cities With 100,000 or More Inhabitants in 1992—Population, 1980 to 1992, and Land Area, 1990." Abortionists by city are from Stanley K. Henshaw and Jennifer Van Vort (editors). *Abortion Factbook, 1992 Edition: Readings, Trends, and State and Local Data to 1988.* New York: Alan Guttmacher Institute, 1992. Table 16, "Number of Abortions, Number of Abortion Providers, Percent of Abortions in Nonhospital Facilities Performing 400 or More Abortions, and Percent of Abortions in Hospitals, by SMSA of Occurrence, 1987 and 1988." The cities with 70% or greater minority populations are El Paso, Laredo and Brownsville, Texas; Miami, Florida; Gary, Indiana; Detroit, Michigan; Honolulu, Hawaii; Jersey City, New Jersey; Washington, D.C.; Hartford, Connecticut; and Atlanta, Georgia. The cities with 10% or less minority populations are Eugene, Oregon; Spokane, Washington; Lincoln, Nebraska; Green Bay, Wisconsin; Boise City, Idaho; Cedar Rapids, Iowa; Springfield, Missouri; Sterling Heights, Livonia and Warren, Michigan; and Sioux Falls, South Dakota.

3   $(79\%/0.338)/(21\%/0.662) = 7.4$.

4   John Benditt. "Special Report: Second-Trimester Abortions in the United States." *Family Planning Perspectives,* November/December 1979, p. 359.

5   "Abortion and the Holocaust: Twisting the Language." 'Religious' Coalition for Abortion Rights. 1987.

6   Undated letter from Mrs. Mattie Byrd (mother of Belinda Byrd, who died 27 January 1987), quoted in Feminists for Life of America *amicus* brief in the *Webster vs. Reproductive Health Services* case, No. 88-605.

136. How Many Abortions Are Committed for the "Hard-Cases"?

Introduction

As of September 1996, 98 of the world's countries had actual or practical abortion on demand. In every one of these countries, *without exception*, the anti-lifers first legalized abortion for one or more of the classic "hard-cases"—life of the mother, rape, incest and fetal deformities (eugenics).

In Western countries, pro-abortionists continue to use the "hard-cases" as powerful propaganda tools to defend legalized abortion. Every time pro-life activists try to enact the slightest restriction on rampant and unregulated abortion, the pro-abortionists rely on two psychological ploys: (1) the specter of women being sent back to the "back alleys," and (2) women suffering from the "hard-cases" being denied abortions.

This propaganda has persuaded the public that the "hard-cases" are extremely common. A 1990 national Wirthlin poll found that the average person believes that an incredible 21% of abortions in the United States are committed for rape and incest.[1]

The Reality

Table 19 is a summary and analysis of U.S. abortion statistics for 1980-1996. We chose this period because the absolute numbers of legal abortions in the United States rose significantly each year from 1967 to 1979, and finally stabilized in 1980.

This table is the most valuable weapon in the pro-life activist's statistical arsenal. There is no way to attack its veracity, because all of its statistics come from *pro-abortion* sources, and all of its assumptions err in favor of the pro-abortionists.

Several crucial points stand out when you examine Table 19:

- The "hard-cases" of the mother's life, rape, incest and fetal deformities (eugenics) account for only about 0.7% of all abortions in the United States each year. This means 99.3% of all abortions are committed "to save the mother's lifestyle" (actual reasons the aborting mothers give are in the next Question, and they confirm these numbers).

- Abortion is nothing more nor less than a convenient cover-up for fornication, because 82% of all mothers getting abortions are unmarried. More than half of all women who abort have had no children.

- The widespread availability of contraception does *not*, as sex educators and school-based clinic advocates assert, lead to decreased abortions because 57.5% of all women who abort were using contraception when they conceived.

- Millions of women use abortion *as* birth control in the United States. More than 40% of women who abort were not using any kind of contraception when they became pregnant; more than half of all women who abort have had abortions before; and nearly 10% of women who abort have had at least *three* abortions before.

1 Results of a 1990 Wirthlin poll described in "The Week." *National Review*, 3 December 1990, p. 12.

Table 19

Analysis
of United States Abortion Statistics

Average Annual Numbers of Abortions, 1980 to 1996: 1,558,000 (100.0%)

Characteristics of Aborting Women[2]

Marital Status
- Unmarried 1,277,000 (82.0%)
- Married 281,000 (18.0%)

Percentage of Pregnancies Aborted
- Total 28.6%
- Married 8.7%
- Unmarried 57.5%

Prior Legal Abortions (1996 figures)
- None 46.1%
- One 30.6%
- Two 14.5%
- Three or more 8.8%
- Total repeaters 53.9%

Race
- White 1,031,500 (66.2%)
- Minority 526,500 (33.8%)

Age
- Under 15 .... 14,200 (0.9%)
- 15 to 17 .... 154,500 (9.9%)
- 18 to 19 .... 224,000 (14.4%)
- 20 to 24 .... 527,700 (33.9%)
- 25 to 29 .... 334,900 (21.5%)
- 30 to 34 .... 188,500 (12.1%)
- 35 to 39 .... 90,400 (5.8%)
- 40 and over 23,800 (1.5%)

Prior Births
- None 850,500 (54.5%)
- One 342,600 (22.0%)
- Two 236,400 (15.2%)
- Three 85,000 (5.5%)
- Four or more 43,500 (2.8%)

Contraceptive Use[1]

No use of contraception (abortion as birth control) 662,150 (42.5%)

Failed contraception 925,850 (57.5%)

When Abortions Were Committed[2]

To 10 weeks. 1,208,500 (77.6%)

11 to 20 weeks 339,400 (21.8%)

21 or more weeks 10,100 (0.6%)

The "Hard-Cases"

Mother's life or health[3]. 5,610 (0.36%)

For rape and incest[4] 1,270 (0.08%)

For fetal birth defects[5] 3,750 (0.24%)

Total "hard-cases" .... **10,630 (0.68%)**

Non-therapeutic ("lifestyle") abortions .... **1,547,370 (99.32%)**

References and Calculations for Table 19

1 Stanley K. Henshaw and Jennifer Van Vort. "Abortion Patients in 1994-1995: Characteristics and Contraceptive Use." *Family Planning Perspectives*, July/August 1996, pp. 140-148.

2 Stanley K. Henshaw and Jennifer Van Vort. *Abortion Factbook, 1992 Edition: Readings, Trends, and State and Local Data to 1992*. New York: The Alan Guttmacher Institute, 1992. Appendix "Trends, State and Local Data to 1988." Stanley K. Henshaw and Jennifer Van Vort. "Abortion Services in the United States, 1991 and 1992." *Family Planning Perspectives*, May/June 1994, pp.100-112. 1993-1996 figures based on extrapolation of 1980-1992 trends; in no case was there a radical or significant change in trends during 1980-1992.

3 This percentage is derived from the aggregate results of studies of why more than half a million women had abortions, as follows; (1) Office of Public Health of the Louisiana Department of Health and Hospitals, compilation of State of Louisiana "Report of Induced Termination of Pregnancy" forms (#PHS 16-ab), Item 9d, "Reason for Pregnancy Termination," 1975 -1988. 114,231 of 115,243 abortions (99.1%) for mental health and 863 (0.75%) for physical health. (2) D.B. Paintin, M.D., Department of Obstetrics and Gynecology, St. Mary's Hospital Medical School, London, England. "Late Abortions." *The Lancet*, 11 November 1989, p. 1158. This study found that only 966 of 358,074 abortions reported in the United Kingdom for 1987 and 1988 were for a "specified medical disorder." (3) J.J. Rovinsky and S.B. Gusberg. *American Journal of Obstetrics and Gynecology*, 98:11-17 (1967). There were 57,228 deliveries at New York's Mount Sinai Hospital from 1953 to 1964. During the same period, 69 abortions were committed for physical health reasons. Totals are 1,898/529,533 = 0.36%.

4 About one-third of all rape victims are postmenopausal or have not yet reached menarche (first menstruation), and are therefore usually sterile [R.B. Everett and G.K. Jemerson, "The Rape Victim." *Obstetrics and Gynecology*. 50, 1977, p. 88. Also data from Dr. Charles Pratt, Survey of Family Growth Division, National Center for Health Statistics, and Planned Parenthood-World Population (PP/WP), summarized in testimony by Rep. Thomas J. Bliley, Jr., (R-Va.) on 25 July 1983, and reprinted in the next day's *Congressional Record*]. Of those victims who are of childbearing age, 32.1% have been rendered *permanently* sterile due to elective surgery or environmental effects. Finally, 34.3% of all non-sterile women of childbearing age are *temporarily* sterile due to contraceptive use [U.S. Department of Commerce, Bureau of the Census. Reference Data Book and Guide to Sources, *Statistical Abstract of the United States*, 1995. Washington, D.C., U.S. Government Printing Office. Table 107, "Contraceptive Use By Women, 15-44 Years Old: 1990"]. This means that (100% - 33%) X (100% - 32.1% - 34.3%) = 22.5% of rape victims were capable of becoming pregnant at the time of the attack. A woman can become pregnant only about five days out of a typical 28-day cycle, if the survival time of the sperm and the egg are both taken into consideration. Furthermore, even if all conditions are ideal and both man and woman are fertile, and intercourse takes place on *every fertile day*, it will take an average of *five months* (or a total of 25 possible fertile days out of five 28-day cycles) to achieve pregnancy [R. Pearl. *The Natural History of Population*. New York: Oxford University Press, 1939, pp. 72-79, and V. Seltzer. "Medical Management of the Rape Victim." *Journal of the American Medical Women's Association*, 32, 1977, p. 141]. Men in the United States have an infertility rate (due to natural or surgical causes) of about 25%. However, as a class, rapists have a much higher degree of erectile or ejaculatory dysfunction (57%) serious enough to render them sterile. Rape is legally defined as penetration only; ejaculation need not occur. Of those *nonsterile* rapists who penetrated, only about half deposited sperm [C. Groth, A. Nicholas, and Ann Wolbert Burgess. "Sexual Dysfunction During Rape." *New England Journal of Medicine*, 6 October 1977, pp. 764-766, and M. Dahlke, et al. "Identification of Semen in 500 Patients Seen Because of Rape." *American Journal of Clinical Pathology*, 68, 1977, p. 740]. Conclusion: On the average, (100% - 33%) X (100% - 32.1% - 34.3%) X (25/140) X (100% - 57%) X 50% = 0.86%, or fewer than 1% (8.6 per 1,000) women who are raped in the United States become pregnant.

The average number of rapes committed in the United States during 1980-1996 came from the 1995 *Statistical Abstract*, Table 289, "Forcible Rape—Number and Rate, By Selected Characteristics: 1970 to 1988." 1989-1993 figures are from the 1995 *Statistical Abstract*, Table 315, "Forcible Rape—Number and Rate: 1970 to 1993." 1994-1996 figures are estimates. The underreporting factor appeared in the 1990 *Statistical Abstract*, unnumbered table, "Police Reporting Rates for Personal and Household Crimes: 1975 to 1987," p. 168. 1988-1996 figures are assumed equal to the 1987 figure of 53.2%. The result is an average of 147,755 rapes committed each year in the United States. The average number of legal abortions committed each year is calculated elsewhere in this chapter. Conclusion: An average of (147,755 X 0.86) = 1,271 rapes result in pregnancy each year. An average of 1,558,000 abortions have been committed each year since 1980, when the current level of about 1.5 million abortions per year was reached. *If every rape-caused pregnancy ended in abortion*, a maximum of (1,558,000/1,271) = one out of every 1,226 abortions would be committed for rape. This is 0.082% of all abortions (under one-hundredth of one percent).

5 David A. Grimes, M.D. "Second-Trimester Abortions in the United States." *Family Planning Perspectives*, November/December 1984. Grimes quotes a range of 1,500-3,750 abortions per year for serious birth defects. For the purposes of this table, the higher number is used.

Table 20

Why Do Women Have Abortions?

Reason Given by Women	% Responding by Age						Most Important Reason
	14-18	18-19	20-24	25-29	30-44	Total	
"A baby would change my life."	92	82	75	72	69	76	16
"I can't afford a baby right now."	73	73	70	64	58	68	21
"I have problems with my relationship."	37	46	56	55	50	51	12
"I'm not ready for the responsibility."	33	40	35	25	18	31	21
"I don't want others to know I was pregnant or having premarital sex."	42	41	35	21	22	31	1
"I'm not mature enough to have a baby."	81	57	28	7	4	30	11
"I have all the children I want."	12	23	31	51	26	8	8
"Husband or boyfriend wants me to abort."	23	29	25	18	20	23	1
"The fetus has a possible health problem."	9	13	12	14	17	13	3
"My health isn't good enough."	3	4	7	8	15	7	3
"My parents want me to abort."	28	12	4	3	2	7	1
"I am a victim of rape or incest."	1	1	1	1	1	0	1
Other	2	5	8	5	8	6	1
							100

Reference: Aida Torres and Jacqueline Darroch Forrest. "Why Do Women Have Abortions?" *Family Planning Perspectives*, July/August 1988, pp. 169-176, Table 1.

137. Why Do Women Say They Have Abortions?

Numbers can only go so far in helping others understand women's motives for having abortions. There is nothing as persuasive as actually surveying women in abortion centers and asking them why they think they must have abortions.

The Alan Guttmacher Institute (AGI) did exactly this in 1988. The AGI surveyed 1,900 women in 38 states who were waiting for abortions, and asked them to fill out a form that detailed their motives for aborting.

The results of this survey are shown in Table 20. They are fascinating, and we can draw many conclusions from them. For example:

■ According to the women themselves, the "hard-cases" of mother's health, rape, incest and fetal deformity (eugenics) account for only 7% of all abortions. Pro-lifers should remember that abortionists and health professionals have found that pregnancies that threaten mothers' physical health or lives are very rare indeed (see Question 84 for details). Also, careful study of statistics reveals that very few women become pregnant from rape or incest (see Question 86). Finally, we must remember that many women who abort for eugenic reasons may believe their preborn child is severely handicapped based on various pre-natal tests, but the odds reveal that most of these babies are perfectly healthy.

■ Most women who have abortions, regardless of their ages, say "a baby would change my life." This seemingly innocuous statement shows just how drastically the "Culture of Death" has infected the thinking of the Western world. Most people now see a baby as a curse and a burden instead of a precious gift. The AGI poll shows that husbands, boyfriends and parents have this attitude, too.

■ The percentages of some excuses, such as "I can't afford a baby right now" and "I'm not ready for the responsibility" do not change with age as much as we might have thought. These excuses give us insight into the mentality of women who have abortions, and can increase the effectiveness of sidewalk counselors, crisis pregnancy center or Birthright workers, and others who have contact with mothers contemplating abortion.

The Facts of Life

Pro-Life Organizations

This Appendix consists of vital information on about 100 major pro-life and pro-family organizations in the United States and other English-speaking countries. Each of these groups has a proven track record of fighting the "Culture of Death," and each has experts in various fields willing to assist activists not only in the United States, but worldwide.

A few of the listed organizations, such as La Leche League International, do not officially take a position on abortion, but are involved in an area that may occasionally be of interest to pro-life activists, such as breastfeeding. These organizations have an asterisk (*) listed after their names.

Australia

ACT Right to Life

P.O. Box 333
Civic Square
ACT 2608
Australia
Telephone: 011/61-06-253-3100

Endeavour Forum

79 Church St.
Beaumaris, Vic. 3193
Australia

Pro-Life Victoria

Suite 3
672B Glenferrie Road Hawthorn 3122
P.O. Box 15 Hawthorn
Victoria 3122
Australia

Canada

Alberta Family Life Centre

305A 1324 11th Ave. S.W.
Calgary, AB
T3C 0M6
Canada
Telephone: (403) 228-2190
FAX: (403) 228-2249

Alliance for Life

B1-90 Garry Street
Winnipeg, MB
R3C 4H1
Canada
Telephone: (204) 943-5273

Campaign Life

53 Dundas St. East
Suite 306
Toronto, ON
M5B 1C6
Canada
Telephone: (416) 368-0250
FAX: (416) 368-8575

Canadian Alliance for Chastity Education (CACE)

7 Albert Street
Cornwall, Ontario K6H 4E7
Canada
Telephone: (613) 938-1091

Ireland

....
Family Solidarity News

15 Gardiner Place
Dublin 1
Ireland
Telephone/FAX: 011/353-1-746-463

....
Society for the Protection of Unborn Children

Ard Na Greine
Eaton Brae
Dublin 14
01-071488
Ireland

....
Youth Defense

312 Crumlin Road
Dublin 12
988 792
Ireland

New Zealand

....
Humanity

P.O. Box 26-113
Epsom
Auckland 3
New Zealand
Telephone: 011/64-09-376-2101

New Zealand Society for the Protection of Unborn Children

Box 12-286
Thorndon
Wellington
New Zealand

Philippines

Families for Family

c/o Winternitz and Associates
7th Floor Golden Rock Bldg.
168 Salcedo Street, Legaspi Village
Makati, Metro Manila
Philippines
Telephone: 011/63-2-817-4121
FAX: 011/63-2-817-2761

Pro-Life Philippines

San Lorenzo Ruiz Center
2002 Jesus Street
Pandacan, Manila
Philippines
Telephone/FAX: 011/63-2-521-3887

South Africa

Doctors For Life

P.O. Box 61897
Bishopsgate 4008
South Africa
Telephone: 011/27-031-306-0972

LEARN

P.O. Box 210
Meadowsland 1851
Gauteng
South Africa

Pro-Life

P.O. Box 1601
Cape Town
8000
South Africa
Telephone: 011/27-21-61-4261

United Kingdom

ALERT

27 Walpole St.
London SW3 4QS
United Kingdom
Telephone: 011/44-171-730-2800
FAX: 011/44-171-730-0710

LIFE

Life House
1A New Bold Terrace
Leamington Spa
Warwickshire
CV32 4EX
United Kingdom
Telephone: 011/44-192-631-6737
FAX: 011/44-192-633-6497

PLAN

56 Woodhall Lane
Welwyn Garden City
Harts AL73TF
United Kingdom

Society for the Protection of Unborn Children

5-6 Matthews Street
London SW1P 2JT
United Kingdom
Telephone: 011/44-171-222-5845
FAX: 011/44-171-222-0630

United States

Abortion & Recovery Research

Vincent Rue, Ph.D.
111 Bow Street
Portsmouth, New Hampshire 03801-3819
Telephone: (603) 431-1904
Area of expertise: Abortion (post-abortion trauma and research)

Abortion Lawsuit Project

Family Concerns, Inc.
Post Office Box 550168
Atlanta, Georgia 30355
Area of expertise: Abortion (lawsuits against abortionists)

Alliance for Chastity Education (ACE)

Post Office Box 11297
Cincinnati, Ohio 45211-0297
Area of expertise: Chastity education

American Academy of Medical Ethics (AAME)

4205 McAuley Boulevard, #420
Oklahoma City, Oklahoma 73120-5504
Telephone: (405) 751-6111 or 1-(800) 972-6853
Periodicals: *Issues in Law and Medicine* and *The Healing Ethic*
Area of expertise: Physicians opposing abortion and euthanasia

American Center for Law and Justice (ACLJ)

1000 Regent University Drive
Post Office Box 64429
Virginia Beach, Virginia 23467
Telephone: (804) 579-2489
FAX: (804) 579-2836
Web site address: http://www.aclj.org
Area of expertise: Constitutional Law (First and Fourteenth Amendments)

American Family Association (AFA)

Post Office Drawer 2440
Tupelo, Mississippi 38803
Telephone: (601) 844-5036
Periodicals: AFA *Journal*
Web site address: http://www. gocin.com/afa/home.html
Area of expertise: Pornography in the mass media

American Life League (ALL)

Post Office Box 1350
Stafford, Virginia 22555
Telephone: (540) 659-4171
FAX: (540) 658-2586
Periodicals: *Celebrate Life!* and *Communique*
Web site address: http://www.ahoynet.com/~all
Areas of expertise: Abortion (chastity, education and legislation), euthanasia

American Rights Coalition (ARC)

Charlie Wysong
Post Office Box 487
Chattanooga, Tennessee 37401
Telephone: (615) 756-7065 or 1-800-634-2224
Area of expertise: Abortion (lawsuits against abortionists)

Americans against Abortion (AAA)

Melody Green
Last Days Ministries, Post Office Box 70
Lindale, Texas, 75771-0070
Telephone: (903) 963-8671
Area of expertise: Abortion (education)

Americans United for Life (AUL)

343 South Dearborn Street, Suite 1804
Chicago, Illinois 60604
Telephone: (312) 786-9494
Periodical: *Studies in Law and Medicine*
Areas of expertise: Abortion and euthanasia (litigation)

Baptists for Life

Post Office Box 3158
Grand Rapids, Michigan 49501
Telephone: (616) 669-5040
FAX (616) 669-9558
Area of expertise: Abortion

Bethany Christian Services

901 Eastern Avenue, NE
Grand Rapids, Michigan 49503
Telephone: (616) 459-6273
Web site address: http://www.bethany.org/
Area of expertise: Adoption

Birthright

Post Office Box 98363
Atlanta, Georgia 30359
Telephone: (404) 451-6336 or 1-(800) 550-4900
Area of expertise: Abortion (crisis pregnancies)

Catholic League for Religious & Civil Rights

Post Office Box 2409
Bala-Cynwyd, Pennsylvania 19004
Area of expertise: Defense of Catholic Faith

Catholics United for the Faith (CUF)

827 North 4th Street
Steubenville, Ohio 43952
Telephone: (614) 283-2484 or 1-800-693-2484
FAX: (614) 283-4011
Periodical: *Lay Witness*
Areas of expertise: Apologetics and abortion (education)

Catholics United for Life (CUL)

3050 Gap Knob Road
New Hope, Kentucky 40052
Telephone: (502) 325-3061
New Hope, Kentucky 40052
Web site address: http://www.mich.com/~buffalo/
Areas of expertise: Abortion (education and sidewalk counseling)

Center for the Rights of the Terminally Ill (CRTI)

Post Office Box 54246
Hurst, Texas 76054
Telephone: (817) 656-5143
Area of expertise: Euthanasia

Christian Action Council (CAC)

109 Carpenter Drive, Suite 100
Sterling, Virginia 20164
Telephone: (703) 478-5661
Periodical: *CareNet Communication Brief*
Web site address: http://www.goshen.net/CareNet
Area of expertise: Abortion (crisis pregnancies and post-abortion counseling)

Christian Advocates Serving Evangelism (CASE)

Post Office Box 450349
Atlanta, Georgia 30345
Area of expertise: Legal defense of Christian activists

Christian Coalition

Pat Robertson
Post Office Box 1990
Chesapeake, Virginia 23320
Telephone: (800) 325-4746
Periodical: *Christian American*
Web site address: http://www.cc.org/
Area of expertise: Politics

Citizens United Resisting Euthanasia (CURE)

812 Stephen Street
Berkeley Springs, West Virginia 25411
Telephone: (304) 258-LIFE
Periodical: *Life matters*
Web site address: http://www.awinc.com/partners/ bc/compass/lifenet/
cureinfo.html
Area of expertise: Euthanasia

Collegians Activated to Liberate Life (CALL)

Post Office Box 259806
Madison, Wisconsin 53725
Telephone: (608) 256-CALL
FAX: (608) 256-8999
Area of expertise: Abortion (education)

Concerned Women for America (CWA)

Mrs. Beverly LaHaye
370 L'Enfant Promenade SW, Suite 800
Washington, DC 20004
Telephone: (202) 488-7000
Periodical: *Family Voice*
Web site address: http://www.cwfa.org
Area of expertise: Family issues

Couple to Couple League (CCL)

Post Office Box 111184
Cincinnati, Ohio 45211
Telephone: (513) 471-2000
Periodical: *Family Foundations*
Web site address: http://www.missionnet.com/~mission/cathlc/ccl/index.html
Areas of expertise: Breastfeeding and NFP

Eagle Forum

Mrs. Phyllis Schlafly
Post Office Box 618
Alton, Illinois 62002
Periodical: *The Schlafly Report* and *Educational Reporter*
Web site address: http://www.eagleforum.org
Telephone: (618) 462-5415
Areas of expertise: Family issues and politics

Educational Research Analysts

Mel and Norma Gabler
Post Office Box 7518
Longview, Texas 65601
Area of expertise: Monitoring public school textbooks

Elliott Institute

David Reardon
Post Office Box 7348
Springfield, Illinois 62971-7348
Telephone: (217) 546-9522 or 1-(800)-634-2224
Periodical: *Post-Abortion Review*
Area of expertise: Abortion (post-abortion trauma)

Family Research Council (FRC)

700 13th Street NW
Washington, DC 20005
Telephone: (202) 393-2100
Periodicals: *Washington Watch* and *Family Policy*
Web site address: http://www.frc.org/
Areas of expertise: Pro-family legislation and education

Feminists for Life of America

733 15th Street, NW Suite 1100
Washington, DC 20005
Telephone: (202) 737-3352
Area of expertise: Abortion (authentic feminist viewpoint)

Focus on the Family

Dr. James Dobson
8655 Explorer Drive
Colorado Springs, Colorado 80920
Telephone: (719) 531-3400
FAX: (719) 531-3499
Periodicals: *Citizen* and *Focus on the Family Physician*
Web site address: http://iclnet93.iclnet.org at pub/resources/text/focus
Areas of expertise: Abortion (education), chastity and family issues

Free Speech Advocates (FSA)

6375 New Hope Road
New Hope, Kentucky 40052
Telephone: (502) 549-5454
Area of expertise: Constitutional law (First and Fourteenth Amendments)

Home School Legal Defense Association (HSLDA)

Paeonian Springs, Virginia 20129
Telephone: (540) 338-5600
Periodical: *The Home School Court Report*
Area of expertise: Home schooling (legal defense)

Human Life International (HLI)

4 Family Life
Front Royal, Virginia, 22630
Telephone: (540) 635-7884
FAX: (540) 636-7363
Periodicals: *HLI Reports, HLI Special Reports* and *HLI Update*
Web site address: http://www.hli.org/
Areas of expertise: Abortion (international), contraception, euthanasia, sex education and natural family planning

International Anti-Euthanasia Task Force (IAETF)

Post Office Box 760
Steubenville, Ohio 43952
Telephone: (614) 282-3810
Area of expertise: Euthanasia

International Association of Parents and Professionals for Safe Alternatives in Childbirth (NAPSAC) *

Route 1, Box 646
Marble Hill, Missouri 63764
Telephone: (314) 238-2010
Area of expertise: Breastfeeding

Jewish Anti-Abortion League

Post Office Box 262
Gravesend Station
Brooklyn, New York 11223
Telephone: (718) 336-0053
Area of expertise: Abortion

Jews Opposing Euthanasia

Rabbi Yonah Fortner
National Synagogue of the Physically Handicapped
6451 Charlesworth Avenue
North Hollywood, California 91606
Telephone: (818) 985-2429
Area of expertise: Euthanasia

JUDEA

2723 Avenue J
Brooklyn, New York 11210
Telephone: (718) 258-8675
Area of expertise: Pro-life/pro-family issues (education and Jewish outreach)

La Leche League International (LLLI) *

96616 Minneapolis Avenue
Post Office Box 1209
Franklin Park, Illinois 60131
Telephone: (312) 455-7730
Area of expertise: Breastfeeding

Lawyers for Life

Post Office Box 26275
Kansas City, Missouri 64196
Telephone: (816) 221-1617
Areas of expertise: Legal aid and networking

Legal Action for Women (LAW)

Post Office Box 11061
Pensacola, Florida 32524-1061
Telephone: 1-800-962-2319 or 1-800-UCANSUE
Periodical: *Abortion Malpractice Report*
Area of expertise: Abortion (lawsuits against abortionists)

Life After Assault League (LAAL)

1336 West Lindberg Street
Appleton, Wisconsin 54914
Telephone: (414) 739-4489
Area of expertise: Assisting women who are victims of rape or incest

Life Dynamics Incorporated (LDI)

Mark Crutcher
Post Office Box 2226
Denton, Texas 76202
Telephone: (817) 380-8800
FAX (817) 380-8700
Periodical: *Life Activist News*
Area of expertise: Abortion (education, research and lawsuits against abortionists)

Life Education And Resource Network (LEARN)

Reverend Johnny Hunter
Post Office Box 6357
Virginia Beach, Virginia 23456
Areas of expertise: Abortion and chastity education for African-Americans

Lutherans for Life

Post Office Box 819
Benton, Arkansas 72015
Telephone: (501) 794-2212 or 1-(800) 729-9535
Area of expertise: Abortion

Methodists for Life

109 East Mill Street #2
Yale, Michigan 48097
Telephone: (313) 387-2452
Area of expertise: Abortion

National Association for Abstinence Education (NAAE)

6201 Leesburg Pike, Suite 404
Falls Church, Virginia 22044
Telephone: (703) 532-9459
Area of expertise: Chastity education

National Association of Evangelicals

1023 15th Street NW, Suite 500
Washington, DC 20005
Telephone: (202) 789-1011
Web site address: http://nae.goshen.net/
Area of expertise: Constitutional law (First Amendment)

National Chastity Association

Post Office Box 402
Oak Forest, Illinois 60452
Telephone: (708) 687-1767
Area of expertise: Chastity education

National Conference of Catholic Bishops (NCCB)

Secretariat for Pro-Life Activities
3211 4th Street NE
Washington, DC 20017-1106
Telephone: (202) 541-3070
Periodical: *Life at Risk*
Areas of expertise: Abortion (education) and euthanasia

National Democrats for Life

1500 Massachusetts Avenue NW
Washington, DC 20005
Telephone: (202) 463-0940
Area of expertise: Politics

National Legal Center for the Medically Dependent and Disabled

Post Office Box 441069
Indianapolis, Indiana 46204
Telephone: (317) 632-6245
Periodical: *Issues in Law and Medicine.*
Area of expertise: Euthanasia

National Organization of Episcopalians for Life (NOEL)

10523 Main Street, Suite 35
Fairfax, Virginia 22030
Telephone: (703) 591-6635
Area of expertise: Abortion

National Organization for Post-Abortion Reconciliation and Healing (NOPARH)

St. John's Center
3680 Kinnickinnic Avenue
Milwaukee, Wisconsin 53207
Telephone: (414) 483-4141 or 1-800-593-2273
Area of expertise: Abortion (post-abortion trauma and counseling)

National Pro-Life Religious Council

1430 K Street NW, #500
Washington, DC 20005
Telephone: (202) 393-0703
Area of expertise: Abortion

National Right to Life Committee (NRLC)

419 7th Street NW
Washington, DC 20004
Telephone: (202) 626-8800
FAX: (202) 737-9189
Periodical: *NRL News*
Web site address: http://www.nrlc.org/nrlc
Areas of expertise: Abortion (education and legislation) and euthanasia

Northwest Family Services

Rose Fuller
4805 NE Glisan Street, Suite #238
Portland, Oregon 97213
Telephone: (503) 215-6377
Areas of expertise: Chastity and NFP

Nursing Mothers Counsel *

Post Office Box 50063
Palo Alto, California 94303
Area of expertise: Breastfeeding

Open ARMS (Abortion Related Ministries)

Post Office Box 1056
Columbia, Missouri 65205
Telephone: (314) 449-7672
Area of expertise: Abortion (post-abortion trauma)

Orthodox Christians for Life

Box 805
Melville, New York 11747
Telephone: (516) 271-4408
Area of expertise: Abortion

Pharmacists for Life International (PFLI)

Bogomir Kuhar
Post Office Box 1281
Powell, Ohio 43065-1281
Telephone: 1-(800) 227-8359
FAX: (614) 881-5520
Periodical: *Beginnings*
Areas of expertise: Contraceptives and abortion (abortifacients)

Physicians for Compassionate Care (PCC)

William Toffler, M.D., President
716 SW Cheltenham Street
Portland, Oregon 97201
Telephone: (503) 245-0919
Area of expertise: Euthanasia (education and politics)

Pope Paul VI Institute

Thomas W. Hilgers, M.D.
6901 Mercy Road
Omaha, Nebraska 68106
Telephone: (402) 390-6600
FAX: (402) 390-9851
Area of expertise: NFP

Population Research Institute

Steven Mosher
5119A Leesburg Pike #295
Falls Church, Virginia 22041
Periodical: *PRI Review*
Web site address: http://www.pop.org
Areas of expertise: Abortion (international) and population control

Presbyterians Pro-Life

Box 11130
Burke, Virginia 22009-1130
Telephone: (703) 569-9474
Area of expertise: Abortion

Priests for Life

Fr. Frank Pavone
Post Office Box 307
Rochester, New York 10573-0307
Telephone: (914) 937-8243
Periodical: *Priests for Life*
Web site address: http://www.priestsforlife.org
Area of expertise: Abortion (education of priests)

Project Rachel

C/O Milwaukee Archdiocese
Post Office Box 2018
Milwaukee, Wisconsin 53207
Telephone: (414) 769-3391
Area of expertise: Abortion (post-abortion trauma)

Pro-Life Action League

Joe Scheidler
6160 N. Cicero Avenue #210
Chicago, Illinois 60646
Telephone: (312) 777-2900
Area of expertise: Abortion (education and direct action)

Protestants Against Birth Control (PABC)

2654 Kinnickinnic Avenue
Milwaukee, Wisconsin 53207-2151
Telephone: (414) 483-3399
Area of expertise: Contraception and abortion (abortifacients)

Republican National Coalition for Life

5009 Harvest Hill Road
Dallas, Texas 75244
Telephones: (214) 387-3830 or (214) 387-4160
Area of expertise: Abortion (education and politics)

The Rockford Institute

934 North Main Street
Rockford, Illinois 61103-7061
Telephone: (815) 964-5053
Periodical: *Religion and Society*
Area of expertise: Family issues

Rutherford Institute

1445 East Rio Road
Charlottesville, Virginia 22906-7482
Telephone: (804) 978-3888
Area of expertise: Litigation (defense of free speech)

Seton Home Study School

1350 Progress Drive
Front Royal, Virginia 22630
Telephone: (540) 636-9990
Periodical: *Seton Home Study School*
Area of expertise: Home schooling

Stop Planned Parenthood International (STOPP)

Jim Sedlak
Post Office Box 8
La Grangeville, New York 12540
Telephone: (914) 473-3316
Periodical: *The Ryan Report*
Area of expertise: Abortion (research and local activism against Planned Parenthood)

United Church of Christ Friends for Life

Post Office Box 255
Tellford, Pennsylvania 18969
Telephone: (215) 257-6328
Area of expertise: Abortion

Victims of Choice (VOC)

124 Shefield Drive or Post Office Box 6268
Vacaville, California 95688
Telephone: (707) 448-6015
Area of expertise: Abortion (post-abortion trauma)

Women Exploited by Abortion (WEBA)

Route 1, Box 821
Venus, Texas 76084
Telephone: (214) 366-3600
Area of expertise: Abortion (post-abortion trauma and counseling)

Women for Faith and Family (WFF)

Post Office Box 8326
St. Louis, Missouri 63132
Telephone: (314) 863-8385
Area of expertise: Family issues

World Federation of Doctors Who Respect Human Life

Box 508
Oak Park, Illinois 60303
Telephone: (708) 848-3835
Area of expertise: Physicians opposing opposition and euthanasia

The Facts of Life

Appendix B

Demographic Summaries of the World's Nations

Continental and Regional

Continent and Region Names (Number of Nations)	1997 Population	Land Area (Sq. Kilometers)
North America (2)	297,711,000	19,348,753
Central America (8)	131,890,000	2,481,366
The Caribbean (12)	35,979,000	230,500
South America (14)	328,073,000	17,794,598
THE AMERICAS (36)	**793,654,000**	**39,855,217**
Northern Europe (10)	94,455,000	1,744,547
Western Europe (7)	182,231,000	1,107,505
Eastern Europe (6)	97,451,000	882,056
Southern Europe (12)	148,088,000	1,315,347
Former USSR (12)	292,043,000	22,100,900
EUROPE (47)	**814,268,000**	**27,150,355**
Northern Africa (7)	170,523,000	8,526,767
Western Africa (17)	213,470,000	6,139,188
Central Africa (8)	85,009,000	6,612,253
Eastern Africa (16)	237,700,000	6,355,347
Southern Africa (5)	53,741,000	2,674,778
AFRICA (53)	**760,444,000**	**30,308,333**
Western Asia (16)	160,929,000	4,540,340
Central Asia (9)	1,378,048,000	6,781,478
Southern Asia (10)	530,783,000	4,488,032
Eastern Asia (7)	1,430,943,000	11,761,877
ASIA (42)	**3,500,704,000**	**27,571,727**
Australia and N.Z. (2)	22,209,000	7,984,349
Island Nations (11)	7,231,000	554,878
OCEANIA (13)	**29,440,000**	**8,539,227**
WORLD TOTALS (191)	**5,898,509,000**	**133,424,860**
Developed Countries (58)	**1,052,813,000**	**35,623,761**
Developing Countries (133)	**4,845,697,000**	**97,801,098**

Summaries

Population Density (Persons/Sq. km.)	Total Fertility Rates			1997 Population Growth Rate (percent)
	1965	1997	1965-1995 Change	
15	2.0	2.1	6%	1.0
53	7.9	3.1	-61%	2.0
156	5.3	2.6	-50%	1.2
18	5.6	2.6	-52%	1.4
20	**4.6**	**2.5**	**-45%**	**1.4**
54	2.1	1.9	-11%	0.3
165	2.0	1.6	-22%	0.5
110	2.5	2.0	-21%	0.2
113	3.1	1.3	-58%	0.3
13	2.9	2.3	-22%	0.5
30	**2.6**	**1.9**	**-29%**	**0.4**
20	7.4	4.1	-44%	2.3
35	7.0	6.5	-8%	3.1
13	6.2	6.5	6%	2.8
37	7.2	6.5	-9%	2.8
20	6.2	3.9	-36%	2.6
25	**7.0**	**5.8**	**-17%**	**2.8**
35	6.7	4.5	-33%	2.7
203	6.4	4.1	-36%	2.1
118	6.2	3.0	-52%	1.7
122	5.9	1.8	-70%	0.9
127	**6.2**	**3.0**	**-52%**	**1.6**
3	2.8	1.8	-36%	1.2
13	6.0	4.1	-32%	2.2
3	**3.6**	**2.4**	**-34%**	**1.4**
44	**5.6**	**3.1**	**-44%**	**1.5**
30	**2.5**	**1.9**	**-24%**	**0.7**
50	**6.2**	**3.4**	**-46%**	**1.7**

The Facts of Life

National Summaries (See notes by column,

Nation	1997 Population	Land Area (Sq. Kilometers)
North America		
Canada	29,127,000	9,976,139
United States	268,584,000	9,372,614
Central America		
Belize	224,000	22,965
Costa Rica	3,576,000	51,100
El Salvador	6,102,000	21,041
Guatemala	11,530,000	108,889
Honduras	5,751,000	112,088
Mexico	97,490,000	1,958,201
Nicaragua	4,435,000	130,000
Panama	2,781,000	77,082
The Caribbean		
Bahamas	286,000	13,878
Barbados	257,000	430
Cuba	11,357,000	110,861
Dominican Republic	8,252,000	48,734
Guadaloupe	446,000	1,760
Haiti	6,804,000	27,750
Jamaica	2,643,000	10,990
Martinique	407,000	1,060
Puerto Rico	3,889,000	8,897
St. Lucia	147,000	622

pp. 374-375)

Population Density (Persons/Sq. km.)	Total Fertility Rates			Abortion Law Status	1997 Population Growth Rate (percent)
	1965	1997	1965-1995 Change		
3	2.1	1.8	-16%	F	1.2
29	2.0	2.1	+8%	F	1.0
10	3.6	2.7	-27%	F	2.4
70	4.8	2.9	-41%	B	2.3
290	7.1	3.6	-49%	B	2.0
106	6.9	5.2	-26%	A	2.5
51	8.5	4.4	-48%	A	2.7
50	8.2	2.7	-67%	B	1.9
34	7.6	4.6	-39%	A	2.7
36	5.9	2.5	-57%	A	1.9
21	2.3	2.2	-7%	C	1.5
598	4.0	3.3	-16%	F	0.2
102	4.5	1.6	-64%	F	0.9
169	6.7	2.9	-57%	A	1.8
253	4.5	3.9	-14%	C	1.4
245	6.2	4.6	-26%	C	1.6
241	6.5	2.0	-69%	F	1.1
384	3.6	2.8	-22%	C	1.2
437	3.6	2.0	-45%	F	0.6
237	4.2	3.6	-15%	F	0.6

National Summaries (continued)

Nation	1997 Population	Land Area (Sq. Kilometers)

The Caribbean (continued)

Nation	1997 Population	Land Area (Sq. Kilometers)
St. Vincent/Grenadines	119,000	388
Trinidad and Tobago	1,373,000	5,130

South America

Nation	1997 Population	Land Area (Sq. Kilometers)
Argentina	35,033,000	2,766,889
Bolivia	8,230,000	1,089,581
Brazil	164,320,000	8,511,965
Chile	14,583,000	756,945
Colombia	37,380,000	1,138,914
Ecuador	11,323,000	283,561
French Guiana	156,000	86,117
Guyana	720,000	214,969
Netherlands Antilles	189,000	960
Paraguay	5,641,000	406,752
Peru	24,927,000	1,285,216
Suriname	443,000	163,265
Uruguay	3,265,000	177,414
Venezuela	21,862,000	912,050

Northern Europe

Nation	1997 Population	Land Area (Sq. Kilometers)
Denmark	5,218,000	43,077
Estonia	1,640,000	45,100
Finland	5,112,000	338,127
Iceland	269,000	103,000

Population Density (Persons/Sq. km.)	Total Fertility Rates			Abortion Law Status	1997 Population Growth Rate (percent)
	1965	1997	1965-1995 Change		
306	3.8	2.0	-48%	F	0.8
268	3.8	2.5	-34%	B	1.1
13	3.4	2.7	-19%	B	1.1
8	7.3	4.2	-42%	B	2.2
19	5.6	2.5	-56%	A	1.2
19	4.0	2.5	-37%	A	1.5
33	5.7	2.4	-59%	A	1.7
40	7.3	3.2	-57%	B	2.0
2	5.0	3.1	-39%	B	4.0
3	6.1	2.2	-64%	F	-0.5
197	4.7	2.2	-53%	F	0.5
14	6.3	4.0	-36%	A	2.7
19	7.2	3.2	-56%	B	1.8
3	6.7	2.3	-66%	B	1.6
18	3.3	2.2	-35%	C	0.7
24	5.9	2.8	-53%	A	2.1
121	2.1	1.6	-23%	F	0.2
36	2.2	2.1	-7%	F	0.5
15	1.5	1.9	+21%	F	0.3
3	3.0	2.1	-32%	F	0.8

National Summaries (continued)

Nation	1997 Population	Land Area (Sq. Kilometers)
Northern Europe (continued)		
Ireland	3,573,000	70,284
Latvia	2,791,000	64,500
Lithuania	3,928,000	62,500
Norway	4,349,000	323,895
Sweden	8,906,000	449,964
United Kingdom	58,669,000	244,100
Western Europe		
Austria	8,074,000	83,853
Belgium	10,122,000	30,519
France	58,726,000	551,500
Germany	82,068,000	356,910
Luxembourg	411,000	2,586
Netherlands	15,645,000	40,844
Switzerland	7,185,000	41,293
Eastern Europe		
Bulgaria	8,726,000	110,912
Czech Republic	10,472,000	78,907
Hungary	10,365,000	93,032
Poland	39,139,000	312,677
Romania	23,265,000	237,500
Slovakia	5,484,000	49,027

Population Density (Persons/Sq. km.)	Total Fertility Rates			Abortion Law Status	1997 Population Growth Rate (percent)
	1965	1997	1965-1995 Change		
51	4.7	1.8	-61%	B	0.3
43	2.0	2.0	—	F	0.5
63	2.4	1.9	-20%	F	0.7
13	2.4	1.9	-20%	F	0.3
20	1.8	2.2	+17%	F	0.5
240	2.0	1.9	-8%	F	0.3
96	2.2	1.4	-37%	F	0.5
332	2.0	1.7	-16%	F	0.2
106	2.5	1.7	-32%	F	0.5
230	1.6	1.5	-10%	F	0.4
159	3.1	1.8	-42%	F	0.8
383	2.1	1.6	-23%	F	0.6
174	1.8	1.7	-9%	B	0.7
79	2.4	1.7	-27%	F	- 0.3
133	2.4	1.9	-20%	F	0.2
111	2.2	1.7	-22%	F	0.1
125	2.4	2.1	-14%	B	0.4
98	2.8	2.0	-29%	F	0.1
112	2.4	1.9	-20%	F	0.5

National Summaries (continued)

Nation	1997 Population	Land Area (Sq. Kilometers)
Southern Europe		
Albania	3,483,000	28,748
Bosnia and Herzogovina	4,750,000	51,125
Croatia	4,713,000	56,546
Greece	10,766,000	131,990
Italy	58,485,000	301,268
Macedonia	2,274,000	25,712
Malta	376,000	316
Montenegro	682,000	13,806
Portugal	10,655,000	92,389
Serbia	10,241,000	88,438
Slovenia	1,984,000	20,227
Spain	39,680,000	504,782
Former USSR		
Armenia	3,608,000	29,800
Azerbaijan	7,975,000	86,600
Belarus	10,495,000	207,600
Georgia	5,816,000	69,700
Kazakhstan	17,641,000	2,717,300
Kyrgyzstan	4,910,000	198,500
Moldova	4,528,000	33,700
Russia	150,498,000	17,075,400
Tajikistan	6,467,000	143,100
Turkmenistan	4,238,000	488,100
Ukraine	51,821,000	603,700

Population Density (Persons/Sq. km.)	Total Fertility Rates			Abortion Law Status	1997 Populatio Growth R (percer
	1965	1997	1965-1995 Change		
121	5.7	2.4	-59%	F	1
93	2.5	1.8	-26%	F	
83	2.5	1.8	-26%	F	
82	2.7	1.3	-50%	F	
194	2.8	1.1	-60%	F	
88	2.5	1.8	-26%	F	
1,189	3.6	2.4	-32%	A	
49	3.0	1.6	-44%	F	
115	3.5	1.3	-63%	B	
116	2.5	1.8	-26%	F	
98	2.4	1.7	-27%	F	
79	3.7	1.2	-69%	B	
121	5.1	2.3	-55%		
92	4.5	2.6	-43%		
51	2.3	2.0	-14%		
83	2.4	2.1	-14%		
6	4.1	2.8	-31%		
25	5.1	3.8	-25%		
134	2.9	2.6	-11%		
9	2.4	2.1	-14%		
45	5.9	4.2	-30%		
9	3.0	1.9	-38		
86	2.3	2.0	-1		

A
E$
Li
Mo
Suc
Tun
West

West

Benin
Burkina
Cape Ve
Cote d'I
Gambia,
Ghana
Guinea
Guinea-Bis
Liberia
Mali
Mauritania
Niger

National Summaries (continued)

Nation	1997 Population	Land Area (Sq. Kilometers)
Former USSR (continued)		
Uzbekistan	24,046,000	447,400
Northern Africa		
lgeria	29,735,000	2,381,741
ypt	63,292,000	1,001,449
ya	5,635,000	1,759,540
rocco	30,378,000	446,550
an	32,085,000	2,505,813
sia	9,169,000	163,610
ern Sahara	228,000	268,064
ern Africa		
	5,884,000	112,622
Faso	10,961,000	274,200
rde	461,000	4,033
oire	15,784,000	322,463
he	1,051,000	11,295
	18,795,000	238,533
	6,804,000	245,857
au	1,179,000	36,125
	3,428,000	111,369
	9,905,000	1,240,192
	2,410,000	1,025,520
	9,567,000	1,267,000

Population Density (Persons/Sq. km.)	Total Fertility Rates			Abortion Law Status	1997 Population Growth Rate (percent)
	1965	1997	1965-1995 Change		
54	5.3	3.4	-37%	F	2.1
12	8.5	4.4	-48%	C	2.2
63	6.1	3.8	-38%	A	2.2
3	8.1	6.1	-24%	A	3.7
68	8.8	3.0	-66%	B	2.1
13	7.0	5.6	-21%	B	2.8
56	8.3	2.2	-74%	F	1.7
1	6.1	5.3	-13%	B	2.5
52	7.1	7.1	—	A	3.3
40	6.4	6.5	+3%	A	2.7
114	3.1	1.8	-42%	F	2.9
49	7.4	7.4	—	A	3.4
93	6.6	6.0	-10%	F	3.1
79	6.8	5.9	-14%	F	3.0
28	7.0	7.0	—	F	2.2
33	5.3	5.9	+12%	F	2.4
31	6.8	6.8	—	F	4.5
8	7.1	7.1	—	A	2.8
2	6.5	6.5	—	A	3.2
8	7.1	7.1	—	A	3.5

National Summaries (continued)

Nation	1997 Population	Land Area (Sq. Kilometers)
Western Africa		
Nigeria	107,824,000	923,768
Sao Tome and Principe	147,000	964
Senegal	9,562,000	196,722
Sierra Leone	4,979,000	71,740
Togo	4,729,000	56,785
Central Africa		
Angola	10,785,000	1,246,700
Cameroon	14,301,000	475,442
Central African Republic	3,327,000	622,984
Chad	5,815,000	1,284,000
Congo	2,616,000	342,000
Equatorial Guinea	442,000	28,051
Gabon	1,187,000	267,667
Zaire	46,535,000	2,345,409
Eastern Africa		
Burundi	6,529,000	27,834
Comoros	588,000	2,235
Djibouti	435,000	23,200
Ethiopia and Eritrea	64,117,000	1,221,900
Kenya	30,688,000	580,367
Madagascar	14,752,000	587,041
Malawi	10,518,000	118,484

Population Density (Persons/Sq. km.)	Total Fertility Rates			Abortion Law Status	1997 Population Growth Rate (percent)
	1965	1997	1965-1995 Change		
117	7.1	6.3	-11%	A	3.2
153	7.1	5.4	-25%	B	2.6
49	7.3	5.9	-20%	A	3.1
69	6.5	6.5	—	B	2.5
83	6.6	6.6	—	A	3.6
9	6.4	7.4	+15%	C	3.1
30	6.5	5.6	-15%	B	2.9
5	5.5	6.3	+14%	A	2.0
5	6.0	5.9	-3%	A	2.1
8	6.3	6.3	—	B	2.3
16	5.6	6.0	6%	A	2.6
4	4.0	5.6	+40%	A	1.4
20	6.2	6.8	+10%	A	3.0
235	6.8	6.8	—	B	2.2
263	3.6	2.4	-32%	B	3.5
19	6.6	6.6	—	A	2.0
52	6.7	7.1	5%	B	3.1
53	8.8	5.9	-33%	A	2.9
25	6.6	6.6	—	A	3.2
89	7.3	7.7	+4%	B	1.7

National Summaries (continued)

Nation	1997 Population	Land Area (Sq. Kilometers)

Eastern Africa (continued)

Nation	1997 Population	Land Area (Sq. Kilometers)
Mauritius	1,157,000	2,040
Mozambique	18,898,000	801,590
Reunion	693,000	2,500
Rwanda	9,054,000	26,338
Somalia	7,361,000	637,657
Tanzania	30,119,000	945,087
Uganda	21,352,000	235,880
Zambia	9,891,000	752,614
Zimbabwe	11,548,000	390,580

Southern Africa

Nation	1997 Population	Land Area (Sq. Kilometers)
Botswana	1,458,000	581,730
Lesotho	2,085,000	30,355
Namibia	1,762,000	824,292
South Africa	47,420,000	1,221,037
Swaziland	1,017,000	17,364

Western Asia (Middle East)

Nation	1997 Population	Land Area (Sq. Kilometers)
Bahrain	634,000	678
Cyprus	749,000	9,251
Gaza Strip	810,000	381
Iraq	21,483,000	438,317
Israel	5,430,000	20,770
Jordan	4,439,000	97,740

Population Density (Persons/Sq. km.)	Total Fertility Rates			Abortion Law Status	1997 Population Growth Rate (percent)
	1965	1997	1965-1995 Change		
567	3.9	1.8	-55%	A	1.1
24	6.6	6.0	-10%	F	3.7
277	4.6	3.7	-21%	A	2.0
344	8.2	8.6	+4%	B	2.7
12	7.2	6.4	-11%	A	3.1
32	7.1	5.9	-16%	B	2.5
91	6.8	7.4	+9%	B	2.5
13	7.1	6.2	-14%	C	2.6
30	8.4	4.2	-49%	B	1.6
3	7.7	4.7	-38%	A	2.4
69	6.1	4.5	-27%	A	2.4
2	6.0	6.0	—	F	3.4
39	6.1	3.8	-38%	F	2.6
59	7.2	4.6	-36%	B	2.9
936	2.7	2.2	-18%	F	2.8
81	4.5	3.9	-14%	F	0.9
2,126	2.5	1.8	-26%	F	3.5
49	7.7	5.4	-30%	F	2.9
261	4.2	2.7	-35%	F	2.5
45	8.7	5.3	-39%	F	3.8

National Summaries (continued)

Nation	1997 Population	Land Area (Sq. Kilometers)

Western Asia (Middle East) (continued)

Nation	1997 Population	Land Area (Sq. Kilometers)
Kuwait	1,809,000	17,818
Lebanon	3,845,000	10,400
Oman	1,887,000	212,457
Qatar	549,000	11,000
Saudi Arabia	19,826,000	2,149,690
Syria	16,582,000	185,180
Turkey	65,918,000	779,452
United Arab Emirates	3,181,000	83,600
West Bank	1,556,000	5,638
Yemen	12,232,000	517,968

Central Asia

Nation	1997 Population	Land Area (Sq. Kilometers)
Afghanistan	20,202,000	652,090
Bangladesh	133,896,000	143,998
Bhutan	1,861,000	47,000
India	969,963,000	3,287,590
Iran	71,879,000	1,648,000
Maldives	279,000	298
Nepal	22,578,000	140,797
Pakistan	138,753,000	796,095
Sri Lanka	18,636,000	65,610

Southern Asia

Nation	1997 Population	Land Area (Sq. Kilometers)
Cambodia	11,272,000	181,035

Population Density (Persons/Sq. km.)	Total Fertility Rates			Abortion Law Status	1997 Population Growth Rate (percent)
	1965	1997	1965-1995 Change		
102	8.6	3.2	-63%	F	1.6
370	5.8	2.8	-52%	A	2.0
9	7.4	6.6	-11%	A	3.5
50	7.0	5.3	-25%	A	2.4
9	7.6	6.2	-19%	B	3.0
90	8.3	5.9	-29%	A	3.7
85	5.7	3.2	-43%	F	2.0
38	7.2	4.1	-43%	A	4.6
276	2.4	2.1	-14%	F	2.6
24	8.0	7.1	-12%	A	3.3
31	7.2	6.9	-4%	A	5.2
930	8.0	4.3	-47%	A	2.3
40	6.0	5.9	-3%	B	2.3
295	6.1	3.6	-41%	F	1.8
44	6.7	5.9	-12%	A	3.2
936	4.0	3.2	-20%	B	3.5
160	6.9	5.3	-23%	F	2.4
174	7.3	6.0	-18%	B	2.6
284	4.7	2.2	-53%	A	1.1
62	5.9	4.3	-27%	A	3.3

National Summaries (continued)

Nation	1997 Population	Land Area (Sq. Kilometers)
Southern Asia (continued)		
Indonesia	210,161,000	1,904,569
Laos	5,103,000	236,800
Malaysia	20,559,000	329,749
Myanmar (Burma)	46,670,000	658,190
Philippines	73,817,000	300,000
Singapore	2,952,000	618
Taiwan	21,862,000	32,267
Thailand	61,592,000	513,115
Viet Nam	76,795,000	331,689
Eastern Asia		
China, People's Rep.	1,225,400,000	9,596,961
Hong Kong	5,553,000	1,045
Japan	126,215,000	377,801
Macau	501,000	16
Mongolia	2,623,000	1,566,500
North Korea	24,226,000	120,538
South Korea	46,426,000	99,016
Oceania		
Australia	18,772,000	7,713,363
Brunei Darussalam	307,000	5,765
Fiji	791,000	18,274
French Polynesia	229,000	3,650

Population Density (Persons/Sq. km.)	Total Fertility Rates			Abortion Law Status	1997 Population Growth Rate (percent)
	1965	1997	1965-1995 Change		
110	6.1	2.7	-55%	A	1.6
22	6.0	6.8	+13%	A	2.8
62	5.9	3.3	-44%	F	2.2
71	6.5	3.9	-40%	A	1.8
246	6.2	3.6	-42%	A	1.9
4,777	3.0	1.6	-44%	F	1.1
678	4.2	1.5	-64%	F	0.9
120	6.7	1.8	-73%	B	1.2
232	6.8	3.5	-48%	F	1.7
128	6.3	1.8	-71%	F	1.0
5,314	2.4	1.3	-48%	B	0.0
334	2.3	1.6	-29%	F	0.3
31,325	2.3	2.4	+7%	B	1.2
2	6.3	4.3	-31%	F	2.6
201	7.7	1.9	-75%	F	1.7
469	5.5	1.5	-73%	C	1.0
2	2.8	1.8	-36%	F	1.3
53	4.5	3.9	-14%	A	2.6
43	4.7	2.8	-42%	F	1.1
63	5.3	2.1	-61%	C	2.2

National Summaries (continued)

Nation	1997 Population	Land Area (Sq. Kilometers)

Oceania (continued)

Nation	1997 Population	Land Area (Sq. Kilometers)
Guam	161,000	541
Micronesia	128,000	704
New Caledonia	190,000	18,441
New Zealand	3,437,000	270,986
Papua New Guinea	4,492,000	462,840
Solomon Islands	426,000	28,896
Tonga	107,000	747
Vanuatu	181,000	12,189
Western Samoa	219,000	2,831

···

Notes by Column

Column (1): Countries are arranged by continent and region in accordance with United Nations standard protocol.

Column (2): 1997 estimated populations of each nation, based on historical 1995 data and projected 2000 data. 1997 figures are calculated by using the projected population growth rate for the time period 1990-2000. Reference: U.S. Department of Commerce, Bureau of the Census. Reference Data Book and Guide to Sources, *Statistical Abstract of the United States*. Washington, D.C.: U.S. Government Printing Office, 1993 (113th Edition). Table 1,374, "Population, By Country, 1980, 1990, and Projections: 2000." Only those countries, sovereignties, and dependencies with a projected 1997 population of more than 100,000 are tallied; these 191 countries account for 99.98% of the world's total population and 97.93% of its total land area.

Column (3): National land area in square kilometers. United Nations. *Statistical Yearbook* (38th Edition). New York: United Nations, 1993. Table 11, "Population by Sex, Rate of Population Increase, Surface Area and Density."

Columns (5) and (6): Total Fertility Rate (TFR) means the average number of children that would be born to all women in a country if they all lived to the end of their childbearing years (ages 15-44). Source of TFR information: The World Resources Institute, in Collaboration with the United Nations Environment Program and the United Nations Development Program. *World Resources 1994-5: Guide to the Global Environment*. New York: Oxford University Press, 1994. Table 16.2, "Trends in Births, Life

Population Density (Persons/Sq. km.)	Total Fertility Rates			Abortion Law Status	1997 Population Growth Rate (percent)
	1965	1997	1965-1995 Change		
297	4.9	3.1	-37%	F	2.4
181	6.6	4.5	-32%	C	2.0
10	3.5	2.2	-37%	B	1.7
13	3.1	2.0	-37%	F	0.5
10	6.6	4.6	-30%	B	2.3
15	8.0	5.0	-37%	F	3.4
144	3.8	2.6	-30%	B	0.8
15	3.3	2.5	-25%	B	2.2
77	3.4	2.6	-24%	F	2.3

Expectancy, Fertility and Age Structure, 1970-95." Total fertility rates given in the table are for the periods 1970-1975 and 1990-1995. These rates are assumed to be representative of their midpoints, i.e., 1972 and 1992. The 1965 and 1997 rates are exponentially extrapolated using the average 1972-1992 rate.

Column (8): Abortion law status. The following categories are shown;

A — full protection or rigidly controlled life of the mother exception

B — exceptions *not* including mother's mental and physical health, such as rape and incest or eugenics

C — exceptions including mother's mental and physical health (practical abortion on demand)

F — abortion on demand under the law.

References: (1) United Nations. *Abortion Policies: A Global Review* (three volumes). New York: United Nations, 1993. (2) International Planned Parenthood Federation. Wall chart entitled "Abortion Laws Worldwide." England: IPPF, 1993, and updates.

Column (9): U.S. Department of Commerce, Bureau of the Census. Reference Data Book and Guide to Sources, *Statistical Abstract of the United States*. Washington, D.C.: U.S. Government Printing Office, 1993 (113th Edition). Table 1,374, "Population, By Country, 1980, 1990, and Projections: 2000."

The Facts of Life

Pro-Abortion and/or Population Control Organizations

Academy for Educational Development (AED)[1]
African Center for Applied Research on Population and Development[3]
African Development Bank[3]
African Development Foundation[3]
African Institute for Economic and Social Development[3]
African Institute for Economic Development and Planning[3]
African Medical and Research Foundation[3]
African Social Studies Programme[3]
Africare, Inc.[1]
AIDS Coalition to Unleash Power (ACT-UP)
Alan Guttmacher Institute (AGI)[1]
American Academy of Child Psychiatry (AACP)
American Academy of Health Administration (AAHA)[2]
American Academy of Pediatrics (AAP)[2]
American Association for the Advancement of Science (AAAS)[2]
American Association of Maternal & Child Health
American Association of the United Nations (AAUN)
American Association of University Women (AAUW)[2]
American Atheists
American Baptist Churches USA[2]
American Bar Association (ABA)
American Civil Liberties Union (ACLU), Reproductive Freedom Project[1]
American College of Nurse-Midwives (ACNM)[3]
American College of Obstetrics and Gynecology (ACOG)
American College of Osteopathic Obstetricians and Gynecologists (ACOOG)
American College of Osteopathic Pediatricians (ACOP)[2]
American Ethical Union[2]
American Federation of Teachers (AFT)
American Friends Service Committee (AFSC)
American Gay Atheists (AGA)

American Genetic Association (AGA)[2]
American Group Psychotherapy Association (AGPA)
American Home Economics Association (AHEA)[2]
American Humanist Association (AHA)
American Indian Health Care Association
American Jewish Congress (AJC)
American Library Association (ALA)
American Medical Association (AMA)[2]
American Parents Committee
American Pharmaceutical Association[2]
American Protestant Hospital Association (APHA)
American Psychiatric Association (APA)[2]
American Psychoanalytic Association (APA)
American Psychological Association (APA)
American Public Health Association (APHA)[1]
American Society of Mammologists
American Student Medical Association (ASMA)
American Veterans Committee (AVC)
American Women's Medical Association (AWMA)
Americans Against Human Suffering (AAHS)
Americans for Democratic Action (ADA)[2]
Americans for Indian Opportunity
Americans United for Separation of Church and State
Animal Liberation Front (ALF)
Animal Rights Activists for Choice (ARAC)
Ansell Incorporated[3]
Arab Centre for Information Studies on Population, Development and
    Reconstruction[3]
Arab Gulf Programme for United Nations Development Organizations[3]
Asia and Pacific Programme for Development Training and Communication
    Planning[3]
Asia Foundation[1]
Asian and Pacific Development Center[3]
Asian Center for Population and Community Development[3]
Asian Development Bank[3]
Asian Forum of Parliamentarians on Population and Development[3]
Asian Institute of Management[3]
Asian Population and Development Association[3]
Associated Country Women of the World[3]
Association for Population/Family Planning and Information Centers (APFPIC)[1]
Association for Voluntary Surgical Contraception (AVSC, formerly AVS)[1,2]
Association of Planned Parenthood Physicians (APPP)
Association of Women in Psychology (AWP)
Australian International Development Assistance Bureau[3]
Australian National University, International Population Dynamics Program[3]

Baptist Joint Committee on Public Affairs
Belgian Administration for Development Co-operation[3]
Brown University, Population Studies and Training Center[3]
Canadian International Development Agency (CIDA)[3]
CARE, Inc.[2]
Caribbean Community[3]
Caribbean Epidemiology Centre[3]
Carnegie Foundation
'Catholics' for Free Choice (CFFC)[1]
Center for Constitutional Rights (CCR)
Center for Development and Population Activities (CDPA)
Center for Population Communications (CPC)
Center for Population Options (CPO), International Center on Adolescent
    Fertility[1]
Center for Reproductive Law and Policy (CRLP)
Center for War/Peace Studies[2]
Center for Women's Policy Studies
Central Conference of American Rabbis (CCAR)
Centre for Applied Research on Population and Development[3]
Centre for Development and Population Activities (CEDPA)[3]
Children's Aid Society
Children's Defense Fund (CDF)
Church of Satan
Citizen's Advisory Council on the Status of Women
Clergy Consultation on Abortion
Clergy Consultation Service
Coalition of Black Trade Unionists
Coalition of Concerned Black Americans
Coalition of Labor Union Women
Columbia University, Center for Population and Family Health[1,3]
Committee for International Cooperation in National Research in Demography
    (CICRED)[1]
Committee in Solidarity with the People of El Salvador (CISPES)
Common Cause
Concern for Dying (CFD)
Congressional Black Caucus
Constitutional Rights Foundation[2]
Consumer Action Now
Cornell University, The Population and Development Program[3]
Council for the Development of Economic and Social Research in Africa[3]
Council of Population and Environment[2]
Council on Economic Priorities[2]
Council on Environmental Quality[2]
D.K. Tyagi Fund[1]
Danish International Development Agency (DIDA)[3]

The Facts of Life

Development Associates, Inc.[1]
Development Services International of Canada (DSI)[1]
Dual & Associates, Inc.[1]
Early Money Is Like Yeast (EMILY)
East-West Population Institute, East-West Center[1]
Eastern Virginia Medical School, Contraceptive Research and Development
    Program (CONRAD)[3]
Education, Training and Research Association
Environmental Action (EA)
Environmental Policy Center (EPC)
European Association for Population Studies[3]
Family Care International, Inc. (FCI)[1]
Family Health International (FHI)[1]
Family Planning International Assistance (FPIA)[1]
Family Service Association (FSA)
Federal Ministry for Economic Co-operation (Germany)[3]
Federation of American Scientists
Federation of Jewish Philanthropists
Federation of Organizations of Professional Women
Federation of Protestant Welfare Agencies
Feminist Majority Foundation
Feminists for Animal Rights (FAR)
Fertility Awareness Network (FAN)
Finnish International Development Agency (FIDA)[3]
Florence Crittenden Association of America
Florida State University, Center for the Study of Population[3]
Ford Foundation[3]
Friends of Family Planning (FFP)
Friends of the Earth (FOE)[2]
Fund for a Feminist 'Majority'
Futures Group[1,3]
General Service Foundation (GSF)[3]
Genetics Society of America (GSA)[2]
Georgetown University, Center for Population Research[3]
Girls Clubs of America[2]
Global Committee of Parliamentarians on Population and Development[1]
Global Fund for Women
Global Tomorrow Coalition, Inc. (GTC)[1]
Harvard University, Center for Population Studies[3]
Health Services International, Inc. (HSI)[1]
Hemlock Society
Hewlett [William and Flora] Foundation[3]
Hollywood Policy Center
Hollywood Women's Political Caucus
Human Rights for Women

Institute for Population Problems (Japan)[3]
Institute for Resource Development, Westinghouse (IRD)[1]
Institute of Public Health (Japan)[3]
Institute of Southeast Asian Studies[3]
Inter Press Service, Third World News Agency[3]
Inter-African Committee on Traditional Practices Affecting the Health of Women
    and Children in Africa[3]
Inter-American Children's Institute[3]
Inter-American Parliamentary Group on Population and Development[3]
Intercollegiate Association of Women Students
International Alliance of Women (IAW)[3]
International Catholic Migration Commission[3]
International Children's Centre[3]
International Committee for Contraception Research[3]
International Confederation of Midwives[3]
International Contraception, Abortion, and Sterilization Campaign
International Council of Women[3]
International Council on Management of Population Programmes (ICOMP)[1]
International Development Center of Japan[3]
International Development Research Center[3]
International Federation for Family Health[3]
International Federation for Family Life Promotion (IFFLP)[1]
International Federation for Home Economics[3]
International Federation of Business and Professional Women[3]
International Federation of Medical Students Associations[3]
International Federation on Aging[3]
International Food Policy Institute[3]
International Geographical Union, Commission on Population Geography[3]
International Health Society[3]
International Institute for Environment and Development (IIED)[1]
International Institute for Rural Reconstruction[3]
International Institute for Vital Registration and Statistics[3]
International Labor Organization (ILO)[1]
International Monetary Fund (IMF)
International Organization for Chemical Sciences in Development[3]
International Organization for Migration[3]
International Planned Parenthood Federation (IPPF)[1,2,3]
International Projects Assistance Services (IPAS)[1,3]
International Reference Center for Abortion Research
International Research Institute for Reproduction[3]
International Science and Technology Institute, Inc. (ISTI)[1,3]
International Statistical Institute[3]
International Union for the Scientific Study of Population (IUSSP)[1,3]
International Women's Health Coalition (IWHC)[1]
Izaak Walton League of America

Japan International Co-operation Agency[3]
Japanese Organization for International Cooperation in Family Planning, Inc. (JOICFP)[1,3]
Jessie Smith Noyes Foundation[3]
John Short & Associates, Inc. (JS&A)[1,3]
John Snow, Inc. (JSI)[1,3]
Johns Hopkins Program for International Education in Gynecology and Obstetrics (JHPIEGO)[1]
Johns Hopkins Program for International Education in Reproductive Health[3]
Johns Hopkins University, Department of Population Dynamics[3]
Johns Hopkins University, Population Communication Services (PCS)[1,3]
Johns Hopkins University, Population Information Program (PIP)[1,3]
Junior League
Juvenile Law Center
Kansas State University, Department of Sociology, Population Research Laboratory[3]
Latin American Council of Social Sciences[3]
Leadership Conference on Civil Rights
League of Arab States, Population Research Unit[3]
League of Women Voters (LWV)[2]
Los Angeles Regional Family Planning Council (LARFPC)[1]
Macro International, Inc.[3]
Management Sciences for Health (MSH)[1,3]
Margaret Sanger Center[1]
Marie Stopes International (MSI)[1,3]
Medical Committee for Human Rights
Mexican-American Legal Defense and Education Fund
Mexican-American National Women's Association (MANA)
Ministry of Development Cooperation (Norway)[3]
Mobilization for Survival
Mother and Child International[3]
Ms. Foundation for Women
National Abortion and Reproductive Rights Action League (NARRAL, formerly NARAL)[1]
National Abortion Federation (NAF)[1]
National Academy of Sciences (NAS), National Research Council, Committee on Population[3]
National Alliance for Optional Parenthood
National Association for the Advancement of Colored People (NAACP)
National Association for the Laity (NAL)
National Association of Community Health Centers
National Association of Cuban-American Women
National Association of Neighborhood Health Centers
National Association of Reproductive Health Centers
National Association of Social Workers

National Audobon Society[1,2,3]
National Black Feminists Organization (NBFO)
National Black Women's Health Project
National Center for Policy Alternatives
National Coalition of Black Lesbians and Gays
National Commission for the Protection of Human Rights
National Committee for Children and Youth
National Conference of Black Lawyers
National Conference of Commissioners on Uniform State Laws
National Council de la Raza
National Council of Churches (NCC), Church World Service[1]
National Council of Negro Women
National Council of Obstetrics and Gynecology (NCOG)
National Council of Puerto Rican Women
National Council of Women of the United States
National Council on Family Relations
National Education Association (NEA)
National Emergency Civil Liberties Committee (NECLC)
National Family Planning and Reproductive Health Association (NFPRHA)[1]
National Family Planning Forum (NFPF)
National Gay and Lesbian Task Force (NGLTF)
National Hispanic Lawyers Association
National Indian Health Board
National Institute of Child Health and Human Development (NICHD)[1]
National Medical Association (NMA)
National Organization for Women (NOW)
National Organization of Non-Parents (NON)
National Resources Defense Council[2]
National Student Nurses Association
National Welfare Rights Association
National Wildlife Federation (NWF)[2]
National Women's Health Network (NWHN)
National Women's Law Center
National Women's Political Caucus
Negative Population Growth (NPG)[2]
Nicaraguan Network
North American Man-Boy Love Association (NAMBLA)
OPEC Fund for International Development[3]
ORT - International Corporation[3]
Overseas Development Administration (Great Britain)[3]
Oxfam International[3]
Pan American Health Organization (PAHO)[3]
Parent-Teacher Association (PTA)
Parents Aid Society
Partners of the Americas[3]

The Facts of Life

Pathfinder International[3]
Peace Science Society International[2]
Pennsylvania State University, Population Research Institute[3]
People for the American Way (PAW)
People for the Ethical Treatment of Animals (PETA)
People's Anti-War Mobilization
Philippine Center for Population Development[3]
Physicians' Forum
Planned Parenthood Federation of America (PPFA)[2,3]
Planned Parenthood Federation of Canada (PPFC)[2,3]
Planned Parenthood/World Population
Planning Assistance
Population Action International (PAI)[3]
Population Association of America (PAA)[1]
Population Communications International (PCI)[1]
Population Concern[1]
Population Council[1,3]
Population Crisis Committee (PCC)[1,2]
Population Environment
Population Institute[3]
Population Investigation Committee[3]
Population Planning and International Health[1]
Population Reference Bureau (PRB)[1,3]
Population Resource Center (PRC)[1]
Population Services International (PSI)[1,2,3]
Population-Environmental Balance[1]
Press Foundation of Asia[3]
Princeton University, Office of Population Research[1,3]
Program for International Training in Health, University of North Carolina
    (INTRAH)[1]
Program of Appropriate Technology in Health (PATH)[3]
Project HOPE[2]
Puerto Rican Legal Defense and Education Fund
Radical Women
Rainbow Coalition
RAND Corporation[1]
Regional Employment Programme for Latin America and the Caribbean[3]
'Religious' Coalition for Reproductive Choice (RCRC, formerly RCAR)[1]
Reproductive Health Media Strategies Project
Reproductive Health Technologies Project
Republicans for Choice
Research Triangle Institute (RTI)[1,3]
Revolutionary Communist Party of the USA (RCP)
Rockefeller Foundation[3]
RONCO Consulting Corporation[1,3]

Royal Academy for Islamic Civilization[3]
SANE
Sex Information and Educational Council of the United States (SIECUS)[2]
Sierra Club[1]
Social Development Center (SDC)[1]
Socialist Workers Party
Society for Adolescent Medicine
Society for the Psychological Study of Social Issues
Sociologists for Women in Society
South Pacific Commission[3]
Spartacist League
Statistical Institute for Asia and the Pacific[3]
Student American Medical Association
Swedish Agency for Research Cooperation with Developing Countries[3]
Swedish International Development Agency (SIDA)[3]
Teen Line Connection (TLC)
Traditional Republicans
Transnational Family Research Institute (TFRI)[1,3]
Triton Corporation[1]
Tulane University, International Health Program[1]
Tulane University, School of Public Health and Tropical Medicine[3]
Unitarian Service Committee of Canada[3]
Unitarian Universalist Service Committee[3]
United Automobile Workers Union (UAW)
United Nations Center for Human Settlements (UNCHS, "Habitat")[3]
United Nations Commission for Latin America and the Caribbean (UNCLAC)[3]
United Nations Department for Development Support and Management Services[3]
United Nations Department for Economic and Social Information and Policy
    Analysis[3]
United Nations Department of International Economic and Social Affairs
    (UNDIESA)[1]
United Nations Department of Policy Coordination and Sustainable
    Development[3]
United Nations Department of Technical Cooperation for Development[1]
United Nations Development Programme (UNDP)[3]
United Nations Economic and Social Commission for Asia and the Pacific
    (UNESCAP)[3]
United Nations Economic and Social Commission for Western Asia (UNESCWA)[3]
United Nations Economic Commission for Africa (UNECA)[3]
United Nations Economic Commission for Europe (UNECE)[3]
United Nations Environment Programme (UNEP)[3]
United Nations Food and Agricultural Organization (UNFAO)[1,3]
United Nations Industrial Development Organization (UNIDO)[3]
United Nations International Children's Emergency Fund (UNICEF)[3]
United Nations International Fund for Agricultural Development (UNIFAD)[3]

The Facts of Life

United Nations International Labor Organization (UNILO)[3]
United Nations Population Fund (UNFPA)[3]
United Nations World Bank[1,3]
United Nations World Food Programme[3]
United Nations World Health Organization (UNWHO)[1,3]
United States Agency for International Development (USAID)[3]
United States Fund for Population Activities (USFPA)[1]
United States Jaycees[2]
University of Chicago, Ogburn/Stouffer Center for the Study of Population and Social Organization[3]
University of Connecticut, Center for International Community Health Studies[3]
University of Exeter, Institute of Population Studies[3]
University of Keele, Centre for Health Planning and Management[3]
University of Michigan, Department of Population Planning and International Health[3]
University of Michigan, Population Studies Center[3]
University of Montreal, Department of Demography[3]
University of North Carolina, Carolina Population Center[3]
University of Pittsburgh, Graduate School of Public Health, Population Program[3]
University of Southern California, Department of Sociology, Population Research Laboratory[3]
University of Texas at Austin, Population Research Center[3]
University of the West Indies, Advanced Training and Research in Fertility Management[3]
University of Wales, College of Cardiff, Sir David Owen Population Centre[3]
University of Western Ontario, Population Studies Centre[3]
University Research Corporation (URC)[1,3]
Urban League
Voluntary Human Extinction Movement (VHMENT)
War Resisters League
Western Consortium for Public Health, International Health Programs[1,3]
White House Conference on Children and Youth
Wilderness Society[2]
Wildlife Society[2]
Women in the Senate and House (WISH)
Women Judges Fund for Justice
Women of All Red Nations (WARN)
Women Strike for Peace
Women's Action Alliance (WAA)
Women's Equity Action League (WEAL)
Women's International League for Peace and Freedom
Women's Legal Defense Fund
Women's Lobby
Women's Medical Association (WMA)
Women's National Abortion Action Coalition (WNAAC)

Women's National Democratic Club
Working Group on Traditional Practices Affecting the Health of Women and
    Children[3]
Workmen's Circle
World Assembly of Youth (WAY)[3]
World Association of Girl Guides and Girl Scouts (WAGGGS)[3]
World Conservation Union[3]
World Education, Inc.[3]
World Federalists, U.S.A.[2]
World Federation of Health Agencies for the Advancement of Voluntary Surgical
    Contraception (WF/SC)[1,3]
World Medical Association[2,3]
World Neighbors[1]
World Population Society (WPS)[1,3]
World Resources Institute (WRI)[1,3]
World University Service of Canada[3]
World Young Women's `Christian' Association (WYWCA)[2,3]
Worldview International Foundation[3]
Worldwatch Institute[1,3]
Yale University, Economic Demography Program[3]
York University, Centre for Research on Latin America and the Caribbean[3]
Zero Population Growth (ZPG)[1,2,3]

---

1 Groups listed as "Nongovernmental Organizations in International Population and Family
   Planning" in the *Population Briefing Paper*, December 1988, issued by the Population Crisis
   Committee, 1120 19th Street NW, Suite 550, Washington, DC 20036-3605.

2 Groups listed as "Sponsoring Organizations" at the antinatalist conference titled "The International
   Convocation on the World Population Crisis." This conference was sponsored by the Planned
   Parenthood Federation of America and was held 19-20 June 1974 at the Hotel Americana in New
   York City.

3 United Nations Population Fund (UNFPA). *Guide to Sources of International Population Assistance
   1993* (Eighth Edition). New York: United Nations, 1993.

The Facts of Life

HLI's Major Branches

HLI Africa

P.O. Box 48527
Roosevelt Park 2129
Transvaal
South Africa
Telephone/FAX: 011/27-11-678-2792
E-mail: prolife@iafrica.com

HLI Asia

Suite 302, Our Home Condominium
Malakas cor Matulungin St.
Teacher's Village, Diliman
Quezon City
Philippines
Telephone: 011/632-434-9031
FAX: 011/632-434-9033
E-mail: hliasia@ibm.net

HLI Australia

P.O. Box 205
Broadway 2007
Australia
Telephone: 011/612-211-2793
FAX: 011/612-211-6324
E-mail: hliaust@ozemail.com.au

HLI Austria

Kolblgasse 15-1-9
A 1030 Wien
Austria
Telephone/FAX: 011/43-1796-6529
E-mail: hli-aut@hli.vol.at

HLI Belgium

Pro Vita
A. Geuderestr. 19
B-2800 Mechelen
Belgium
Telephone: 011/32-15-422-814
FAX: 011/32-1542-3734
E-mail: 100714650@compuserve.com

HLI Canada

191 Granville St.
Vanier, ON K1L 6Y3
Canada
Telephone: 1/613-745-9405
FAX: 1/613-745-9868
E-mail: nstn1281@fox.nstn.ca

HLI Costa Rica

Apartado 5849-1000
San Jose,
Costa Rica
Telephone: 011/506/286-1929
FAX: 011/506-255-1481
E-mail: aleal@cariari.ucr.ac.cr

HLI Croatia

Pozeska 11
55223 Vetovo
Croatia
Telephone/FAX: 011/385-34-267-067
E-mail: antun.lisec@public.srce.hr

HLI Czech Republic

Zazmoli 9
622 00 Bruno
Czech Republic
Telephone: 011/42-5-02-922-30
FAX: 011/42-5-02-921-66

HLI El Salvador

Vida Humana Internacional
C. El Adriatico, #20
Colonia Jardines de Guadalupe
San Salvador, El Salvador
Telephone: 011/503-243-6319
FAX: 011/503-243-1279
E-mail: silavida@es.com.sv

HLI Europa

ul. Jaskowa Dolina 47/2
80-286 Gdansk-Wrzeszcz
Poland
Telephone: 011/48-58-46-10-50
FAX: 011/48-58-46-10-01
E-mail: hlieu@beta.nask.gda.pl

HLI Germany

Kieler Str. 24
D-45145 Essen
Germany
Telephone: 011/49-201-876-1112
FAX: 011/49-201-876-1113
E-mail: hligermany@aol.com

HLI Guatemala

Aprodem
15 Avenida #40-49 zona 8
Guatemala
Telephone: 011/502-472-1272

HLI Ireland

39 Mountjoy Square
Dublin 1
Ireland
Telephone: 011/353-1855-2504
FAX: 011/353-1855-2767

HLI Madras

Our Lady of Lourdes Shrine
Perambur, Madras 600011
India
Telephone: 011/91-44-619-100

HLI Miami

Vida Humana Internacional
4345 SW 72nd Ave. suite E
Miami, FL 33155
Telephone: (305) 662-1497
FAX: (305) 662-1499
E-mail: vhi@shadow.net

HLI New Zealand

Family Life International
P.O. Box 91271,
A.M.S.C.
Auckland
New Zealand
Telephone: 011/649-358-3122
FAX: 011/649-357-0832
E-mail: fli_ak@iconz.co.nz

HLI Nicaragua

Anprovida
Apartado C-098
Managua,
Nicaragua
Telephone: 011/505-278-5183
FAX: 011/505-278-2568

HLI Nigeria

45 Ibadan Rd
P.O. Box 1225
Ijebu Ode, Ogun State
Nigeria
Telephone: 011/234-37-434556
FAX: 011/234-37-431675

HLI Visayas/Mindanao

Level III
Cebu Caritas Building
Padre Gomez St.
6000 Cebu City
Philippines
Telephone: 011/63-32-212-657
FAX: 011/63-32-91843

HLI Russia

13-95, Aviacionnaja St.
Moscow 123182
Russia
Telephone/FAX: 011/7-095-490-6894
FAX: 011-7-095-292-9778

HLI Sri Lanka

"Lake Side"
Charles William Mawatha
Wennappuwa
Sri Lanka

HLI Ukraine

Ave. Majakovskovo 29b-125
253217 Kiev
Ukraine
Telephone/FAX: 011/44-547-00-05
Telephone: 011/44-547-51-87
E-mail: hli-va@hli-va.ru.kiev.va

....

HLI UK

PO Box 4771
London
SE9 4XA
United Kingdom
Telephone: 011/44-181-857-9950
FAX: 011/44-181-859-6177
E-mail: greg@hliuk.demon.com

Index

Z

Get Others to Face the FACTS!

Order Additional Copies of *The Facts of Life*

It is *vital* that the information in *The Facts of Life* be disseminated far and wide in order to plant new seeds of life in the killing fields of this culture of death. Order copies now for:

- ☑ Your Pastor & Parish
- ☑ Your Relatives
- ☑ Talk Show Hosts
- ☑ Your Library
- ☑ Your Newspaper Editor
- ☑ Your Elected Officials
- ☑ Your Friends
- ☑ Your Local Respect Life Office
- ☑ Your Schools
- ☑ Others

1-5 copies: $19.95 (US) ea. ★ 6-10 copies: $17.95 ea. ★ 11-20 copies: $15.95 ea. Add $4.00 shipping and handling to the first book and .50 cents for each additional book. Excellent bulk rates available for larger orders. Call 1-800-549-LIFE.

✔ Yes!

Send me _____ copies of *The Facts of Life* (#M601) at $_____ each. Total enclosed: $_____.

☐ My check or money order is enclosed, made payable to **HLI**.
☐ Charge my: ☐ Visa   ☐ MasterCard   ☐ Discover

Number: _____ Expiration Date: ____/____

Signature: _____

L037
My Name: _____

Address: _____

City: _____ State:_____ Zip:_____

Please rush copies directly to (attach additional sheets if necessary):

_____   _____

_____   _____

_____   _____

Mail payment and this form to: HLI, 4 Family Life, Front Royal , VA 22630 USA.

To order by credit card, call toll free: 1-800-549-LIFE

We are involved in a struggle between the Culture of Life and the Culture of Death...

Each of us must decide: Will we join the battle or retreat into apathy? What kind of world will your children and grandchildren inherit? What will you say when asked by them: "What did *you* do to fight this evil?"

Human Life International (HLI) is the world's largest, most experienced international pro-life/pro-family organization. With 85 branches in 57 countries, HLI spreads the Gospel of Life through service, advocacy and education. HLI's outreach is through intercessory prayer, printed materials, global and local conferences, the world wide web, video and audio cassettes, missionary activities, reasearch and the mass media.

With your donation of $25 or more, HLI will send you *HLI Reports*, an informative and timely newsletter, and other material that will enable you to stay up-to-date and be informed. You will be motivated, inspired and equipped to take part in the epic struggle that is shaping the future of mankind.

"You are doing the most important work on earth!"
—Pope John Paul II, speaking to Fr. Paul Marx, founder and chairman of HLI

- -

Please send me:

- ☐ *HLI Reports*, the monthly, 16 page newsletter packed with articles, book reviews and insider information
- ☐ *Special Report*, the monthly, 12 page "front lines" dispatch from Fr. Paul Marx, Fr. Matthew Habiger, Fr. Richard Welch and others
- ☐ *HLI Update*, the monthly, 4 page world-wide news report on pro-life/ pro-family activities
- ☐ HLI's FREE catalog of the world's best pro-life/pro-family books, booklets, pamphlets, videos, audio cassettes and more
- ☐ Information about HLI's newsletters and other materials in languages other than English. Specify language:_____

My donation to HLI of $_____ is enclosed:

☐ My check or money order is enclosed, made payable to **HLI**.
☐ Charge my: ☐ Visa   ☐ MasterCard   ☐ Discover

Number: _____ Expiration Date: ____/____

D035 Signature: _____

Name: _____

Address: _____

City: _____ State:_____ Zip:_____

Mail payment and this form to: HLI, 4 Family Life, Front Royal , VA 22630 USA.

To order by credit card, call toll free: 1-800-549-LIFE

Other Materials Available from HLI

Faithful for Life — Fr. Paul Marx, OSB. The pioneer Apostle of Life tells his life story, describing his fifty years as a priest and his role as a leader in the pro-life/pro-family movement.

Item #: A611   Item #: A612
Softcover $12.95   Hardcover $17.95

Blood of the Martyrs — Fr. Richard Welch, CSR. Story of a Catholic priest in the Rescue movement and how he put his faith into action. Takes the reader into the mind and struggles of someone who want to address the evils of contraception, sterilization and abortion.

Item #: Z605   Book $8.00

Deadly Deception — James W. Sedlak. Exposes the deceptive tactics of International Planned Parenthood in the Western Hemisphere. A great resource for all pro-lifers!

Item #: P203   Item #: P402
Pamphlet .25¢   Bklt. $4.00

Humanae Vitae — Pope Paul VI. Best translation of this historic and prophetic encyclical on Love, Life and the Family.

Item #: C404   Bklt. $3.00

Veritatis Splendor — Pope John Paul II. Powerfully reaffirms the vital connection between man's behavior and truth; clarifies the nature of moral truth.

Item #: C415   Bklt. $2.25

Envangelium Vitae — Pope John Paul II. Proclaims the Gospel of Life to the world, drawing distinct lines between the Culture of Life and the Culture of Death.
    Item #: C614   Book $3.25

Euthanasia: Recent Declaration of Popes and Bishops — Offers the definitive statements by the Church on euthanasia throughout the years.
    Item #: C402   Bklt. 95¢

The Truth and Meaning of Human Sexuality — The Pontifical Council For the Family. Offers practical guidelines to parents on educating their children for chastity. Presents to the reader the beauty and meaning of true love.
    Item #: C616   Book $3.00

Familiaris Consortio — Pope John Paul II. The Church's guide for the preparation and promotion of family life.
    Item #: C403   Bklt. $3.25

- ✂

Order Form   To order by credit card, call: 1-800-549-LIFE

Name: _____
L038
Address: _____

City: _____ State: _____ Zip: _____

☐ My check or money order for $_____ is enclosed, made payable to **HLI**.
☐ Charge my: ☐ Visa ☐ MasterCard ☐ Discover

  No.: _____ Exp.: ___/___ Signature: _____

Item #:	Quantity	Price	Total
		Shipping and Handling	$4.00
		Grand Total Enclosed	

Please allow 4-6 weeks for delivery of materials.

Mail payment and this form to:
HLI, 4 Family Life, Front Royal , VA 22630 USA.

Join Human Life International on the World Wide Web!

http://www.hli.org

Human Life International on the Web is providing information around the clock, without media distortion or bias. With just the click of a button, people around the globe can read our latest publications, learn more about our informational programs, research our positions on a variety of family life issues, check out our latest press releases, plan ahead for upcoming conferences and seminars, and much more.

Now the web is no longer comprised of simple static pages of text and graphics; it has advanced with technology to become multimedia and interactive. HLI has advanced with it. A visit to the HLI Website will dazzle the viewer with moving graphics, online audio and video clips, interactive forms, online bookstore, and a comprehensive keyword search engine. Without sacrificing timely information and scholarly research, a hallmark of our organization, these new technologies will prove to be invaluable means for getting the message out to as many people as possible, as quickly as possible.

Visit our site often. We continually update it with news and information that's crucial to our mission of spreading the word in defense of human life. Save our site as a bookmark, or favorite, for easy access at just the click of a button.

Come and See HLI on the Web!

About the Author

Brian Clowes, Ph.D., author of *The Pro-Life Activist's Encyclopedia*, is an engineer, teacher and pro-life activist. Father of five sons and one daughter, Dr. Clowes writes about life and family issues with a degree of passion and clarity matched only by his experience. Dr. Clowes is the Director of Human Life International's Pro-Life/Pro-Family Training Institute.

About Human Life International

Human Life International (HLI), founded by Rev. Paul Marx, OSB, PhD, is the world's foremost pro-life, pro-family education and training apostolate. HLI promotes the sanctity of life and the dignity of the family by teaching and fostering chastity, marriage preparation, Natural Family Planning and Catholic orthodoxy. HLI opposes modern-day threats to life and the family, including contraception, sterilization, abortion and euthanasia.